Home Remodeling For Dummies®

Cheat Sheet

W9-AVN-769

Health and safety items to consider for a remodeling project

When planning a remodeling project, health- and safety-related modifications should be your top priority. You may want to consider the following:

- ✔ Installing smoke detectors, carbon monoxide detectors, and radon detectors
- ✔ Testing for lead and asbestos and doing any necessary abatement
- ✔ Installing and repairing handrails
- ✔ Upgrading electrical systems
- ✔ Replacing faulty electrical wiring
- ✔ Grounding an electrical system
- ✔ Installing a child-safe garage door and opener
- ✔ Using tempered glass as shower doors
- ✔ Replacing unsafe appliances
- ✔ Repairing or replacing your furnace
- ✔ Surrounding a swimming pool with protective fencing

Contractor lingo

- ✔ General contractors who build residential subdivisions, custom homes, commercial buildings, and industrial buildings are known as *building contractors* or *builders.*

- ✔ General contractors who remodel commercial buildings are known as *tenant improvement contractors* or *commercial remodelers.*

- ✔ General contractors who remodel homes are known as *residential remodeling contractors, remodeling contractors,* or *remodelers.*

Four steps to evaluating bids

1. Narrow the playing field.

2. Make sure that everyone knows exactly what you want.

3. Make sense out of the prices.

4. Compare and select the winning bid.

For all of the details, see Chapter 10.

...For Dummies: Bestselling Book Series for Beginners

Home Remodeling For Dummies®

Cheat Sheet

What the building inspector looks for

After a remodel, the building inspector checks all of the following. You should too.

- ✔ Grading around the house provides proper drainage.

- ✔ Exterior materials meet code and workmanship is satisfactory.

- ✔ Lock sets work and meet code. (Deadbolt locks should have a thumb turn on the inside, not a key.)

- ✔ Attic/crawlspace access is adequate/safe.

- ✔ Gas lines are connected properly (with flex tubing from valve to appliance).

- ✔ Smoke detectors work and are installed where required.

- ✔ Electric connections are proper throughout the house and at the service panel.

- ✔ Electrical circuit breakers are labeled correctly on service panel.

- ✔ Electrical outlets and switches work properly.

- ✔ Ground-fault circuit interrupters (GFCIs) work.

- ✔ Light fixtures are installed properly and work.

- ✔ Appliances (especially cooktop and vent hood) are connected properly.

- ✔ The water heater is strapped down.

- ✔ The water heater pressure relief valve works.

- ✔ There are no penetrations through the firewall between the garage and house.

- ✔ Penetrations throughout house are sealed or finished properly.

- ✔ Roof, gutters, and roof vents are properly installed and flashed.

- ✔ Plumbing and fixtures work and are installed properly.

- ✔ Sliding glass doors, windows in or near doors, shower doors, and enclosures and mirrored closet doors are made of tempered glass.

...For Dummies: Bestselling Book Series for Beginners

Praise for Home Remodeling For Dummies

"If you are in the mood to remodel, before you hire a contractor, hire Jim and Morris Carey. This book is easy to understand, puts you way ahead of the curve, and your friends will never say you're just a bubble left to plum."
— Chuck Woolery, television personality

"For anyone just thinking about remodeling a home in any way, STOP everything and go directly to your nearest bookstore where you will find this extraordinarily informative book that covers every question anyone might have — the directness and simplicity of the writing makes it a joy to read!"
— Christina Ferrare, model

"The Carey Brothers are no strangers to this field. James and Morris Carey are 3rd generation contractors and specialists in residential remodeling. This book should be required for homeowners on a budget."
— Stan Kohler, Associated Press Graphics

"James and Morris Carey are two of the most down-to-earth, credible individuals I have ever worked with. They made the task of working around the house simple and understandable. Their book is perfect for the anti-handyman who has a fear of hammers and saws."
— Bob Agnew, Operations Manager, Program Director KNBR Radio

"*Home Remodeling For Dummies* not only helps do-it-yourselfers, but it benefits people like me who are hire-it-outers. After reading James' and Morris Carey's book, I know how to plan, stay within a budget, find sensible financing, and obtain bids on a project. I have a 50-year-old home, so I know I will use this book as a guide for my future remodeling needs."
— Eugenia Chapman, author of *Clean Your House and Everything In It* and *Find Your House and Everything In It*

"*Home Remodeling For Dummies* is a must-read for anyone who buys a fixer-upper. The Carey Brothers explain exactly how to turn a dump into your dream home."
— Ray Brown, co-author of *Home Buying For Dummies* and *House Selling For Dummies*

 ™

References for the Rest of Us! ™

BESTSELLING BOOK SERIES FROM IDG

Do you find that traditional reference books are overloaded with technical details and advice you'll never use? Do you postpone important life decisions because you just don't want to deal with them? Then our *...For Dummies*® business and general reference book series is for you.

...For Dummies business and general reference books are written for those frustrated and hard-working souls who know they aren't dumb, but find that the myriad of personal and business issues and the accompanying horror stories make them feel helpless. *...For Dummies* books use a lighthearted approach, a down-to-earth style, and even cartoons and humorous icons to diffuse fears and build confidence. Lighthearted but not lightweight, these books are perfect survival guides to solve your everyday personal and business problems.

> *"More than a publishing phenomenon, 'Dummies' is a sign of the times."*
> — The New York Times

> *"...you won't go wrong buying them."*
> — Walter Mossberg, Wall Street Journal, on IDG Books' ...For Dummies books

> *"A world of detailed and authoritative information is packed into them..."*
> — U.S. News and World Report

Already, millions of satisfied readers agree. They have made *...For Dummies* the #1 introductory level computer book series and a best-selling business book series. They have written asking for more. So, if you're looking for the best and easiest way to learn about business and other general reference topics, look to *...For Dummies* to give you a helping hand.

4/98

HOME REMODELING FOR DUMMIES®

by Morris Carey and James Carey

Foreword by Dom DeLuise

IDG BOOKS WORLDWIDE

IDG Books Worldwide, Inc.
An International Data Group Company

Foster City, CA ♦ Chicago, IL ♦ Indianapolis, IN ♦ New York, NY

Home Remodeling For Dummies®

Published by
IDG Books Worldwide, Inc.
An International Data Group Company
919 E. Hillsdale Blvd.
Suite 400
Foster City, CA 94404
www.idgbooks.com (IDG Books Worldwide Web site)
www.dummies.com (Dummies Press Web site)

Library of Congress Catalog Card No.: 98-86811

ISBN: 0-7645-5088-8

Printed in the United States of America

10 9 8 7 6 5 4 3 2 1

1B/RU/QY/ZY/IN

Distributed in the United States by IDG Books Worldwide, Inc.

Distributed by Macmillan Canada for Canada; by Transworld Publishers Limited in the United Kingdom; by IDG Norge Books for Norway; by IDG Sweden Books for Sweden; by Woodslane Pty. Ltd. for Australia; by Woodslane (NZ) Ltd. for New Zealand; by Addison Wesley Longman Singapore Pte Ltd. for Singapore, Malaysia, Thailand, Indonesia and Korea; by Norma Comunicaciones S.A. for Colombia; by Intersoft for South Africa; by International Thomson Publishing for Germany, Austria and Switzerland; by Toppan Company Ltd. for Japan; by Distribuidora Cuspide for Argentina; by Livraria Cultura for Brazil; by Ediciencia S.A. for Ecuador; by Ediciones ZETA S.C.R. Ltda. for Peru; by WS Computer Publishing Corporation, Inc., for the Philippines; by Unalis Corporation for Taiwan; by Contemporanea de Ediciones for Venezuela; by Computer Book & Magazine Store for Puerto Rico; by Express Computer Distributors for the Caribbean and West Indies. Authorized Sales Agent: Anthony Rudkin Associates for the Middle East and North Africa.

For general information on IDG Books Worldwide's books in the U.S., please call our Consumer Customer Service department at 800-762-2974. For reseller information, including discounts and premium sales, please call our Reseller Customer Service department at 800-434-3422.

For information on where to purchase IDG Books Worldwide's books outside the U.S., please contact our International Sales department at 650-655-3200 or fax 650-655-3297.

For information on foreign language translations, please contact our Foreign & Subsidiary Rights department at 650-655-3021 or fax 650-655-3281.

For sales inquiries and special prices for bulk quantities, please contact our Sales department at 650-655-3200 or write to the address above.

For information on using IDG Books Worldwide's books in the classroom or for ordering examination copies, please contact our Educational Sales department at 800-434-2086 or fax 317-596-5499.

For press review copies, author interviews, or other publicity information, please contact our Public Relations department at 650-655-3000 or fax 650-655-3299.

For authorization to photocopy items for corporate, personal, or educational use, please contact Copyright Clearance Center, 222 Rosewood Drive, Danvers, MA 01923, or fax 978-750-4470.

 is a trademark under exclusive license to IDG Books Worldwide, Inc., from International Data Group, Inc.

About the Authors

James and Morris Carey, known as the Carey Brothers, are nationally-recognized experts on home building and renovation. They share their combined 40 years of experience as award-winning, licensed contractors with millions nationwide through a weekly radio program and syndicated newspaper column, both titled "On The House." With wit, enthusiasm, and clarity, the Carey Brothers' Associated Press syndicated newspaper column and four-hour radio broadcast offer people money-saving tips on building, remodeling, and repairing homes. The column, with accompanying graphics, appears in dozens of newspapers across the country including *The Los Angeles Times, Cleveland Plain-Dealer, San Diego Union-Tribune, New Orleans Times-Picayune* and *San Francisco Examiner.*

These third-generation contractors hold twelve-year broadcast careers in radio and television. They deliver user-friendly, hands-on advice in their radio program, which is carried coast-to-coast weekly, via satellite, to a rapidly growing network of more than 170 stations. The program also is broadcast via live remote from home and building expos nationwide. The Careys presently appear as regulars on the Family Channel's *Home and Family* television program, hosted by Cristina Ferrare and Michael Burger, and have appeared as guests on national and local television programs, including *Vicki* and ABC-TV's *Home Show* and *Caryl & Marilyn: Real Friends,* among others.

Recognized for their efforts in answering immediate and constant structural concerns by the public in the hours and days following the devastating October 1989 earthquake, the Carey Brothers and KCBS in San Francisco received the George Foster Peabody Award, broadcasting's most prestigious honor, for their outstanding contributions towards "comprehensive, intelligent, and useful coverage." Morris and James continue to own and operate a successful home remodeling and construction firm, Carey Bros., and have been named to *Remodeling* magazine's Hall of Fame "Big 50," which recognizes top achievers in the industry and have been honored as one of the nation's top 500 companies by *Qualified Remodeler* magazine.

In addition to their syndicated column, they authored a how-to book, *Cost-Effective Home Upgrades,* published by Ortho Books, 1992. And Morris was a regular contributor to *Remodeling Contractor* and *The Journal of Light Construction.* They currently author a column for *Home Magazine's Best Selling Home Plans.*

The brothers are ardent supporters of Habitat for Humanity, both locally and nationally. They were the founding fathers of the first California chapter of the National Association of Remodeling Industry (NARI), with James serving as the chapter's first president. James resides with his family in Brentwood, California, where he is a former member of the City Planning Commission and Design Review Board. Morris lives in Pittsburg, California, where he formerly produced a locally televised broadcast of Pittsburg City Council meetings for students, seniors, and shut-ins.

For relaxation, the brothers enjoy golfing — describing themselves as "true hackers." Admitted "homebodies," Morris and James are forever remodeling their own homes. "It gives us something to do in our spare time," quips Morris. James enjoys family camping, while Morris delights in working in the garden with his wife, and loves being a grandfather.

Homeowners can receive answers to their specific home renovation and repair questions by calling the Carey Brothers toll-free number, 1-800-REPAIR-IT (737-2474), during their radio program, Saturday from 9 a.m. to 1 p.m. Eastern Standard Time; via e-mail at careybro@onthehouse.com; fax at 1-888-44-CAREY (442-2739); and through their Web site at www.onthehouse.com.

ABOUT IDG BOOKS WORLDWIDE

Welcome to the world of IDG Books Worldwide.

IDG Books Worldwide, Inc., is a subsidiary of International Data Group, the world's largest publisher of computer-related information and the leading global provider of information services on information technology. IDG was founded more than 25 years ago and now employs more than 8,500 people worldwide. IDG publishes more than 275 computer publications in over 75 countries (see listing below). More than 90 million people read one or more IDG publications each month.

Launched in 1990, IDG Books Worldwide is today the #1 publisher of best-selling computer books in the United States. We are proud to have received eight awards from the Computer Press Association in recognition of editorial excellence and three from *Computer Currents'* First Annual Readers' Choice Awards. Our best-selling ...*For Dummies*® series has more than 50 million copies in print with translations in 38 languages. IDG Books Worldwide, through a joint venture with IDG's Hi-Tech Beijing, became the first U.S. publisher to publish a computer book in the People's Republic of China. In record time, IDG Books Worldwide has become the first choice for millions of readers around the world who want to learn how to better manage their businesses.

Our mission is simple: Every one of our books is designed to bring extra value and skill-building instructions to the reader. Our books are written by experts who understand and care about our readers. The knowledge base of our editorial staff comes from years of experience in publishing, education, and journalism — experience we use to produce books for the '90s. In short, we care about books, so we attract the best people. We devote special attention to details such as audience, interior design, use of icons, and illustrations. And because we use an efficient process of authoring, editing, and desktop publishing our books electronically, we can spend more time ensuring superior content and spend less time on the technicalities of making books.

You can count on our commitment to deliver high-quality books at competitive prices on topics you want to read about. At IDG Books Worldwide, we continue in the IDG tradition of delivering quality for more than 25 years. You'll find no better book on a subject than one from IDG Books Worldwide.

IDG BOOKS WORLDWIDE

John Kilcullen
CEO
IDG Books Worldwide, Inc.

Steven Berkowitz
President and Publisher
IDG Books Worldwide, Inc.

Eighth Annual
Computer Press
Awards ≥1992

Ninth Annual
Computer Press
Awards ≥1993

Tenth Annual
Computer Press
Awards ≥1994

Eleventh Annual
Computer Press
Awards ≥1995

Dedications

To my wife, Carol, for her love, support, and encouragement during our 17 years together and particularly during this project when my notebook computer accompanied us on vacations to Hawaii and Alaska. And to my son Chris (13) and daughter Jamie (6) for their patience and understanding when Daddy wasn't available for activities because he was chained to his computer. Often, they simply wanted to use the computer themselves.

— James Carey

I would like to dedicate this book to the millions of do-it-yourself readers, viewers and listeners who have been instrumental in helping to make The Carey Bros. a household name among home remodeling and home improvement enthusiasts nationwide. Thank you one and all!

I would also like to dedicate this book to my co-author, business partner, and kid brother, James.

It was late in October of 1964. The day I left home to join the navy. I clearly remember holding him in my arms. Back then he was known as Jamie. I hugged him, told him that I loved him, and assured him that I wouldn't be gone for very long. I was 18 and he was 6. That was 34 years ago. Since then, I have had the distinct pleasure of watching him grow to manhood. He has become a loving husband, a super father, and my life-long business partner. We have worked side-by-side as carpenters, contractors, radio talk-show hosts, television personalities, authors, and businessmen for nearly two decades. I rely on his strength of character and integrity, his steadfast support of our goals, and his reassuring words when things go wrong. Through good times and bad he has always been there for me, and I will be forever thankful that I have had the good fortune to be blessed with such a wonderful brother.

I would also like to dedicate this book to my beautiful wife, Carol, who I have never stopped loving since we met in 1962. She is my confidant, my personal support system, my research assistant, my best friend, my lover, and a very sexy grandmother. On top of all that, she and my son Morris III run Carey Bros., the remodeling company that James and I created. I am so very proud of them.

To Ricky, Doreen, Jennie, Dawn, Lisa, Robin, Shayne, Stephanie, D.J., Sammy, Moe the 4th, Wendy, Nick, Daniel, and Mikayla: To be blessed with a loving family is the most special success of all. In life, it is the only important success. Through good times and bad I will love you all.

— Morris Carey

Authors' Acknowledgements

There are many people who contributed both directly and indirectly to the success of this book. While there are too many to list, we would be remiss without naming a few.

We wish to thank Jim Wall, Kathy Gargalikis, Louis Kidwell, the city of Brentwood, California, everyone at the city of Concord, California, Building Department, Sam Crabtree, George Kiskaddon, Alan Wickstrom, Hoyt Hart II, Esq., Dave Kahane, and Eugene Skuratowicz for their technical expertise.

Special thanks to Tim Green and Don Logay for using their writing talent by coming through in the home stretch when we were running out of time and there remained gobs of information that we wanted to include in this book. Thank you, guys.

At IDG Books, we want to thank Kathy Welton and Holly McGuire for making this book happen and giving us the opportunity to share our passion with you. Also, special thanks to Tim Gallan, Tammy Castleman, and Patricia Pan for their editorial expertise. Thanks to them, all of our i's got dotted, t's crossed, and ne'er a participle dangled.

Most people would agree that a picture is worth a thousand words. While this book does not contain pictures, it is filled with plenty of wonderful illustrations that help make sense of many of the tales and tasks that we describe throughout this book. Our thanks to Tony Davis for his illustrative genius.

At Carey Bros. Remodeling Company, special thanks to Morris D. Carey, III (Morris' son), and Carol Carey (Morris' wife), Carol Grady, Aunt 'Peps' (our 80-year-young receptionist), and the entire staff of our remodeling company for doing such a super job while our attention has been focused on this book and other projects.

At On The House Syndication (our media company), many thanks to Steve Raucher and Lori Martin for their encouragement and support — and for keeping our radio affiliates happy. What's the affiliate count, guys?

Publisher's Acknowledgments

We're proud of this book; please register your comments through our IDG Books Worldwide Online Registration Form located at http://my2cents.dummies.com.

Some of the people who helped bring this book to market include the following:

Acquisitions, Development, and Editorial

Senior Project Editor: Tim Gallan

Acquisitions Editor: Holly McGuire

Copy Editors: Tamara Castleman, Patricia Yuu Pan

Technical Reviewer: John Rohosky

Editorial Manager: Leah P. Cameron

Media Development Manager: Heather Heath Dismore

Editorial Assistant: Donna Love

Editorial Coordinator: Maureen Kelly

Production

Associate Project Coordinator: Tom Missler

Layout and Graphics: Lou Boudreau, Linda M. Boyer, J. Tyler Connor, Angela F. Hunckler, Todd Klemme, Heather N. Pearson, Brent Savage, Janet Seib, Kate Snell

Proofreaders: Christine Berman, Kelli Botta, Vickie Broyles, Nancy Price, Rebecca Senninger, Janet M. Withers

Indexer: Sharon Hilgenberg

General and Administrative

IDG Books Worldwide, Inc.: John Kilcullen, CEO; Steven Berkowitz, President and Publisher

IDG Books Technology Publishing: Brenda McLaughlin, Senior Vice President and Group Publisher

Dummies Technology Press and Dummies Editorial: Diane Graves Steele, Vice President and Associate Publisher; Mary Bednarek, Director of Acquisitions and Product Development; Kristin A. Cocks, Editorial Director

Dummies Trade Press: Kathleen A. Welton, Vice President and Publisher; Kevin Thornton, Acquisitions Manager

IDG Books Production for Dummies Press: Michael R. Britton, Vice President of Production and Creative Services; Beth Jenkins Roberts, Production Director; Cindy L. Phipps, Manager of Project Coordination, Production Proofreading, and Indexing; Kathie S. Schutte, Supervisor of Page Layout; Shelley Lea, Supervisor of Graphics and Design; Debbie J. Gates, Production Systems Specialist; Robert Springer, Supervisor of Proofreading; Debbie Stailey, Special Projects Coordinator; Tony Augsburger, Supervisor of Reprints and Bluelines

Dummies Packaging and Book Design: Robin Seaman, Creative Director; Jocelyn Kelaita, Product Packaging Coordinator; Kavish + Kavish, Cover Design

♦

The publisher would like to give special thanks to Patrick J. McGovern, without whom this book would not have been possible.

♦

About the Technical Reviewer

John Rohosky, AIA, is a San Francisco Bay-area licensed architect and contractor with more than 25 years experience in residential design, building, and remodeling. His projects include designing homes from the ground up, story additions, kitchen and bath remodels, foundation replacements, decks and garden structures, and seismic retrofits (for earthquake sturdiness). In addition to design, John provides construction management services, performs building inspections, conducts feasibility studies for a range of building projects, and is a construction litigation consultant. In his free time, John swims in the frigid waters of San Francisco Bay.

Contents at a Glance

Cartoons at a Glance

By Rich Tennant

page 67

page 171

"First of all, the stupid elves never return my phone calls and now I find out they put the roof on without the nougat sealer."

page 229

page 327

"I don't know why we're building a family room when this seems to be the room we all want to congregate in."

page 5

"You said you wanted me to add space to the kitchen."

page 377

"To preserve the beauty and durability of the dental molding, we put fluoride in the trim paint."

page 283

Fax: 978-546-7747 • E-mail: the5wave@tiac.net

Table of Contents

Foreword

· ·

*W*hen I was a teenager, growing up in Brooklyn, New York, I was in charge of one household job that was all mine — the straightening of bent nails. I got to be very good at it. My father's workbench had an enormous vise with a convenient flat area that was great for straightening nails.

You would have to tap in this direction and then that direction and those wounded nails would almost look okay. I was also asked from time to time to nail one of these straightened creatures, and it was oh so hard to get one of those babies in the wood because you would have to tap the head of the nail like this and it would bend and then you would have to tap it from the northwest while still applying pressure in the southeast if you were to sink it. I always hammered those used nails in and bent them of course, and then I'd flatten the side of the nail into the wood and my father's angry voice would go up an octave or two.

I shall never forget the day in wood shop at school. The teacher handed me some brand-new nails and I was shocked: You mean that people actually used new nails? You gotta be kidding! I couldn't believe it. My father worked for the Sanitation Department; he was a good, hard-working man, and he kept bringing home these bent nails. For years, the DeLuise family used only and exclusively bent and used nails.

You can imagine how betrayed I felt when I realized that the rest of the world was using new nails to hold their wood together.

I am friends with Morris and James Carey because every time we have done a project together, they have used new nails, and I am so very grateful for that. I shall be their friend forever. We met while I was appearing on their television show called *Home & Family,* and from the first moment we hit it off just like old friends. Bingo!

Recently, I had a gazebo installed in my home, and Morris and James were entirely in charge of the installation. I realized then that work and fun can go together and you can still be very productive — big time. These men (who are really only grown-up boys) are so filled with knowledge about how to fix and improve, to restore and embellish, to enhance and renovate, to protect and repair within an inch of your life, that it's not even funny. And to top it all off, whenever we get together, (Morris, James, and Dom) we all have only one wife's name to remember: Carol! Carol! Carol! All of our wives are named Carol. As far as I am concerned, that is enough of an omen to know the hardware store god has spoken.

I use brand spanking new nails and a song in my heart whenever I hammer now.

You can bet there was a smile on my lips and lots of joy in my heart when the gazebo installation was completed in one day by Morris and James Carey. The job was done in record time and is solid as a rock and growing. There is no way I wouldn't want and cherish a book written by the Carey brothers on how to complete all those household chores around your home and garden, and all the while doing it with a smile on your face.

No matter what anyone tells you, I think the Carey Brothers are very knowledgeable, but only because they use brand-new nails. You better believe it.

Dom DeLuise

Introduction

•••

When IDG Books assigned us the task of writing this book, more than one person with whom we are acquainted suggested that it should be called *Home Remodeling By Dummies*. While neither of us claims to be a mental giant, when it comes to home remodeling, we have had more than our share of experiences, having designed and remodeled several hundred homes.

Unfortunately, when the subject of home remodeling is the topic of discussion, many people are either on the giving or receiving end of a remodeling horror story. While we have had the occasional trying project, we, fortunately, have more than our share of success stories.

One thing that neither of us has ever been accused of is not having passion for what we do. We are both very passionate about our work, and we love what we do. We have a special affinity for home remodeling because of the incredible metamorphosis that occurs when converting a tired, old space into a place of beauty and cheerfulness.

Thus, our goal in *Home Remodeling For Dummies* is to share with you what we have learned in our nearly two decades as home remodeling contractors in the hopes that your remodeling ventures will be exciting, enjoyable, and educational. Moreover, we hope that your remodeling dream becomes a reality that brings you and your family many years of comfort and pleasure.

How to Use This Book

This book is a reference, meaning that you don't need to read it from cover to cover. (Though you'd really make us feel good if you did.) We wrote the chapters as self-contained packets of information, so, for example, you don't have to read Chapter 19 to understand Chapter 20.

The Index is quite thorough, and so is the Table of Contents. If you already have topics in mind, look them up and start reading. No assembly required.

Who Needs This Book

If you're considering any sort of home remodel — large or small — this book can help. We emphasize the importance of planning and research, so our advice applies whether you're adding a new family room or installing a new sink.

What We Assume About You

You do NOT have to be a handyman or a do-it-yourselfer to benefit from the information in this book. In fact, we assume that you have very little knowledge regarding the nuts-and-bolts of even the simplest remodeling or repair job.

We don't try to teach how to pour a foundation, frame a wall, or wire a kitchen. We do tell you what's involved in these and many other tasks so that you can keep tabs on your contractor and ask the right questions before and during the remodeling process.

We assume that you find the planning and legal aspects of home remodeling rather intimidating, so we spend a lot of time explaining in plain English stuff like the bidding process, contracts, and liens.

How This Book Is Organized

The chapters in this book are organized into seven parts. Here's what they present:

Part I: Making the Big Decision to Remodel

The chapters in this part are all about planning. First, we help you decide whether you should remodel or move to a new home. Then we start talking about costs and how over-remodeling can make a home difficult to sell. If you decide to remodel, we help you to plan your budget by examining costs in relation to the investment you're making in your home. Finally, we end this part by listing some resources that can help you decide what and how you want to remodel.

Part II: Laying It All Out

If Part I is all about planning, then Part II is about even more planning. In fact, this may be the most important part in this book. We describe what goes in to drawing up plans. Then we help you find worthy contractors and explain the bidding process. We show you what a remodeling contract should look like and explain what a mechanic's lien is. We also help you prepare for the stresses for remodeling, and we end by discussing a few miscellaneous legal issues.

Part III: Foundation and Framing

This part describes the very beginnings of a large remodeling job: building the floor, walls, and roof. The chapters follow the order of an actual construction: first demolition, then the foundation and flooring, then the wall framing, and finally the ceiling and roof. We provide advice on the pros and cons of various materials, and we help you understand what's going on while your contractor does all of the work.

Part IV: Closing It All In

If Part III is about the skeleton, then Part IV is about putting some meat on those bones. We help you select the right doors and windows, roof covering, and exterior siding.

Part V: Energizing the Walls

Anything that goes in or on the wall frame is covered in this part. First we cover plumbing, heating, and electrical concerns. Then we give the lowdown on insulation. Finally, we discuss drywall options.

Part VI: Interior Finishes and Final Touches

If the remodeling process were like baking a cake, then this part is about applying the icing. We cover painting, tile, and flooring. And to top things off, we provide advice on getting the final inspection and making the final payment.

Part VII: The Part of Tens

Like all ...*For Dummies* books, this one ends with top-ten lists. We give you ten important things to remember about the remodeling process, and we also offer you ten tips that should save you some money.

Icons Used in This Book

We'd like to think that every word in this book is important, but the truth is, some passages are more important than others, so we use these little pictures (called icons) to point them out.

This icon flags text that's important and not to be forgotten.

When we go out on a limb to suggest that you should or shouldn't do something, we use this icon. It's represents your basic good idea.

When we discuss something that involves a lot of jargon or a decent amount of math, we flagged it with this icon.

This icon points out dangers and health hazards that you should be wary of.

When we feel like telling a little story, you'll see this icon.

Where to Go From Here

If you're just considering a remodeling project and don't know how to get started, may we suggest that you carefully read Parts I and II. If you're interested in a specific topic (like aluminum siding versus vinyl siding or how to have a lien released), look it up in the Table of Contents or Index.

Part I

Making the Big Decision to Remodel

The 5th Wave   By Rich Tennant

"I don't know why we're building a family room when this seems to be the room we all want to congregate in."

In this part . . .

We continually harp on the need for planning. In order for you to complete a successful remodel, you have to do a lot of legwork up front, even if (or especially if) you plan on hiring someone else to do the actual remodeling work. In this part, we help you to evaluate the costs and benefits of remodeling, and we provide tips on gathering information and managing spending.

Chapter 1

Improve Rather Than Move

· ·

In This Chapter

▶ The pros and cons of moving versus improving

▶ What to look for when considering a move

▶ The hidden costs of moving

· ·

*W*e can hear them now. The great call of the wild. Actually, that's an understatement. A more apt description would be *the roar of the irate*. What are they? They are the battle cries of malcontent homeowners everywhere living in cramped, outdated and, in some cases, unsafe housing. "I can't live another day without a second bathroom in this house!" Or, "This kitchen is so small, it's driving me nuts!" And, "The closets in this house are too tiny and we don't have enough of them!" These are just a few examples. Sound familiar? They do to us. We have heard all these complaints and more countless times during our nearly twenty years as remodeling contractors. They may be familiar words to you as well. Chances are that you have either thought or spoken them yourself. It's no wonder you picked up this book.

Cramped quarters, outdated finishes, and the need to make general repairs and perform routine maintenance are fuel for the raging multi-billion dollar residential remodeling market. Industry statistics report that residential remodeling topped $125 billion in 1996 and that there appears to be no end in sight. That explains why mega home centers designed to cater to the pro and do-it-yourselfer alike are springing up in communities all across this land. Is remodeling popular? If you have any doubt, simply visit your local home center to witness the frenzy of activity taking place within its walls. Chances are you'll fear for your life as determined do-it-yourselfers go barreling down crowded aisles, guiding overflowing shopping carts and plywood-filled hand trucks to a seemingly endless line at the checkout stand.

So you've decided to remodel. Or have you? Well then, you're in the right place because the purpose of this chapter is to help you weigh the relative pros and cons of improving your home versus moving.

Once upon a time

Many years ago, we worked with a couple who called us because they were trying to decide whether to remodel or move. Their list was long: remodel the kitchen, remodel a bath, widen the entry hall, install new entry doors, install new flooring throughout the home, paint the entire interior and exterior, and add on a new master bedroom suite complete with up-scale bathroom and walk-in closet. In short, they wanted to bring their '60s rancher up to date. Watching them go through all the emotions was interesting. First, they felt despair. "What are we to do with this home that no longer suits our needs?" Then, we got involved and they shifted from despair to hope. "Can we possibly have all of the things that we want where we want them?" We call this the old "cake and eat it" syndrome. We digested the information that they gave us and presented them with a couple of solutions and preliminary costs for the proposed work. Another emotional change — from hope to anger. We can remember their words as if they were spoken only moments ago: "It's going to cost how much? You've got to be kidding!"

They then did what most people whom we have dealt with over the years have done in that situation: They threw us out of their house. Just kidding! They went shopping for a new house, triggering yet another emotional shift from anger back to hope. The questions and concerns continued. Would they be able to find the home of their dreams within the price that they could afford? Would the home be located in a neighborhood as nice as their existing one? Would the people be as friendly? Would the schools be as good? Would the children make new friends easily? Could they still go to the same church and would shopping be as convenient? And, last but not least, how would the move affect their commute to

work? Whoa, fear upgraded to anxiety. They were clearly overwhelmed. The interesting fact is that this couple is the rule and not the exception.

After they began to find answers to each of these questions, they realized that they could not have the home that they wanted by moving. After considering *all* the costs, remodeling was not only the most cost efficient alternative, but it also met their emotional needs as well. Emotions shifted from anxiety to excitement as they anticipated having the home of their dreams in the neighborhood of their dreams. *Cake and eat it big time!* Finally, after working with them for several months and generating many designs and cost estimates, they were ready to "go for it." "Go ahead and put the paperwork together," they said. We were thrilled to be able to help make their dreams come true, and besides, we needed the money. We agreed to meet the following Thursday evening to sign the contract.

Thursday evening rolled around, and we met as scheduled. We all studied the final documents one last time, and then the moment of truth arrived. It was time to sign on the dotted line. Just as the pen was poised to ink her signature, the wife broke down and began to cry, explaining that it was all too emotional and that she simply couldn't sign that evening. There went the excitement. We agreed to meet the following evening to try again. We did, and with big smiles everyone signed, and we were off and running. As is always the case during a remodeling project, especially with one of such magnitude, emotions ran high and low. Fortunately, when complete, their home was magnificent, they were happy, and we got paid. So this is one of those stories where everyone lives happily ever after.

If you're like most folks, you will experience several forms of emotion before proceeding with a remodel. Excitement, fear, anger, and anxiety are some of what you have to look forward to. And even after the decision has been made and the work begun, moments of doubt or remorse still arise now and again. These moments can grow frequent in the middle third of your project when the work seems to be taking forever. Fortunately, these feelings are all but forgotten when the work is complete and you begin to enjoy your newly remodeled home.

Going on Safari, or Hunting for a House

Have you gone home shopping yet? If not, your project probably isn't large enough to warrant it; you haven't found the time; or you have yet to receive the preliminary cost estimates for the work that you want done. Whichever, you will most likely end up going house hunting. Our experience has been that almost everyone considering a sizable remodel does. And we recommend it because it provides a good reality check, and you can really get a feel for what's out there. Look for the following:

- Lot size
- Density (the number of homes per acre of land)
- Architectural diversity
- Modern floor plan and design trends

When compared to their current homes, the postage stamp lots, minimal clearance between houses, and narrow streets dismay most people. Conversely, they are almost always impressed with the up-to-date finishes, fixtures, and creature comforts that are a staple in newer homes. How can you help but be impressed when comparing olive green appliances to brushed stainless steel? In reality, our clients regularly supply us with design ideas that they have come upon while wading through model homes.

Determining Needs and Budget

We placed a lot of emphasis on design thus far. That's because it is the element that affects most people. After all, space and appearance are the reasons that most people consider remodeling in the first place. We classify these as needs. The other, equally deciding factor on whether to improve or move is budget. *Budget* can be defined as the amount of money that you are willing to invest in your home. Affordability and return on investment usually dictate budget. Certainly you don't want to build more than you can afford or what you could reasonably expect to get if you were to sell sometime down the road. We promise to cover the cost versus value topic more thoroughly in Chapter 2. In the meantime, suffice it to say that economics plays a major part in the decision to improve versus move.

In our experience, remodeling is almost always more cost-effective than moving — all costs considered. In our story in the sidebar, "Once upon a time," we discuss the fact that our clients had found that they could get more for their money by remodeling than moving to new digs. We have seen this scenario played out time after time in the last twenty years. However, your decision to remodel doesn't result by simply comparing our remodeling estimate to the cost of a new home. You have to consider other costs — *hidden costs.*

Hidden costs are those costs that go part and parcel with a move, but are frequently overlooked when making the comparison to remodeling. Some of these costs have tangible values that can be arrived at quite easily, such as real estate commissions and moving expense. Others of these costs are less tangible, more difficult to value, and can have emotional as well as economic impact. We cover some of these hidden costs a little later in this chapter. Irrespective of the type of cost, a cost is a cost, and it must be carefully evaluated when making the decision to move or improve.

Is remodeling for everyone? Not hardly. Earlier, we stated that remodeling is *almost always* more cost-effective than moving. Sometimes needs well exceed what a home is capable of offering. For example, local zoning may not allow you to construct what your needs dictate. Or the estimated cost to turn your remodeling dream into reality may make your home the palace of the neighborhood, rendering pennies on the dollar invested.

One of the most common ways of making this happen is by overbuilding. This condition occurs when you invest so much money in your home that it puts its value well beyond the average value of other homes in your neighborhood. Consequently, you may have the neatest home since sliced bread but can end up in serious financial trouble when it comes time to sell. Chapter 2 describes, in detail, how this can happen and what you can do to avoid it.

What Have You Got to Lose?

In our experience, one of the single biggest factors influencing a family's decision to improve rather than move is schools. Parents are as reluctant to pull their children from a good school environment as the youngsters are to say farewell to established friendships. A move often means a change of schools and the need, from the child's point of view, to start all over again.

What value can you place on friendship?

If you've been in your neighborhood for any length of time, you've probably grown attached to certain things. Take your neighbors, for example. Friendships may date many years, perhaps even several decades. The thought of not being able to go next door to borrow a cup of sugar from Millie is more than some people care to consider, no matter what the cost. To say that an important and unique support system develops among neighbors would be a gross understatement. As a culture, our home and our neighborhood are important anchors. However, some people have been in their homes for years and couldn't begin to tell who their neighbors are. This, fortunately, is the exception and not the rule. These people are less concerned about neighbors and more concerned about the quality of the neighborhood. What is the difference between neighbors and neighborhood? Neighbors are the human element of the neighborhood. They are, for the most part, the emotional attachment that we have to a neighborhood. The neighborhood, on the other hand, consists of much more than just the neighbors. School, church, shopping, and work are just a few of the other elements that comprise a neighborhood. Moreover, their proximity to home and the comfort and convenience that each offers has a decided impact on the decision to improve rather than move.

Aside from the emotional impact, stress surrounding a move can result in behavioral problems and sometimes poor grades. Church and shopping don't have quite the same decision-making weight on a proposed move as schools do. How do they differ? Schools have attendance boundaries. Churches and shopping centers don't. A move across town (in some cases, across the street) frequently requires a transfer to a different school. And with school crowding what it is, any leniency that was once enjoyed is virtually nonexistent. On the other hand, you can move across town or even to a neighboring town and still elect to attend the same church. However, if you and your family have an active church life, living near the church definitely has its advantages.

Shopping is altogether different. We grew up in a small town where everything you could ever want or need was within a few blocks: The grocery store, drug store, cleaners, hardware store, bank, and barber were all within walking distance. Although this condition still exists in many neighborhoods, as with our neighborhood, the corner market no longer exists or has been replaced by a commercial strip center or a conglomeration of major national chain stores. So if you're in a neighborhood where shopping is convenient (even if it isn't within walking distance) and the alternative is to live in an area where you'll be required to drive quite a ways, you may want to stay put.

Moving Has Hidden Costs

One of the most significant hidden costs of moving is general repairs that must be made in order to sell your home. On top of the necessary repairs are improvements that you may need to make in order to make your home attractive to a potential buyer. For example, one of the first things that you should do when considering selling your home is to have it inspected by a professional home inspector. The home inspector should have no vested interest in the repairs and should provide, in writing, a detailed report of the condition of the property and include recommendations regarding its repair. A well-detailed report will also offer a range of repair costs to give you an idea of what you can expect to spend if you were to make all of the needed repairs. It is not unusual to spend 1 to 5 percent of the home's value making repairs.

A home inspection is only one of many inspections that may be required by a buyer to assess the condition of your property. Other inspections include the following:

- Fireplace inspection by a certified chimney sweep
- Roof inspection by a roofing professional
- Pool or spa inspection by a certified pool inspector
- Under special conditions, a structural engineer may be required to evaluate the integrity of certain aspects of construction
- A soils engineer may be needed where drainage is an issue

Each of these inspections can cost from a few hundred dollars to a thousand dollars or more. Because the seller is usually responsible for these costs, tack them on to the cost of selling your home. As if that isn't enough, you can be sure that one of the first things a good buyer will do is request that the home be professionally inspected by the inspector(s) of his choice. And nine times out of ten the inspector(s) will not only list most of the items that your inspector discovered, but he will also find a few of his own items that require attention.

Ergo, if you are under the impression that you'll be able to pack up and move into new accommodations leaving the existing abode as-is, wake up and smell the humus. While an as-is sale is an alternative, you will be expected to discount the selling price accordingly. We are by no means suggesting that you not have the home inspected. On the contrary, we are strong supporters of home inspection — both for the seller and the buyer. On the flip side, if you decide to stay, most of the repairs can probably be spread out over time so that the cost isn't quite such a sting to the old bank account. By the same token, if you plan to add on or remodel, many of the required repairs can be integrated into other work, which reduces repair costs substantially.

Chapter 2

Home Improvement Cost-Limit Rules: Show Me the Money

● ●

In This Chapter

▶ How to get the best bang for your remodeling buck

▶ The importance of planning

▶ When enough is too much

▶ How to avoid building a white elephant

● ●

Getting the most for your home improvement dollar is a primary concern if you are planning to remodel your home — whether you are simply replacing a bathroom faucet or remodeling the entire kitchen. Return on investment is a significant consideration in every remodeling project. This return includes resale value, the prevention of costly repairs, and diminished upkeep costs. For example, installing an inlaid, sheet vinyl floor is more expensive than installing cushion vinyl squares; however, the inlaid vinyl is more abrasion resistant and, because it is has fewer seams, provides a more water-resistant surface. The additional 50 to 75 percent spent on inlaid sheet vinyl flooring pays big dividends in lasting-quality. The moral: Less is more. Less money invested up front may end up costing you more money down the road.

As a homeowner or a prospective homebuyer, you probably have several projects in mind. If you are like most people, you have neither the time nor the resources to accomplish all of them. Therefore, you must prioritize. In Chapter 1, we touch upon two fundamental elements of prioritizing — needs and budget. Needs can best be described as the remodeling "wish list." The budget is the amount of money that you want to invest to make your improvements. Another way of describing the two is dreams and reality. The reality is that no matter how big your budget may be, you reach a point of diminishing returns. That's called overbuilding.

So, by the time you are ready to come up for air at the end of this chapter, we are confident that you will be able to stretch your remodeling dollar using good planning and sorting out your needs and budget. In short, you'll discover how good planning can prevent your dream from becoming a nightmare.

Planning, Planning, Planning

Each year, we do several seminars for people considering remodeling. We begin each seminar by sharing with them the three most important steps to a successful remodeling project:

- ✔ The first, we tell them, is planning.
- ✔ The second step is to do more planning.
- ✔ The third step is, you've got it, planning.

We use several examples to drive this point home, but the one that seems to work the best involves moving a wall: Moving a wall on paper with an eraser is easier than moving the real McCoy with a hammer and a pry bar.

What does planning have to do with budget and overbuilding? Lots! One of the first and most important steps in the planning process is to compare your home to other homes in the neighborhood. You do not want to over-build for the neighborhood. Overbuilding your home can make it pricier than the market can bear when it comes time to sell. Whether you plan to sell your home or stay in it, you are wise to keep an eye on local home values to help prioritize improvement projects.

Establishing home values in your neighborhood can involve a bit of investigative work. One simple way is to comb through real estate ads in your local newspaper. Many newspapers also publish a list of recent sales, complete with prices. A real estate appraisal is another sure means of establishing home values in your neighborhood, although more costly than some of the other alternatives. We believe the best resource is your local real estate professional. Most will provide a detailed market analysis, usually at no charge.

Where to draw the line

In a healthy real estate market, the general rule is to avoid making improvements that will increase your home's value to more than 20 percent above typical values in your neighborhood. In a sluggish market, you should avoid pushing the remodeled value above typical values. If you live in a neighborhood with mixed values, hold the remodeled value below top values in the neighborhood, irrespective of the state of the real estate market. For example, say that your home is worth $170,000 and is located in a neighborhood where the typical value is $200,000. In a healthy market, set a $70,000 limit on the remodeling budget for a total remodeled value of $240,000 ($200,000 plus 20 percent). In a soft real estate market (using the same values), you should hold the line at about $30,000 on improvements that will raise the home's value to $200,000, the typical value of homes in the neighborhood.

If, however, the real estate market is currently prosperous and you plan to move five years down the road, it is advisable to temper your remodeling budget by limiting it to the typical value of homes in your neighborhood. While we have yet to meet anyone who can predict the future with any degree of certainty, we do know that prosperous economic times are cyclical and, therefore, should be a consideration when you know, in advance, that you will not be hanging your hat in the current home forever.

Unfortunately, these parameters may mean that the pricey kitchen cabinets for your dream kitchen or the proposed family room add-on may jack up the home's value well above what can be considered reasonable for the neighborhood. On the flip side, under-improving a home can make it tough to sell. For example, if your three bedroom, one bath home is surrounded by four bedroom, two bath homes, your best bet is to bring your home up to snuff with others in the neighborhood before considering other improvements.

Special rules for special needs

As with any rule, there are exceptions. Families with special needs may find it necessary to exceed our suggested improvement cost cap.

A larger kitchen with an ample eating area, more spacious bathrooms with double lavatories, an additional half or full bathroom, an above-average-sized family room, a bonus room, and one or more additional bedrooms are examples of improvements that appeal to a larger-than-average family. In fact, large families commonly do one or more of these projects.

By the same token, a family with an elderly parent or college-age child may find an in-law unit to be the perfect improvement. Families with members who are physically challenged may require custom alterations such as wider door openings, an elevator or chair lift, a wheelchair-accessible shower, or wider hallways. Many of these projects are not mainstream and, therefore, do not lend the best return on the remodeling dollar. However, in terms of comfort and convenience, the yield is well above average.

Don't build a white elephant

Making improvements to suit your family's unusual needs may be your best alternative. On the other hand, too many ultra-personal improvements may put your home so far out of the mainstream that you'll not only have trouble recouping your investment, but you may also have trouble attracting a buyer when you decide to sell. We call this a *white elephant.* Don't make that mistake. If we had a nickel for every time a client has said, "We're never going to sell this house — we'll die here," we'd have a lot of nickels. We suggest that you not act on this premise.

Resale should *always* be a consideration when remodeling, even if you don't intend to sell. The one thing that's for certain in life is that nothing is for certain. Although you may not plan to sell, circumstances down the road may force you to. Therefore, whenever possible, make improvements that will appeal to the masses. Unusual colors, shapes, sizes, finishes, and details can be a turnoff to most buyers. A 400-square-foot family room may be perfect for your family, but at one and a half times the size of the average family room, it is a nightmare for most people to furnish. So go ahead and customize your home; just be sure that it isn't too custom.

What Came First, the Kitchen or the Egg?

Of the hundreds of people that we've dealt with over the years in our remodeling business, only a handful had initial budgets that came anywhere close to their needs. In fact, one of the biggest challenges that we have as remodeling contractors is to help people hone needs and budget so that a project becomes "doable." Our job is not to get the homeowner to spend more money. The ultimate goal is to create solutions that will improve home value and personal comfort within a budget that is both affordable and that makes "dollars and cents" sense. This mission should be held by any professional assisting you in the planning process be it an architect or designer. No small task!

List your needs and prioritize them. By setting priorities, you make sure that the most important and financially sensible jobs get done first. Although setting priorities seems like the most obvious place to begin, many people begin investing time and money on low-priority improvements when more pressing improvements should first be addressed. For example, a family room addition may be an attractive and value-adding project to your home. It can, however, be practically worthless if your kitchen is outdated and its wiring dangerously substandard. A priority list clearly shows that a new family room is a "could," a new kitchen is a "should," and updating the wiring is a "must." Adding a new family room would be like putting a fresh coat of paint on rotted wood.

When struggling with more projects than you have money, some projects may end up at the bottom of the list or be dropped altogether. That's precisely why you need to set priorities — to help ensure that the "musts" get done before the "shoulds" and that the "shoulds" get done before the "coulds."

Here's a sample wish list with someone's higher-priority projects listed first:

- Remodel kitchen
- Replace windows
- Install new front door
- Install new wall-to-wall carpet
- Install new powder room flooring
- Retile shower in kids' bathroom
- Paint living room and dining room
- Install two skylights in hall
- Install new roof

A Tug of War

Refining your needs and budget can be a lot like a tug of war. Be prepared to do lots of bargaining. If you think that your needs will match those of your spouse or significant other, you're in for a big surprise. It's not as easy as agreeing on a new kitchen. More important, where is the kitchen ranked on each of your priority lists? And if it isn't the first item on both of your lists, will you have enough money left in the budget once more important priorities are addressed?

Come into my parlor

The first step in the remodeling process for our construction firm is a telephone call from a homeowner considering remodeling. The call generally consists of a discussion of what the caller wishes to have done to his home. We also lay out the services that we provide and even discuss approximate costs for proposed projects whenever possible. An in-home meeting to expand upon our telephone discussion and to have a first-hand look at the home follows this telephone exchange. It is at this in-home meeting where the preliminary needs and budget discussion occurs.

Many years ago when we first began our remodeling business, these in-home visits would include only one of the decision-makers. We would spend several hours discussing needs, budget, possible design solutions, and gather a war chest of information used to create a preliminary design. A couple of weeks later, with the design complete, we would meet to review it. More often than not, more than one of the primary decision-makers would be at this meeting. Why the change? Most people perceive the first meeting as a mundane process that doesn't take more than one person.

On the other hand, everyone is excited to attend the design review meeting to see the design.

It wasn't long before we discovered that this was a recipe for disaster. The otherwise calm initial meeting became conflict resolution at the design review meeting. The party present at the in-home meeting invariably became the object of criticism by the other decision-making party. Consequently, we were back to the drawing board (literally), often starting from scratch. At the least, this can be an imposition for everyone involved and, at best, can be quite costly in design fees. Not to mention the fact that the planning process is dragged out, which can lead to construction delays and cost increases. Goes to show you just how naïve we were. We expected that one person could represent the needs and budget for all parties. What we didn't realize at the time was that the needs and budget discussion is a process and not simply an event. Moral: All parties *must* be present during all aspects of the planning process. It saves time, money, and marriages.

Chapter 3

Dollars and Sense: How Much Is Too Much?

"Darling, I love you but give me Park Avenue."

*I*n the classic television show, *Green Acres,* Oliver Douglas (Eddie Albert) and his beautiful wife Lisa (Eva Gabor) were forever trying to improve the comfort and appearance of their newly acquired home, a dilapidated farmhouse in the country.

He wanted "fresh air"; she wanted "Times Square." If Lisa had had her way, every room would have been adorned with a lavish crystal chandelier. Oliver, on the other hand, was quite content to have a simple light bulb suspended from a bare electrical cord. It was an ongoing conflict that provided a highly humorous thread throughout the program's long run.

Making matters even worse, the brother and sister remodeling team of Ralph and Alf — the comical "Monroe Brothers Construction Company" — were forever working on or bungling the improvements that Lisa and Oliver *could* agree on.

Thus, we make point number one: Lisa and Oliver Douglas didn't do their homework. They didn't have a *plan*. We're not referring to a blueprint or a floor plan — we're talking about a *master* plan — an overall idea of what they were doing, and in what order it was to be done. They had no idea what to do first, but they tore the house apart anyway.

The lesson to be learned from point one? On TV, it's funny. At your house, it isn't!

If you're like most people, you want it all — and you want it now. By the same token, unless you're independently wealthy, you're wise to perform your remodeling work in *planned* phases. That's precisely why we suggest that you first develop an overall master work plan. It allows the work to be done sensibly and cost-effectively over a period of time without constantly taking two steps forward and one step back.

One example of this hits rather close to home — in fact, *our* home. A house that one of us purchased some years back had a family room that was too small. But other necessary remodeling work took precedence over enlarging the family room, and the project had to be put on the back burner.

Among the more immediate projects were concrete patios and paths at different areas surrounding the home. Because a master plan that included a future family room expansion had been developed at the onset, no concrete was poured in the location where the family room expansion would ulti-mately be located.

The master plan saved the unnecessary expense of pouring concrete and later removing it and repouring it elsewhere to make way for the family room work.

In this instance, a couple of old axioms are well worth remembering: Plan your work and work your plan, and haste does indeed make waste.

Wants versus Needs versus Budget

Throughout this book, we speak often and emphatically about what we believe are the two most important elements of any home improvement project: needs and budget.

Needs are also linked to, and preceded by, wants. Here's the difference. A leaking roof that is in dire need of replacement is a must-do — a *need*. On the other hand, a steaming hot tub surrounded by a spacious new multi-level redwood deck engulfing the back yard is certainly not needed — it is undeniably a *want*.

Although some wanted improvements could be classified as borderline needs (you may want a new roof to improve the appearance of your home), most wants fall into the less critical planning categories of "could we" or "should we."

Over the years, we have found that not everyone can agree on exactly what items should be classified as could we, should we, or we must. Yet, you're better off to find this out early on in the planning process rather than later — after lots of time and money have been invested in multiple designs and cost estimates.

Later in this chapter we will discuss how to further prioritize your needs by breaking them down into less general categories.

A Little Communication Goes a Long Way

If you're interested in avoiding the waste of precious time and equally precious money, we have one word for you: communicate! Write this word down — it's important; we'll wait.

So what do you need to talk about? Lots! Start with wants and needs and then weigh them against your budget. If your family is like most, each person has a different idea of what she wants and what she thinks is needed, and most give little thought as to what degree your remodeling budget will be impacted.

What you are likely to find is that *you* may be the only one in your family who believes that you *need* a new kitchen. On the other hand, everyone may agree that your home needs a new kitchen but can't agree on how much to invest.

By the same token, you may have a difficult time seeing the "need" for the larger family room that other family members are lobbying for.

Don't expect to resolve all, or even most, needs and budget issues in one sitting. Although most decisions can be hammered out in the course of a few meetings, channels of communication need to remain open throughout the entire project.

The outcome of these discussions means a better relationship with your designer, architect, and contractor — and a happier home environment overall.

Children should be seen and often heard

As adults, you may have difficulty seeing things through the eyes of your children. Consequently, we have found that children are often the *forgotten* family members. Yet they can have much to offer when it comes to planning an improvement.

We can recall doing a project that, among other things, involved a whole house window replacement. One of the family members, a teenage girl, suggested that the window in her room "stick out." After a brief discussion, we determined that she was suggesting a bay window with a cushion seat, which she envisioned as a great place to read while being surrounded by the outdoors.

Sometime after the project was finished we had the opportunity to pay the family a visit. Her bay window was neatly adorned with several colorful pillows and a collection of her favorite dolls. As it turned out, the bay window also improved the floor space in her room and greatly enhanced the exterior appearance of the home — and the home's resale value — a couple of unexpected bonuses.

Kids can have valid thoughts and observations if you just give 'em a listen.

Asking questions is okay

As we've said before: A little communication goes a long way. Simply taking the time to consider the feelings of all family members can elicit full support of a project which, in turn, generates family unity and excitement — a couple of things that can come in especially handy during a stressful remodeling project.

However, communication isn't only important among family members. We encourage our clients to be as communicative with us as possible during their remodeling project. We know that this policy is in sharp contrast to the way many contractors like to operate. Many are of the philosophy that customers are to be seen and not heard. Others would just as soon never see their clients. This attitude has helped contribute to the poor reputation that plagues remodeling contractors.

Many contractors forget that most of their customers are quite unfamiliar with the construction process and, therefore, tend to have many questions. Some contractors are put off by these questions and often complain that the customer is telling them what to do.

When choosing a contractor, be sure that he or she is comfortable with the prospect of your asking lots of questions. If not, we suggest you find someone who is. Your questions and ideas should be welcome — and communication is the key.

We've all heard the remodeling horror stories. The project came in way over budget; the contractor didn't finish the project anywhere near on time; and the process was almost unbearable. Sound familiar? Our experience is that many of these nasty misadventures could have been avoided had the homeowner taken more time in the planning stages of the project.

We'll say it again: The first step to a successful remodeling project is lots and lots of planning. For example, if you're considering a kitchen remodel in time for a June wedding, serious planning should start in the fall of the prior year.

Serious planning means that you're doing more than just thumbing through an occasional remodeling magazine you picked up while standing in the grocery checkout line. In our opinion, serious home improvement begins when you actively seek out information related to all aspects of your proposed project. If this strikes a cord, you'll want to be sure to tune into Chapter 7 where we will discuss this subject in great detail.

Unless you intend to put every bit of spare time and energy into planning your improvement (and most people can't), you should be prepared to spend a minimum of six months doing your homework. "But," you say, "the contractor told us that he can begin the work immediately and that we can make decisions along the way." WRONG! You're setting yourself up for disaster. The contractor who suggests doing business this way is one you definitely want to avoid.

Makin' a List, Checkin' It Twice . . .

Listing your needs and then prioritizing them makes the planning process much easier and creates much less confusion in the long run. Also, by setting *priorities,* you make sure that the most important and financially sensible jobs get done first.

This process helps ensure that the "musts" get done before the "shoulds," and that the "shoulds" get done before the "coulds." With good planning, you may even have money left over to do a few of those highly desirable "coulds."

These three basic categories can be further expanded into seven types of considerations:

- Health and safety/building code
- Cost control
- Needed repairs
- Improved appearance
- Improved function
- Improved lifestyle
- Pure luxury

Take a closer look at each category and what you should be considering.

Health, safety, and building code items

In all cases, health and safety items should be your number one priority. You may, for example, want to consider the following:

- Installing smoke detectors, carbon monoxide detectors, and radon detectors
- Testing for lead and asbestos and doing any necessary abatement
- Installing and repairing handrails
- Upgrading electrical systems
- Replacing faulty electrical wiring
- Grounding an electrical system
- Installing a child-safe garage door and opener
- Using tempered glass as shower doors
- Replacing unsafe appliances
- Repairing or replacing your furnace
- Surrounding a swimming pool with protective fencing

Improvements for the elderly, infirm, or the physically challenged are other worthy health and safety improvements. These may include the installation of lever door hardware, safety grab bars, faucets with more user-friendly handles, easy-access ramps, wider hallways and door openings, and a chair lift.

What's the deal with radon?

Radon is a naturally occurring radioactive inert gas that results from disintegrating uranium in the earth. It typically makes its way into homes through cracks in concrete floors or basement walls and floors.

When allowed to infiltrate the home, radon can cause health problems and, thus, should be monitored and prevented. Among the most effective means of dealing with this problem is to patch cracks with caulking and various other types of patching compounds. In addition, an exhaust system can be installed in a basement or crawl space to remove potentially harmful levels of radon.

Fortunately, radon is not a problem for most people in the United States. Its existence is primarily limited to the Rockies, the Midwest, and New England.

And what about asbestos and lead?

More than radon, lead and asbestos affect more homes than any other potential health hazards. Asbestos can be found in various construction materials used to build homes prior to 1978. Lead, on the other hand, was used in the formulation of lead-based interior and exterior house paints.

Fortunately, the United States government banned the use of both asbestos and lead in 1978. Accordingly, if your home was built prior to 1978 and you suspect that it might contain lead and/or asbestos, we strongly suggest that you immediately go to Chapter 16 for more information on this subject. Do not pass GO; do not collect $200.

Childproofing your kitchen against potential accidents is another worthy project. Protective locks and cabinet latches, electrical outlet covers, protective cook top covers, and an oven door lock are a few of the many inexpensive safety devices that can make the kitchen infinitely safer for the little people in your house.

Controlling household costs

Like health and safety, household *cost control* items should rank high on your priority list. As remodelers, we consider these *must* projects. Unfortunately, many homeowners fail to comprehend the benefits that can result from performing one or more of these items. Those who do, enjoy lower utility bills, decreased maintenance costs, or the prevention of what may now be a small repair from growing into a large and expensive undertaking sometime down the road.

Essentially, projects that control household costs are money savers — both now and in the future. Replacing energy-inefficient single pane windows with new double or triple pane windows is an excellent example of a cost control project. What makes these projects increasingly popular is that, as with the window example, they not only lower your utility bills, but they also improve comfort and enhance your home's appearance — and they are a plus at time of resale.

While replacing an old "gas-guzzling" furnace may not improve appearance, it *will* make your home more comfortable and lower the amount of money paid to your local utility company each month. This option is worth considering if your monthly bills are sky high.

A penny saved is a penny . . . well, you know. The following projects all rank high as endeavors that will help you control monthly household costs:

- ✔ Insulating walls, floor, and ceiling
- ✔ Adding weather-stripping around exterior doors and windows
- ✔ Caulking gaps and penetrations in siding
- ✔ Repairing or replacing a leaking roof

Basic improvements

Basic repairs are those projects that show up on most "honey-do" lists throughout the year.

Most of the projects in this category are simple fix-its or cleaning tasks that take little more than some good old-fashioned elbow grease. Caulking around the bathtub, getting rid of mildew, patching wallboard, repairing a dripping faucet, removing countertop stains, cleaning and buffing a kitchen sink, replacing broken door hinges, and repairing curling vinyl are just a few examples.

However, not *all* basic repairs are small, inexpensive, or easy do-it-yourself projects. Replacing a tired old range or worn out carpeting and replacing and regrouting shower tile may require professional assistance.

The basics are just that. Give them your attention first — before the spiffy "wants."

Cosmetic improvements

These are projects that have a great effect on the appearance of your home — or what is more affectionately known as "curb appeal." With cosmetic improvements, a little can go a long way.

However, not all cosmetic and improved appearance projects are inexpensive. Unfortunately, many of these projects just end up being quick fixes for seriously needed repair work — all sizzle and no steak.

Two such projects are roofing and painting. In an attempt to make a quick sale, the seller of a property often slaps a fresh coat of paint on the home's exterior without regard to proper preparation. The appearance of the home may be improved from the curb, but up close, significant repair work may necessitate another paint job the following year.

The same holds true for a roof. Often an old, leaking roof with curled shingles is covered with a new layer of roofing without regard to the condition of the roof sheathing. Most people know that a leaking roof will damage the wallboard or plaster inside the home. What many people don't know is that more often than not the roof sheathing is also damaged, requiring repair before a new roof is installed.

Thus, the only means of thoroughly inspecting and repairing roof sheathing is to remove all layers of the existing roof cover. Don't get talked into making appearance upgrades by contractors who offer unbelievable prices with the promise of being in and out quickly. Doing so is like putting new chrome wheels on your car with tires that are bald. It may look good, but you don't have much to look forward to when you're doing 70 mph on the freeway!

With that in mind, you can truly improve the appearance, livability, and value of any home by adding the following:

- A new roof
- A fresh coat of paint
- Wallpaper
- Paneling
- Crown mold
- Chair rail
- A new garage door
- New landscaping
- A new entry door and lockset
- Shutters
- A greenhouse window
- Skylight

You may have trouble assigning actual dollar amounts to many of these projects for the sake of return at time of resale; still, a large number of these improvements can make all of the difference in the world when it comes time to sell your home.

Without needed repairs and/or a few well-thought-out cosmetic improvements, your home can sit on the market indefinitely. Therefore, the ten or fifteen thousand dollars that you may have been willing to knock off your selling price would probably be better spent in making needed repairs and some cosmetic improvements that would allow you to increase the asking price and ultimately ensure a quicker sale.

Peas storage hot, peas storage cold

One virtually universal project with every client who walks into our remodeling showroom is the need for more or improved storage. No one ever seems to have enough closet or storage space. Many homeowners have considered a room addition just to gain additional storage space. Pure overkill.

Many people are actually able to dramatically improve storage by simply better organizing the space they *already* have — which can be done for a fraction of the cost of adding on. This process has become so popular that a host of specialty companies now do nothing more than rearrange, rework, and reorganize your existing storage and closets.

Let your fingers do the walking through the "closets" section of the Yellow Pages of your local telephone directory. You're sure to find plenty of companies who will visit your home for a complimentary consultation and cost estimate.

Additionally, a wide assortment of shelving and storage components can be found in almost any home center.

Functional improvements

No one's home ever seems to be quite as functional as he would like it. Remodeling projects that make your home function more efficiently are among the most practical home improvement projects.

Cosmetic and appearance-type projects give your house lots of sparkle but add little substance. Just the opposite is true of projects that make the home more functional.

Some functional improvements are fairly simple:

✔ Adding a cabinet or countertop

✔ Adding cabinet accessories such as a spice rack, pull out, or lazy Susan

✔ Adding a modern appliance

Improvements that make the home function more efficiently aren't always small, easy, and inexpensive. An additional bathroom for the children, for instance, or a larger garage for improved workspace may be just the ticket. And these projects mean a call to your local contractor — keeping in mind the tips and advice found in this book. So don't even think about hiring a contractor without first reading and rereading Chapter 9.

Lifestyle improvements

Although generally expensive, lifestyle improvements have the greatest overall impact on the home and its occupants — and, might we add, the greatest appeal.

More than any other category, these projects personalize a home. They can turn a cookie-cutter tract home into a charming custom abode or a dazzling showplace. These highly personal improvements are why most people choose to remodel rather than move.

Examples of lifestyle improvements include the following:

- A master bathroom remodel to accommodate the needs of two income earners
- A bedroom addition that doubles as a home office
- A family room addition or a larger family room to accommodate a media center, a game table, or other sources of entertainment
- A master bedroom suite that includes a sitting area, a large walk-in closet, and a bathroom with a whirlpool tub to relax in at the end of a long day's work
- An in-home gym for the health-conscious family

Do you have a room that would jump to life with the addition of a greenhouse window — or a crackling fireplace? Your imagination and pocketbook are the only limitations, so let your imagination soar.

Your home is your castle

Earlier in this chapter, we talk about the importance of differentiating between wants and needs.

Luxury improvements are almost always *wants,* although you can find exceptions. A swimming pool is a good example. Considered to be a luxury improvement, most people use a pool solely for recreation — and to cool off in after sunbathing. Yet some people have a pool for health or therapeutic purposes. Thus a want becomes a need.

Unfortunately, luxury improvements are usually so user-specific that the return on investment can be very poor, especially if the improvements over-improve the home relative to the neighborhood values.

Two (or three) birds with one stone

The beauty of some improvements is that they satisfy more than one category. For example, a new roof purchased as an appearance improvement can also classify as a health and safety improvement and/or a household cost control improvement. A roof with a good fire rating helps the home resist fire, making it safer. The new roof also curtails any leaks that can result in expensive repair bills to roof sheathing and wallboard, making it a cost containment improvement. When a new roof consists of slate or other rare and costly materials, it can even be classified as a luxury improvement.

Projects that fall into more than one category are considered among the most cost-effective — and desirable.

However, if the money is available and higher-priority improvements have been taken care of, you may be able to justify luxury improvements such as a pool, a sauna, a gourmet kitchen with commercial grade appliances and top-of-the-line counters and finishes, or a state-of-the-art home theater.

Have Your Cake and Eat It, Too

Although most people remodel to make their home more enjoyable and more functional rather than to increase its value, few families stay in one house forever.

Therefore, resale value should be kept in mind when planning home improvements. Remember that the real cost of an improvement is based on the purchase price less the selling price. For example (according to statistics gathered by *Remodeling* magazine), the average cost nationally for a bathroom remodel in 1997 was $8,563, with an estimated resale value of $6,582 — a 77 percent return on investment. Therefore, the *real* cost of a bathroom remodel, considering *resale value,* would be $1,981 ($8,563 − $6,582 = $1,981).

Location, location, location

Not everyone can expect a 77 percent return on investment. Your return may not be quite as generous. On the other hand, you may be among those with a dollar-for-dollar return. Or you may even make money on your improvement!

Many factors influence the return on your remodeling dollar, such as geography. The experts tell us that if you live in San Francisco, your return on investment on that bathroom remodel mentioned earlier can be as high as 125 percent, which is in sharp contrast to the anticipated return for that same project in say, Albany, New York, where the projected return is a mere 40 percent. Still nothing to sneeze at, but you should be aware of the potential return — based on geographical location — before you proceed.

The following factors influence return on investment:

✔ Property values

✔ Local labor and material costs

✔ Regional popularity of a particular project

✔ Condition of the real estate market

✔ Average value of homes in your neighborhood

✔ Style of the improvement

✔ Amount of time the improvement has been in place

If you're unsure of what kind of return to expect on your investment, check with a few local realtors for their opinions before you sign on the dotted line.

As we discuss in Chapter 2, a sluggish real estate market can significantly diminish your home value and, in turn, any improvements that you've made. By the same token, your return in a prosperous real estate climate can be a hefty one. Also, the average value of homes in your neighborhood has a profound effect on your return.

Your luxury bath may have cost more than the value of your run-of-the-mill-bathroom neighborhood can handle. This goes back to our discussion on over-improving in Chapter 2. Time is an equally important factor. For the purposes of their report, the "Cost versus Value" prognosticators' estimated values are conditional upon a home being sold in one year.

Even though few homeowners put newly remodeled homes on the market, predicting further into the future becomes dicey. However, everyone agrees that the payback percentage for any prudent remodeling job should increase in the long term.

Beat the clock! Tick, tock . . .

Other, less tangible, factors affect the return on your remodeling dollar. A home that sits with a for sale sign in the front yard for an extended period can negatively affect your bottom line.

However, a safe, well-maintained, up-to-date home — one that contains a host of modern amenities with mass appeal — speeds the sale of a home. And the sooner your home sells, the more likely you are to get top dollar.

Moreover, a quick sale may also mean avoiding pending price increases in the construction cost or purchase price of your *new* home. Not to mention the fact that a sudden increase in interest rates can make qualifying for your new loan more difficult and result in substantially higher interest payments.

Other, indirect benefits of remodeling can only be realized on April 15th when the tax man comes calling. Depending upon your specific circumstances, the cost of home improvements can increase the *cost basis* of your home, which can mean big savings in capital gains taxes when it comes time to sell. Keep in mind that the cost basis of your home is the sum of the original purchase price of your home along with the cost of all improvements made to it.

Thus, if the purchase price of your home was $100,000 and you added a swimming pool that cost $10,000, the cost basis (considering no other improvements for the sake of this example) would be $110,000.

Quality is like money in the bank

Another major factor that influences the value of your remodeling work is the *quality* of the work. When it comes to construction and residential remodeling, the word "quality" is one of the most abused words in the business.

Beauty may indeed be in the eye of the beholder, but quality work isn't one bit subjective — it either is or isn't. And when it's *not,* money spent to improve the appearance and value of your home may do just the opposite.

So how do you avoid ending up with a liability instead of an asset? Simple! You treat everything that you do to your home as an investment. After all, for most of you, your home is the single largest investment that you will ever make. Why, then, would you ever want to do anything that could potentially weaken that investment? This investment attitude pays big dividends. Your improvements will look better, last longer, and require less maintenance.

Insist on quality products and quality work. It pays — really!

Beauty and the beast

Labor and material are the two variables that most control the quality of a job. Being cost-conscious certainly is good business, but not when it steps over the line to becoming penny wise and pound foolish.

One of the quickest ways to shoot yourself in the foot is by hiring unskilled labor to perform work that is best left to the professional. While remodeling isn't like building a bridge, it can involve hundreds, even thousands of details. To expect every contractor to be *equally* proficient with all of these details is foolhardy. While we have had experience with craftspeople who are able to do many things very well, they are the exception and not the rule.

Our advice: Only hire qualified craftspeople. For example, if you are planning to have your house painted, you should be shopping for a painting contractor. After you narrow the scope of painting contractors, visit previous jobs to see their work first hand. Also, use this opportunity to sound out past clients.

The same holds true for material. Many contractors attempt to make their estimate for a project attractive by specifying inferior material. After all, the faucet for your new kitchen can cost less than $50 — or well over $500. The irony is that at first glance, the two may be difficult to tell apart. However, the proof is in the pudding. What can be so different about the two faucets? Lots! Table 3-1 outlines the differences in the two faucets. This example can be used with virtually any product incorporated into your remodeling project.

Table 3-1	Materials and Cost	
Part	*$50 Faucet*	*$500 Faucet*
Valve construction	Plastic	Brass
Washer construction	Rubber	Ceramic
Trim construction	Plastic	Brass
Finish material	Paint	Powder coating
Hose construction	Rubber	Metal reinforced rubber

Compare apples to apples

Don't get us wrong. We aren't suggesting that you may always need a $500 faucet for your new kitchen. We *are*, however, suggesting that you think twice about selecting the bargain-basement model.

Price and quality aside, information on all the products that you choose for your project should be given to all contractors bidding the work. Each bid you get should be based on the same price level for all components. This is the only surefire way to generate an apples-for-apples bid. Anything less results in confusion and disappointment.

So what's it worth?

Everyone has his or her own personal idea of which particular projects will offer the greatest return on investment, and just how *much* they will increase values with a potential buyer at time of resale, or how much of an increased *finance value* it will create for your home with your friendly lending institution.

To this end, each year *Remodeling*, a home improvement industry trade journal, publishes its annual "Cost vs. Value Report." Table 3-2 examines the cost versus value of various remodeling projects for 1997-98.

Check and see how this information relates to your wants and needs, your priorities, and your budget. Then sit down and start makin' a list and checkin' it twice.

Table 3-2	Cost versus Value for Remodeling Projects		
Job	*Job Cost*	*Resale Value*	*Cost Recouped*
Minor kitchen remodel	$22,509	$20,340	90%
Two-story addition	$56,189	$48,943	87%
Master suite	$37,388	$32,527	87%
Attic bedroom	$23,002	$19,839	86%
Family-room addition	$32,558	$27,904	86%
Bathroom remodel	$8,563	$6,582	77%
Deck addition	$5,927	$4,356	73%
Replace siding	$5,099	$3,593	71%
Home office	$8,179	$5,679	69%
Replace windows	$5,976	$4,042	68%

Chapter 4

How Will You Pay for It?

. . . .

In This Chapter

▶ Finding the money to pay for your dream home

▶ Paying with cash

▶ Getting various types of loans

▶ Finding out about second mortgages

▶ Getting the government to help foot the bill

. . . .

*I*n this chapter, we discuss a critical area that often determines the speed and ease of your project's completion — where are you getting the money to fund your remodeling project?

This question is so important that we always ask it in our initial discussion with a prospective client. If payment is not properly planned for, it can ultimately cause confusion, delays, and needless frustration.

You can fund your dream project in many ways. However, those who fail to execute at least one or more of these many options — early in the game — run the risk of seeing their dream project deteriorate into a long, drawn out, wasteful remodeling nightmare.

With home improvements, as in life, money makes the world go 'round . . . smoothly. Best have some before you start. Once the job clock is ticking, needless delays due to funding glitches *can* be expensive. ***Remember:*** When the project begins, time truly does become money.

This chapter gives you a better understanding of the many choices available to you to fund your remodeling project. We also tell you how to shop for a loan and some of the more important questions to ask — questions that can literally save you tens of thousands of dollars in the long run.

Avoiding the Money Pitfall

One of the most important aspects of knowing what to do lies in learning what *not* to do, which brings to mind *The Money Pit,* one of our all-time favorite movies, which stars Tom Hanks and Shelley Long.

In this movie, a young couple buys a fixer-upper, thus unleashing a long string of comedic disasters that should be required viewing for every homeowner facing repair work and/or remodeling.

In one scene, they have need for a plumber. Hanks calls for one, and just as he hangs up the phone, the plumber instantly appears and roars up the driveway behind the wheel of a flashy, late-model Cadillac. Covered in gold jewelry, Mr. Goldchains steps out of his car and instructs Hanks to immediately write him a check — all before Hanks has the opportunity to get a word in edgewise.

Desperate and exasperated, Hanks meekly complies with the plumber's demand and surrenders the money. Keep in mind, Hanks has yet to even tell the plumber *why* he called him out to the home in the first place.

So first watch the movie. Then, if a contractor says, "Show me the money" before he says, "Show me the problem," you'll know how to respond: "No thanks. Next!"

Know How Now or Go Slow Later

Fortunately, most people understand the need for, and importance of, payment information early on, and they are fully aware that that information prevents a whole lot of wheel spinning and needless delays on both sides later down the line.

Put yourself in the position of having spent several months planning a second story addition with your architect or contractor only to find that you're not able to finance the entire project as previously planned. These types of delays will have you asking, "Will we *ever* get this project off of the ground?"

Or worse yet, you're ready to begin the project and learn that the loan funding process tacks on another four weeks. Then your question becomes, "Will we ever get this project *finished?*"

Rest assured that this needless frustration can easily be avoided by doing some financial preplanning and then sharing that information with the contractor of your choice.

Simply put: Discussing finances (project costs and what you're willing to spend) up front can prevent confusion and costly delays later.

Paper or Plastic: How to Pay?

The United States Department of Commerce estimates that total expenditures for remodeling in 1997 exceeded $125 billion. What's more, the remodeling industry has been a $100 plus billion industry for more than a decade and, based on historical growth, the end appears to be nowhere in sight.

So where does all this remodeling money come from? Industry statistics show that the majority of these billions of dollars are borrowed from various lending sources. Refinancing existing mortgages, obtaining new second mortgages, using equity lines of credit, and applying other creative types of financing are among the most popular options for borrowers.

While most projects are financed with borrowed funds, a sizable number of people still choose to pay cash.

But these cash buyers are the exception, not the rule. In fact, many people who have the *ability* to pay cash still choose to borrow — for a variety of reasons ranging from tax implications to keeping back-up reserves at optimum levels.

Cash is king — or is it?

Ultimately, should you pay cash? Unless you are independently wealthy, the answer is probably not.

A significant portion of our customers are seniors, and they almost always prefer to pay cash.

We conclude that this has much to do with the fact that many of these people are products of the Great Depression of the 1930s. They are, by nature, more conservative financially. Also, because of their age, they are more likely to have accumulated savings, which allows them the choice to pay cash. In addition, seniors are not in their primary earning years, which means that any tax incentives that they could otherwise take advantage of do not apply.

In contrast, most young people have not yet had time to develop their savings — or they are upwardly mobile (otherwise known as yuppies) and still living from paycheck to paycheck.

However, if you are a youngster with lots of extra cash, paying cash may be the smart thing to do. On the other hand, if you are young and have lots of available cash, you'll want to consult your tax advisor before making a move.

Age aside, other factors should influence one's decision whether or not to pay in cash.

Cost is a consideration

The *cost* of the improvement can certainly be a deciding factor in the decision to pay cash.

For example, a person with ample savings is more likely to pay cash for a $15,000 bathroom makeover (which may be a fraction of their savings) rather than for a $50,000 kitchen remodel (which can account for the lion's share of their nest egg).

Financial planning experts are always quick to caution people not to liquidate their cash. You should strive to always have savings for unexpected expenses that may arise. To keep savings at a comfortable level and not amass too much debt, many people opt to pay part in cash and finance the balance.

You may be able to earn more money investing your cash than what it would otherwise cost you to borrow the money.

If your savings is generating a 5 percent return and the cost to borrow is 8 percent, the *net cost* of the loan is 3 percent.

```
8%-5% = 3%
```

Conversely, if your investments are yielding a 10 percent return and the cost to borrow is 9 percent, you are then earning 1 percent.

```
(10%-9% =1%)
```

Your savings can be significant depending upon the specific amounts involved. Weigh your options carefully for the best possible scenario.

Subtract Line 12 from Line 3C

A major factor that can influence your decision to pay cash is taxes. Interest expense on loans secured by your home can often be tax deductible. Hence, if you are in a high tax bracket, it may make better sense for you to leave your savings alone and borrow, using your home as collateral.

Doing the organized paper shuffle

You should begin the process of borrowing money right at home. Start by organizing all of your personal financial information (income tax returns, pay check stubs, household expense information, and so on).

Regardless of whom you attempt to borrow money from, the first thing they will want is information about you and lots of it. Trust us, by the time you get the loan, you will have completed so many applications and shuffled so much paper that you'll wonder how many trees gave their lives for your cause.

Being prepared only makes the process less painless and your loan proceed more expeditiously.

The interest expense diminishes your taxable income resulting in less money to Uncle Sam come April 15th. However, certain limitations may preclude you from deducting loan interest. Check with your tax accountant for specific details.

Borrowing more than a cup of sugar

Should you decide that you will *not* be paying cash for your remodeling, then you will be borrowing your funds — and you'll soon find that shopping for a loan is an adventure in itself. The good news is that lots and lots of people out there want to lend you money. The bad news is that the process is confusing at best.

While you can finance your home improvement in various ways, one element is common to most home improvement loan agreements — your home will probably be used as collateral.

With such security, most lenders are anxious to make this kind of loan. And interest rates for *home secured* loans are traditionally lower than other types of consumer credit.

May I please have seconds?

Mortgage. Webster defines it as: 1) the pledging of property to a creditor as security for the payment of a debt and 2) the deed by which this is done.

The root of the word mortgage is *mort,* which is the French word for "dead." Appropriately, most people are in this state by the time they pay off their mortgage. This, however, is not *always* the case.

Bankers are always wishful thinkers living in a perfect world

As the Rolling Stones song says, "You can't always get what you want . . . but if you try sometimes . . . you get what you need."

Your home will most likely be your loan collateral, and the current *loan-to-value ratio* will determine the maximum amount of money that a lender is willing to loan you.

Simply stated, the loan-to-value ratio is the value of your home less the total amount of money you owe on it – expressed as a percentage.

For example, an 80 percent loan-to-value ratio is the most common lender limit. Hence, your existing mortgage balance — added to the amount you wish to borrow — should not exceed 80 percent of your home's appraised value.

Using these criteria, a person with an appraised home value of $175,000, and an existing first mortgage of $95,000 would be eligible to borrow $45,000 ($175,000 value × 80% = $140,000 less the $95,000 first mortgage = $45,000).

While 80 percent is the most common loan-to-value ratio for traditional second mortgages, you do find exceptions to this rule. Some lenders will commonly lend up to 90 percent of the home's value. Keep in mind, the higher the loan-to-value ratio, the greater the lender risk, the higher the interest rate. This principle is the yin-yang of how loans work.

Other factors that affect the amount that you can borrow are your income and the total of all other debts. Essentially, lenders want to see all of your monthly contractual obligations, including your new loan payment, not exceed 40 percent of your family's gross monthly income.

Why? Because the term of a loan can vary greatly. A conventional first mortgage is generally amortized over a 30-year period. Contrast that to a second mortgage that is traditionally amortized over 15 years. (Keep in mind, though, that the term for a second mortgage can also be for as little as three years.)

The elements that most influence the term are

✔ How much money you borrow

✔ How you structure an affordable monthly payment

The most popular type of home improvement financing is a second mortgage. Simply stated, a second mortgage is a lien tacked on to a home that already has a first mortgage. With a favorable credit and payment history, your chances of procuring a second mortgage are quite good.

Second mortgages are particularly appealing to folks with low-interest first mortgages, where refinancing at a higher rate doesn't make sense. You almost always fare better if you leave that 6.5 percent first mortgage alone and tack-on a 10 percent second instead. An exception would be when the balance on your first mortgage is very low. (We discuss refinancing in more detail in the section "Starting from scratch" later in this chapter.)

Bear in mind that mortgages have a pecking order that affects the interest rate. For example, in the event of default and foreclosure, the first mortgage holder can recover funds before the holder of the second mortgage. Due to this increased risk, the rate for a second mortgage is typically one to two points higher than the interest rate for a new first mortgage. Shop for the loan plan that best suits your individual needs.

Starting from scratch

The second most common means of financing a home improvement is to refinance. When refinancing, all existing debt secured by your home is paid off and a new first mortgage is issued. The new first mortgage can be for the amount of the existing indebtedness or can include *cash out* for remodeling or other purchases.

To illustrate, if the appraised value of your home is $200,000, a new first mortgage with an 80 percent loan-to-value ratio would result in your being eligible for a $160,000 loan. If your existing total indebtedness (that is, your mortgage) was only $100,000, you would have $60,000 that could be used to remodel your home.

With a second mortgage, you make two monthly payments — one to each of two lenders. When refinancing, you make only one payment to the primary lender.

Refinancing makes the best sense in the following situations:

- ✓ When the interest rate for a new first mortgage is equal to, or less than, your existing mortgage rate
- ✓ When the combined monthly payment for a first and second mortgage exceeds the monthly payment for a new first mortgage

The disadvantage is that you will probably end up paying more interest in the long run (if you take the loan to full term). The advantage is that you have a more affordable monthly payment when the mortgage is amortized over 30 years.

The loan-to-value limitations, requirement for private mortgage insurance, and debt-to-income ratios with second mortgages (see the preceding section) apply to refinancing as well. Each course of action has its merits, so you need to determine what works best for your particular situation.

What's my line?

A relatively new method of financing your home improvements is with an open-end personal line of credit secured by your home.

With this type of loan, you can apply for the maximum amount of credit that you and your home can qualify for. You can then use part of this amount to pay for your desired home improvements and the balance to pay off other bills, invest in property, or use as you wish.

One of the most appealing aspects of this type of loan is the fact that once approved for a given amount of money, you don't need to keep going back to the well for approval. You can borrow all or only a portion of the funds within your limit of approval.

In the simplest terms, a line of credit secured by your home is a lot like a credit card with a very large credit limit. The difference is that, in most cases, tax laws allow you to deduct the interest on a line of credit secured by your home — credit card interest is not deductible.

Interest rates on home-secured lines of credit are comparable to other, more traditional mortgages and are affected by the same conditions — loan-to-value, credit, term, amount, and so on.

Back to the future

Some lenders consider a portion of the value of the improvement when making a loan. These loans are called *future value* or *future equity loans*. They allow you to borrow more money by including part of the perceived value of the improvements. Most lenders who use this program recognize 50 to 75 percent of the cost of the proposed improvements.

For instance, say that you want to spend $25,000 installing a new roof and replacement windows. If your home has a current market value of $200,000 and your loan balance is $150,000, you can only borrow $10,000 under the 80 percent loan-to-value criteria.

A future equity loan that recognizes 75 percent of the $25,000 allows you to borrow an additional $15,000 for a total of $25,000.

A hundred percent and then some

New and increasingly creative loan programs are popping up everyday to meet consumer needs. Two such programs are the 125 percent and the 135 percent loan programs.

Essentially, these programs allow you to borrow up to 125 percent or 135 percent, respectively, of the appraised value of your home with a $150,000 maximum loan limit. To illustrate, according to the terms of the 125 percent loan, if your home is worth $200,000, and you owe $150,000 against the home, you can borrow $100,000 ($200,000 × 125% = $250,000 − $150,000 = $100,000).

The difference between the two loan programs is credit and income. The 125 percent program is widely available to consumers with good credit and income. The higher loan limit is reserved for people with exceptional credit and above average income. In short, you need to demonstrate that you're a good risk and that you have the wherewithal to repay the loan.

A real plus is that in addition to home improvements, these programs can be used for vacations, loan consolidation, college tuition, a new vehicle purchase, or wherever your imagination takes you.

Bear in mind that interest expense on this type of loan is tax deductible to 100 percent of your home's value. Thus, with an already higher rate due to increased risk, combined with the lack of some deductibility, these loans can end up being a bit pricey. Check with your tax accountant for more specific information.

Borrowing from your uncle (Sam)

The government of the good old U.S. of A. can also be of help when searching for money to pay for your remodeling. No, they're not likely to give it to you, but you may qualify for a government program that offers lower interest rates, relaxed qualifying standards, a higher loan-to-value ratio, or any combination of creative financing possibilities.

One such program is the FHA Title I loan. This loan program is guaranteed by the Federal Housing Administration and has several advantages:

- ✔ The program can be used to finance improvements up to 100 percent or more of your home's value.
- ✔ No formal appraisal is required.
- ✔ The turnaround time can be much shorter than conventional forms of financing.

The downside is that the FHA Title I program has a limit of $25,000, and loan proceeds can only be used for non-luxury projects such as remodeling a kitchen or bathroom, or installing a new roof. Examples of projects that don't qualify are a swimming pool, spa, or decking. And while the fees and turnaround time can be attractive, interest rates can be on the high side due to the low equity requirements. Still, this kind of loan can be far more attractive than using a credit card as credit card interest is *not* tax deductible.

Brother, can you spare a dime?

One last avenue for financing your remodeling dream is to negotiate a loan *not* secured by real estate. This alternative may include borrowing from a family member, a friend, or your friendly local bank, savings and loan, or credit union.

These funding options can also be used as an add-on to other loans.

For instance, when refinancing or adding a second mortgage, you may fall a few hundred — or a few thousand — dollars short of the total amount needed to accomplish your goals. If so, one of these programs can be used to pick up the slack, provided that the monthly payments are affordable.

Aside from paying a potentially higher interest rate, keep in mind that you won't be able to deduct the interest expense on loans such as these. A call to your friendly tax accountant is in order when considering one of these alternatives.

A loan from your local bank, credit union, or savings and loan doesn't always mean higher interest rates, though. Most lenders will lend at more favorable rates when a car, boat, or other personal property secures the loan. You may even be able to borrow against investments such as stocks, bonds, insurance, profit sharing, and retirement plans.

Let me give you my card

You may want to consider funding your remodel by using a credit card. Due to high interest rates, credit cards should be a last resort and, in any event, should be considered only for small projects or portions of larger ones. In the case of a kitchen remodel, you may opt to use a credit card to purchase a new appliance or a plumbing fixture, for example.

Chapter 5
A Direct Look at Non-Direct Costs

In This Chapter
▶ How a building permit can save you money and even your life

▶ A look at costs you (or your contractor) may not have considered

▶ Who has the last word about what you can and can't build

*W*hen it comes to building, the Uniform Building Code (UBC) is the law. The UBC requires planning and building permits. The fees you pay to get the permits translate into non-direct costs for you (as opposed to direct costs like concrete, lumber, and carpentry, to name a few).

These fees are normally paid for by the contractor (when one is involved) and should, therefore, be included in your cost estimate. If, on the other hand, you will be doing the work yourself, they are costs that you want to definitely be aware of as they can take quite a bite into your remodeling budget.

Besides the building permit, you (or your contractor) also have to pay for the following:

✔ Plan review or plan check fee. This fee covers the cost of a city planner's time to review your plan to ensure that it complies with local planning ordinances such as property line setbacks, height, and design.

✔ Plumbing permit.

✔ Mechanical permit.

✔ Electrical permit.

✔ Insulation permit.

Not all projects require a building permit. For example, fences not over six feet, retaining walls not over four feet, painting, papering, and similar finish work do not require a permit. One-story detached accessory buildings used as tool and storage sheds, playhouses, and similar uses are also excluded, provided that the projected roof area does not exceed 120 square feet.

By the same token, if you are replacing kitchen counters, which requires the removal and reinstallation of a sink and cook top, you probably don't need a building permit, but you may need to pull plumbing and electrical permits. When in doubt check with your local building department.

Although the law of the land, it can be amended by both state and local planning and building agencies. Therefore, it is always a good idea to check with your local building department to determine when (and for what) permits will be needed.

As you pour through this chapter, we hope to make you aware of the importance that planning ordinances and building permits play in your remodeling project — if for no other reason, to avoid a run-in with the law. Moreover, we want you to have a sense of the costs associated with "playing by the rules" so that you can budget accordingly.

Being Penny Wise and Permit Foolish

In an attempt to save money, some people avoid the planning and permit process. Their rational is, "Why get the government involved? Uncle Sam is not going to stick his nose into my business. A home is a man's castle and no one is going to tell me what I can and can't do to it."

This attitude is foolish and potentially dangerous. It can be a recipe for disaster.

Contrary to popular belief, getting a permit is *not* like sending an engraved invitation to the tax assessor. Actually, the permit process is designed to protect you, your family, and the community from potential health and safety hazards. As you will discover in the "Go Ahead, Make My Day" section of this chapter, the inspection process that goes part in parcel with obtaining permits is done to determine that the work performed meets minimum building code and not a means of harassing the homeowner.

Well-thought-out public planning and stringent building codes save lives and lessen the risk of property damage. Get a permit. You won't be sorry.

Peter Piper Picked a Peck of Pickled Permits

Doing work without a permit can be expensive. Prior to selling a home, improvements that were made without a building permit may need to be demolished or, at a minimum, reworked to satisfy code. We have seen cases where paneling, wallboard, and framing needed to be removed in order to expose electrical wiring so that it could be inspected *after the fact*. Getting a permit and doing the work right the first time would have been far less expensive than the corrective work. What's more, substandard work exposes you, your family, and your neighborhood to risk.

The problem is that not everyone can agree on what constitutes "substandard work." Precisely our point.

Quality is a word that is really abused. Consequently, what one builder considers a "well-built, structurally sound building" may be a house of cards to another. What one electrician looks upon as a professionally wired job, may be viewed as an accident waiting to happen by someone else.

How Much Is That Permit in the Window?

Although permit costs can vary slightly from community to community, the Uniform Building Code establishes permit fees. Table 5-1 outlines many of the building permit fees from the UBC.

Table 5-1	Uniform Building Code Building Permit Fees
Total Valuation	*Fee*
$1 to $500	$21
$5.01 to $2,000	$21 for the first $500 plus $2.75 for each additional $100, or fraction thereof, to and including $2,000
$2,001 to $25,000	$62.25 for the first $2,000 plus $12.50 for each additional $1,000, or fraction thereof, to and including $25,000
$25,001 to $50,000	$349.75 for the first $25,000 plus $9 for each additional $1,000, or fraction thereof, to and including $50,000
$50,001 to $100,000	$574.75 for the first $50,000 plus $6.25 for each additional $1,000, or fraction thereof, to and including $100,000
$100,001 to $500,000	$887.25 for the first $100,000 plus $5 for each additional $1,000, or fraction thereof, to and including $500,000
$500,001 to $1,000,000	$2,887.25 for the first $500,000 plus $4.25 for each additional $1,000, or fraction thereof, to and including $1,000,000
$1,000,000 and up	$5,012.25 for the first $1,000,000 plus $2.75 for each additional $1,000, or fraction thereof

Thus, if the total value of your remodel is $30,000, your building permit fee would be $394.75 ($349.75 for the first $25,000 plus $45 for the remaining $5,000). For the purpose of establishing the permit fee, many building departments use the value of the work given to them by the contractor or owner. Some, on the other hand, assign values based on an established rating system.

A Real-World Example

Here is an example used by the city of Brentwood, California. They use a 600 square foot addition with a 400 square foot awning. They rate the cost of construction of a wood frame building at $67.60 per square foot plus $3.00 per square foot for air conditioning for a total of $70.60 per square foot. They figure the awning value at $10 per square foot. By the way, these values are conservative by any standard.

A little quick math reveals that the valuation of the addition is $42,360 and the awning $4,000 for a total valuation of $46,360. The building permit fee based on this value is $395. As it happens, the city of Brentwood uses the building permit fee schedule from the 1991 UBC. So if you attempt to calculate the fee by using the UBC fees from Table 5-1, you'll come up with a higher number.

That takes care of the building permit. Keep in mind that other fees generally accompany the permit such as plan review, and permits for electrical, plumbing, and mechanical work.

In this city of Brentwood example, the "plan check fee" is $256.75, which is 65 percent of the building permit fee. The 65 percent value is a standard derived from the Uniform Building Code.

Other fees included in this example are an "energy plan check fee" of $70, an "office automation fee" of $7.22, an "electric permit" for $87.80, a "plumbing permit" for $143.90, and a "mechanical permit" for $79.55.

The energy plan check fee is used to ensure that the proposed improvements meet current energy planning requirements. This fee is not to be confused with *energy compliance engineering,* which is required if your proposed improvements don't meet the standard compliance package. The cost for energy compliance engineering can range from $100 to $500 depending upon the complexity of the project. Energy compliance engineering is done by an independent engineering firm or sometimes by a heating contractor.

Electrical, plumbing, and mechanical permits are required if your project contains any electrical, plumbing or mechanical work. Thus, if you are adding an electrical outlet, running hot or cold water lines, or extending a heat duct into a room addition, you need electrical, plumbing and mechanical permits. The fees for these segments of work are minimal compared to the overall picture. Several means are used to determine the fees for each of these crafts.

Most building departments have a base permit issuance fee and then charge by the outlet, fixture, or device. The electrical permit for Brentwood is $87.80. This amount encompasses an issuance fee, 30 receptacles and 10 lights, a plan check fee, and an office automation fee. Building departments are increasingly including an office automation fee which covers the cost of upgrading manual record-keeping and accounting tasks to more streamline computer automated systems that help to take a little "red" out of the red tape.

The plumbing permit and the mechanical permit fees also include issuance fees, plan check fees, and office automation fees. The plumbing permit is calculated by the number of fixtures (water heater, sinks, toilets, and so on) and the mechanical permit by the number of furnaces, vents, and other mechanical devices.

Some communities calculate these permit fees without regard to the number of outlets, fixtures, or devices. They simply multiply the square footage of the improvement. For instance, one of the communities that we do work in charges $.0325 per square foot for each craft for which a permit is issued. Thus, an electrical permit for a 600 square foot addition is $19.50. Accordingly, plumbing and electrical permits would be similarly priced — as a function of the square footage of work.

The grand total for the permits and fees for the city of Brentwood example is $1,040.22 or just over 2 percent of the total valuation. In most cases, permits range from 2 to 5 percent of the total valuation of the work.

Hold on, we're not done yet. You also have to worry about school fees, drainage fees, grading permits, or encroachment permits.

- ✔ A **school facilities fee** is typically not required on remodeling work where no addition is being built. When adding on, this fee normally doesn't kick in unless the project is over 500 square feet. Therefore, a 600 square foot addition in the city of Brentwood requires a school facilities fee of $1,104. This fee is limited to certain states and is, in most cases, paid directly to the local school district.

- ✔ Some communities also assess a **drainage fee** that is based on the *new impervious area*. In other words, if the soil is covered and can't absorb rainwater naturally, the water must be discharged into a municipal storm drain system. Increased use of the storm drain system means more maintenance and repair costs and the need for increased income to offset these costs. Ergo, the drainage fee. This fee also accounts for increased capacity for detention basins, ponds, channels, and streams to prevent flooding. Expect to pay in the neighborhood of $.35 per square foot of new impervious area. By the bye, the drainage fee for a swimming pool alone can run in the neighborhood of $300.

✔ A **grading permit** is normally not required for a residential addition. This permit is generally reserved for new construction only. The same is true for community facilities fees (fire and police services), park and trail fees, and street improvement fees.

✔ An **encroachment permit** is required when your improvements infringe into the public right-of-way. Most home remodeling projects don't require an encroachment permit because they rarely infringe upon public rights-of-way such as streets and sidewalks. Be prepared to cough up $500 to $600 for an encroachment permit. The good news is that the lion's share of this fee constitutes a deposit. Only about 20 percent of the total fee is collected for the permit. The balance is refunded when the work is complete and the building department is assured that it doesn't have to make repairs to the public right-of-way.

Go Ahead, Make My Day

The building inspector is an enforcer of sorts, but not the Clint Eastwood kind of enforcer. We've yet to see an inspector walk on to a job toting a 357 magnum and point it at the contractor while asking, "Well, do you feel lucky?" Drama aside, building officials really do have the powers of a law enforcement officer. Now you know why we get along so well with our local building officials.

The building inspector determines that all the work — building, plumbing, electrical, and mechanical — meets prevailing building codes. He is the objective third party who has public safety in mind while evaluating the work. Keep in mind that you are part of that public!

The building inspector should never be confused as a job superintendent or on-the-job instructor. He'll be the first to tell you that he has better things to do than write up correction notices for work that's not up to snuff. The quickest way to get on your inspector's bad side is to make him your job superintendent. Do you really want to make an enemy of the person who has both the powers of a law enforcement officer and the authority to approve your remodeling project?

Many people fear that aside from inspecting their remodeling work, the building official will traipse through their home on a witch-hunt in search of building code violations. Not true! An inspector is there to inspect the work for which the permit was issued — no more, no less.

Sometimes, though, this work may require a visit to various locations throughout the home.

For instance, the installation of a new roof requires a building permit. A standard condition for this permit, and for any permit issued in the U.S., is that a smoke detector be installed in each of the bedrooms in the home. Hence, when the inspector makes his final inspection of the roofing project, he will also check to see that the smoke detectors have been installed as required.

Keepin' Your Distance

The first step in the permit process is plan review by your local planning department. Plan review is done to determine that your proposed project does not encroach into property line setbacks established for your lot. The *setback* is the minimum allowable distance from the property line to a structure on your property.

Building setbacks vary from neighborhood to neighborhood and according to zoning. Also, they are usually different at various locations on the property. To illustrate, you may have a side yard setback of five feet on one side of your home and ten feet on the opposite side.

By the same token, your rear yard setback may be twenty feet. So, if the back of your home is currently 35 feet from the rear property line, you can extend the back of the house up to 15 feet (35 – 20 = 15) — provided that no other restrictions prevent this.

The only time that you need to deal with setback requirements is when adding on. There are, however, a couple of interesting exceptions to this rule — a greenhouse window and a fireplace.

In both instances, a greenhouse window and a fireplace (not constructed within existing living space) will stick out beyond the face of the existing exterior wall. Although these improvements may put your home only one to two feet closer to the property line, that may be just enough to nix the improvement or require a variance.

A *variance* is the permission to deviate from a specific local zoning regulation. Typically, this approval is given by a member of the planning staff or the city planning commission. Keep in mind, a variance applies only to a zoning regulation. Building regulations or "codes" have no variance provision.

Most communities are reluctant to approve a variance request unless a definite hardship is present that prevents a homeowner from enjoying the same rights as his neighbor. However, a variance is usually granted if the deviation or exception would not have a detrimental impact on adjacent properties or affect substantial compliance with the regulations.

Variances can be issued for encroachment into a setback, exceeding height limitations, and lot coverage requirements, to name a few. The variance approval process can be quite complex, depending upon the request and the community.

The application fee to obtain a variance generally ranges from $100 to $200. Our advice is to look for possible alternatives before requesting a variance. The variance process can be time consuming and costly.

Determining setbacks is not always as easy as whipping out the old measuring tape to make a measurement from the house to the property line. Every now and then the property line can't be located. When such is the case, a civil engineer must be called in to survey the property to map lot lines.

Unsuspecting homeowners often confuse the fence line with the property line. While the two are often one in the same, it isn't always so. Thus, don't be surprised if, in the wake of a survey, your neighbor orders you to remove *your* fence from *his* property. Consider the bright side. That's better than the building inspector telling you that the foundation for your new addition encroaches into your setback. Oops!

The fee for surveying property lines for the average single family lot can range from $500 to $2000 depending upon the size and configuration of the lot and the lay of the land. Hilly lots and lots with several angles are more complex to survey and, therefore, are on the more expensive end of the scale.

Chapter 6

Overspending

. . . .

. . . .

*E*very homeowner who ventures into the world of home remodeling and/or repair must come to respect — and, when possible, avoid — four little words: "While you're at it."

Sounds pretty innocent, you say? Uttering these potentially explosive words can wreak havoc, bust budgets, and turn once straightforward remodeling projects into monstrous catastrophes.

The context in which these words are spoken is what makes them dangerous. Typically, homeowners say these words to their contractor when requesting more work — "While you're at it, why don't you add a skylight?" In the construction industry, this request is known as a *change order* — two more words you must come to respect — a written addendum to the contract that specifies a change or group of changes that the owner and the contractor mutually agree upon.

A change here or there is certainly to be expected with most any remodel, no matter how well planned. Unfortunately, one while-you're-at-it too many can trigger big delays and major overspending. You may end up scrambling for cash to pay for your job and wondering if your home will ever be back to normal. Worse yet, you may spend too much money, making your investment nearly impossible to recoup.

Look at change orders — and the "While you're at it . . ." phrase — as remodeling credit cards. In fact, you can best understand the potential danger for any project-in-progress if you simply exchange the word *change* (in change order) to *charge* order.

This chapter tells you how to avoid the change order merry-go-round. It also helps you decide when a change order is worth the trouble, tells you how to best protect yourself, and warns you of what to expect when a change order takes place.

Planning for Change

Change orders cause delays, overspending, communication difficulties, and a host of other problems that can make an already difficult experience virtually unbearable. If you're frightened, then we've done our job. We want to instill just enough healthy fear to cause you to go the extra mile when planning your project.

Life would be a whole lot simpler for all parties if change orders didn't enter the scheme of things; most reputable contractors that we know would be very happy if they never had to do a change order. They are the contractors who suggest the three Ps of remodeling: planning, planning, and planning.

Making allowances

Many people mistakenly believe that planning begins with a floor plan and ends when the ink is dry on the contract. Actually, it is the period from the creation of the floor plan to the final preparation of the contract that is the most crucial time in the planning process. It is during this time that any questions, generalizations, or confusion must be honed and resolved to ensure a successful remodeling adventure.

For instance, the contract for your new kitchen remodel may include labor to install a new ceramic tile floor along with an allowance for tile. Budget allowances are frequently used for items that have yet to be chosen such as appliances, tile, plumbing fixtures, and flooring. Remember that an allowance should never be arbitrary and should always be accompanied by a sample of what can be purchased within the value being allowed.

For example, if as part of your remodeling you are installing new wall-to-wall carpeting throughout your home, your contract should include an allowance for this budget item. The *value* is based on the number of square yards of carpet needed and the quality of the goods being installed, pad included.

So, if the carpet allowance is three thousand dollars and you need 100 yards of carpet, you are being allowed $30 per yard, installed ($3,000 ÷ $100 = $30). You must insist that the contractor present you with a sample of the carpet and pad that falls within the allowance amount. The manufacturer, weight of the goods, and the thickness and style of the pad should all be noted in your contract.

This method applies to all allowance items. If the contractor includes an appliance allowance of $4,000 in your contract, she should also have included a list of appliances, their make, and their model so that you can determine that you are satisfied with what you're getting.

Unprofessional contractors often include unrealistically low allowances. Their philosophy is that their pricing is then lower, which gives them an edge in getting the job. Sadly, after they have the job, they typically bury the consumer with change orders for upgrades.

Allowance items can count for a good chunk of a project, so make absolutely sure that you are satisfied with the appearance and quality of the products being used to establish the allowance. If you don't, you have broken one of the fundamental rules of good planning and are headed down a dangerous path.

Pay now or pay more later

The contractor who suggests making decisions after the job has begun is committing one of remodeling's greatest crimes. Often, in order to generate quick cash, he suggests that the job be started right away. When queried about finish selections, he invariably responds by suggesting that they can be "made along the way." Avoid this contractor like the plague.

Finish selections are the finish materials that you choose to have incorporated into your remodeling project. Finishes are materials for which choices can be made that influence the appearance of your remodeling project. For example, typically you don't choose concrete for your foundation, studs for your framing, or pipes for your plumbing. However, almost everyone chooses a door style, wall finish, tile size and color, paint color, and carpet style — to name a few.

A six-panel door, a polished brass, single-lever faucet, and a pink one-piece toilet are examples of finish selections. To make a finish selection complete, it should include a manufacturer name, model and/or style number, and finish and/or color number, and installation accessories.

Whenever possible, make all selections before your remodeling project begins. This way, the contractor has a head start on ordering material and supplies, which contributes to an orderly, on time, and in budget project.

Finding out — before your job begins — that the kitchen tile you want takes eight weeks to get is far easier than scrambling around looking for an alternate or, worse yet, stopping the project for eight weeks.

Having the information in advance gives you ample time to make choices without being under tremendous pressure. And, if necessary, you can wait to begin the project until all the finishes that you want are available for prompt installation. After all, you don't often remodel a bathroom or your kitchen, so you may as well have what you want.

We know from our experience as remodeling contractors that choosing *all* finishes before the job begins is sometimes unrealistic. However, the fewer decisions to make after the job begins, the smoother the job goes. Besides, you need to reserve as much of your mental energy to deal with the hustle and bustle of remodeling. Just the day-to-day changes, exciting as they may be, can zap your mental energy. The fewer decisions you have to make, the clearer your head, and the less stressful your remodeling experience will be.

Hurry now, don't delay

Change orders can cause delays, and delays almost always cost money. Delays also come with other, equally important consequences.

Many people plan a remodeling project to be completed in time for a special event. Be it a holiday, wedding, anniversary party, or other event, they want the project finished on time so that they can share their "new home" with friends and family. Others plan family vacations around the remodeling. Most people prefer to be close to home while the work is going on so that they can monitor the progress and be available should questions arise. Thus, delays can significantly magnify the inconvenience homeowners experience — especially when the bathroom remodeling won't be complete in time for Aunt Freda and Uncle George's long-awaited visit.

In most cases, homeowners can avoid this scenario. Strive to err on the side of too much planning. If your family is visiting in June, begin planning for the bathroom remodel in October or November of the previous year.

Good planning does not take things down to the wire. Thus, if the visit is in June, the plan should be to have the bathroom completed no later than May 1st. Since the average bathroom remodel takes about eight weeks, the project should begin no later than March 1st.

Here's a good rule to follow when it comes to planning: Be prepared to spend twice the time on planning that the project is expected to take. Therefore, using our bathroom example, if the project is going to take eight

Bread and butter

The only way that a contractor can rack up the standard 20 percent in change orders is if you allow it.

Way back when we were young remodelers, we were comparing notes with a friend who had been in the remodeling business for years. The subject of change orders entered our discussion, and we found ourselves beaming with pride at what, even then, was a 2 percent change order rate. Our friend began laughing uncontrollably.

When we asked him why he was laughing, he replied that we would never make it as remodeling contractors with such a low number of change orders. He proudly asserted that he "sold" an average of 20 percent in change

orders. He went on to say that change orders were his bread and butter and that they accounted for his overhead and profit on a job.

Through the years, we have heard several variations of this story from different contractors. The common thread among these contractors is that they always seem to be struggling or, as in the case of our friend, are no longer in the remodeling business. We suspect that our friend's "change order" attitude carried over to other areas of his business that contributed to his failure.

The moral of the story is that your best defense against unscrupulous change orders is a strong offense. And the best offense is good planning.

weeks to complete, begin serious planning sixteen weeks (approximately four months) before job start. Hence, our suggestion to begin in October or November of the previous year. See Chapter 7 for insight into how you can best spend your time and energy during this four-month planning period.

Take My Change Order, Please!

Good planning doesn't mean that you won't have any change orders. However, the more thorough the planning, the less likely you are to make changes. An occasional change is normal; constant and excessive change orders are a sure sign of poor planning.

We track our change order rate by computer. We are proud to say that, in nearly two decades of remodeling, we have maintained a charge order rate of less than two percent. We attribute this to the extensive planning that we do before the contract is ever signed — let alone the first nail driven. Compare this value to the industry average of twenty percent in change orders.

Getting it in writing

Never agree to a verbal change order. Read our lips: *A change order must always be in writing.* There, now that's off our chests. Verbal agreements can trigger what is affectionately referred to as *selective amnesia.* With verbal agreements, people tend to remember only those elements of the agreement that are generally in their favor. This problem is simple to solve: Put it in writing. Remember, if it's not it writing, chances are good that you won't get it.

The change order should spell out, in detail, the additional work requested. Make sure that *every* change order includes the following:

- ✔ Shop drawings
- ✔ Specifications
- ✔ Fixed-price cost estimate
- ✔ Adjustments to the completion date
- ✔ Payment terms

The change order should also state the original contract sum, the total dollar amount of all change orders to date, and the revised total contract sum. This information helps keep a handle on the amount of money you fork over to your contractor. Good contract management can mean the difference between using a petite salad fork and an ominous pitchfork.

If you have the money, I have the time and materials

Be it a contract or a change order, a *time and materials agreement* can strain your relationship with your contractor. A time and materials agreement allows the contractor to charge you for his work as he goes. Typically, the contractor charges you for several levels of labor. For example, your project may require a laborer to dig holes for a foundation, carpenters for framing, and some site supervision to coordinate the work. (If such is the case, chances are that you will pay a higher rate for site supervision than for the other two labor categories because the task of supervision is performed by a person with extensive construction and management experience who, in turn, commands a higher wage.)

In addition, the contractor charges you for material purchases, including any delivery charges (or labor to and from the store to pick up material and supplies).

One more time on time and materials

Why is a time and materials agreement an option? Two words: inexperience and greed.

Inexperienced contractors, who are not seasoned bidders, view time and materials as an opportunity to perform work without the risk of defeat if they present a bad bid. With a fixed price, they must perform the work for the agreed upon price. Every dollar above that cuts into their profit. And depending on just how bad the bid is, there may be no profit. In some cases, the contractor may be lucky to make wages. Worse, he may walk from the job and leave you hanging.

On the other hand, some greedy homeowners, in an attempt to save money, view time and materials as the panacea. These people would just as soon manage the project themselves.

Accordingly, they watch every move that the contractor and the crew make to ensure that they are getting work for every penny they spend. If they think that too much material has been delivered to their job, they complain that the contractor is being wasteful with their money. Conversely, if the contractor is short material and makes a trip to the store, these homeowners insist that had the contractor ordered enough material in the first place, they wouldn't be subject to additional pick-up and delivery charges.

Ironically, some top quality contractors use time and materials quite successfully. Unfortunately, we classify them as the exception and not the rule. Disputes over money almost always go hand-in-hand with time and materials work.

A time and materials agreement typically allows for an overhead and profit markup that can range from 10 to 50 percent, depending on how the contractor structures his agreement.

Things generally begin to unravel with a time and materials agreement when the homeowners feel that they aren't getting their money's worth for the labor. Homeowners begin to scrutinize the workers' work habits. If the workers are not constantly moving or if they make a mistake that requires correction — such as a trench in the wrong location or a wall framed incorrectly — the homeowner goes ballistic: "Why do I have to pay for your workers' idiotic mistakes when they are supposed to know what they're doing?"

 Avoid open-ended change orders. Wherever possible, a change order should contain a fixed price for the additional work, which helps avoid the money-haggling disputes that are often part and parcel with a time and materials change order.

A *fixed sum agreement* obligates the contractor to perform the work included in the contract for the agreed upon sum. If she spends more money than she originally estimated, she ends up with less profit. Conversely, if the project goes well and costs come in better than budget, the contractor enjoys a bit of a bonus. Keep in mind that even the change orders with fixed sums can be a tough pill to swallow.

Unfortunately, contractors cannot always provide a fixed price when creating a change order. One example is damage repair work that is not readily obvious, such as water-damaged floorboards or wall framing concealed by a tub, tile, or shower pan. Damage repair to roof sheathing is routinely excluded from a roofing contract. Most good roofers do, however, include a time and materials clause along with a labor rate for the work.

If the work must be performed on a time and materials basis, be sure to have the contractor include the labor rate at which the work will be billed. Additionally, when asked, some contractors do include a ceiling or "not-to-exceed" amount in their estimate, which can offer an added level of assurance.

The price of doing change orders

People are often mortified to find that the cost for additional work on a change order is almost as much as the original contract, and they are convinced that the contractor is trying to rip them off.

Inevitably, additional work costs more than it would have if the work had been included as part of the original contract. Some of the factors that can contribute to what may seem like an excessively high price are

- ✔ Delays
- ✔ Extra shipping costs
- ✔ Additional overhead expense for the contractor

Most reputable contractors also include an administrative charge as part of the change order cost. This charge covers the additional scrambling that he must do to pull all of the details of the change together. Such details include the following:

- ✔ Change order paperwork
- ✔ Cost estimates
- ✔ Drawings (if required)
- ✔ Time needed to get prices, delivery information, and so on

Other contractors have a minimum change order charge, regardless of the cost. The contractor uses a $50 or $100 minimum fee to cover the cost of document preparation and extra management expense. So, if you are changing the style of baseboard to be installed throughout your home, you may still get hit with a small minimum fee for paperwork even though the cost of the baseboard stays the same. Overall, this charge is a small price to pay to keep your job organized and to ensure that all parties involved with the change receive ample notification. A good contractor is as skilled with his pen as he is with his hammer.

Chapter 7

Information Gathering: Resources and Techniques

*P*roperly thinking a project through can save everything from time and money to perhaps even your marriage. Think we're kidding? You'd be surprised at how many divorced people got that way because they started a remodeling project without a plan. Thus, if you want out of a marriage quickly, we suggest that all you do is try adding a room — or remodeling the kitchen — without a working plan. You'll be single before the wallboard goes up. Works every time.

One of the most important aspects of planning is gathering information. This step is also the most fun. Gathering information is the process of imagination whereby you transform rough ideas into mental pictures — and product samples into dream rooms and spectacular floor plans.

Information gathering is a lot like shopping. Sometimes you're only window-shopping — getting ideas and/or doing some future planning. Other times, you actually make your purchase. Planning a remodel or home improvement is the same. First, you window-shop (or shop for windows) . . . then, later on during the construction phase of your project, you make the actual purchase based on your earlier plan.

Gathering information can be as simple as thumbing through the latest remodeling ideas magazine from the checkout counter to enrolling in a class at your local community college. In either case, the goal is to arm yourself with as much information as you can to assist with the design development of your project and to help you become a better-educated consumer.

Showrooms

We began our remodeling business nearly two decades ago here in California, and we were one of only a handful of full-service remodeling contractors in the area who had a showroom. We knew instinctively that a showroom would enhance our ability to help our customers paint a mental picture of their project. Customers would have the opportunity to see, first hand, the products and materials specified for their remodel.

Our instinct was right. Not only did the showroom increase sales, we had happier customers and fewer problems during construction. Why? Because customers liked the opportunity to review materials in advance, and in the comfort and convenience of one location.

Perhaps, as more customers continually become better educated consumers — demanding every assist and tool available to ensure the best job possible — then you may start seeing more showrooms in contractors' offices. Until that time, you know what to look for and what will provide you with the best planning assistance.

Although showrooms may still be scarce, showrooms generally have increased dramatically both in number and in size. In addition, we frequently send our clients to *specialty showrooms* whenever necessary. For instance, when a customer wants to look at a vast selection of plumbing fixtures and fittings (more than our showroom could ever accommodate) we send them to our wholesale plumbing supplier who has a complete product showroom of his own.

Mega Home Centers

Another relatively new resource for information is the mega home center. These establishments have more building products under one roof than Hawaii has pineapple. You can find a reasonable selection of almost any home remodeling product at one of these colossal concerns. The growth of these mega home centers dramatically has improved the consumer's ability to gather information and to make on-the-spot product comparisons. These operations often staff knowledgeable clerks who can also provide valuable information and product insights.

Keep in mind that many of these home centers cater to the do-it-yourselfer. Product lines frequently vary from what you can find at wholesale houses that cater to the building professional. For example, the selection of plumbing fixture choices at a home center may be a fraction of what is available from a plumbing supply house. The grade or quality of a fixture or faucet likely isn't up to par with finer lines available at a contractor supply house. But home centers can be helpful in getting the "idea" juices flowing.

Finally, don't be fooled by the low price leader! Home centers may be an excellent resource for the do-it-yourselfer but can be a disadvantage when working with a contractor. Contractors tend to buy products from wholesale outlets with which they have long-standing relationships. Thus, contractors know what to expect in terms of product quality and customer service. Good contractors look for better-than-average quality. This tactic results in a product that lasts longer and looks better than a lower quality product — and that means fewer repair or replacement problems down the road. Keep this approach in mind while shopping, pricing products, and putting your project budget together.

Finding Information in the Information Age

There has never been a time in the history of the world when information has been so readily available. To say that information is literally at your fingertips would not be an exaggeration — and especially true regarding home remodeling. Aside from the showrooms and retail outlets we mention in this chapter, you can tap into a veritable plethora of home remodeling information in many ways.

Magazines and newspapers

You can't even run to your local grocery store for a jug of milk and a loaf of bread without being surrounded by a dozen or more home remodeling magazines at the checkout counter. The list of titles is almost endless. From home plans to decorating, these publications serve as one of the most popular sources of information for many people. These magazines are widely available, inexpensive, and chock-full of four-color photos, informative articles, and hints and tips. Even the advertisements can be a source of valuable ideas.

The home and garden and real estate sections of most newspapers also can be great sources of information. These sections invariably offer a range of tips, tidbits, and features that can satisfy your thirst for information quite nicely.

Books: Time to get cracking

Need still more home remodeling information? Crack a book — by far one of the most valuable sources of remodeling information and ideas. But then, you knew that because your nose is planted squarely in one of the best.

You'll find no shortage of books on any aspect of remodeling. Better bookstores have an entire section devoted to home and garden and usually contain just about any book on any subject you could ever hope to delve into. The most important factor in choosing a book or books is to find one that works for you.

Although we are strong advocates of having a few good "how-to" manuals around the house for remodeling projects, buying them can become a major investment of both dollars and space. A trip to the local library often is just enough to get the information you need. The library is one of the most highly underrated resources available. Get (book) crackin' by visiting your local library.

In addition to your library or bookstore, the U.S. government offers a wide variety of informational home remodeling handbooks that are free for the asking. Drop a line to the Consumer Information Center, Pueblo, Colorado 81009, and request a free consumer information catalog. You receive a treasure trove of information for anyone preparing to remodel or repair their home.

Other excellent resources for free information include

- State and local contractor licensing agencies
- Industry and professional trade associations such as the National Association of Home Builders, the National Association of the Remodeling Industry, and the National Kitchen and Bath Association
- Consumer agencies such as the Better Business Bureau

Radio: The theater of the mind

Radio has been dubbed the "theater of the mind." For the last dozen years we have had the opportunity to perform in this theater with our home improvement radio program, *On the House with the Carey Bros.* This program, now in its 12th year (the last six in national syndication), provides listeners with a forum to get answers to their remodeling and repair questions.

While we like to think of our program as *the* definitive resource for answers to home improvement questions, we are but one of many local, regional, and national home remodeling radio programs across the country.

TV: A picture is worth 999 words

As recently as a decade ago, the one or two home remodeling television shows that existed were limited to only the Public Broadcasting System. Today, almost every network or station has at least one (and in many cases, several) "how-to" shows. Although these programs once were reserved exclusively for weekend broadcast, you can now see the shows 24 hours a day, seven days a week, 52 weeks a year.

The fact that television shows seem to move at light speed doesn't always allow viewers to fully absorb the information. Folks can't simply turn off the set and feel confident they can do what they just finished watching.

We have a two-word answer for getting around this problem: *home videotape*. By videotaping the program, you can view segments repeatedly until you can confidently perform the demonstrated project and/or process. Consequently, many home remodeling TV programs offer videotapes of the show and accompanying plans or other descriptive materials for a nominal fee.

When it comes to learning how to perform a do-it-yourself task, few instruments are as consistently effective as the *instructional videotape*. The techniques and information that these tapes offer used to be available only through seminars at local home centers, adult education classes, or the local college. Now, by the magic of videotape, you can bring the seminar right into the comfort of your own home. The best part is that you can attend class at your convenience and at your own pace.

Instructional videotapes can help you get a job done, but they can be weak on presenting new and exciting ideas. But hey, presenting new ideas is not their primary purpose, and you do have many, many other sources for creative remodeling input. We suggest that you use 'em all.

Home shows

One of the best means of gathering ideas and information is a home show or home expo. These events typically occur in the spring and fall when consumers traditionally pursue remodeling, maintenance, and repair projects.

Home show promoters fill an event hall or convention center with vendors peddling their products and services in the comfort of a well-lit, air-conditioned facility. This is window-shopping, big time, under the big top! Windows, doors, roofing, fireplaces, cabinets, counters, tile, appliances, flooring, wall finishes, shower enclosures, plumbing fixtures, lighting, home furnishings, home automation, and landscaping are just a sampling of the many products on display at the average home show.

In addition, expect to find lots of service providers at most shows. Designers, space planners, architects, contractors, engineers, decorators, and representatives of industry trade associations are almost always on hand. This venue can help facilitate the process of shopping for a design professional and/or contractor.

Information-packed seminars are almost always a part of any home remodeling expo. Topics usually include how to hire a contractor, kitchen remodeling tips, bathroom remodeling tips, and how to pay for your project, among others. Local professionals usually host these seminars. For instance, a local mortgage company may host a seminar on paying for your project. Thus, you not only get some much-needed information, you also make a valuable contact.

The best part is the price of admission. You can spend the entire day strolling through a home show for less than the cost of a ticket to the movies. Unfortunately, refreshments are no less expensive at a home expo than the movie theater. Thus, be sure to bring lots of cash for snacks.

The Internet

Popular, generic Internet search engines include www.yahoo.com, www.altavista.digital.com, www.excite.com, www.hotbot.com, and www.lycos.com. A visit to any one of these sites on the World Wide Web enables you to search for anything, anywhere.

However, when looking for building and remodeling products and service information, your best bet is to use an industry-specific engine. You can find, in much greater detail, information specifically devoted to your remodeling project.

A couple of building-industry search engines that come to mind are www.BuildingOnline.com and www.Build.com. Both of these sites search thousands of remodeling and building products and service Web sites and have been on-line since early 1995. As a result of their early presence on the Web, these sites have among the most thorough and, hence the best, resources in gathering information.

Computer software

Some architectural-type design programs first let you design a floor plan and then bring the plan to life via 3-D images. The software even enables you to "walk" from room to room to experience every nook and cranny of your new creation. The experience is truly mind-boggling — unbelievable until you actually try it for yourself. You may never do another remodel by the seat of your pants again. You can find most such software affordably priced below $50 at bookstores and software retailers.

Part II
Laying It All Out

In this part . . .

We help you find, evaluate, and hire contractors. You're not going to be happy with your remodeling project if you hire the wrong person to do the job. We can help ensure that you avoid that mistake. We also help you make sense of contracts, mechanic's liens, and other legal hassles.

Chapter 8

Drawing Up the Plans

• •

In This Chapter

▶ Understanding why plans are important

▶ Knowing who draws the plans

▶ Making the most out of architects, engineers, and designers

• •

*W*hen you have an organized suitcase full of brochures, magazine photos, and product information sheets (see Chapter 7), you're ready to move on to the next stage of the planning phase: drawing up plans. All of your research becomes really valuable at this stage. You can now communicate to a design professional what you want to do to your home, and you have pictures that emphasize every detail. Also, as a result of your research, you have a pretty good idea how much to budget for your project. By the way, if your project is an addition, don't forget to include money for landscaping.

The plans are the single most important part of any building project, no matter how large or small. Consider the plans the central communication device, the project bible. The plans form the only document that every person involved with the project will use — the building department, the subcontractors, and the material suppliers. You need to carefully choose the person who is to create the plan. The person you select not only needs to have a great deal of experience in creating plans, but should also specialize in drawing the type of project you want built.

Why Drawing Plans Is Important in Remodeling

With a remodel, you need to think about the high cost of replacing perfectly good walls, ceilings, floors, windows, and doors. A remodeling design should account for upgrading the plumbing, heating, and electrical systems. A good designer spends a great deal of time attempting to reuse as much of what exists as possible. In the design, you don't remove any walls unless absolutely necessary. Windows convert to doors, doors access new hallways, and old hallways are converted to enlarge rooms. People who specialize in drawing remodels acquire a certain capacity for designing around what exists. This special sensitivity to the cost of unnecessarily removing parts of the home can greatly reduce costs.

Those who draw new projects think a bit differently than remodel designers. With new projects, the order of construction begins with a clean, neatly graded lot. No obstructions lie between the delivery location and the place where the materials will be used. Everything is very orderly and done by the numbers. Contrast that with a remodel, where every wall that comes down poses a new and unusual challenge.

Designers who specialize in commercial projects also differ from remodel designers in their training and experience. Commercial building codes are completely different than residential ones. Even the building materials are different — not to mention the people who are trained to install them.

The point is, if you intend to remodel your home, don't look for help from among the folks in the new-residential or commercial construction industries. They may be excellent in their field, but you don't want them involved in your home remodel. If you plan to remodel, you want an expert in *residential remodeling design*.

Who Draws the Plans?

No law stipulates who can or can't draw a set of plans for a home remodeling project. You can draw the plans yourself or have your neighbor do them. However, some building departments require you to have, literally, a stamp of approval from either a licensed architect or a licensed engineer. Other building departments require such approval only when the job involves structural work. Mind you, this requirement normally has nothing do with the aesthetic value of the project — only its structural integrity. The "stamp" to which we refer is the respective architect or engineer's seal — rubber-stamped onto the plans — and then signed. If you don't have a relationship with an architect or an engineer, you may find it difficult to locate someone to stamp your plans. The engineer takes a great deal of risk stamping plans created by someone else. Here's why: Once the drawings have been stamped, the responsibility for correctness shifts to the person who stamped them. That person becomes responsible for every mistake — no matter who made it — obvious or not. This stamp is usually necessary only when structural work will take place. Kitchen and bath remodels and other remodel projects that don't incorporate structural changes normally don't need to be stamped. Apparently, the government doesn't want it to fall down, but they don't seem to care how it looks. This seems to further support the theory that "beauty — really is — in the eye of the beholder."

How 'bout an architect?

Architects don't generally design small, residential remodeling projects because there's more money to be made doing commercial work, subdivisions, and custom homes. Architects usually work for a percentage of the construction budget. If your remodel will cost $40,000, the architect would charge you between 7 and 15 percent, or somewhere between $2,800 and $6,000. Compare this to a 15 percent commission of $75,000 to design a $500,000 custom home, and you can see why architects shy away from remodels.

Try a designer

The inequity between the extremely high cost of becoming a licensed architect and the very small amount of design money available in the home remodeling industry caused a whole new breed of artist to evolve — the designer. Designers usually offer some other product or service in conjunction with their drawing talent. The consumer gets away with a professional design for less money and can purchase other services and products through the designer. The designer can afford to make a smaller profit on the design when the sale includes other services or products. The customer saves money, and the designer makes enough of a living to propagate his or her vocation. Because designers aren't licensed, they affiliate themselves with architects and/or engineers who perform structural calculations. These licensed professionals then stamp and sign the designer's plans when required.

Designers are everywhere. You may find an appliance store with its own "kitchen designer." Or discover a certified bath designer providing services for a plumbing products company. Home centers now employ folks to design your kitchen or bath on computer while you wait. Designers are even showing up at furniture companies.

Which designer has proved to be the most remodel-savvy of them all? You have it! The design-build remodeler. About one-third of all U.S. remodelers are now designing and remodeling all under one roof. This trend is one-stop shopping at its finest, and people are loving it. Finding good residential remodelers who will bid plans drawn by architects or other separate entities is becoming increasingly more difficult. Where architects once organized building teams, remodelers are now organizing design teams.

In Chapter 9, we include a form that you can use to qualify and hire contractors, architects, engineers, and, yep, even a design-build remodeler. No matter how someone dresses, suit or T-shirt, no one should be above scrutiny. Assembling a good building team can take a while. Take your time and do it right.

Specs

Make sure that the person who is doing the plans creates a thorough set of *specifications*. Specifications amplify the details shown in the plans. Here's how the process works, using a door as an example. The plans show where the door is located and which way it swings. The plan may even indicate the size of the door. But the specifications indicate the exact technique that builders must use to install the door and more detailed information on the door itself, for example: the number of hinges, the door thickness, what the door is made of, and its finish.

Specifications are sometimes included on the plan sheets as *schedules* (door schedule, plumbing fixtures schedule, window schedule, and so on). A schedule is the term used to define a detailed list of information about a specific aspect of the project. For example, a plumbing fixtures schedule lists each plumbing fixture, its location, size, shape, model number, color, and so on. Schedules are normally presented in a spreadsheet format (as shown in Table 8-1). However, a detailed schedule in book form is far more effective. Some remodeling contractors offer estimates that are so thorough they almost replicate a *specifications book*.

Table 8-1	An Excerpt from a Fixtures Schedule				
Location	*Type Fixture*	*Brand*	*Model*	*Finish/Color*	*Handle Type*
Master Bath	Shower valve	Moen	Spiffy	Polished chrome	Clear acrylic
Master bath	Toilet	Kohler	Integra	White	Polished chrome

In addition to the detail associated with an item and the way it gets installed, a good specifications book states who does certain work. With a lighted exhaust fan for example, two different contractors perform the installation — the electrical contractor and the heating contractor. Normally, the heating contractor supplies and installs the fan, the roof flashing, and the duct that connects them. Then the electrician wires the fan into the electrical system. With a gas-fired central heating unit, three contractors are involved. The heating contractor installs the furnace and the ducting. An electrician wires the unit so that the fan motor and automatic pilot light work, and also installs the thermostat wire. The plumber pipes in the gas line. The same three contractors are involved in installing an air conditioner.

Getting Engineers Involved

In addition to the person who does the architectural drawings, several engineers (each with a different specialty) may also have to be involved.

A geotechnical engineer, civil engineer, and structural engineer all help to create the *site plan* (a drawing of the lot with the house on it, also known as the *plot plan*), the structural calculations, and drawings. The civil engineer can be licensed to fulfill all of these tasks, but generally we see specialization in each engineering category. The civil engineer deals with survey and property layout, watershed and drainage, slope control, retaining walls, and so on. The geotechnical (soils) engineer studies the earth and reports on its stability. The structural engineer deals with structural aspects of foundation and building design.

The civil engineer

With larger projects these engineers are always involved in a very big way. With smaller projects, like room additions, their involvement is substantially reduced. For a room addition, a civil engineer may survey the property to insure that the proposed construction is placed the proper distance from property lines and easements. An *easement* is a right of way on your property that is owned by someone else. The local public utility may have an underground sewer line easement on your property. Normally, you are not allowed to build upon, or immediately adjacent to, an easement. The rules vary from one building department to another.

More often than not, planning departments allow fences to be used as property markers, eliminating the need for the surveying talents of the civil engineer. You can also determine easements by asking a title company to provide a plot map of the property. You probably have a map of your lot and the easements thereon among your mortgage documents. How's that for quick and easy civil engineering? It should be noted, however, that a formal survey should be performed whenever a project will be built close to a property line.

Our government: How they perpetuate the "Boston tea party" mentality!

We know of one community whose survey records were — and still are — a mess. To correct the problem, the city politicos require a complete lot survey for each and every addition project. They hope that the new surveys will help to restore their records. Because a full blown lot survey can cost between $1,500 and $3,000, this added expense comes as a big surprise to folks who have planned small room additions in that community. Ain't politics a pain?

Watershed and drainage are thoroughly monitored in new construction. Building agencies want to be sure that consumers aren't being duped into buying a future swamp when they purchase a new home. For a remodel, it is assumed that the property owner knows whether the back yard or basement is flooding and what needs to be done to correct it. Therefore, building agencies are less apt to require you to hire a civil engineer. In other words, why ask you to pay for a report containing information you are already aware of? The requirements for proper drainage, watershed, setbacks, and so on, don't disappear with a small project. In an established neighborhood, the information can be gathered in less expensive ways (for example, owner's testimony, neighbors' testimonies, fence lines, public records, and others).

We don't want to lead you to believe that a civil engineer's work isn't important. It is. When an addition is to be built up against a setback, enlisting the services of a qualified surveyor is wise. No one may notice until later that your measurements were off. You never can tell when a neighbor will call the city planning department and complain that your room addition is too close to their house. All of a sudden you may find yourself tearing out walls and thinking about how inexpensive that survey bid was.

The geotechnical (soils) engineer

The soils engineer tests the ground to determine what it is made of: sand, clay, shale, rock, and so on. Bores, made to depths of about 40 feet or so, reveal the composition. The soils engineer studies the bores and creates a soils report. The structural engineer then uses the report as a guideline when designing the foundation.

The structural engineer

The structural engineer must make many other important determinations involving wind, earthquake, and load calculations. The structural engineer suggests ways to construct a building so that it is sturdy enough to withstand the forces of nature. For a room addition, hiring a structural engineer who specializes in light, wood-frame residential construction is extremely important. We have seen engineers go way overboard designing an addition as if it were the Taj Mahal or a fire station or amphitheater. Don't get us wrong, overbuilding an addition isn't wrong, but it can get ridiculous. We built a home for our cousin that was really well engineered. To prove how convinced we were that it was a sturdy structure, one afternoon we landed a helicopter on the subfloor. No kidding!

Interior Decorators

With a designer and engineers on board, the team still isn't complete. Other experts can be very helpful. For example, a good interior decorator determines how a room will be furnished and decorated. These decisions can affect the location of lighting, windows, doors, built-in cabinets, and, in some cases, wall location. The ability to organize the furniture and accessories in a room is an important aspect of design. Space management, colors, and textures can enhance the beauty of a room. The decorator uses all of these elements to fulfill your needs. If a decorator is not brought in until the end of the project, you could seriously impair the ability to fulfill your needs.

We believe in moderation in all things, and we are very practical. But we have found that many designers don't have a sensitivity to room design. By the same token, interior decorators aren't always sensitive to the costs associated with moving walls, windows, and the like. If you can afford the added cost, a team effort can prove to bring forth a blend of ideas that may evolve into a very special and satisfying result.

Consider a color consultant

Several years ago, we got a call from a fellow from San Francisco who said that he wanted to be a guest on our radio program. He called himself Dr. Color and said he was a color consultant. At that time, we weren't sure what a color consultant did. He said that he was the fellow that folks all over the country called when they wanted a color scheme for a "painted lady" — you know — like the old Victorian homes in San Francisco. Well, most of our listeners don't own painted ladies, so we asked him to do color schemes for our own, respective homes. We wanted to see if his talent would be effective on less intricate architecture.

We had no idea. What he did was incredible. First, he took pictures of both homes. Then, he decided on a series of colors for each and created a color legend. Next, he numbered corresponding color swatches and numbered each part of the home in every photograph — the photos ended up looking like a paint by numbers canvas. There were numbers on the walls, soffits, overhangs, fascias, window trim, corner trim, you name it.

Dr. Color suggested six colors for one home and five for the other. Where most people would use one or two colors to paint a home Dr. Color uses five or six or more. He picks colors from stone, brick, and the surrounding landscape to crate his palette. The point: Some people have better color perception than others. This special ability can enhance the beauty of your home inside and out. At the time, one of us had just painted and the other owned a new home that didn't need paint. As we write, our homes are being painted using the color schemes created by Dr. Color — unbelievable!

Chapter 9

How to Hire the Contractor

In This Chapter

▶ Being your own contractor

▶ Hiring a contractor to do it for you — our special form will help

▶ Hiring a contractor and participating in the work

▶ Hiring a handyman

*T*he art of hiring a contractor is frequently confused with the act of getting bids. All too often the contractor who produces the lowest bid is the one who gets the job. And nothing could be more dangerous to an unwary consumer. The processes are closely related — that's for sure — but hiring a contractor and bidding are completely separate issues. Hiring a contractor involves investigating that person's character, dependability, business stability, and reputation. Bidding simply has to do with pricing a project. So why is it that so many people figure a contractor's price indicates stability or determines character? Yeah, we know, anyone who is nice enough to give a low bid has to be a really great person and therefore deserves the work.

Bidding is a separate issue and we discuss it thoroughly in Chapter 10. But this chapter focuses on hiring a contractor, right after touching on being your own contractor or "owner-builder." But please, before continuing, read the following sentence — out loud — to yourself — in front of a mirror:

A low bid does not constitute credibility on the part of the bidder.

By the by, this fact applies to architects, engineers, subcontractors, and civilians, too.

Being Your Own Contractor

What about being your own contractor? You really aren't required to hire a contractor to make improvements to your own property. The law allows you to do it yourself. That's right. Generally speaking, you don't have to be a licensed contractor to do your own room addition or remodel — or any home improvement for that matter. There are some restrictions in some communities. But, usually they are minor.

Each community has its own set of rules regarding owner-builders. We know of one community that doesn't allow owner-builders to do their own electrical work. In this community, a licensed electrical contractor must do the work.

As an owner-builder you may not need to have a contractor's license, but you are expected to get a building permit where required and to comply with all applicable building codes and ordinances. **Note:** A project can be dismantled later if it is found that a permit was not issued for the work. The discovery of this condition often occurs when a pre-sale home inspection is performed. Awe shucks, and you were getting ready to invest the value of the permit fees into upgraded light fixtures.

Actually, being your own remodeling contractor can be a truly exciting and satisfying experience. As an owner-builder you are guaranteed complete control over every aspect of your project and exactly how it will be built — right down to the very last detail. As the contractor you decide on

- ✔ Construction methods
- ✔ Materials
- ✔ Assembly techniques
- ✔ Project scheduling
- ✔ Budget management
- ✔ Hiring and firing
- ✔ Payroll
- ✔ Pickups and deliveries
- ✔ Safety meetings
- ✔ Equipment

Building inspectors are your friends

A building inspector can prove to be your closest ally. Remember that the cheapest correction cost is the one that is made *before* the project is complete — not *after*. We like to consider the building inspector as a quality control manager. We have saved thousands over the years as a result of building-official assistance. The building inspector ensures that the structure is safe and sound not only for you and your family, but for your neighbors as well, which is really important when it is your neighbor who is doing the remodel.

By the same token, as the contractor, you have no one else to blame when things go sour. When you become your own contractor, you must instantly assume several important responsibilities — many that you may not know existed. For example, when it comes to injury claims you may well be treated as an employer. When someone is injured while working on your property you ultimately may be held responsible. Have you looked into the worker's compensation laws in your state lately? A worker's crippling injury can end up costing you millions — literally everything you own. In California for example, a contractor is not issued a building permit without proof that a valid worker's compensation policy is in effect. Owner-builders are not required to exhibit such proof of insurance. Check your homeowner's insurance policy. Make sure that you have the proper coverage and plenty of it.

No, we aren't trying to scare you. Millions of home improvements have been successfully performed by owner-builders. We of all people truly know about the especially satisfying feeling associated with "doing it yourself." We simply want to make sure that you are aware of the responsibilities that accompany the task. Then, as an informed consumer, you can weigh your potential for risk against your potential for return.

Successful owner-builders generally have an abnormally strong desire to save money. They thrive on what others consider difficult challenges. And they are known to revel in the recognition that follows. One couple even admitted to us that they felt that as owner-builders they had become one with their home. Possible financial rewards coupled with the pleasure of personal involvement are achievements that should not cloud an owner-builder's normally good judgment.

You must consider some factors before calculating how much money you will actually save by doing it yourself. Time off work means lost wages. Not knowing which subcontractor is responsible for what portion of which task can put the project on a collision course with failure. And what if one of the subcontractors you hire accidentally causes a fire? The experts say that an owner-builder can expect to save about 10 percent of the construction cost. This considers the cost to repair mistakes that are normally made and lost wages (figured at $10 per hour). The greater your earning power the less potential for profit.

Most importantly, when you become an owner-builder you, in essence, become an employer. As such, you expose yourself to risks associated with worker injuries and damage to your home by people you have hired. You must not overlook this aspect of your tenure as a remodeler. Unforeseen costs can really sneak up on you here. Before taking on the task of owner-builder, have a meeting with your insurance agent. Find out who pays if an individual in your employ burns down part of your home. Find out what kind of insurance binder you need from each subcontractor that you hire. In our construction company we issue many subcontracts every week. When we discover that a subcontractor's insurance has expired, we require verification of a renewed policy before writing the subcontract.

Hiring a Contractor

Occasionally, even the avid do-it-yourselfer has to hire a contractor. Granted, hiring a specialty contractor to install a roof or redo a countertop is not as complicated as enlisting the services of a general contractor to do a whole-house remodel or a room addition. But fortunately, the task of hiring a contractor — on any level — can be simplified by following a few basic rules.

What to do first

First, call as many contractors as you have time to contact. You will have to call ten to get four responses and ultimately two bids.

Ask each contractor that comes to your home to complete a . . . credit application. That's right: a credit application!

A credit application?

Remember the last time you had to borrow money? Remember the ecstasy you experienced when you decided to get the loan? How about the agony when you were asked to fill out the loan form, the credit application, and the loan docs. Oh, all the paper work!

The lender uses information contained in the credit application to determine how stable a borrower may be. The bank wants to find out whether the borrower is capable of (and likely to) pay back a loan, and in the event of default, how to find the borrower. Yep, even though well armed with ample amounts of background information, lenders still have about a 20 percent default rate. Without credit applications, chances are that the number of disputes between lenders and borrowers would be as high as those between homeowners and contractors. Get the point? Think about it? We spend $2,000 or more on a stereo system that requires four pages (or more) of loan documents to be completed, and yet we hire a contractor to improve our home to the tune of $15,000 or more, and the work is done on a handshake, or the contractor's one page contract.

Over the past two decades, the letters we receive complaining about contractors all begin exactly the same way: "You know, at first he seemed like such a really nice guy."

In some parts of the country, hiring anyone still simply means a phone call and a handshake. The rest of us must follow a few important rules of the road to reduce the chance of failure:

✔ Practically every professional you talk with will be friendly, courteous, and helpful. But business is business, and although friendship is a key to a successful business relationship, it is important to know who you are doing business with from a business standpoint as well.

Fact: The California Contractors State License Board manages over 235,000 licensed contractors. They tell us that 80 percent of the contractors who fail do so not because of their inability to perform their trade, but because they have poor business skills. Poor bidding skills, improper money management, and a lack of understanding of your rights are just a few of the reasons for their failure.

✔ The best bid has nothing to do with a contractor's credibility. The amount of the bid does *not* indicate how or when the contractor will finish the job — or if it will ever be finished!

Our work application, which follows, forces the contractor, architect, or engineering professional who is interested in doing business with you to provide sufficient background information to make a truly informed decision. Have the form filled out no matter how large or small the project is. $500, $5,000 or $50,000, your concern about selecting a reputable person should be the same.

You can also get a credit application (at no charge) from the place where you bank. However, we think that our work application form is more specific to the construction businesses. You want to know where the contractor lives, where he banks, and how long he's been in business and in the community.

Do not accept this form from the applicant unless it is entirely complete and signed. Every blank is important. Also, do *not* use this form without first consulting an attorney in your area.

The instructions in the following sections show you how to use the work application form:

Block #1

You fill out this part. If the applicant doesn't get this information, he may not remember where to return it. Block #1 should contain the full name of the legal owner(s) of the property where the work is to be performed. Also, include the complete property address (street, city, state, and zip). The owner's work phone, home phone, cell phone, pager, and fax number(s) should be included. Don't forget to add a brief description of the kind of work being anticipated and a basic budget, too. If you include a budget, the contractor will know that you are serious and well organized. If you aren't willing to relinquish this value, the contractor will probably assume that you are being coy. Most well-organized professionals know that you have a budget and need that to begin the process. A pro won't do business with you until you are prepared to discuss your budget. And look out for the contractor who comes up with this response to the form: "I really can't help you. I have too much work to be filling out a silly form like this one." This is when you know — for absolutely sure — that the form really works!

Block #2

The company's name goes here. And it should be the company's full, legal name. For proprietorships and partnerships information about the legal name of a company can be cross-checked with the county recorder in the county where the business is located by requesting "Fictitious Business Name" information about a given company. Corporations are listed with the state rather than the county. But verification of a corporate name is just a phone call away and is as easy to do on the state level as a fictitious name statement is to do on a local level.

The company address is as important as the company name. Many companies use post office boxes for their mail. Don't accept a post office box number. You want the address where the business keeps its legal records. In the event of a dispute, you could spend hundreds of dollars to find the place where the company can be served with legal documents.

The business and fax phone numbers are needed more as a convenience than anything else. However, state and city business license numbers and issue dates are very important.

A contractor's license does not turn a jerk into a good person. The contractor's licensing process ensures that applicants (good and bad) are forced to pass an examination about both their trade and the state laws that govern their business. Good applicants will learn; bad applicants will not!

Contractor's licenses are managed in most states by the Department of Consumer Affairs or the Department of Industrial Relations. Normally, these are not the same state agencies that deal with the management of corporations. A company may be in good stead with the state as a corporation but can at the same time be on bad terms with the contractor's licensing agency. The same disparity holds true for county-level and city-level business licenses. The company's federal tax identification number will be a social security number for non-incorporated businesses and a special two part number for companies that are incorporated (for example, 68-145789). You have no idea how valuable this information can be if anything goes wrong — not to mention how many crooks you will catch in the process.

In the case of both state and city licensing, the date of original issue of the license is important. This information tells you how long the company has been working the business and in your area. If a company works in ten different cities, it must have a business license for each of the ten communities.

Work Application

for Contractors, Architects, and Engineers

This form will not be accepted by the property owner unless it is entirely complete.

Block #1 — Name, Address & Phone Numbers (complete this block before submitting it to the applicant).	
Project Description	Budget $
Block #2 — Applicant Company Name (legal company name style)	Office Phone
	Office Fax
Applicant Business Address (where company records are kept)	State Lic. No / Date Issued
	City Lic. No / Date Issued
	Federal Tax ID No

Block #3 — Owner/Officer Name	Title	Home Address	Home Phone

Block #4 — Bank Name	Address		Phone	Acct Type	Acct #

Block #5 — Worker's Comp Insurance Agent	Address		Phone

Block #6 — General Liability Insurance Agent	Address		Phone

Block #7 -- Vendor / Supplier	Contact	Address	Phone

Block #8 — Client Name	Address	Phone	Project Type

I, the undersigned, am an owner or officer of the business named in Block #2, and I hereby authorize the property owner named in Block #1 to contact and question any or all of the parties named in this document for the purpose of evaluating my character, business standing, and credit history.

_____   _____

Signature of Owner or Corporate Officer   Date

A home built without permits or contractors?

An old-timer once wrote to tell us about his father who had built the family home from the ground up with his own two hands. The fellow went on to report that it had been done without a licensed contractor, without permits, and without any government involvement at all. He said the house was over a half century old and that it was in great condition. We wish every home could be built that way, but it just ain't so. Hiring a licensed contractor, like getting a permit, is simply taking the additional step to add another layer of protection to the formula for success.

Block #3

You need to know the name of the owner(s) or corporate officers, their titles, complete home addresses, and home phone numbers. This insight makes serving legal documents easier should a dispute arise. The information given in this block can be checked with the appropriate county or state agency at the time that you confirm the business name information in Block #2.

Block #4

Complete bank information is a must. A business without a bank account may have no assets to manage the work you wish to have performed. You should know if the company is a regular depositor and a long-term depositor. Getting account number information after the fact can prove to be nearly impossible if a judgment is levied against the company. According to the Small Business Administration, small businesses (like remodeling companies) fail at a rate of 96 percent over any five-year period. So a business is especially susceptible to failure within its first five years of operation. Don't be ashamed to ask the bank for its status report on the applicant.

Block #5

Do not have anyone work on your home who does not carry worker's compensation insurance (WCI). If a contractor's employee is injured on your property and the employer does not carry WCI you could be forced to pay medical bills, costs for loss of work, and yes, even costs to retrain the worker in another type of work. The cost could be hundreds of thousands of dollars. Do not accept a copy of the insurance policy from the applicant company. Require that it be sent directly to you by the insurance carrier.

Block #6

Do not have anyone work on your home who does not carry general liability insurance (GLI). If your property is damaged by the applicant company or if an innocent bystander is injured as a result of the applicant company's involvement, you could be held responsible for that company's actions if that company is uninsured and especially if that company has no assets that can be attached to cover the cost of a claim. Do not accept a copy of the insurance policy from the applicant company. Insist that it be sent directly to you by the listed insurance carrier.

Block #7

Talking to people whom the applicant has done and is doing business with is very important. Vendor references can verify how the applicant pays his bills, and in many cases can attest to the financial stability of the applicant.

Block #8

Talking to the contractor's customers — past and current — is extremely important. You should ask the applicant to arrange for you to see the referenced projects. Another person's perception of what is acceptable may be different from your own. The work should be similar in nature to the work you wish to have done. Ask if many changes were made to the job. Ask how the changes related to the original contract sum. For example: If the original contract was $10,000 and the changes totaled $2,000, then the final price ended up 20 percent greater than the original price. A low change-order ratio indicates good planning on the part of the contractor. We are ashamed to tell you that 20 percent is almost an industry standard. The change-order rate at our remodeling company — in 14 years — has never exceeded an annual average of more than 2 percent. Remember, planning is what keeps the *real* cost down. More about this in Chapter 10.

Signature line and date

The form must be signed by an owner — or an officer if a corporation. The signature gives you the right to investigate the applicant. A legal document should always be dated. But here's the real bottom line. If you don't follow through with a thorough investigation of the applicant — and later find out that you could have prevented a problem by doing so — who will you blame?

Finally, don't go through the process of taking all this valuable information unless you intend to use it. Call the vendors, the customers, and the bank. Meet the partners, check out the license numbers, the social security number, and all the phone numbers.

The interview

If the term of the job will exceed a week, then interviewing each prospective contractor becomes extremely important — and don't think that the contractor isn't sizing you up, too. Some things to consider include the following:

✔ Ask if the contractor will have someone else doing the work (such as a working foreman). If so, ask to meet that person in advance of signing a contract. Don't expect suits and ties, but do expect cleanliness. Also, you never know when the workers will be folks who don't speak English. This arrangement can be frustrating if you don't speak their language as well. You can overcome the language barrier by insisting (in the contract) that all workers either speak English or that at least one interpreter be on the project at all times.

✔ Find out what time the applicants like to start work in the morning and when their day ends.

✔ Are they family types? When you have to live in close quarters with someone who will be working in your home for weeks or months on end, you should be sure that you are reasonably compatible. If you have a pet and an applicant doesn't like pets, you can be in a fix.

✔ Is the applicant a talker or a listener? Do you get the feeling the contractor wants to overwhelm you with claims of splendor, magnificence, and grandeur? If the contractor isn't listening now, be advised that it doesn't get better. And after the sale, salespeople go downhill. Not up-hill — downhill!

These are all things you just don't want to find out about *after* you have signed on the proverbial "dotted line."

Hiring a Contractor and Participating in the Work

If you have decided to hire a contractor but would like to participate in some of the work yourself, then go for it. There are contractors who offer "customer participation programs" in which you can perform certain portions of the work. However, you should be aware that the contractor is exposed to greater risk when you are involved. As a novice, you can innocently cause serious damage and literally double the contractor's management expense. Such mistakes also can delay production. Delays can increase the contractor's overhead and thereby reduce his profit. So don't be surprised if your contractor wants to limit your involvement to unskilled tasks such as demolition, excavation, cleanup, trash offhaul, and final janitorial work. Foundation, framing, plumbing, heating, and electrical systems are usually handled exclusively by the contractor.

Painting, flooring, bath accessories, mirrors, and other finish work can be done after the contractor is complete and after the final inspection has been performed. There is little or no contractor risk associated with these tasks. Furthermore, these items are normally not a part of the building inspection.

If you want to participate in the construction of your project, be sure to discuss your desire with the contractor before the contract is signed.

Building Contractors versus Remodeling Contractors

In most states, a licensed general building contractor or "general contractor" is allowed to construct the following

- Residential subdivisions
- Custom homes
- Commercial buildings
- Industrial buildings
- Home remodels
- Commercial building tenant improvements

Even though one license covers all of the tasks we've listed, most general contractors specialize in only one field. In fact, these fields are so different that the industry has developed a list of names that are used to differentiate one type of contractor from another. Here's how it breaks down:

- General contractors who build residential subdivisions, custom homes, commercial buildings, and industrial buildings are known as *building contractors* or *builders.*
- General contractors who remodel commercial buildings are known as *tenant improvement contractors* or *commercial remodelers.*
- General contractors who remodel homes are known as *residential remodeling contractors, remodeling contractors,* or *remodelers.*

The codes and ordinances that govern commercial work are quite different from those that control residential construction. Not to mention the fact that both of these sets of rules constantly change. Also, the basic techniques used in new construction vary greatly from those used in remodeling. For example, new construction begins with new and modern building technology and ends with a real estate agent and a For Sale sign. A remodel involves understanding how to effectively couple new technology with older buildings and building systems. But most importantly, remodeling means working in close quarters with a family who lives at the project.

Now you know what we mean when we say, "A general contractor's license does not a remodeler make!"

The Handyman

Not every job you will do requires that you enlist the services of a licensed contractor. In California, for example, you aren't required to hire a licensed contractor when the total value of the work is less than $300. The handyman is usually more competitive for small projects. If you frequently hire out small projects in your home, consider a handyman. They often advertise in the classified ads.

If it's too good to be true . . .

Recently, a dear friend asked our advice about a remodel. She told us that her handyman quoted her $5,000 to do a bathroom/bedroom addition in her garage. She asked us if we thought the price was fair. We responded by telling her that the price was too low and that it probably would not even cover the cost of the materials. She was infuriated by our response. It was obvious that she had already made up her mind. We felt that she was convinced that she had made a super deal. Our advice to you: "If it seems to be too good to be true, it probably is!" A handyman does not a contractor make, and a wise consumer does not the bait take.

Chapter 10

Getting and Comparing Bids

. . . .

. . . .

Some folks get unbelievably frustrated when they realize that they are going to have to ask a contractor for a bid. You, too, can expect to have such a frustrating experience? With the help of this chapter, maybe not.

A Roofing Example

See if this scenario sounds familiar. Assume that you want a new roof. You call ten roofing contractors, four show up to survey your roof, and you finally end up getting three bids. The bids are $8,000, $16,000, and $23,000 — all for the same house?!? And you can't figure out why the bids are so different.

In a nutshell, here is what went wrong. In this example, only one value is known to all of the bidders — the size of your roof. You didn't tell the roofers what type roofing you wanted, so each roofer simply provided a bid based on his favorite roofing material. You have no idea how often consumers make this mistake. In the case of any project — roofing, flooring, cabinetry — you must first decide on the specific material that you want. For a roof, you select the brand and type of roofing. For a floor, you select the brand, model, and color of carpet, vinyl, and so on. For cabinetry, you select the wood, door and drawer style, and so on. In other words, you need to be as specific as possible about what you want the contractors to bid on.

Getting back to our roofing example, here is what should have happened.

✔ First, go shopping for roofing material. This may involve educating yourself as you go.

✔ Next, select the exact roofing material that you want.

✔ Then, purchase a sample amount of the material to hand out to each bidder.

This effort may take you some time, but it is your house — who better to make that determination? Now, when you call those ten roofing contractors, four may still be all who show up. But when you hand each of them a piece of the roofing material that you selected, the three bids that you finally get will look more like these: $10,000, $9,500, and $10,200 — much closer together than before. Remember also that the cost of installation is directly related to the type of roofing material selected — another reason why selecting the material first helps to level the playing field. By the way, the relationship of material selection and installation cost is true for almost all construction materials — roofing, flooring, wallpaper, painting, you name it. Other aspects of the work such as removal of the old roof and water damage repairs should be handled as separately priced options. Believe it or not, this simple technique of *selecting materials first* is the basis upon which all good bids are collected.

Contractors who are extremely busy frequently submit a higher than normal bid. This tactic becomes more obvious when four or more bids are collected. By the way, a busy contractor isn't necessarily a good one.

Four Steps to Getting Good Bids

Getting a remodeling bid doesn't have to be difficult. With the right tools, it can actually be quite a bit of fun. You need to follow four steps to get and compare bids. You need the following:

✔ A group of qualified bidders

✔ A clear set of plans and/or specifications

✔ A cost breakdown form

✔ A bit of insight into how to compare and select the winning bid

Step 1: Narrow the playing field

To find good bidders, refer to Chapter 9 and reread everything you didn't completely comprehend the first time. Do so again and again until you thoroughly understand the process.

Interlude with an angry painter!

We pen a weekly home improvement newspaper column syndicated by the Associated Press called *On the House*. One article we wrote addressed the issue of how to select a contractor. Part of our advice included contacting the Better Business Bureau, the Contractor's License Board, the contractor's past customers, and current suppliers.

About a week after the column was published, we received an angry letter from a painting contractor in San Francisco. He was upset by the fact that our advice suggested such extensive investigative measures. But he seemed even more outraged by the fact that we said nothing about how to deal with unkind, inconsiderate consumers (his prospective painting customers). He went on to chastise us about how we had failed to mention how rude many customers can be. He was livid about how his prospective clients never asked him into their homes. He said that they often asked him to wait in the garage or on the front porch.

We responded to his letter in our very next column. "As contractors, we have never — not ever — been asked to wait outside. Maybe your sales appointments would be more successful if you bought a new outfit, took a bath, brushed your teeth, combed your hair, oh, and while you're at it, learned to smile."

Qualifying bidders is the single most important step in the bidding process. And don't worry about giving a break to a new, young contractor who you think may deserve a chance. He stands to get plenty of jobs and experience — an abundance of people either won't read this book or won't believe it after they have.

Here's a way to find out just how volatile the remodeling industry really is. Pick up a copy of the phone book and fan through the yellow pages until you get to "contractors, remodeling." Start making calls. You will probably find that a very high percentage of those listed are either disconnected or no longer in service. As the year goes on, the percentage of disconnected numbers usually increases measurably.

Step 2: Make sure that everyone knows exactly what you want

Whether the project is large or small, hire an architect or a designer to prepare a professional set of plans accompanied by a thorough set of specifications. You save nothing by taking shortcuts here. Specifications are an extremely important part of the planning and bidding process. They elaborate on items in the blue prints. For example, the plans may indicate that the bathroom has two sinks. The specifications indicate the brand, model, and color of the sinks, what they are made of, and any special installation instructions (below the tile, above the tile, and so on). A proper bid cannot be made by the best of remodeling contractors when specifications are incomplete. Specifications that are thorough reduce the chance that bidders will make assumptions. And you know what happens when you assume something! By the way, for small projects where plans aren't needed, you're still better off to prepare a thorough set of specifications. Get professional help here also.

Finally, ensuring that the bidders are kept aware of all changes and corrections is in your best interest. During the bidding process, you may discover a discrepancy. If so, you need to contact the bidders and inform them of the error. The idea is not to pull the wool over their eyes, but to work methodically to get the most thorough and correct bid.

You know, most goods sold over the counter are tangible — you can see, touch, and smell the finished product before you buy it. However, just the opposite is true when you shop for a remodel. A remodel doesn't become tangible until it is entirely complete. Therefore, thorough planning is an imperative. Plans and specifications can't make the project tangible, but they can make the prospective event easier for everyone to understand before and during construction.

True or False? A floor plan drawn in crayon on a torn, brown paper bag is acceptable? Definitely false. If you expect accurate bids, you need a top-notch set of plans.

Plans and specifications offer a clear picture of what you want — or would you rather rely on your contractor?

Items that are not completely clear during the bidding process are often reduced to fierce arguments between you and your contractor during the construction process. The only way to insure that a reasonably clear understanding exists during construction is to plan your project with someone who is familiar with remodeling. Get a top notch set of plans and specifications from an experienced designer or an architect who specializes in remodeling.

The professional provides specifications as a part of the plans and/or in the form of a separate book depending on the size and scope of a project. Figure 10-1 shows an example page from a specifications book. Note how thoroughly each item is detailed. A specification book for a larger projects can be quite elaborate — and even get its own binding. With smaller projects the specifications may be several sheets of information stapled to the plans.

Specifications for the Jones Residence Master Suite Addition and General Remodel

MASTER BATHROOM — Plumbing Fixtures

All plumbing fixtures shall comply with the most current version of the Uniform Plumbing Code and state and local ordinances. Plumbing contractor shall insure that all warranties and maintenance guides are turned over to the owner prior to billing for final payment.

Tub: American Standard, Lexington Cast Iron Model #2315.607.020, 60"x32", White

Waste and Overflow: American Standard, Model #2001.456, Polished Brass

Tub Valve: Omega, Futura, Model #24, Two Handle, Deck Mount, Polished Brass

Tub Valve Handles: Omega, Futura, Model #34, Crystal & Polished Brass

Toilet: Pressure Assisted, Elongated. Brand & Model not yet selected (Use Allowance of $475)

Toilet Seat: Kohler, Lustra, Elongated, Model #K62, White

Lavatory: Kohler, Portrait, Self-rimming, 24" Oval, Model #K4521, 8" Centerset, White

Installation Note: Lavatories to be installed in a 1/4" round bead of white silicone caulk.

Faucets: Omega, Futura, Model #45, Two Handle, 8" Centerset, Polished Brass

Faucet Handles: Omega, Futura, Model #55, Crystal & Polished Brass

Figure 10-1:
A page from a specifications book.

Note the comment about the plumbing code. This jargon is S.O.P. (standard operating procedure) for a contractor, but not for store clerks. So, if you intend to purchase certain items yourself (plumbing or otherwise) you will want the store to guarantee your money back in full if what they sell you doesn't comply with all applicable codes and ordinances. Remember, if the building inspector discovers a non-compliant item, you are required to replace it no matter how much it costs or who has to pay for it.

Use allowance items when details are scanty

The allowance you got when you were a kid is nothing like an *allowance* in a remodeling bid. Unlike your parents, your contractor is not giving you a thing when an allowance is included in his bid or proposal.

An *allowance* in a remodeling bid is a dollar value (or budget amount) that corresponds to a category or item of work (for example, light fixture budget, plumbing fixture budget, painting budget, and so on). This practice is commonly used by architects, engineers, designers, and other construction professionals to establish a standard value for all bidders to use when a category or item of work has not been sufficiently detailed in the plans or specifications.

For example, say that you haven't selected your kitchen sink yet, but you don't want to slow up the bidding process. All you have to do is make a notation to the bidders indicating what value you want them to use for the sink. All the sink bids will coincide if this task is done. If you don't designate either a specific sink or an exact budget value, you can count on getting three different sink prices. This practice is acceptable for individual items, small groups of items, or entire categories. Table 10-1 shows an example.

Table 10-1	A Sample List of Allowable Items	
Allowance Item	*Location*	*Allowance*
Sink, faucet, and drain	Kitchen	$500
Sliding glass door	Master bedroom	$600
Light fixtures	All	$1,200
Pressure assisted toilet	Hall bath	$475
Vinyl floor	Master bathroom	$450

A list of allowance items can be annotated onto the plans, included in the specifications, noted in the cost breakdown, or provided to each bidder on a separate sheet of paper like this one. Whatever happens, don't let a bidder establish allowances for you — you do it.

With allowance items, if the value of the allowance in the contract is greater than what is needed to make the actual purchase, the contractor normally refunds the difference to the client. On the other hand, if a greater sum of money is needed to purchase an allowance item, it comes out of your pocket — yep — even if the contract is for a fixed price. And it doesn't make any difference who decided on the allowance in the first place — you, the designer, or the contractor — the same rule applies. Can you see where things can get expensive if you let a contractor establish the allowances?

The down side of allowances

Unscrupulous contractors will suggest their own allowance values to reduce their bid in hopes of getting the client to sign on the dotted line. In a kitchen remodel, for example, a contractor may assign cabinetry, countertops, and appliances as allowance items, bragging that the items can be purchased for the values she included. The problem arises when you finally decide to purchase the items and discover a major budget deficit. Knowing what you know now, how could you possibly let an individual bidder suggest an allowance value!

Often the contractor purchases the allowance item for less than the allowance amount and "keeps the change." Read your bidder's contract to see if this issue is addressed. If not, look out!

Don't get scammed — specify exact details for every item of work. If you can't do that, be sure to stipulate an allowance value. To do so successfully, you must be aware of the prices of the items stipulated. If not, you will likely run out of money before the project is completed. Allowances should not be taken lightly.

If your contractor establishes your allowances and those allowances make up 20 percent (or more) of your construction contract, then you may be in for big-time budget problems.

Step 3: Make sense out of the prices

To make sense out of various bids, provide a blank price breakdown form to each bidder. The price breakdown form establishes a uniform pricing format, so that bidding differences and errors can be easily found. The cost breakdown also allows you to determine that at least some value is included in the bid for every category of work on the project. Additionally, the pricing divisions of labor, material, and fixtures provide yet another level of detail — and clarity.

You can't possibly be expected to understand and compare bids if you don't force the issue with a cost breakdown form. Before you pass out the form to your bidders, make sure to mark those categories of work that are not included in your bid with NIC (not in contract) or NA (not applicable). Also, don't forget to stipulate allowance values for those items of work that are not yet completely detailed in the plans or specifications.

We filled in the blanks in our example cost breakdown (see Table 10-2) so that you can see what it is supposed to look like when you get it back from the contractor (although the contractor will probably hand-write the numbers). Note the five columns: Category, Labor, Material, Fixtures, and Total. Column 1 describes the category of work. Column 2 is used when either labor or installation costs are included in the total price. Column 3 is used when material, rentals, or fees are included in the total price. Column 4 is used when fixtures are included in the total price. Column 5 includes the subtotal for each category and the total bid amount. You would be absolutely amazed if you knew how many mistakes can be found when you compare bids presented in a uniform format. Don't expect every price in every category to be broken down. Often subcontractors will not break their bids down for the contractor.

Table 10-2	A Sample Cost Breakdown			
Category	*Labor*	*Material*	*Fixtures*	*Total*
Permits and fees	$125	$1,075		$1,200
Temporary facilities (toilet, power, phone, security fence)	$450		$450	
Excavation (earth removal)	$2,000			$2,000
Demolition	$1,600	$200		$1,800
Foundation	Sub bid	Sub bid		$3,400
Carpentry labor — rough	$6,000			$6,000
Lumber and rough hardware		$6,000		$6,000
Plumbing	$1,500	$1,500	$1,500	$4,500
HVAC and sheetmetal	Sub bid	Sub bid	$2,300	$5,500
Electrical	Sub bid	Sub bid	$750	$2,200
Windows/sliding patio doors/skylights		$5,000		$5,000
Drywall	$1,300	$650		$1,950
Stucco	Sub bid	Sub bid		$3,800
Roofing	Sub bid	Sub bid		$900
Painting	Sub bid	Sub bid		$875
Insulation	Sub bid	Sub bid		$250
Doors & millwork		$675		$675
Garage door & opener	Sub bid	Sub bid		$1,260
Cabinetry	$800	$3,400		$4,200
Countertops	Sub bid	Sub bid		700
Shower surrounds, tub, decks, and walls	Sub bid	Sub bid		$3,275
Finish carpentry		$1,300		$1,300
Finish flooring	Sub bid	Sub bid		$3,000
Appliances				NIC
Mirrors & medicine cabinets	$75	$75		$150

Category	Labor	Material	Fixtures	Total
Shower doors	$75	$175		$250
Landscape and irrigation				NIC
Concrete flatwork				NIC
Fences, gates, and decking				NIC
Cleanup	$1,780			$1,780
Supervision	$4,160			$4,160
Contingency				$6,650
Overhead				$7,300
Profit				$8,000
Total Bid				**$88,525**

Many contractors don't like to provide price breakdowns. They feel that doing so gives their competition an unfair advantage. Others feel that too much information in the hands of an "uneducated consumer" can be more trouble than it's worth. Oh, and some contractors are just lazy. We suggest that you don't do business with a home remodeler who is afraid to break down his prices for you. Most banks that do construction loans have their own cost breakdown form. By the way, some refer to them as "construction breakdown" forms. Chances are, your banker will be happy to give you a copy.

Step 4: Compare and select the winning bid

When it comes to knowing what the right price should be, most folks draw a blank. You may know what you want to spend, or how much you can afford, but that isn't the same as knowing the correct price. That's why most people rely on competitive bidding — getting many bids. By comparing one price to two or three (even four) others, you will eventually be able to determine what is fair and reasonable. Contractors who have been around for a while know who the good bidders are by years of trial and error. You don't have that same luxury. That's why you must be so careful about who you select to do the bidding and the form in which the bid is returned. Even then, understanding the bids requires lots of patience and study on your part.

And don't be fooled by the low bidder. A really low bidder — like a really high one — has probably made a mistake. As a general contractor, we get five bids for each category of work and then average them. We then use the average value of that category as a bench mark from which to compare all of the bids in that category. Again, this procedure is performed for each category of work. The bids in a given category that are more than 10 percent higher or lower than the category average are thrown out and the most thorough of the remaining bids is selected. Using this formula sometimes leaves us with only one bid to select from in some categories.

You probably don't want to hear this, but be careful if the returned bid totals are all over the board. Chances are, the plans or specifications just aren't thorough enough or you haven't correctly selected your contractors — or both. When this happens, you should start again from scratch. On the other hand, when most of the bids are within about 10 percent of each other, you've done the job correctly.

With the return of the bids often comes the insatiable desire to use the low bidder no matter what. So how does the low bidder arrive at the low bid anyway? Here are a few reasons why you may rationalize using the low bidder:

✔ You are certain that the low-priced contractor has a lower overhead.

✔ The estimator made a mistake, and you get to take advantage of it.

✔ The contractor is trying to "buy" a job (bidding low to get needed work).

For some reason, the high bidder is often seen as the crook and the low bidder as a friend — or a fool — who can easily be taken advantage of.

An old saying says, "If it's too good to be true — it probably is." If the price in a low bid really is too low, who suffers? You, the contractor, or both of you? No, we don't suggest that you use the high bidder either. The answer really is simple. To get and compare good bids, you must qualify the bidders, provide thorough plans and details, and carefully compare the prices at the category level. Finally, take the average of the bids, and don't use anyone who is more than 10 percent higher or lower than that average.

Chapter 11

The Contract

*W*hat literature about contracts would be complete without some mention of the proverbial gentlemen's agreement — and the inimitable handshake between two people that binds their commitments to each other for all eternity? Certainly not this book. However, our understanding is that Pope Julius II never did get around to paying Michelangelo in full for the fine paint job he did on the ceiling of the Sistine chapel. Could it possibly be that the legendary handshake isn't all that it is made up to be?

Handshake or not, our experience with construction contracts has taught us that if it isn't in writing, chances are you won't get it. Somewhere between 40 to 70 percent of the way through a remodeling project both contractor and customer are often faced with a phenomenon known as *selective amnesia* where one or both forget important aspects of what they originally agreed to. At this point, the value of a handshake diminishes substantially and a well-detailed, clearly-written construction agreement begins to look mighty inviting.

We guarantee that this chapter will guide you through the ins and outs of construction contracts — and you can have our handshake on it.

Contract Basics

A small project like replacing a doorknob or fixing a leaky faucet shouldn't involve any more paperwork than an invoice for the repair and a check for the final payment. On the other hand, larger projects are a whole different ball game. With big projects, a good contract is invaluable. Misunderstandings during big-budget home improvements that may cost hundreds, yep, even thousands of dollars, can be prevented with a thorough agreement between the owner and the contractor.

How many money-related issues are addressed in a well-written remodeling contract, you ask? The fact is, practically every word in a remodeling contract can be reduced to a money issue in one way or another. Certain parts of the contract explain exactly what you will get in return for your money. Where other parts, like start and finish dates, indirectly address money issues. Think about it. Start and finish dates relate to how long the project will take and therefore how long you will be inconvenienced. What is your time worth and how much will it cost you in the way of additional inconvenience if your project runs unusually late? We could go on, but we're pretty sure that you get our point.

The remodeling contract basically defines the following:

- *Who* is responsible for *what*.
- *When* and *where* the work will happen.
- *Why* the work is happening.
- *How* to recover if something goes wrong.

The basic contract agreement is a single document that ties all the other project documents together (plans, specifications, change orders, subcontracts, payment schedule, production schedule, and so on). Most importantly, a good contract is *bilateral,* providing equal protection for all parties involved. Unfortunately, a thorough contract tends to be awfully wordy. We don't like contracts that are hard to read — the kind containing language that would confuse a Harvard law professor.

The amount of protection that can be offered to a consumer in a thorough contract is simply amazing. Even the statements that seem to benefit only the contractor give the consumer a choice and a chance to back out if there is an objection. For example, the contract may stipulate that a certain interest rate will be charged for late payments. When you know in advance what the proposed late charge is, you can object and negotiate a value that is more to your liking or not sign the contract at all. More importantly, if the contract doesn't stipulate a value, who knows what rate might be awarded if you lost a suit against the contractor.

We found the following contract in a local stationery store.

CONSTRUCTION CONTRACT

DATE: _____CONTRACTOR'S LICENSE NO.: _____

GENERAL CONTRACTOR_____PHONE_____

ADDRESS_____CITY_____STATE____ZIP_____

OWNER'S NAME_____PHONE_____

OWNER'S ADDRESS_____CITY_____STATE____ZIP_____

JOB ADDRESS_____CITY_____STATE____ZIP_____

The undersigned, as owners of the following described real property,

STATE OF_____COUNTY OF_____BK._____PG._____

DESCRIBED AS LOT_____TRACT_____

hereby contract with and authorize you as Contractor, to furnish all necessary materials, labor and workmanship, to install, construct and place the improvements, in accordance with the plans and specifications as attached or described on reverse which, by reference, are incorporated hereby, and in accordance with the terms set forth

hereinafter, for the total sum of materials and labor to cost $_____payable as set forth hereinafter;

Down payment $_____Balance of $ _____to be financed for_____ months.

Monthly installments of $ each, payable on   day of each month until paid in full.

This order shall become binding upon acceptance thereof by Contractor and shall not be deemed to be a bid in any sense of the word. However, upon acceptance of same by Contractor, it shall thereafter be treated as a contract between the undersigned owners and the Contractor.

Contractor to perform all work in good and workmanlike manner. He will at all times maintain proper workman's compensation insurance and shall comply with California Contractor's License regulations.

This agreement shall not be binding on Contractor unless properly accepted by the Contractor, by an officer or member of Contractor's firm, and is not subject to cancellation except by mutual written consent of all parties hereto. Full acceptance of this contract by Contractor is contingent upon his securing loan for account of owner, if loan is hereby applied for.

This contract may not be assigned by Contractor without the prior written approval of owner, which approval shall not be unreasonably withheld, and that where the term "Contractor" is used herein, it shall be construed to mean assigns, and the terms and agreements herein contained shall bind, apply and inure to the heirs, assigns, successors, executor and administrators of the parties hereto.

It is understood and agreed that all payments hereunder shall be at the office of the Contractor or of the assignee.

Contractor shall have_____ days to accept in writing this offer and if he does not so accept this offer shall be deemed null and void. At any time before written acceptance owner may revoke this offer by giving written notice of such revocation to Contractor or his authorized representatives.

It is agreed that no payment shall be made hereunder until Contractor has furnished to owners written Waivers of Mechanics' Liens by Sub-Contractors who have worked on said job as of the date on which payment is due.

_____
OWNER

_____
OWNER

ACCEPTANCE

The undersigned accepts the terms of the contract set forth herein above and agrees to faithfully perform according to the terms and conditions thereof.

DATE:_____   _____
REPRESENTATIVE FOR CONTRACTOR

_____
CONTRACTOR

The neat thing about a one-page contract is that it isn't very threatening. You don't have too much to read, and you find little or no confusing terms to challenge your command of the English language. On the other hand, the one-page contracts that we have found typically *do not* address consumer rights. In short, they provide protection for the contractor and almost *no* protection for you.

Frankly, a one-page contract just doesn't have enough space to protect you legally when you're agreeing to spend thousands of dollars. The next section presents a better contract.

A Full-Fledged Contract (Actually, Just a Summary)

We thought about showing you an entire multi-page contract — word for word. We decided that you would probably be bored to death. In the end, we thought it would be more effective if we hit on the high points and presented many of the important clauses that are most often left out of a one- or two-page construction contract. Keep in mind that this is presented as general information only, and because of varying state laws, we suggest that you confer with an attorney before using any of the information presented here.

The cover page

The cover page has always been the easiest page for us to understand. It usually contains large type, sometimes a picture or two, and often a good deal of white space. The cover page generally includes the following:

- ✔ Type of contract: stipulated sum (fixed price), time and materials, and so on
- ✔ Parties to the agreement (name, address, and so on)
- ✔ Price (numeric and written)
- ✔ Payment schedule or a reference to it
- ✔ Start and finish dates

The cover page also briefly identifies the project, provides room to list the other contract documents such as plans, specifications, and so on, and furnishes a place for the parties to sign. Some states provide for a cooling-off period, which allows the homeowner several days to cancel the agreement without penalty. We like for the contract to stipulate the existence of this *right of rescission* in boldface type.

A contract between two or more parties is designed to do two things: specify who is responsible for what and determine what to do in the event that a disagreement arises. A contract that properly covers the latter can be invaluable in arbitration or court.

Identification of the agreement and the parties

Most contracts do a good job of identifying the parties involved. And although you certainly know who you are, what about the contractor? If you haven't checked her out, do so before signing the contract. Make sure that the contractor's business name is legally correct (see Chapter 9). The address listed should be the one where his legal records are kept — not a post office box. Also, the contractor's license number should be listed somewhere on this page. You would be amazed at how often consumers are duped by contractors who actually aren't licensed. Finally, a contract date and number help to identify the agreement as a specific and unique document.

The meat of the contract

You're likely to run into one of these types of contracts:

- ✔ Stipulated sum
- ✔ Time and materials
- ✔ Management

The stipulated sum contract

With a stipulated sum contract, you pay a fixed price that can only be modified by a written change (called a *change order*) to the work. We like the stipulated sum contract best of all. It boasts a fixed price and puts the entire responsibility of completing the work on the shoulders of the contractor. Plus, we think that establishing a price before the work begins makes a great deal of sense.

Even the price of a stipulated sum contract can grow by leaps and bounds if you aren't careful. Impulse buying on your part, during construction, can easily double the work — and the cost. Not a healthy direction if the budget is limited.

Be careful not to sign a stipulated sum contract that does not include a detailed estimate. In a stipulated sum contract, you pay a specified amount for a task no matter how much it costs the contractor. The estimate can be high or low, but the price is fixed — a known value.

The time and materials contract

While time and materials contracts are great for small repair jobs costing under a couple hundred dollars, we are uncomfortable with them overall. In a time and materials contract, the price is not fixed and is therefore an unknown commodity. You only pay for the actual time (labor) and materials used at your project. With a time and materials contract, comparison shopping is difficult at best. As a consumer would you rather sign a contract where the price stays the same no matter what it costs, or would you rather sign a contract where every job cost — necessary or not — *increases* the price you pay? With time and materials, the contractor with the lowest labor rate or the lowest markup can ultimately end up being the most expensive choice.

The management contract

This type of contract causes us some concern, which is our nice way of saying that we don't like it. In the management contract, the contractor works as a consultant for a fee equal to a percentage of the contract — usually 10 percent. If the contract amount is $25,000, the contractor's fee is $2,500, plus expenses. When the amount of the work increases, so does the contractor's fee. We are uncomfortable about recommending a method where a conflict of interest is automatically built in. The work covered by a management contract can be for a specified sum or for time and materials — usually the latter. And if you read the preceding section, you already know how we feel about time and materials. But more importantly, the management contract shifts a certain amount of responsibility to the homeowner. Even partial responsibility for a large home remodel is not a risk to be taken lightly.

The project and the plans

In this part of the contract, the project is titled and then related to specific documents that detail the work to be done. Plans, specifications, and all other relevant documents really need to be a part of such a clause. A right of rescission notice also should be included in the contract in those states where a *buyer cooling off* period is required by law.

> **Notice to owner:** You, the owner, may cancel this transaction at any time prior to midnight of the third business day after the date of this transaction without penalty. See the attached notice of cancellation form for an explanation of this right.

Plan on using the latest version

During the planning phase of a project, your contractor may have been given several different versions of your plans and specifications. So at contract time, be sure that the final version of the plans (the set that you have *approved for construction*) is properly referenced in the contract (by sheet number and revision date). Also, be sure that the same set of plans is also signed by you and the contractor. To the same extent, this holds true for specifications, estimates, payment schedules, and other documents that are frequently revised during the bidding process.

We like to see all of the project-related documents in the project section of a contract. The average contractor likes to mention the plans and specifications in just that manner. We think that the statement ought to include the plan sheet numbers, the most current plan revision date, and the name of the designer or architect who did the drawings. If specifications are separate from the plans, they should be identified by title, date most recently revised, name of the person who prepared them, and total number of pages. For example: Pages 1 through 25 inclusive of the Specifications Book for the Smith Project, revised March 12, 1998, prepared by Sarah Q. Very detailed.

Each and every page of these documents should be read and initialed by both parties at the contract signing. When both parties have signed copies of these documents — along with the reference to them in the contract — both can easily determine exactly who agreed to what at a later date.

The price

Make sure that the price is printed as both a numeric sum and as a written value ($5,000 — five thousand dollars and no cents). Doing so almost completely eliminates any chance for a misunderstanding about the agreed price.

The payment schedule

The payment schedule is yet another really important part of the remodeling contract. For smaller projects, we suggest a simple payment schedule like the one presented in Table 11-1. The schedule is very specific about when a payment is due and for how much.

Table 11-1	A Sample Payment Schedule
Stage of Project	*Payment*
Downpayment at contract signing	$1,000
At wallboard complete	$10,000
At cabinets installed (including countertops)	$15,000
Upon completion of the work	$5,500
10 Percent retention (paid 30 days after completion)	$3,500

For larger projects, a more sophisticated method is recommended. In this case, the payment schedule on the cover page is replaced with a statement indicating that a separate payment schedule exists. Such a statement may read as follows: "Payments shall be made in accordance with the example payment schedule attached and marked Exhibit A." (You may notice that our payment schedule is very similar to the cost breakdown we show you in Chapter 10. Isn't it amazing how versatile basic project information can be?)

Expanded payment schedule

In our sample expanded payment schedule, shown in Table 11-2, payments are based on a percentage of completion, substantiated by calculations made in a construction breakdown format:

1. **First, the percentage of completion for each category of work is estimated by the contractor.**

2. **Each percentage is converted to a dollar value and those values are then subtotaled.**

3. **The value of the work completed ($2,740) is divided by the contract subtotal ($68,653).**

   The result is 4 percent — the percentage of work completed. This value is then used to determine the percentage of cleanup, supervision, contingency, overhead, and profit. Completion of each of the five categories is directly proportional to the rest of the work. Therefore, in this example, each of the five can be considered 4 percent complete.

4. **Finally, the dollar values of the last five items are extended and added to the billing amount.**

And you thought that creating an accurate way to substantiate the percentage of work completed would be difficult.

Table 11-2	A Sample Expanded Payment Schedule		
Category	*Total*	*% Complete*	*$ Complete*
Permits and fees	$1,200	100%	$1,200
Temporary facilities	$450	20%	$90
Excavation	$2,000	50%	$1,000
Demolition	$1,800	10%	$180
Foundation	$3,400		
Carpentry labor — rough	$6,000		
Lumber and rough hardware	$6,000		
Plumbing	$4,500		
Hvac and sheetmetal	$5,500		
Electrical	$2,200		
Windows/sliding patio doors/skylights	$5,000		
Drywall	$1,950		
Stucco	$3,800		
Roofing	$900		
Painting	$875		
Insulation	$250		
Doors and millwork	$675		
Garage door and opener	$1,260		
Cabinetry	$4,200		
Countertops	$700		
Shower surrounds, tub decks and wainscot	$3,275		
Finish carpentry	$1,300		
Finish flooring	$3,000		
Appliances	NIC		
Mirrors and medicine cabinets	$150		
Shower doors	$250		
Landscape and irrigation	NIC		

(continued)

Table 11-2 *(continued)*			
Category	*Total*	*% Complete*	*$ Complete*
Concrete flatwork	NIC		
Fences, gates, and decking	NIC		
Subtotal	**$68,653**	**4%**	**$2,740**
Cleanup	$1,780	4%	$71
Supervision	$4,160	4%	$166
Contingency	$6,650	4%	$266
Overhead	$7,300	4%	$292
Profit	$8,000	4%	$320
Totals	**$88,525**		**$3,855**

Heavy-duty contract jargon

The second page of a good contract is where things begin to look crowded and technical. But bear with us. You may end up discovering rights — and some responsibilities — that you never knew existed.

Article 1: The work

1.1 Good Construction Co. shall perform the Work required by the Contract Documents. The Contract Documents are complementary, and what is required by any one shall be as binding as if required by all.

Article 1 states that all the contract documents are complimentary. If, for example, no ceiling fixtures are shown on the plan, but some other contract document says that ceiling fixtures are included, then you get ceiling fixtures — whether they are in the plans or not.

Article 2: Time of commencement and substantial completion

2.1 The Work to be performed in accordance with this Agreement shall be Commenced and Substantial Completion shall be achieved as noted on the first page of this Agreement and is subject to authorized adjustments. When the Date of Commencement is delayed as a result of conditions beyond the control of Good Construction Co., the date of Substantial Completion shall be extended by an equal number of work days.

Article 2 expands on start and finish dates shown on the contract cover page. It says that the dates are subject to *authorized adjustments,* which means that the parties can mutually agree to change the dates. Also, the dates can be changed in accordance with other rules set forth in this contract (labor disputes, foul weather, and so on). It also says that if the start date is legitimately delayed, then the end date is extended accordingly. That's fair.

Article 3: Contract sum

3.1 The Owner shall pay the Contract Sum to Good Construction Co. in current funds for the performance of the Work, subject to additions and deductions as may be authorized by Change Order or as provided elsewhere in the Contract Documents.

3.2 The Contract Sum is determined with reference to Good Construction Co.'s Cost Breakdown, attached herewith, and is set forth on the first page of this Agreement.

Article 3 deals with the contract amount. Paragraph 3.1 relates that the owner will pay the contractor in *current funds* (the money currently in use) — no wooden nickels here. And that the amount cannot be altered without a written change order. **Note:** This clause prevents the contractor from changing the amount of the contract without your written permission.

Paragraph 3.2 states that the contract sum is equal to the total noted in the contractor's cost breakdown. This paragraph also makes the contractor's cost breakdown a part of the contract documents. Finally, Paragraph 3.2 stipulates that the contract sum (total price) is shown on the cover page.

Article 4: Progress and final payment

4.1 Based upon Applications for Payment submitted to the Owner by Good Construction Co., the Owner shall make Progress Payments on account of the Contract Sum to Good Construction Co. as provided in the Progress Payment Schedule. All payments shall be due on the day indicated.

4.2 Any moneys not paid in accordance with the Contract Documents shall bear interest from the date payment is due at 1% per month (12% ANNUAL PERCENTAGE RATE).

4.3 Final payment, constituting the entire unpaid balance of the Contract Sum, shall be paid by the Owner to Good Construction Co. no more than 30 days after the Work is entirely complete.

4.4 A salesperson's commission shall be paid out of the Contract Sum, which will be paid to the salesperson prorated in proportion to the Progress Payment Schedule.

Article 4 elaborates on when progress payments and the final payment are to be made. In Paragraph 4.1, the contract states that progress payments (payments made in conjunction with the progress of the job — see the expanded payment schedule earlier in this chapter) shall be made in accordance with the payment schedule. Paragraph 4.2 establishes the rate for a late charge — pretty standard. In Paragraph 4.3, final payment is due and payable only when the job is entirely complete — the final payment is usually equal to about 10 percent of the total contract amount. Paragraph 4.4 is required in all home improvement contracts in the state of California when a sales commission is paid. The existence of commissioned salespersons in the home improvement industry is common throughout the country.

Article 5: Contract documents and oral claims

5.1 The Contract Documents, which constitute the entire agreement between the Owner and Good Construction Co., are listed herein and, except for Modification issued after execution of this Agreement, shall include only those other documents as enumerated therein.

5.2 The Contract Documents consist of this Agreement, the Cost Breakdown, the Plans, and Specifications, all written Addenda mutually agreed upon and issued prior to the execution of this Agreement, and all written Modifications mutually issued by the Owner and Good Construction Co. after execution of the Contact such as Change Orders. THIS AGREEMENT CONSTITUTES THE ENTIRE AGREEMENT BETWEEN THE OWNER AND GOOD CONSTRUCTION CO. AND SUPERCEDES ANY PRIOR WRITTEN OR ORAL AGREEMENTS, THERE ARE NO OTHER REPRESENTATIONS, ORAL OR WRITTEN, BETWEEN THE OWNER AND GOOD CONSTRUCTION CO. RELATING TO THE SUBJECT MATTER CONTAINED IN THIS AGREEMENT, WHICH ARE NOT FULLY EXPRESSED OR REFERENCED HEREIN.

5.3 By executing the Contract, Good Construction Co. represents that it has visited the location of the Work and has reasonably familiarized itself with obvious local conditions under which the Work is to be performed.

Article 5 is pretty important because it lists all the documents that are part of the contract (plans, specifications, cost breakdown, and so on). Paragraph 5.2 states that anything you were previously told is not true unless it was agreed to in writing. This statement should remind you to be certain that everything you want is in the contract. Not every contract includes this reminder, but it should.

Paragraph 5.3 is very important. Here, the contractor tells you that he has visited the site and that he is familiar with the conditions at your project. This clause forces the contractor into a position of responsibility regarding site conditions, whether he visited the location or not (which is often the case when a salesperson or estimator is involved and visits the site in the contractor's stead).

The contract stipulates that the plans and specifications are a part of the contract but doesn't indicate that they have to be high-quality plans and specifications. Be sure that your plans represent exactly what you want. KEEP ASKING QUESTIONS UNTIL YOU ARE SURE.

Article 6: Owner

6.1 The Owner shall furnish all surveys and a legal description of the location of the Work.

6.2 Except as provided in Paragraph 7.5, or unless noted otherwise in the Contract Documents, the Owner shall secure and pay for necessary approvals, easements, assessments, and charges required for the construction, use or occupancy of permanent structures, or permanent charges in existing facilities. This shall include, but is not limited to, street improvement fees, park dedication fees, lot improvement tax, or sewer and other assessment fees.

6.3 If Good Construction Co. fails to correct defective Work or persistently fails to carry out the Work in accordance with the Contract Documents, the Owner, by a written order, may order Good Construction Co. to stop the Work, or any portion thereof, until the cause of such order has been eliminated.

6.4 The Owner realizes that during the performance of the Work the area where the Work will be performed, and many of the areas adjacent to it, may be extremely dangerous and pose severe safety hazards, and the Owner shall alert Good Construction Co. to all known or suspected hazards.

6.5 The Owner shall be entirely responsible for Owner's own general safety, or that of Owner's family and pets, for anyone whose acts or omissions may be the direct responsibility of the Owner, for anyone directly or indirectly employed by the Owner, or for anyone whose acts or omissions the Owner may be liable, and not attributable to the intentional and wrongful acts or negligence of Good Construction Co.

6.6 The Owner, at Owner's own expense, shall remove, protect, and/or store any and all personal property at the location of the work including, but not limited to rugs, drapes, furniture, decorations, utensils, shrubs, and planting (inside or outside). Good Construction Co. shall not be held responsible for damage to any items of personal property.

6.7 Unless specifically noted otherwise in the Contract Documents, the Owner shall be entirely responsible for all costs related to existing building code violations, hidden or not, hidden defects of every kind, dry rot, fungus damage, structural pest, faulty or outdated plumbing lines, other mechanical or structural defects, and other conditions such as floors not flat or level, walls out of plumb, and rooms out of square.

Article 6 is the section that describes the stuff that you are responsible for. The obligations aren't unusual, but the costs associated with a couple of them can be quite considerable.

Paragraph 6.1 requires you to provide a survey of the property, which can cost $1,500 to $3,000 or more. Occasionally, a land survey is required by the building inspector even though it was not required by the building department at permit time. Include the cost of the survey into your budget just in case.

Paragraph 6.2 says that you have to pay all city fees of any kind. Be careful here because some fees are not levied until the end of the project (such as a sewer connection fee). Ask questions if this clause exists.

Paragraph 6.3 gives you the right to stop payment if things aren't going right. However, you must first submit your complaint to the contractor in writing.

You are required by Paragraph 6.4 to notify the contractor of any hazards known to you. You may assume that an abandoned septic tank is not a danger until someone on the construction crew falls in and follows up with a lawsuit. Can you imagine the smell?

In Paragraph 6.5 you are advised that a construction project poses many dangers, and you are responsible for protecting yourself and your family. In other words, if one of your children falls through a hole surrounded by a proper barrier, you may not be able to blame the contractor.

Paragraph 6.6 makes you responsible for protecting your personal property. Most remodeling contractors do not want the risk associated with handling your electronic equipment, furniture, silver, china, crystal, and so on. You will more than likely be the one to take down the drapes, empty the cabinets and closets, and store the family trinkets and photos.

The cost to repair existing problems such as code violations, rot, termites, and other damage is, as Paragraph 6.7 reminds you, your responsibility. For example, if your contractor tears out a wall to discover an extremely dangerous electric panel, the cost of repair is yours.

Article 7: Contractor

7.1 Good Construction Co. shall supervise and direct the Work, using its best skill and attention and shall be solely responsible for all construction means, methods, techniques, sequences, and procedures, and for coordinating all portions of the Work.

7.2 Unless specifically noted otherwise in the Contract Documents, Good Construction Co. shall provide and pay for all labor, materials, equipment, tools, construction equipment and machinery, transportation, and other facilities and services necessary for the proper execution and completion of the Work, whether temporary or permanent.

7.3 Good Construction Co. shall at all times enforce strict discipline and good order among its employees.

7.4 Good Construction Co. guarantees to the Owner that all materials and equipment incorporated in the Work will be new unless otherwise specified, and that all Work will be of good quality, free from significant faults and defects, and in conformance with construction industry standards and the Contract Documents. All Work not conforming to these requirements may be considered defective.

7.5 Unless otherwise provided in the Contract Documents, Good Construction Co. shall pay all sales taxes which are legally enacted on the date of this Agreement, shall secure and pay for building, mechanical, plumbing, and electrical permits, and for all building inspections necessary for the proper execution and completion of the Work.

7.6 Good Construction Co. shall give all notices and comply with all laws, ordinances, rules, regulations, and lawful orders of any public authority bearing on the performance of the Work.

7.7 Good Construction Co. shall be responsible for the acts and omissions of its employees, Subcontractors and their agents and employees, and other persons performing any of the Work under a contract with Good Construction Co.

7.8 Unless specifically noted otherwise elsewhere in the Contract Documents Good Construction Co. shall match new interior and exterior finishes and construction details as closely as possible to those which exist. Exact type, style, color, and pattern match of new products and materials to existing products and materials cannot be guaranteed.

Article 7 is also pretty important: The contractor's responsibilities are listed here. Paragraphs 7.1, 7.2, and 7.3 give the contractor the right to determine how the project is built, explain that the contractor is responsible for all labor, materials, and so on, and guarantee that the conduct of his employees will be well disciplined.

Paragraph 7.4 is one that really counts. Here the contractor guarantees that the work will be good quality. In other words, free from significant faults and defects. The catch-all statement, "in conformance with construction industry standards" subjects the contractor to scrutiny by industry experts.

In 7.4 the contractor also agrees that only new materials will be used on the project unless noted otherwise. This clause is important because it prevents material from being reused without your permission — very important in remodel construction.

In Paragraphs 7.5 and 7.6, the contractor agrees to pay all applicable taxes and follow the rules of all appropriate authorities — building and otherwise. This clause may not seem very important at contract time, but in a situation where a disagreement results, your contractor's promise "to comply with the law" can be invaluable.

In Paragraph 7.7, the contractor agrees that he will be responsible for the acts and omissions of his employees and subcontractors. This guarantee is especially important when a subcontractor goofs up. Ever hear a contractor say, "Hey, I didn't do it. The subcontractor is responsible. He has to come back and fix it"? According to Paragraph 7.7, the contractor is completely liable to you for all subcontractor goof ups.

Paragraph 7.8 is a really important blanket statement. Here, the contractor warrants that new and old construction details will match as closely as possible. More often than not, remodeling plans don't show these important details (siding and window details, molding, door hardware, and so on). The very worst thing that a first time guest can say is, "Oh, what a lovely re-model." A person who doesn't know that your home has been remodeled can only know the remodel occurred if the new room size and/or construction details don't match the rest of the home. How embarrassing!

Article 8: Miscellaneous provisions

8.1 This Contract shall be governed by the law of the place where the Project is located.

8.2 All claims or disputes between Good Construction Co. and the Owner arising out of or relating to the Contract Documents or the breach thereof, including the interpretation and enforcement of the provisions of this Paragraph 8.2, shall be decided by an arbitrator in accordance with the Construction Industry Arbitration Rules of the American Arbitration Association. Notice of the demand for arbitration shall be filed in writing with the other party to this Agreement and with the American Arbitration Association and shall be made within a reasonable time after the dispute has arisen. The award rendered by the arbitrator shall be final, and judgment may be entered upon it in accordance with applicable law by any court having jurisdiction thereof.

8.3 If either party becomes involved in arbitration or litigation arising out of this Agreement or its performance, the court or tribunal in such arbitration or litigation, or in a separate suit, may award reasonable cost and expenses of arbitration and attorney's fees, including expert witness fees, to the party who recovers judgment.

8.4 The Owner or Good Construction Co. may assign their rights and interests under this Agreement only with the prior written consent of the other; which consent shall not be withheld unreasonably.

You may think of Article 8 as that standard legal reference that you always see in contracts. You know — only there because the attorney says so. Wrong! Look closely: Article 8.2 is an arbitration clause — arbitration is less expensive and more expedient than our conventional court system. Paragraph 8.3 is an attorney's fee clause. If this clause isn't in your contract, you may have to pay your attorney even if you win a suit. And with today's legal fees, an attorney can cost more than the claim. Last but not least, Paragraph 8.4 prevents your contractor from selling his contract to someone else without your permission. Yes, it happens.

Article 9: Time and schedule

9.1 All time limits stated in the Contract Documents are of the essence. Good Construction Co. shall expedite the Work and achieve Substantial Completion within the time specified in this Agreement. If Good Construction Co. delays Substantial Completion of the Project without reasonable cause as noted in Paragraph 9.3, it shall pay the Owner $200.00 per Work day for each Work day of delay beyond the Date of Substantial Completion.

9.2 The Date of Substantial Completion of the Work is the date as signified by the approved final inspection as certified by the convening building official, or when the Owner can occupy, utilize, or continue the Work in conjunction with the use for which it was intended, whichever occurs first. If certain minor portions of the work are deemed unsatisfactory or incomplete, then correction of such unsatisfactory work shall be handled as customer service work and shall be deemed not to affect the Date of Substantial Completion of the Work.

9.3 If Good Construction Co. is delayed at any time in the progress of the Work by changes ordered in the Work, by labor disputes, fire, unusual delay in transportation, adverse weather conditions which cannot be reasonably anticipated, unavoidable casualties, or any causes beyond Good Construction Co. reasonable control, or by any other cause which may justify the delay, then the Date of Substantial Completion shall be extended.

9.4 Within 5 days after Commencement of the Work Good Construction Co. shall prepare a Production Schedule in calendar form, which Good Construction Co. shall distribute to all parties concerned with the Work. The Production Schedule shall indicate work days, Good Construction Co. holidays, a brief description of the Work to be performed each work day by Good Construction Co. and when Work required by the Owner must be performed and/or completed. Work performed by the Owner shall be commenced in conjunction with the actual progress of the Work, not the Production Schedule, except that said work shall be performed by the Owner in a period of time equal to the time allowed in the Production Schedule.

Article 9 puts money in your pocket — $200 per day of delay — if the contractor fails to meet his schedule. Part of the article allows the contractor reasonable delays. We find that most folks are less worried about reasonable delays and more concerned about the contractor not showing up on the job for days or weeks at a time. A contractor may have a difficult time proving that long repeated absences are reasonable. But then that is exactly why Paragraph 9.1 is important.

Paragraph 9.4 promises a production schedule in calendar form. Having a schedule gives you and your family an idea as to when the various events are scheduled to occur and, thus, time to personally prepare for them.

Article 10: Payments and completion

10.1 Payments shall be made as provided in Article 4 of this Agreement.

10.2 Payments may be withheld from Good Construction Co. by the Owner in an amount equal to the Work in question due to significantly defective Work not remedied, or persistent failure by Good Construction Co. to carry out the Work in accordance with the Contract Documents.

10.3 Final payment shall not be due until Good Construction Co. has delivered to the Owner a complete release of all liens arising out of this Agreement. If any lien remains unsatisfied after all payments are made, Good Construction Co. shall refund to the Owner all money the latter may be compelled to pay in discharging such lien, including all costs and reasonable attorney's fees.

10.4 The Contractor's Contingency is maintained by Good Construction Co. to offset losses that may occur as a result of bidding variations and price increases experienced by Good Construction Co. Contractor's Contingency is not refundable to the Owner, and cannot be increased unless additional Work is added in conformity with this Agreement.

When it comes to money, a couple of rights are granted in Article 10 that we think you will probably want in the contract you sign. Paragraph 10.2 gives you the right to withhold payments when the contractor's work gets sloppy. Paragraph 10.3 forces the contractor to provide you with releases of all liens prior to final payment and requires him to refund money where liens exist when you have already paid for the work. If your attitude is, "Oh heck, if it (a lien) happens, I'll never get the refund anyway" — you probably won't.

Article 11: Protection of person and property

11.1 Good Construction Co. shall be responsible for initiating, maintaining, and supervising all safety precautions and programs in connection with its employees, its Subcontractors and their employees, and its Sub-subcontractors and their employees who are involved with the

Work. Good Construction Co. shall give all notices and comply with all applicable laws, ordinances, rules, regulations, and orders of any public authority bearing on the safety of persons and property and their protection from damage, injury, or loss. Good Construction Co. shall promptly remedy all damage or loss to any real or personal property caused by Good Construction Co., any Subcontractor, any Sub-subcontractor, or anyone employed by any of them, except by anyone for whose acts or omissions of the Owner, or anyone employed by the Owner, or by anyone for whose acts the Owner may be liable (see Paragraph 6.5) and not attributable to the fault or negligence of Good Construction Co.

We lovingly refer to Article 11 as the "safety and repair" paragraph. Here, the contractor agrees to comply with all federal, state, and local safety regulations. The latter portion of the paragraph advises the owner that the contractor will repair everything that he, his crew, or his subcontractors break. Was this clause in your last home improvement contract? Did anything by chance get broken that didn't get fixed?

Article 12: Insurance by owner and contractor

12.1 Contractors liability insurance shall be purchased and maintained by Good Construction Co. to protect it from claims under worker's compensation acts and other employee benefits acts, claims for damages because of bodily injury, including death, and from claims for damages, other than to the Work itself, to property which may arise out of the result from Good Construction Co. operations under this Agreement, whether such operations be by Good Construction Co. or by any Subcontractor or anyone employed by any of them. This insurance shall be written for not less than any limits of liability specified in the Contract Documents, or required by law whichever is the greater. Certificates of such insurance shall be made available to the Owner upon Owner's written request.

12.2 The Owner shall be responsible for purchasing and maintaining Owner's own liability insurance, and at Owner's option, may maintain such insurance as will protect him against claims which may arise from the operations under this Agreement.

12.3 The Owner shall purchase and maintain property insurance upon the entire Work to the full insurable value thereof. This insurance shall include the interests of the Owner, Good Construction Co., Subcontractors, and Sub-subcontractors in the Work and shall insure against the perils of fire and extended coverage and shall include "all risk" insurance for physical loss or damage including without duplication of coverage, theft, vandalism, and malicious mischief.

Paragraph 12.1 specifies that the contractor will carry worker's compensation insurance and to what extent. Be absolutely sure to get insurance binders from your contractor's insurance carrier, not the contractor (see why in Chapter 10). Paragraphs 12.2 and 12.3 stipulate the kind of insurance coverage that you are required to carry. Don't let anyone perform major work on your home without this protection. Today, everyone is sue crazy. No matter how reputable your contractor is, you never know what will happen when someone is seriously injured on your property.

Article 13: Changes in the work

13.1 The Owner, without invalidating this Agreement, may request Changes in the Work, consisting of additions, deletions, or modifications which shall become effective when approved by Good Construction Co. in its reasonable discretion. The Contract Sum shall be adjusted accordingly. All such changes in the Work shall be authorized in writing as signified by a written Change Order signed by the Owner and Good Construction Co. The Contract Sum may be changed only by written Change Order.

Although this article is among the shortest of our examples, Article 13 is one of the most valuable. This statement requires your signature before any changes can be made to the original contract price. This clause is a must. It protects you from arbitrary charges levied by the contractor. Bet you never heard of that happening before? Not!!!

Article 14: Termination of the contract

14.1 If the Owner fails to make any payment required by this Agreement for a period of five (5) days after it is due, Good Construction Co., upon five (5) days written notice to the Owner, and without prejudice to any other remedy, Good Construction Co. may terminate this Agreement and recover from the Owner payment of all Work executed and for any proved loss sustained upon any materials, equipment, tools, and construction equipment or machinery, including reasonable profit and damages applicable to the Project.

14.2 If Good Construction Co. defaults or persistently fails or neglects to carry out the Work in accordance with the Contract Documents, the Owner may, after ten (10) days written notice to Good Construction Co., and without prejudice to any other remedy, Owner may make good such deficiencies and may deduct the cost thereof from the payment then or thereafter due Good Construction Co. or, at his option may terminate the Contract and may finish the Work by whatever method he may deem expedient.

Article 14 outlines when and how a termination can be instituted, offering guidelines for both the contractor and the owner. In 14.1, the contractor earns the right to be paid for all properly completed work. In 14.2, the owner is given the right to repair faults at the contractor's expense.

Article 15: Notice to owner

15.1 Under the California Mechanics Lien Law any contractor, subcontractor, laborer, supplier, or other persons who help to improve your property, but is not paid for his/her Work or supplies, has a right to enforce a claim against your property. This means that after a court hearing, your property could be sold by a court officer and the proceeds of the sale used to satisfy the indebtedness. This can happen even if you have paid your contractor in full if the subcontractors, laborers, or supplies remain unpaid. To preserve their right to file a claim or lien against your property, certain claimants such as subcontractors or material suppliers are required to provide you with a document entitled "Preliminary Notice." Original (or prime) contractors and laborers for wages do not have to provide this notice. A Preliminary Notice is not a lien against your property. Its purpose is to notify you of persons who may have a right to file a lien against your property if they are not paid. (Generally, the maximum time allowed for filing a claim or lien against your property is ninety (90) days after completion of your project.) TO INSURE EXTRA PROTECTION FOR YOURSELF AND YOUR PROPERTY, YOU MAY WISH TO TAKE ONE OR MORE OF THE FOLLOWING STEPS.

1. Require that your contractor supply you with a payment and performance bond (not a license bond), which provides that the bonding company will either complete the project or pay damages up to the amount of the bond. This payment and performance bond as well as a copy of the construction contract should be filed with the county recorder for your further protection.

2. Require that payments be made directly to subcontractors and materials suppliers through a joint control. Any joint control agreement should include the addendum approved by the Registrar of contractors.

3. Issue joint checks for payment, made out to both your contractor and subcontractors or material suppliers involved in the project. This will help to insure that all persons due payment are actually paid.

4. After making payment on any completed phase of the project, and before making any further payments, require your contractor to provide you with unconditional lien releases signed by each material supplier, subcontractor, and laborer involved in that portion of the Work for which payment was made. On projects involving improvement to a single family residence or a duplex owned by individuals, the persons signing these releases lose the right to file a claim against your property. In other types of construction, this protection may still be important but may not be as complete.

CONTRACTORS ARE REQUIRED BY LAW TO BE LICENSED AND REGU-LATED BY THE CONTRACTOR'S STATE LICENSE BOARD. ANY QUES-TIONS CONCERNING A CONTRACTOR MAY BE REFERRED TO THE REGISTRAR. CONTRACTOR'S STATE LICENSE BOARD, 9835 GOETHE ROAD, SACRAMENTO, CALIFORNIA 95827. MAILING ADDRESS: P.O. BOX 26000, SACRAMENTO, CA 95826.

Article 15 must be included in every home improvement contract written in the state of California. It clearly outlines state mandates regarding a California consumer's rights and is written in plain English. The experience we have at our remodeling company is that consumers do read this statement and that they do take advantage of the rights expressed. And so they should. You can use many of these procedures to protect yourself regardless of where you live. For example, two-party checks can be written in any state. Also, joint control is common nationwide. You may also want to check with the Department of Consumer Affairs or the Department of Industrial Relations in your state to find out what other rights you have. Many states publish informative consumer articles on how to deal with contractors and contracts.

Joint control is where a third party (with construction savvy) reviews construction progress and authorizes payment distributions. Such companies charge a fee, which is paid by the owner.

By the way, the primary contractor is the one whom you directly contract with. If you contract directly with a general contractor, then that contractor is the primary contractor and everyone he contracts with (on your behalf) is a secondary contractor. If you contract directly with an electrical contractor, then that contractor is a primary contractor and everyone she contracts with (on your behalf) is a secondary contractor.

A Contractor Makes Contracts

Don't be embarrassed about insisting on a thorough contract. Having a contract that is all-encompassing is of mutual advantage to you and your contractor. The contractor isn't a crook if he doesn't possess a contract that addresses the issues we have brought to bear here. But, you certainly have every right to an agreement that protects you in the various ways that we have described. The American Institute of Architects (AIA) has a pretty good contract and so does the Association of General Contractors (AGC). Copies may be available at your local library.

Chapter 12

Mechanics' Liens

• •

In This Chapter

▶ Defining Mechanics' Lien

▶ Dealing with a Mechanics' Lien

• •

*T*he Mechanics' Lien Law is probably one of the most complex — and least understood — aspects of a home improvement project or mainte-nance and repair transaction. Actually, scratch the word "probably" — make that definitely. In fact, our experience is that this particular law, while both powerful and often useful, is just as confusing to contractors as it is to homeowners.

Your understanding of both the law itself and the steps that you should follow in the process can prevent you from paying twice for any phase of your project, and safeguard you from the possibility of losing your house to a disgruntled creditor in a nasty foreclosure sale because a material or a service bill was not paid.

However, explaining the inner-workings of the Mechanics' Lien Law in minute detail can make an *already* confusing subject even *more* confusing. So in this chapter, we offer only what we believe you should be most con-cerned with when it comes to understanding both liens and how they relate to remodeling or repairing your home. On top of that, we offer a bit of wisdom, understanding, and education to serve as a step-by-step guide through this minefield of potential pitfalls, needless messy legal problems, and possible financial risk.

In the end, the success of your project has more to do with your contractor's ability and integrity — and your ability to get along with him — than any other aspect of the process. Your main focus all along should be on finding a good contractor — one who can be your ally instead of your enemy. If you master the principles in Chapters 9 and 10, chances are, this chapter will probably only entertain and educate you.

The Big Picture

Any homeowner in the United States who employs outside labor and material for the improvement or repair of her home is vulnerable to the Mechanics' Lien Law.

Because this law is based on state statutes and civil codes, every state can present unique issues. However, this chapter covers the similar concepts and reasoning that each state employs.

To better understand the basics of the Mechanics' Lien Law, you need to understand the actual words themselves (according to Webster's Dictionary):

 ✓ **Mechanic:** An artisan. One who provides a handicraft for a living. A craftsman skilled in the use of tools.

 ✓ **Lien:** A legal claim, whereby one person retains the property of another until some debt or obligation is paid.

The Mechanics' Lien Law is a relatively new addition to modern law in our society. A version of the original, ancient Mechanics' Lien Law was first enacted in California in the mid-1870s — about 1,600 years after its first introduction to protect the money lenders and craftsmen toiling in ancient Rome.

Today, a Mechanics' Lien is still the most powerful protection that a contractor or material supplier has in ensuring that he is paid for services rendered. The Mechanics' Lien continues to be a mighty legal instrument that represents a claim against real property or a structure on real property. The lien instrument effectively makes the real property responsible for the *claimant's* — the person filing the lien — unpaid services.

Don't Lien on Me

"Pay me or I'll slap a lien on your property!" are ten little words that you don't want to hear in connection with your remodeling or repair project. These are, indeed, fighting words — generally uttered by an angry, frustrated contractor to a defensive homeowner as a result of what is usually a dispute over workmanship, money, or both.

Unfortunately, these dreaded words don't necessarily have to come only from one's chosen contractor. They are a legitimate threat by nearly any person or company in the food chain of your particular project who can demonstrate that they supplied labor and/or material to improve/repair your home or other real property and that they have not received payment in accordance with the terms of the job's contract.

Going back, way back

The Mechanics' Lien Law is an age-old concept dating back to ancient Rome. Its roots appear in early laws dictated by the constitution of Marcus Aurelius, (Emperor of Rome A.D. 161–180), who, in the second century, ordered that a lender of money for home improvements had the right of *hypotheca* — a Latin word meaning the right of a homeowner to offer one's property and/or land as security to ensure that a debt would be repaid as agreed. The lender had the right to take possession of either that property, land, or both if necessary, to satisfy that debt for improvement funds, materials, or both, if unpaid as agreed.

During the Renaissance period in Europe, many of the original societal concepts of both Roman and Greek cultures were revived, dusted-off, and re-employed to restore a sense of order to a floundering, troubled European society.

Thus, you find that French civil law — mainly implemented in the Middle Ages, based on ancient Roman edicts, and still in effect today — rules that architects and workmen who provide labor or furnish materials for a building project are preferred over other creditors for claims, debt settlement, and prompt payment.

The list of prospective lien claimants can include any material suppliers, such as those furnishing concrete, lumber, roofing, and so on; subcontractors such as electricians and plumbers; and even laborers whom your contractor employs to clean up your job. Basically, your potential lien liability is as vast as the number of specialists and suppliers involved in your specific project.

What's potentially even worse, and even more scary, is that you can pay your contractor — as agreed — and still be hit with a Mechanics' Lien if your contractor fails to pay a material supplier for your project. Under the terms and provisions of the Mechanics' Lien Law, the supplier then has a legal right to record a lien against your property for the amount of money that they can prove is due per your work agreement.

You, then, are faced with one of two lousy choices: pay for the material a second time or risk foreclosure of your home to satisfy the debt for the material.

Your Who's Who of Claimants

A lien cannot be filed against your property arbitrarily, or by just anybody involved in your project. The services must have been provided at the request of the property owner or by an authorized *agent*. For example, the general contractor of record and/or any of their subcontractors, sub-subcontractors, architects, builders, or any other person having some charge of construction can serve as the property owner's agent. (By the way, material suppliers are not considered agents of the property owner.)

As long as the work is indeed authorized, a Mechanics' Lien can be filed by the following parties:

- ✔ All persons and laborers furnishing labor and/or material to improve your property
- ✔ Architects
- ✔ Contractors
- ✔ Equipment rental companies
- ✔ Licensed land surveyors
- ✔ Machinists
- ✔ Registered engineers
- ✔ Subcontractors

After reading the foregoing list, you may think that everyone and his brother has the power to file a lien against your property, but that's not completely true. A moneylender, tenant, and the supplier to a material supplier cannot file a Mechanic's Lien. In addition, in states that have contractor licensing requirements, an unlicensed contractor may not file a Mechanics' Lien.

A Preliminary Notice Puts First Things First

With few exceptions, a claimant must first properly serve what is called a *Preliminary Notice.* The failure to properly serve a Preliminary Notice makes recording and executing a Mechanics' Lien impossible. However, a Mechanics' Lien may be filed after a tardy Preliminary Notice has been delivered. A Preliminary Notice should be sent via certified mail — return receipt requested. General contractors and persons performing labor for wages are not required to serve a Preliminary Notice.

A Preliminary Notice — also known as a *Prelim* or *20-Day Notice* — is a notice served on the property owner, the construction lender, and the general contractor. It is dubbed a 20-Day Notice because it must be served no later than twenty days after the claimant first supplies labor, material, or equipment to the job. One is shown on the following page.

CALIFORNIA PRELIMINARY 20-DAY NOTICE
(PUBLIC AND PRIVATE WORK)
IN ACCORDANCE WITH SECTION 3097 AND 3098, CALIFORNIA CIVIL CODE

YOU ARE HEREBY NOTIFIED THAT . . .

CONSTRUCTION LENDER or
Reputed Construction Lender, if any

_____

_____

_____

has furnished or will furnish labor, services, equipment or
materials of the following general description:

_____

_____

for the building, structure or other work of improvement
located at:

_____

Owner or PUBLIC AGENCY
or Reputed Owner (on public work)
(on private work)

The name of the person or firm who contracted for the
purchase of such labor, services, equipment, or materials:

_____

An estimate of the total price of the labor, services,
equipment, or materials (furnished or to be furnished is):

_____

NOTICE TO PROPERTY OWNER
**If bills are not paid in full for the labor, services,
equipment, or materials furnished or to be furnished,
a mechanic's lien leading to the loss, through court
foreclosure proceedings, of all or part of the your
property being so improved may be placed against the
property even though you have paid your contractor
in full. You may wish to protect yourself against this
consequence by (1) requiring your contractor to
furnish a signed release by the person or firm giving
you this notice before making payment to your
contractor or (2) any other method or device that is
appropriate under the circumstances.**

ORIGINAL CONTRACTOR
or Reputed Contractor

The person or firm giving this notice is required,
pursuant to a collective bargaining agreement, to pay
supplemental fringe benefits into an express trust fund
(described in Civil Code #3111). Said fund is
identified as follows:

_____

_____

Mailed this Date: _____

_____
(signature)   (title)

Tardy is as tardy does

Unfortunately, not all service or material providers send a Preliminary Notice. Yet, if the project goes awry, they are always among the first to threaten with a lien. Can they? Well, yes and no.

They *can* file a tardy Preliminary Notice. However, the claimant can then only recover for labor and/or material supplied within 20 days prior to the service of the notice and all services provided thereafter. The claimant may be able to lien, but he may not be able to recover his entire claim.

This notice is designed to advise all the aforementioned parties (particularly the owner) of individuals or firms that are supplying services to improve the owner's property. It describes the nature of these services, who contracted the services, and the value of the service. As a practical matter, this Preliminary Notice alerts a homeowner to any and all potential Mechanics' Lien claimants.

For example, a run-of-the-mill room addition may involve a dozen or more subcontractors and material suppliers. However, unless each party files a Preliminary Notice as prescribed by law, the owner likely has no way of knowing who is supplying services to improve his home. Consequently, the homeowner won't know to whom he is indebted.

Keep in mind, a Preliminary Notice is just that, a notice. As an unsuspecting homeowner, you may be terrified to receive a 20-Day Notice that is, incidentally, usually sent by registered or certified mail. You may confuse the notice with an actual lien, or fear that it is the prelude to a soon-to-follow lien against your home.

Actually, you should be grateful for every 20-Day Notice you receive. The notice enables you to determine to whom you may owe money for services or materials provided.

Save all the Preliminary Notices you receive. Before making any progress payments — partial payment for work already performed — assure that each of these potential claimants has been paid either by issuing joint checks or by obtaining conditional or other lien releases from the party being paid. Information on joint checks and lien releases can be found later in this chapter.

Because many contractors or material suppliers do not routinely serve Preliminary Notices, insist that your general contractor provide you with a complete list of each and every supplier of material or services that you should know about.

What do you then do with this information? You protect yourself and your home. You use your list, or your stack of Preliminary 20-Day Notices, to ensure that all parties have been paid before making payment-in-full to your general contractor.

Please Release Me

You have several options to guarantee that you won't be subject to a Mechanics' Lien, but one of the most popular is a simple little document called a *Lien Release*. Most contractors will routinely provide these forms; however, the forms can be found at most office product stores.

Your Lien Release can either be a Conditional Waiver and Release (referred to as a *Conditional Lien Release*) or an Unconditional Waiver and Release (frequently called a *Full Lien Release*).

Conditional Lien Releases

Subcontractors or material suppliers typically give the general contractor a Conditional Lien Release. The general contractor may give the homeowner a Conditional Lien Release in exchange for either partial or full payment by check. The document is conditional only until the check has cleared the bank — it then becomes an Unconditional Lien Release.

In order to protect you, your general contractor should require Conditional Lien Releases from all of his subcontractors and material suppliers prior to issuing payment for their services. Moreover, you should require Conditional Lien Releases from your general contractor for progress payments made in conjunction with your contract. You should also require your general contractor to submit Unconditional Lien Releases from subcontractors and material suppliers for those phases of the work covered by a particular progress payment.

Unconditional Lien Releases

In contrast to Conditional Lien Releases, an Unconditional Lien Release is issued by a contractor without any conditions — such as having to wait until a check clears the bank. It can be issued by all of the same parties as listed above. The individual issuing an Unconditional Release is, essentially, giving up the right to claim a lien against the property in question. Consequently, this is about the best protection a homeowner can have from being hit with a lien. Since an Unconditional Lien Release eliminates the need to wait for a check to clear the bank, this type of release is almost always issued in exchange for a certified or cashier's check.

Essentially, you want some guarantee that the money you pay to your general contractor for others' services does indeed flow through to them. The prospect of a Mechanics' Lien arises when the funds stay fully with the general contractor instead of going out as payment to subcontractors.

In addition, insist that your general contractor provide you with *piggyback lien releases* with each progress payment. For example, if your first progress payment is $5,000, you should receive a Conditional Lien Release in exchange for your check. When making your second progress payment of say, $10,000, you should receive an Unconditional Lien Release for the first payment of $5,000 and a Conditional Lien Release for the current $10,000 payment. This process continues for all payments right through the final payment. The basic difference is that the $5,000 check has cleared the bank and the $10,000 check has not. Thus, the contractor (or other potential claimant) wants to hang on to the right to lien until the funds from your bank have landed squarely in the contractor's bank.

Do *not* make final payment to your general contractor without first receiving Unconditional Lien Releases from *all* parties that served a Preliminary Notice. (The same applies to any party who has not provided a Prelim but who you know provided services to your project.)

Two-party or not two-party

Although Lien Releases are among the most convenient and, hence, prevalent means of avoiding a Mechanics' Lien, some other methods deserve consideration. A *two-party* or *joint check* is one such method.

You can issue joint checks to the general contractor and a subcontractor or material supplier. Or, the general contractor can issue joint checks to a subcontractor and a material supplier.

For example, suppose that the general contractor is supplying manufactured cabinets for your new kitchen. Furthermore, your agreement with your general contractor requires you to make a substantial progress payment upon delivery of the cabinets to your home.

You can make the check for the progress payment payable to your general contractor *and* the cabinet supplier. You will know who the cabinet supplier is by the Preliminary Notice he serves you. However, if you don't receive notice, you can ask your general contractor for the supplier information and write your check accordingly.

Keep in mind that the joint check system is in addition to — not in lieu of — the Lien Release system we discuss earlier. You should require Lien Releases in all cases. The joint check system simply serves as another layer of consumer protection.

Although joint checks are an effective means of lien prevention, they can be burdensome for you and your general contractor. Many contractors (generals and subs) object to joint checks because they involve added management and running around. Joint checks also subject the general contractor to a certain loss of control on the project that can be quite disadvantageous to all parties — except the party being paid.

Using our cabinet supplier example, requiring the general contractor to pay the cabinet supplier in full for the cabinets — by virtue of the joint check method — can strip him of some much-needed leverage. If, for example, during installation the contractor discovers that some of the cabinets are in some way defective, he may not be able to hold payment as leverage in expediting the necessary repairs.

Most homeowners have the same concern — "I know if I pay him, he'll never come back to finish the work." Sadly, money talks and, well, you know the rest of the story. Never get ahead on payments and by all means never pay for work that is not complete or is not in keeping with the contract documents. When in doubt, discuss things with your contractor to make sure that everyone is on the same page.

Keep in mind that joint checks don't have to be an all-or-nothing situation. You and your general contractor can agree up-front about joint checks. Or you may want to issue joint checks for only the services that put you at the greatest financial risk — the big-dollar items. You may want to suggest joint checks for items such as lumber (when building a big addition), cabinets (for a kitchen remodel), roofing (when re-roofing the entire house), or windows (when doing whole-house window replacement).

The key to using the joint check method is to agree upon it in advance with your contractor and to spell it out in the contract to avoid any misunderstanding.

Opponents of this system suggest that fund control is their job as the general contractor. And to a degree, this is true. However, some contractors out there are excellent craftspeople but less-than-astute businessmen, and they have trouble managing their own funds let alone anyone else's. In such cases, the joint check system is a perfect match.

A la escrow

An alternative to the joint check system is fund management by an independent agency, such as a construction management company or an architectural firm. Both of these entities are set up to provide detailed project accounting, including site inspections, to ensure that progress payment requests correspond to actual progress on the job.

The personnel are trained to identify potential problems or glitches that justify retaining funds until the issue is resolved. This arrangement is quite common on commercial projects and rather large residential remodeling projects. It is rarely seen with most mainstream, residential remodeling projects.

This system often appeals to the contractor who is more adept as a craftsperson than as a businessman. It allows him to do what he does best without being knee-deep in the financial administration. On the other hand, contractors who are astute business people often find that this added level of management can act as a barrier between them and the owner.

This escrow-type alternative isn't cheap either. Be prepared to pay 5 to 10 percent of the total contract value for third-party management. In the case of a $50,000 project, this fee can range from $2,500 to $5,000. So carefully weigh the benefits against the costs before choosing to go this route.

Help Is on the Way

If you receive a Mechanics' Lien, don't panic.

Your world's not ending. In fact, less than one percent of all Mechanics' Liens are ever enforced. However, you must deal with any such lien promptly and professionally.

Individuals filing a Mechanics' Lien face statutory time limitations. For example, suppliers and subcontractors must record a Mechanics' Lien within 30 calendar days after the date on which a Notice of Completion is recorded. If no such notice is recorded, a lien must be recorded within 90 days after the entire project is complete or 60 days after all labor ceases.

A general contractor must record a Mechanics' Lien not later than 60 calendar days after the date on which a Notice of Completion is recorded or 90 days after completion of the entire project.

After the Mechanics' Lien is complete, the County Recorder must record it. At this point, the lien appears on your property's title.

A Mechanics' Lien is worthless unless and until an action to foreclose begins, and that has to happen within 90 days of the date the lien was recorded. If the claimant fails to enforce the lien within this time period, the Mechanics' Lien becomes null and void.

In addition, the lawsuit to enforce the Mechanics' Lien must be filed by the claimant (or the claimant's attorney) within 90 days in the *proper judicial district.* Typically, the proper judicial district is the judicial district where the property is located.

Don't feel alone if your mind is numb with all this information. It's just the nature of construction law. Keep in mind that most Mechanics' Liens are resolved well before any foreclosure process begins. Arbitration and mediation are among the two most popular means of dispute resolution.

Arbitration is a process wherein a neutral third party — a judge of sorts — hears both sides of the story and issues a final decision. The American Arbitration Association has a set of boiler plate rules that are a part of many modern construction contracts. This arbitration clause requires the parties involved to seek arbitration in the event of a dispute. See Chapter 11 for more information on arbitration.

Like arbitration, mediation is an alternative to hiring an attorney and going to court. The basic difference between arbitration and mediation is that in mediation, the mediator is an independent third party who acts as a facilitator and not a judge. The mediator serves as a go-between among the parties in a dispute. The mediator can make suggestions and attempt to engineer a resolution but cannot require a settlement. We like to think of a mediator as the construction industry's marriage counselor. Unfortunately, mediation is not always successful in solving the dispute; in which case it can end up in court.

Rewinding the tape

If payment is made to satisfy a lien, or the prescribed amount of time to foreclose expires, the lien must be released from the property, which requires a Release of Mechanics' Lien. You complete and record this form with the County Recorder in the county where the original lien was recorded.

Often, the matter is resolved or the prescribed amount of time expires and no one remembers to record the Release of Lien. Thus, in a year or so when you are attempting to obtain consumer credit, the lien appears out of the blue just to raise your blood pressure. Even though the lien is no longer valid, it must be expunged with a recorded Release Of Lien.

Job bond, not James Bond

As with most things in life, there's more than one way to skin a cat. Consequently, there's more than one way to deal with a Mechanics' Lien.

You can require that your contractor supply you with a *payment and performance bond* that provides that the bonding company will either complete the project or pay damages up to the amount of the bond. In short, it's an insurance policy. And in order for your contractor to obtain such a bond, he must have a *bonding line of credit.* You should file the payment and performance bond, as well as a copy of the construction contract, with the County Recorder for your future protection.

A payment and performance bond usually costs from 1 to 5 percent of the contract amount, depending on the contractor's bonding ability. The homeowner generally pays for the bond since this is a job cost and not a cost of doing business. A small price for the piece of mind, wouldn't you say?

To say that a payment and performance bond is rarely used would be a gross understatement. In nearly two decades and hundreds upon hundreds of jobs, we have yet to be asked by a homeowner to post a payment and performance bond — even though we have a bonding line of credit.

Keep in mind that not all contractors are capable of obtaining such a bond. A contractor's inability to obtain a payment and performance bond may indicate his financial incapacity. To qualify for a payment and performance bond, the contractor must have an excellent track record when it comes to the business side of the profession. The contractor must provide credit references, client references, and financial data that demonstrate that the contractor is a good risk to a bonding company. Contractors that don't have good vendor or client references and a poor credit rating are not likely to qualify for a bonding line of credit, which may be enough to remove that particular contractor from consideration.

Although you may not require a payment and performance bond from the contractor, the fact that the contractor does, indeed, have a bonding line of credit is another level of assurance that you are dealing with a business person and not just a good tradesperson.

The fact that a contractor cannot obtain a payment and performance bond isn't always a bad sign and isn't necessarily reason to go with another contractor. It is simply one of many factors used to help you determine who to select as your contractor.

Don't confuse this type of bond with a surety bond, which many states with contractor licensing require. A *surety* or *contractor's bond* is a bond that guarantees performance of a contract; however, it is minimal by any standard. The average surety bond will range between five and ten thousand dollars — a drop in the bucket for a sizable remodel. Thus, if the contractor screws up and you attempt to get financial satisfaction from the contractor's surety bond, you may be disappointed to find that it is a fraction of the total job.

A Mechanics' Lien Release Bond is another alternative. After a Mechanics' Lien is recorded, a property owner, general contractor, or subcontractor may record a Mechanics' Lien Release Bond, which frees the property of the Mechanics' Lien. Once such a bond is recorded, the real property described in the bond is released from the Mechanics' Lien and, more importantly, any action to foreclose on the lien.

When you have a Mechanics' Lien Release Bond, that bond acts as a substitute for your home as the object to which the Mechanics' Lien attaches and against which the Mechanics' Lien may be enforced. Thus, when such a bond is recorded and a foreclosure action is pending, the property owner is entitled to a full dismissal of the Mechanics' Lien foreclosure action and the claimant must proceed against the bond principal and surety. In other words, once you have a Mechanics' Lien Release Bond, the person chasing you for the money must now chase the bonding company.

The Mechanics' Lien must also be released along with any claimant-generated lawsuit that may be pending to foreclose upon your property.

Chapter 13

How Will You Live?

*O*ver the years, we've heard our share of incredible, mind-boggling horror stories about home remodeling projects that ever so slo-o-o-wly escalated from a simple roof repair, or the creation of a new dream kitchen, into a nightmare of epic proportions.

Like clockwork, these stories surface every spring, at the start of the home improvement season — in newspaper articles and on television news exposé programs — and continue on through summer as a reminder to be aware and to beware.

You can be assured of seeing the usual cast of sympathetic characters, ranging from the young, suburban couple enduring an 18-month bath remodel to the unfortunate, elderly person who always overpays for shoddy workmanship — and the corresponding line-up of usual suspects: unlicensed, greedy, and/or incompetent contractors.

And just as sure as blooms reappear and the swallows return to San Juan Capistrano, each spring another cast of like characters find each other and again agree to launch another raft of what can only be called projects from hell.

These unpleasant tales always begin with high expectations — "We were so excited about our new bathroom" or "We could hardly wait to cook our first meal in our new gourmet kitchen" — and inevitably, they end with only massive remorse.

Setting aside disasters created by shoddy workmanship, incompetent contractors, or out-and-out fraud — which can be avoided by using your common sense and reading Chapter 9 — most remodeling horror stories are, in reality, a combination of poor planning and Murphy's Law — everything that can go wrong does go wrong — creating a major remodeling snafu as a result. Take a look at Figure 13-1 to see all the potential hassles and inconveniences associated with a remodel.

Figure 13-1:
The realities of your home becoming a construction site.

Thus, you hear: "I thought that it would never be finished" or "I felt like a prisoner in my own home." Sadly, these projects-gone-bad can even put once-happy, long-term marriages to the test. (In some cases, after months of noise and disruption, sawdust turns to divorce dust.)

In almost every story, the problems can be traced back to a case of not looking before you leap. Although a new kitchen or fixing a leaky roof may sound great, few homeowners actually think any further than envisioning the finished project. Yet, we all know it just doesn't magically appear.

Granted, the excitement and lifestyle benefits that you first envision are still present when the project is finished — but the process of getting to that point, if far more stressful and disruptive than you ever bargained for, can dampen your spirits and dull any eventual enjoyment that you may originally envision.

The key word to keep in mind is planning: planning for and/or making provisions to avoid as much stress as possible. After all, just having Aunt Jane and Uncle Harry over for a weekend is stressful enough, let alone opening your home to a band of strangers who come in, say "hello," and then start literally ripping your home apart.

In the course of the average home remodeling project, you may have in the neighborhood of 20 or more people working in, or on, your home.

If you are like most people, the prospect of having this many strangers visit your home can bring up issues of everything from privacy and safety to security — and sanity.

Moreover, anticipating the added stress during the remodeling can — just like checking into the hospital — in itself, cause stress.

Now that we've risked having you frantically looking for other, more rewarding and less taxing ways to spend your remodeling dollars, let us tell you how you can make remodeling less painful, less stressful, and far, far more rewarding.

It's Déjà Vu All Over Again

Although most people probably don't classify their brush with remodeling as one of life's greatest adventures, the experience doesn't always have to be a negative one. *Au contraire,* it can be very interesting, highly educational, and quite rewarding, especially if you choose to get involved in the project.

However, most people are so focused on the results of their remodeling project that they pay little or no attention to planning for the day-to-day matters of living through their project. Suddenly, they awaken one morning to hammering, sawing, and the fact that their home is absent a bathroom, or that where once was a kitchen is now a big empty space. Cold, hard reality sets in very quickly — with chaos and bitterness often not far behind.

Yet much or most of this grief can be avoided with good-old, basic preplanning and truly reasonable expectations. The notion that the planning process ends when the building plans are complete, the contractor is chosen, and the finishes are selected is a sure invitation to a steady stream disappointments and on-going disasters.

A key part of success in the planning process is to create, for the lack of a better term, a *survival plan* — put simply, a plan of how you and your family (pets included) will live through your remodeling experience.

Although a plan is important for all remodeling projects, it is *critical* if you plan to remodel a kitchen, bathroom, bedroom, or laundry room.

Most of us can afford to spare the living room, dining room, family room, or garage for a while, but few of us function as well without a kitchen for brewing a morning cup of java or a bathroom in which to, uh, brush your teeth.

Our mission in this chapter is to help you prepare a survival plan that will assist you in getting through your project so that you stay in control of your life and your remodeling.

Survival Plans

One of the first and most important aspects of a sound survival plan is to acknowledge that things around the house will be "different" (putting it mildly) during your remodeling work. No matter how much planning you do or how little you believe that your home remodeling project will affect you, you will experience a higher level of stress than your normal day-to-day lifestyle.

Bring in the clowns

One of the most obvious changes around your home during a remodeling or repair project is the addition of people — lots of people — and not just any people. These folks are carpenters, plumbers, electricians, tile setters, carpet layers, and so on — and they rip out walls and tear up floors while running into, out of, and around your house.

With these people also comes noise — lots of noise — the kind of nerve-jangling, ear-shattering, piercing noise that can only be created by hammers, electric saws, and the occasional jack hammer. If you're not used to this kind of noise, it'll likely drive you up the wall — if you still have a wall.

So what do you do? Throw 'em all out — talk about a job delay — wave the white flag in defeat, or do you simply roll up your sleeves and deal with it? We suggest choosing Door Number Three.

Timing trials

You've no doubt heard the old saying, "Timing is everything." Timing is certainly one of the best ways to eliminate stress during a remodeling project.

The biggest mistake that many people make is either beginning a project at the least advantageous time or pushing a project to be completed in time for a special event — such as a birthday party, graduation, or wedding.

Throughout this book, we repeatedly stress the importance of timing. If you are scheduling a reception in your home for a June wedding, the planning for any spruce-up remodeling should start at least nine months before the date you want to see the project completed. Plan to have the work wrapped up by March or April so you can concentrate your energy on planning your party and entertaining your guests — in your beautiful new whatever — and not be stressed-out trying to pull together the final details of your remodeling project.

Many contractors try to talk clients into commencing the work hastily, for a variety of reasons. (For instance, the contractor may have an open schedule or may need to get some cash-flow going.) They suggest that "We get things going now, and then we'll make decisions along the way." This is indeed a recipe for disaster. Would you pack for a vacation, load everyone into the family car, back out of the driveway, and *then* start asking where everyone wants to go? We don't think so.

As with vacations, make as many remodeling decisions and selections as possible *before* beginning your project. This is your number-one, guaranteed stress reducer during the remodeling process. If you don't see the logic here, we don't want to vacation with you.

Put it on the job calendar

You should have a clear understanding of what your contractor expects from you and your family, what sacrifices you need to make, and to what extent your day-to-day living is going to be affected by their work.

If this information isn't clear to you, pry it out of your contractor — your survival depends on it!

A *job calendar* is one of the most useful means of expressing this information. The calendar should note events such as when you have to give up a bathroom or move out of your kitchen. It should also let you know when a wall between your existing home and the new addition will be blown out.

The job calendar is a complete schedule of events (in calendar form) from the beginning to the end of your remodeling project. It is created by your contractor and is used to schedule material deliveries, subcontractor work schedules and, best of all, completion! This is where the contractor uses his knowledge of construction to designate how long a specific phase of the project will take. This is extremely important to prevent subcontractors from bumping into one another yet keep things on a tight schedule to finish the job as expeditiously as possible.

Never begin a remodeling project without a job schedule, even if (especially if) you will be the contractor. Therefore, it should be a requirement of your contract with the contractor that a job schedule be provided before the work begins.

In addition, the contractor should update the calendar whenever changes are made that will affect the schedule. The contractor should also update the calendar if the job falls behind or is ahead of schedule. This is especially important if you will be involved in the work. You should know in advance so that you can arrange for time off from work and so on to meet your commitment to the job.

By the same token, the contractor should have a clear understanding of your needs — along with any limitations that you may have. You are responsible for communicating this information to your contractor. Don't wait for her to ask the right questions. She may be assuming that you're just tough — ready and able to endure the rigors of remodeling.

For instance, if you are redoing your kitchen, it is reasonable to expect your contractor to give you at least a week's notice to get your cabinets packed up. That way, you will have ample time to gather storage boxes, pack the goods, and find temporary storage. Anything less is just one more stress factor adding to an already stressful situation.

Living with boxes and dust

Chances are that you'll feel a bit disoriented and cramped during the remodeling process. Things like cooking utensils, bath towels, books, and other personal items have to move from their tidy place into boxes and temporary storage until they can be returned to their new homes. Suddenly, your once-spacious home is crammed with stacks of dusty storage boxes. And boxes — along with any furniture that you move to make way for the remodeling — can turn your home into a frustrating and dangerous maze.

Survival in the dust bowl

Most people can't believe the amount of dust that results from even the most minor remodeling. These people work furiously to keep their home dust free. Unfortunately, their efforts are futile because they don't realize that no barrier can completely keep dust from appearing in almost every room of the home.

The vibration from the inherent hammering and sawing causes dust that resides on walls and ceilings throughout the house to become airborne, ultimately covering virtually everything in the home.

The best way to deal with dust is to have the contractor install temporary plastic sheeting over doors and other openings to keep the dust confined substantially — although never completely — to the construction areas.

However, by boxing things up, you protect your personal items from the remodeling area. Furniture can be torn, scratched, or soiled. Pictures and decorative items can be damaged or destroyed, and the dust alone that remodeling produces can be enough to eighty-six the sensitive entrails of your electronics.

Have plenty of boxes, packing material, and temporary storage space. If the garage or storage shed is already heaping or affected by the work, consider renting a storage space to store furniture and personal items until the coast is clear and things are back to normal.

Keep only those items that you know you'll use during your remodeling. The more space you have, the less cramped you'll feel, and the less stressful the experience will be.

Place any electronics that must remain (such as a computer or stereo system) in a "clean room"; make sure to tape off the windows and doors to eliminate the infiltration of dust. Cover the electronic equipment when not in use — but be sure to turn off their power first to prevent overheating.

Furniture and other personal items that are well out of harm's way can be covered with inexpensive plastic painter's drop cloths that can be found in the paint section of your local home center. Cardboard boxes surrounded by duct tape is another proven method of preventing your favorite table from getting knocked around. On the other hand, if the furniture is in the line of fire, it should be moved completely out of the area to avoid damage.

Rub-a-Dub-Dub, Where's My Tub?

In order to save time and money, some people prefer to have both bathrooms remodeled at the same time. (Don't take for granted that the contractor will work on the bathrooms in tandem. Although the most cost-effective means of remodeling two bathrooms is to do them simultaneously, it can also be the most chaotic for the homeowner.) While this situation doesn't generally require moving out of the house, it can present quite a challenge when it comes to personal hygiene (especially if you live in a one-bath home).

The good news is that even the most extensive bathroom remodel can generally allow for replacing the toilet at the end of each workday. You may have to settle for tooth brushing and a daily sponge bath at the kitchen sink, but more personal functions can be performed in a makeshift bathroom — even one surrounded by studs, plaster, and plywood.

Don't assume that your contractor will automatically replace the toilet each day — you must make it a condition of your contract. Because this request involves extra work, your contractor will probably include this cost in his estimate. The slight additional cost for this task is minimal compared to the convenience and cost savings of remodeling all your bathrooms at once.

Most people don't consider the alternative of a portable construction toilet because of personal health, privacy, and convenience. On the other hand, a portable toilet for the crew actually enhances your privacy. And if a sponge bath at the kitchen sink is too much like roughing it, you can always ask to shower at a friend's home. Alternatively, you can rent or borrow a tent trailer or travel trailer for the project's duration.

If you decide not to rent a portable toilet, be prepared to allow the crew to use your private bath. More information on this, along with other preconstruction plans, can be found in Chapter 14.

If any of these options become a consideration for your sanity, make sure to include the expense in budgeting the overall job cost.

Kitchen Kvetchin'

Never attempt a kitchen remodel without making provisions for a temporary kitchen. You can put your temporary kitchen almost anywhere — although we find that the most popular locations are the dining room, garage, and family room.

Outfit your temporary kitchen with the following items:

- A few base cabinets from the kitchen and some countertops (plywood tops work just fine)
- At least one cabinet with a bank of drawers for utensil storage
- Bottled water
- Camping stove or hot plate
- Disposable paper plates and plastic utensils
- Microwave oven
- Refrigerator

You'll be surprised at how well you'll get along until your new kitchen is ready. And, although a bit challenging, you may find life with a temporary kitchen adventurous — and fun too.

We're Movin' on Out

Many people face the dilemma of living at home during the remodeling process or moving out altogether.

In our experience, very few people need — or choose — to move out completely. With good planning, stress management, and on-going communication with your contractor, staying in your home is quite doable.

In fact, being out of your home can be more stressful than living in it during the remodeling, with one exception: a whole-house remodel that affects a majority of the home — kitchen, all bathrooms, the bedrooms, and a number of the living areas.

Several of our clients have even taken brief vacations during their projects as a way to relieve stress. This option works especially well when all of the design decisions are made and the job no longer requires customer feedback. If something does come up that requires consulting the homeowners, we simply call them. (Yes, we do request that they leave us a telephone number where we can reach them while they're away.)

Kids (And Pets) Need Planning, Too

Pay close attention to the needs of small children and pets during the remodeling experience.

Kids often don't understand what is happening to their home and why so many strangers are visiting. Take time to explain what plans you have for your home — and the events that will take place. As the work progresses, children may need occasional reassurance that their home and their lives will soon be back to normal, assuming it was normal before the remodeling began, that is.

Children respond well to routines. Therefore, your best bet is to keep the children's schedules as normal as possible, including playtime at home. If their play space or bedrooms are not affected by the work, allow the children to play there, so long as it is safe and they are supervised.

Under no circumstances should children be allowed to wander through the house without supervision — especially if they can potentially come into contact with the remodeling area. A jagged pipe, loose electrical wiring, or nails sticking out of a board can cause serious injury or even death.

Although the yard will likely be cluttered with tools, equipment, material, and debris storage, try to keep an area clear for the children to safely play outdoors. Doing so helps make them feel safe and releases any fear or stress that they may be feeling about the remodeling.

Whereas children are quite resilient, pets can be devastated by the remodeling experience. The noise, the strangers, and the disruption can cause a pet great anxiety. And, unless the pet is under constant supervision or confined to a secure space, you face a risk that the pet may run away or become lost.

Unfortunately, gates that typically remain closed to keep animals safe are often left open by workmen, which allows pets to escape. Consider investing in an animal crate. The pet should be placed in the crate in an area of the home or yard farthest from the construction hustle and bustle.

Another pet-management alternative for consideration is to get your pets microchipped. Microchipping is a very fast, painless procedure in which a chip about the size of a grain of rice is implanted between the animal's shoulders. If the pet becomes lost and is turned into the pound, Humane Society, or a veterinarian's office, they can scan the chip and locate the owners.

It is also an appropriate time to make sure that your pets are current with all their vaccinations. Keep in mind that a frightened dog will sometimes bite, and the last thing you want to mar your remodeling experience is an impounded cat or dog and the associated legal fees.

With lots of love, attention, and reassurance, pets can get through the process unscathed.

Chapter 14

Preconstruction Preparation

· ·

In This Chapter

▶ Creating and implementing your own "construction conduct" agenda

▶ Maintaining communication during the project

▶ Managing inconsiderate workers

· ·

*D*ave orders the temporary toilet; Bill plans on where to put the trash; and *you decide where you're going to park the car. The remodel begins. The next morning, the trash ends up in the temporary toilet, and the temporary toilet has been not-so-strategically placed in the trunk of your brand new Subaru. Whoops!*

Here's a scene that is a bit more realistic. You arrive home after a hard day at work. In your entry hall, you discover a large ashtray filled with the world's most disgusting assortment of cigarette butts. Could this really happen to you? It doesn't have to.

The planning required to ensure a relatively smooth remodel is endless. The *preconstruction conference* is an important phase of planning that should take place just before the actual construction work begins. Whether you are an owner-builder or hiring a contractor, the preconstruction conference is a must. At this time you iron out all those important personal details that are not normally covered in the contract documents. You know, like management of the alarm system, loud music, job start time, weekend work, and so on.

If you are hiring a contractor, the preconstruction conference should be attended by the following parties:

✔ You and your significant other

✔ The construction person who will be responsible for the daily management of the project

✔ The person who estimated the project

✔ The foreman or project manager

As you can see from this list, the conference can also act as an initial meeting place for everyone involved in the project. If you intend to act as your own contractor, all of your subcontractors and anyone who will be working directly for you should be present.

You can use the information in this chapter to create your own preconstruction meeting agenda, as well as to begin to prepare yourself for some of the realities of any new construction.

The Preconstruction Conference

The preconstruction conference allows you to do the following:

- Indicate what you expect from everyone associated with your project.
- Provide a copy of your paperwork to everyone in attendance, ensuring that everyone is on the same page.
- Take notes for transcription and distribution. You can appoint someone to act as secretary while you concentrate on the agenda.

The following sections contain the issues that we like to discuss.

The production binder and mailbox

Deciding on a central location where project documents can be reviewed and exchanged is an absolute must. All you need is a three-ring binder (or a large folder or file box). Advise everyone that the binder will contain all of the important documents related to the project such as

- Building permit set of plans
- Building department inspection card
- Finish schedule and/or project specifications (see Chapter 10)
- Production calendar (see Chapter 10)
- Change orders
- Product installation information
- Warranties
- Other relevant paper work

Playing telephone

Whether you hire a contractor or employ your own crew, be prepared for an increased phone bill. The alternative — a temporary phone installation — can cost a fortune. Apart from the additional calls that will be made at your expense anyway, with a temporary phone, you can expect to pay several additional costs:

✔ Deposit

✔ Installation fee

✔ Disconnect charge

✔ Anything else that your local phone company demands

If an addition is being built, an outside extension can easily be added. For simplicity, a cordless phone can be used.

In any event, clearly state that your phone is not to be used for *personal calls.* Don't forget to monitor your phone bill. We once had to terminate an employee who racked up several hundred dollars in 900 calls on a customer's phone. Needless to say, we paid the bill.

Locate the production binder in a spot outside the construction area so that it won't have to be moved during the project. Doing so avoids creating confusion. Everyone should know the binder's location. The same spot also can be used as the *project mailbox* where notes can be exchanged. A mailbox is especially important if you normally leave home in the morning before the workers arrive and don't return until after they finish for the day. An on-sight post office gets used with amazing frequency. Blank paper and a pencil are must-have supplies at this location. (Secure the pencil with a piece of string to prevent it from traveling.)

Communications

Exchange telephone, fax, pager, and cell phone numbers. You can expedite matters by having your personal phone list prepared in advance. Designate numbers as personal or work, explain when and where you can normally be reached, and note if any restrictions apply. Also, ask your contractor or subcontractors to bring along their lists. If an emergency occurs, you won't want an answering service between you and the person who can solve your problem. Remember, no matter how qualified the crew is, problems do arise. Copies of the phone lists should be placed in the project folder or posted on a wall at the project mailbox location.

Safety

A construction site can be a deadly place. Reinforcing bars stick straight up out of concrete supports, electrical wiring is exposed, broken glass, razor sharp sheetmetal edges, open trenches, floors missing that used to exist, and walls where none were before. The need for safe thinking on the job is a must.

Insist on a weekly safety meeting (California requires contractors to have one *at least* every ten working days). Have the crew gather to discuss safety-related experiences. Nothing makes everyone on the job more aware of the ever-present danger on a construction site than a weekly reminder from a coworker, especially when someone spins a yarn about an old injury or an accident once witnessed. The thought may sound a little sadistic, but you would be amazed at how much safer a job becomes when true-life accident experiences are shared among the crew.

Here are a few really important safety rules that we suggest you implement:

✔ **Make sure that all tradespersons are notified to stop work when a guest enters the work area.** Most guests are typically not familiar with the dangers present on a construction site. Power tools are capable of hurling wood splinters, nails, and other dangerous items long distances — and at high speeds. One crooked blow from a framing hammer can send a sharp nail reeling across a room at an extremely high speed — more than fast enough to put an eye out.

✔ **Realize that if you aren't careful, you also can pose a danger to workers.** Entering the work area too quietly can startle a worker, causing an interruption in concentration that results in a serious injury. If you hear a power tool operating, wait until it stops, then speak loudly, and announce your intention to enter the work area.

✔ **Don't even let people work on your property unless a first aid kit — capable of handling 25 persons — is located in a conspicuous, easy-to-get-to location.** We like to place ours near the telephone with a list of emergency phone numbers and the address of the nearest hospital and medical facility. If you are hiring a contractor, you can expect him to provide the first aid kit. If not, be sure to supply one yourself.

✔ **Don't forget the fire extinguishers.** The universal ABC type puts out all types of fires. A minimum of two should be standing by at all times. Place one near the job phone and one at the other end of the project. If you are hiring a contractor, you can expect him to provide the fire extinguisher. If not, be sure to supply one yourself.

Work hours and work days

Advise everyone at the preconstruction conference how you and your neighbors feel about work hours and agree on a schedule that satisfies all concerned.

An original Carey Bros. joke

Speaking of the dangers that exist on a job site — did you hear the one about how to tell the difference between a journeyman and an apprentice? The apprentice is the one with the bumps and bruises all over his forehead.

In most communities residents rarely object when construction work begins at 8:00 a.m. or later. If you want to begin earlier, you really should get permission from your neighbors — doing so sort of insures peace in the neighborhood. The same consideration must be made about quitting time, evening work, and working on weekends. Remember, the construction project lasts only for a few weeks or months. Your neighbors may be there with you for decades to come. Also, you and yours will occasionally want time off from the mess and noise, which is something you will have to sacrifice if workers remain evenings and weekends.

Alcohol and drugs

Don't forget to discuss alcohol and drug use at the preconstruction conference. Construction is dangerous enough without the unnecessary addition of mind-altering narcotics.

For safety's sake, advise everyone that alcohol and drugs are not allowed on your property. Also, be sure to let all workers know that they are not welcome to come to work when inebriated, intoxicated, stoned, loaded, or otherwise under the influence of mind- or body-altering substances. Don't forget lunch and after work, either. Workers can't get into a bar fight if they don't go into a bar. And you won't have to worry about having your property used as a bar if you don't allow drinking there.

Better safe than sorry. You can end up holding the bag if an intoxicated worker becomes injured on your property. Twisted — yes, we agree — but twisted or not, you don't need the aggravation. Drinking with the crew is perceived by some as really macho, but when a person is involved in an accident immediately after becoming intoxicated on your property, well, be prepared to make several new acquaintances from within the legal profession.

Smoking

Nothing is more offensive than a bunch of filthy cigarette butts strewn over a gorgeous landscape. And even if your landscape isn't ready to be photographed for *Better Homes and Gardens,* debris of any kind most certainly scars its appearance. Yea or nay, the crew needs to know your smoking rules.

Don't be afraid to say no! Our experience is that even the heaviest smoker is anxious to respect your wishes.

If you do intend to allow smoking on your property, then where? Once a smoking area is designated, be sure that someone who represents the smokers is required to bring along a fireproof butt receptacle and a small fire extinguisher. Better safe than sorry.

Loud music

Construction workers love music — especially when it's loud. Sometimes the music gets so loud that you can't hear yourself think. Be sure to discuss the importance of moderation in this area. A 20-year friendship with a neighbor can easily be reduced to a pistol duel if things get too noisy.

Ask the folks at the preconstruction conference to police loud voices, high volume controls, and power tool use — at least until the shadow on the sun dial reaches 8:30 or 9:00 a.m. No, we don't suggest that you delay your start time or not do important work that's noisy. However, planning quiet tasks during early hours may prevent unnecessary bloodshed.

Material storage

Decide on a location to store lumber, hardware, appliances, and other project items. Remember that open access to the work area must be maintained at all times. Also, lumber should be as close to the work area as possible, which can sometimes mean destruction of a beautiful lawn or landscape area — a cost you have to weigh against slowed production.

Organizing the construction site to make it as efficient as possible is to your advantage. Use a scale drawing of your property to designate storage locations for items such as lumber, debris, tools, equipment, and cabinetry. In so doing, the construction will progress more quickly and efficiently, and you'll save money by being so well organized.

Daily cleanup

Cleanliness is next to godliness, or so the saying goes. If you believe that such should be the case on your project, then make sure to stress the importance of daily job cleanup at the preconstruction conference.

You have the right to a safe job and nothing is more unsafe than a messy work area. No matter what kind of remodel is being performed, cleanliness can make a difference. A worker's impression of the level of quality expected is often conditioned in part by the appearance of the job. Workers assume that a clean job means that someone is taking pride in what is going on. Unfortunately, everyone wants everyone else to do the cleaning.

To help ensure cleanliness, inform the parties involved that you will charge them to clean the mess they leave behind. Advise them that you charge the same hourly rate they charge you. Think about all the money you can make cleaning up for the plumber and the electrician. By the way, make sure to include this right in your contract if it doesn't already exist.

Family and friends of the crew

Frequently, one or more members of the construction crew take great pride in your project. So much so that they want to show family and friends. You may want to establish a simple set of rules in advance. Write them down and leave them in the project binder or post them in a conspicuous location. For example: "Your family and friends are welcome to briefly visit for 30 minutes or less. They should at all times be escorted by you and not allowed to wander alone into private areas." Since there is a certain amount of risk involved, you may wish to take a different approach. For example: "We realize that you may wish to show our project to your family and friends. However, our insurance carrier advises us that there is substantial risk involved if someone is injured. Therefore, we would appreciate it if you would refrain from bringing guests to the project."

Job signs

Can you imagine driving up to the front of your house to find that your contractor has posted a 40-foot-wide neon sign that includes blinking dancing girls — in three different colors? If you haven't discussed this issue, chances are, the contractor will assume that you don't care.

The sign may not be 40 feet wide, but, for whatever reason, you may not want it there. If you don't mind a job sign, say so, but be sure to discuss the size you are willing to allow and where you would like the sign to be placed.

Water, sewer, and irrigation lines can be pierced while digging a post hole, so make sure that the contractor has agreed in writing that he will be responsible for any damage caused by its placement.

Inspections

Use the preconstruction conference to determine who will represent you during inspections.

No matter what type of remodel, you can count on at least one inspection. Building inspectors often leave a site without making an inspection unless at least one person is there to act as an escort — and rightly so. Your project may be one of many stops that the inspector has to make that day. Being there to provide assistance reduces confusion, improves the inspector's chance of getting in and out quickly, and provides a representative who can often answer important questions. So don't be surprised if the inspector comes and goes without approving the work when no one is there to represent you. If you will be hiring a contractor to do the work, it will automatically be his responsibility to handle inspections. If you contract the project yourself, you will either have to be there yourself or assign someone to be there.

Furniture and personal items

Be sure to let everyone know what part of your home will be used for storage and designate that area off limits.

Be prepared to incur costs associated with the removal and storage of absolutely everything contained in any room that will be remodeled. And don't forget adjacent areas and hallways.

Carpenters love to hear themselves tinkle. You know, they love to hear the clanking sounds in their tool pouches as they saunter from place to place. Unfortunately, a tool-pouch-adorned carpenter is about three-feet wide. Can you imagine what danger is posed here? Just visualize a swinging hammer handle thrashing your favorite china doll into a thousand pieces.

The Invasion

In your wildest dreams you probably never imagined that so many things had to be considered before beginning a remodel. The bottom line is that when you do a remodel strangers are going to be living with you for weeks or months. At the preconstruction conference (discussed earlier in this chapter), you make sure that you let everyone involved know what you expect. You also make sure that all the rules are written somewhere and that everyone working on the site has a chance to read them. As with any situation that involves the human element, be prepared to provide some ongoing management.

With that out of the way, you need to prepare yourself, your family, and your home for the onslaught of dust, noise, and construction crews.

Temporary toilet

Designating your own bathroom as the construction potty can save you hundreds of dollars. But tradeoffs include

- Reduced privacy
- Sanitation problems
- Potential damage to your personal property

Plan for a worst-case scenario situation by restricting the time that your bathroom can be used by workers (post a sign on the door). Also, remove all valuables, decorations, good towels, and other property that can easily be stained or otherwise ruined by glue-covered hands and muddy construction boots. In fact, we suggest that you limit bathroom provisions to paper towels, toilet paper, and an inexpensive bar of soap. If you can manage living with such conditions, everything should be fine. If not — rent a temporary toilet!

Interruption of utilities

A question asked by most first-time remodelers is, "Will I be without services such as water, lights, or heat during my project?" Good news! A general rule of remodeling warns us that daytime loss of services can be frequent whereas interruptions overnight are extremely rare. As a matter of fact, in the last two decades we haven't had to interrupt overnight services very often — less than five times.

Security

Arranging entry can be a real problem if everyone in your home will be gone before workers arrive. You don't want to leave your doors open, and you don't want to leave a key under the mat because you may end up being burglarized. Passing out one or more keys to workers can prove to be a really serious mistake. Who lost the key when? You may be able to entrust the management of access with a neighbor. However, if you don't want to involve others, look into a combination-operated lock-box like the ones used by realtors. Give the combination to the crew and see how easy secured access can be.

 If you plan to stay in your home during the remodel, chances are that your alarm system won't be needed during the day. Workers will usually be at your home all day long. What better protection could you possibly ask for? Besides, alarms are one way to unnecessarily complicate matters. Coordinating a construction project is confusing enough for workers without asking them to deal with the additional management of an alarm. Most alarm systems offer a secondary code that you can easily program into your system for temporary access, but we suggest that you turn the alarm off each day before work begins.

Debris

Storing construction debris on the project site until enough is collected to fill a dumpster or some other off-haul vehicle is frequently more cost effective than removing it daily or renting a dumpster for a long period of time. Trash collection services charge by weight, volume, and sometimes, a daily rental rate. Daily rental costs can be substantially reduced by on-site trash storage. Except for smaller projects, where trash can be trucked away daily, on-site storage is often the most cost-effective trash management method.

The trick to finding a good trash storage site involves the following:

✔ Locate a large area where easy access is available to the work area as well as to the street.

✔ Try to pick a place that won't offend your neighbors. In communities where daily rental cost is not an issue, dumpsters are left on site until filled.

✔ Place the dumpster where it won't conflict with deliveries or the general flow of traffic.

Landscaping

Room additions, more than interior remodels, can mean a partially damaged landscape. Assume for a moment that the back lawn proves to be the best place to store lumber. You can count on losing your once green patch of heaven on earth to a complete lack of water and sunlight. Sorry, but it gets worse. You also have to deal with the bare path created between the lumber pile and the work area. (Another name for work boots is *land levelers.*) You can insist on having material stored where it will do little or no damage to your landscape, but doing so can often slow things down considerably. Decide on a balance that considers both questions.

Crew size

Don't expect dozens of people to be on the project all at the same time. Such conditions on small projects can be dangerous — not to mention expensive. Confusion and sloppiness are enhanced on small jobs run by hoards of personnel. On some days, no one will report to work. Although the absence of workers may cause the job to seem as though it has been abandoned, keep in mind that off-site tasks must also be accomplished (making a lumber list, picking up supplies, and so on).

On most remodeling projects, at least one person should be on the project every day. However, sometimes a worker's presence for more than an hour or so can be fruitless. For instance, when the drywall finish is performed, only one coat of joint compound can be applied each day. That's four coats in four days, with each coat taking about an hour to apply. During this phase, no other inside work can be performed, and the job site gets pretty desolate.

Remember, too, that one person's work is often dependent on someone else's. You generally won't see the heating contractor, the plumber, and the electrician on the project at the same time. Normally, the electrician can't do his work until the plumber and heating contractors are finished. The why is simple! Wiring can easily be routed around ducts and pipes — the reverse is not so easily accomplished. Also, because placement of heat ducting is less critical than waste lines, the plumber usually starts first.

Elderly people, infants, and children

Everyone working on your project must be notified when an infant or an elderly person will be present during working hours. Dust results from almost every kind of remodel work. Dust that can endanger the health of the very young or old who may have allergies or asthma. Extra measures must be taken to reduce the transmission of even the smallest particles through ductwork and gaps in doors. Temporary partitions and plastic barriers reduce dust flow and tape can be used to temporarily seal gaps in door openings. Tape a layer of plastic over heat registers and cold air returns —

at least during working hours. And if at all possible, don't run heating or cooling systems while sawing or sanding is going on. The mess that can be distributed by a central heating or cooling system is unbelievable. Signs can be used to notify the crew about special rules or conditions — "The great-grandmother behind this door carries a Smith & Wesson."

Divorce dust

No matter how well organized your project is, about 70 percent of the way through you will want to strangle everyone — and we do mean everyone. We call this phenomenon *divorce dust:* the disruption for weeks on end, the lack of privacy, the pressure of decision making, the disagreements with family about colors and styles and who knows what else, and all the while things keep going wrong.

Prepare yourself for this eventuality. Have family meetings about the possibility that it will happen and look to each other for support. Constantly remind each other that your home will soon be so much more beautiful and comfortable than it ever was before.

Chapter 15

The Law: Look Before You Leap

In This Chapter

▶ The laws and how they get on the books

▶ The ins and outs of building permits

▶ A few words on in-law units

*R*ules: They're a fact of life. For example, a trip in the car to the local supermarket to pick up a loaf of bread means following several rules. If you drive by the book, you'll fasten your seat belt, stop at red lights, and won't go any faster than the posted speed limit. The same holds true when it comes to doing a remodel. There are rules (planning, zoning, and building codes) that must be followed to make (and keep) our homes and neighborhoods comfortable, safe, and enjoyable. The requirement to have smoke detectors in your home is no less important than having to wear a seatbelt when driving your car. The smoke detector requirement is only one of many codes designed to be part of the solution and not part of the problem.

You may not need any stinking badges, but when it comes to remodeling, a job without permits is, well, like a day without. . . .

A Rule for All Seasons

We firmly believe that playing by the rules puts you light-years ahead of those who foolishly choose the alternative. For remodeling purposes, "the rules" consist of *planning ordinances* and *building codes*.

Planning ordinances are commonly a county or municipal function, while building codes are comprised of federal rules that states, counties, and cities adopt and modify. Modifications are typically necessary due to local climatic, geological, or topographical conditions.

The building code is outlined in a voluminous document entitled the *Uniform Building Code* (UBC). This code provides minimum standards to safeguard life or limb, health, property, and public welfare by regulating and controlling the design, construction, quality of materials, use and occupancy, location, and maintenance of all buildings and structures within a given community.

Moreover, the UBC is dedicated to the development of better building construction and greater safety to the public by *uniformity* in building laws. The code is founded on broad-based principles that make the use of new materials and modern construction systems possible.

Here are some of the code's provisions as it relates to residential construction:

- Access and exit facilities
- Allowable area
- Construction
- Emergency escapes
- Height
- Light
- Location on property
- Room dimensions (ceiling height, floor area, and width)
- Sanitation
- Smoke detectors
- Ventilation

Because the provision for smoke detectors affects most people performing a remodel, it is an excellent example of the specificity and level of detail that you find in the code. You may be interested to learn that you don't need to be adding a bedroom for this section of the code to apply to your improvement. Indeed, this compliance with this section of code kicks in with virtually any permit that is issued for a home remodeling, including a new roof. As such, building officials figure that they will be able to get more smoke detectors into more homes, thereby making homes, in general, more safe.

ICBO: Not just some junket

The International Conference of Building Officials first enacted the UBC at their annual meeting in 1927. Revised editions of this code have been published since that time at approximately three-year intervals.

Every remodeling job requires a *building permit,* which ensures that contractors adhere to the code. In case you have any misgivings about the importance of obtaining a permit, allow us to quote chapter and verse for the UBC:

> It is unlawful for any person, firm or corporation to erect, construct, enlarge, alter, repair, move improve, remove, convert or demolish, equip, use, occupy or maintain any building or structure or cause or permit the same to be done in violation of the UBC.

On the positive side, anyone may propose amendments to the code. Therefore, if you don't like a particular provision, you can attempt to change it. Just remember that experts in the field of building construction and fire and life safety must hold public hearings in which they carefully review any proposed change.

Any builder worth his or her salt should have a pretty thorough understanding of the code if for no other reason than being the recipient of the proverbial *punch list* (the list of fix-it items that more often than not results from the local building inspector's visit to the job site).

Permit me to require more permits

Unless you are building a storage shed that will contain no heating, electrical, or plumbing, you're going to need a plumbing, electrical, or mechanical permit — or all three.

Plumbing permits authorize plumbing work. The code requirements for that work are in another federal code book — the *Uniform Plumbing Code* (UPC).

The UPC provides consumers with safe and sanitary plumbing systems, while simultaneously allowing latitude for innovation and new technologies. Like the UBC, the UPC is an ordinance that provides *minimum* requirements and standards for protecting public health, safety, and welfare.

Birth of a plumbing code

A little more than 50 years ago, the plumbing industry was in complete disorder. Communities had widely divergent plumbing practices and local jurisdictions used many different, often conflicting, plumbing codes. So, the Western Plumbing Officials Association (now the International Association of Plumbing and Mechanical Officials or IAPMO) formed a committee of plumbing inspectors, master and journeyman plumbers, and sanitary and mechanical engineers to create a basic plumbing document for general use. The committee was assisted by the public utility companies and the plumbing industry. IAPMO officially adopted the first edition of the UPC in 1945.

If, in the course of your home remodeling project, you plan to install a new furnace or air conditioner (or alter the existing system) or a range hood, bath fan, or other ventilating system, you'll need a mechanical permit.

You can find all of the federal requirements for performing this kind of work in — you guessed it — the *Uniform Mechanical Code* (UMC). First published in 1967, the UMC is revised and published at three-year intervals.

Finally, if you intend to "get wired," make sure to have an electrical permit. The code book for electrical work is the *National Electrical Code* (NEC). Don't ask us why it isn't called the Uniform Electrical Code.

Be it wiring for a toaster, light fixture, dishwasher, or garage door opener, the work must be performed in accordance with the code as outlined in the NEC.

Bear in mind that although building, plumbing, mechanical, and electrical codes are federal rules; states, counties, and cities may (and often do) amend or modify these rules to accommodate a given locale's specific health and safety needs.

Oh, Zoning!

Community planning is almost always done at either the county or municipal level — or, in some cases, both. Good community planning involves the fundamental element of *zoning* (a government's right to restrict the use of property in order to protect the community's health, safety, and welfare).

Zoning is the uniquely American way of handling land use. The basic premise was to zone land into districts where all compatible users would share the same designation. Thereafter, they could build as they chose, provided they built within the zoned area and met some minimal standards of height, off-street parking, and other guidelines.

Cousin Louie can't plop his ravioli factory right next door to your home sweet home, thus the distinction between residential and commercial zoning. Moreover, distinctions can be made between the different types of zoning. For example, residential zoning has high-density and medium-density variations. High-density zoning may consist of apartment complexes, condominiums, or other multi-family dwellings.

Medium- or low-density residential zoning typically consists of single family dwellings (homes) that are situated on more generous parcels with an occasional landscape buffer of green space area. Duets or townhouses that share a common wall or property line also fall into this classification.

Zoning regulations prescribe what you can build, where you can build it, and how big it can be. In a nutshell, these regulations are designed to control the height, mass, density, and location of buildings, thereby limiting the intensity of development in order to provide proper natural light, air, and open space.

Some of the more obvious benefits to zoning regulations that hit close to home are land use, height restrictions, and setbacks. Building height is defined as the distance, measured vertically, from the *average grade* upon which the structure rests to the highest point on the building. The slope of the lot is referred to as the grade. Thus, if the lot is high (slopes up) on one side and low (slopes down) on the other — the average point between these two distances would be considered the average grade.

A *setback* is the minimum distance required from the street or property line to the closest point on a building. The aim is to allow you to take full advantage of the view from your property without restricting the same from your neighbor. In addition, generous setbacks permit you and your neighbors to enjoy both the greatest amounts of privacy and natural light available.

The land use regulation of zoning prevents a service station, mini-mart, or junkyard from becoming your next-door neighbor. Although the height restriction may prevent you from adding another story and the setback requirement may not allow you to make your home as large as you would like, you need to consider the more far-reaching, long-term benefits.

These regulations prevent your neighbors from doing the same things. Thus, you can look forward to maintaining a pleasant view with lots of sunshine. What's more, having ample distance between you and your neighbor's home may prevent his kitchen window from having direct line-of-site into your bedroom or bathroom. Good planning does have its rewards.

A Chicken in Every Pot — A Car in Every Garage

Other planning ordinances protect home values, but they can also prevent you from performing certain "improvements" to your home. One such example is a garage conversion whereby the garage is converted into living space.

While not as prevalent today — due to more stringent planning regulations — a garage conversion has traditionally been a means of generating additional living space at a fraction of the cost of adding on to your home.

In days gone by, you only had to remove the garage door, frame in the opening, install a window and some siding, finish the interior, and voilà — instant room. Unfortunately, neighborhoods with converted garages were overrun with vehicles that were previously housed in garages. As a result, many people with converted garages found that their property values had, in fact, decreased.

City planners now require that homeowners replace their garage with additional off-street, covered parking such as a carport or garage. Moreover, the structure must meet setback requirements and stringent design review criteria. Accordingly, garage conversions are a less popular alternative due to the lack of space and/or the increased cost associated with garage replacement.

All things considered, a garage conversion may be one of the most expensive and least cost-effective means of adding space to a home.

The Building Permit

About ten years ago an older fellow called our radio program. "I don't need no stinking building permit," he said. He went on to say that he didn't want the government on his property. And furthermore, he and his dad had built their family home — without permits and without using licensed contractors to help. He also told us that the house had been standing problem free for over 70 years. We complimented the achievement but stood by our guns continuing to recommend getting a permit and using only licensed contractors.

Today, building anything anywhere without a building permit is risky at best. We once saw an entire workshop leveled because it was constructed without a building permit.

When you sell or refinance your home, you will most likely have to produce a building permit for any construction work that you — or a previous owner — have done. There's never a good time to discover that you have to tear down a portion of your home, so we suggest that you get a permit before you start your remodel.

In some communities, the city runs the building department. In others, you call the county, and in some areas, the city and county share jurisdiction. The sign on the door may read community development department, public works department, planning department, building department, one stop building center — or some acronymic mutation. Don't worry about using the correct name, simply call the nearest city or county office and ask the person who answers the phone to tell you where you can get a building permit.

Read the instructions first

Contact your building department before you even begin your precon-struction drawings. You need to find out ahead of time what you must do to guarantee that your project complies with local codes and ordinances. You know, your basic rules, regulations, and restrictions.

If you are planning a room addition or an out building, you also have to comply with certain other ordinances in addition to the building code. These can include zoning, building height restrictions, lot coverage limits, and front, rear, and side yard setbacks — to name a few.

The permit process

The permit process is a two-part operation. It includes plan review and project inspections. Depending on how well your building department is organized, the plan review process ranges from very simple to extremely time consuming.

Better building departments offer a *one-stop building permit center*. Here you walk in, hand your remodeling drawings to a plan checker, pay a fee, wait a half hour or so, and leave carrying a corrected set of plans and a proper set of permits. Don't worry, the building official tells you exactly what permits you need. Your building department may require other permits, but the most common are the building permit, plumbing permit, mechanical permit, and electrical permit.

Although most remodel permits are issued in this manner, some communi-ties take weeks or even months to accomplish the exact same task. You may have to attend a public hearing to get approval for your remodel. The public hearing is a town meeting kind of event where city officials publicly discuss the merits of your project (the general public can also make comments during the hearing). The officials can approve, conditionally approve, or deny your proposal.

Communities that have public hearings for remodels are often very anal and should be handled with kid gloves. Never go to a public hearing without the representation of an architect or designer experienced in such matters. We have often been able to reverse unfair planning commission decisions by appealing to the city council.

Some building departments will review your plans while you wait. Others take two to six weeks for the initial review and another several weeks for corrections. Don't be surprised if the total wait is a month or more.

Be sure to bring your checkbook with you to the building department. Certain fees are paid on the spot — no matter how long the process takes.

The folks at the building department are happy to tell you exactly what you need to get through the permit process. All you need to do is ask. In fact, most building departments do their best to make the process as easy as possible by creating instruction sheets that clearly explain the process and the department's expectations. After you get the instructions, read through them and be sure to discuss them with someone before you leave to clarify any confusion you may have.

Whatever you do, don't apply for a building permit yourself if you are going to hire a remodeling contractor. Don't, don't, don't! Doing so shifts certain liability into your court, and you really don't want that. When your contractor gets the permit, the building department requires him to have the proper state and city licenses and at least the minimum required insurance coverage. If you are going to be an owner-builder, let any specialty contractors (plumber, electrician, and so on) that you hire purchase their own permits as well. Oh, and be sure to get a copy of the permit for your records.

The building inspection — a painfully good thing

You will more than likely begin remodeling soon after acquiring your building permit. Before you can call the building department to request an inspection, you must first understand exactly when each inspection is supposed to performed. Although the permit card briefly explains points at which inspections are supposed to occur, you need to clearly understand what constitutes project-inspection readiness.

Room additions involve a series of inspections:

✔ **Foundation inspection:** Before your contractor can pour concrete into the foundation of your addition, you generally have to have a foundation inspection. The permit card won't say so, but the building department wants to look at your reinforcing steel and other elements that are concealed after concrete is poured. Naturally, this inspection must occur after everything is completely ready for concrete to be poured. This same procedure is true for concrete floors.

✔ **Underfloor inspection:** For wood floors, the *underfloor* inspection is next, which involves checking the floor framing, water, sewer, and heating ducts. The contractor cannot install underfloor insulation until the inspector approves the underfloor work.

✔ **Underfloor insulation inspection:** The underfloor insulation inspection is next. The inspector must approve the floor insulation — in place — before the contractor can install the subflooring.

✔ **Frame inspection:** The next — and most extensive — inspection is the *frame inspection,* which doesn't happen until the walls and roof are framed, sheeted, sided, and fitted with heating, plumbing, and electrical wiring. After the inspector approves all elements of the frame inspection, the contractor can install wall and ceiling insulation.

✔ **Wall and ceiling insulation inspection:** Sometimes the building department foregoes insulation inspections and accepts a certificate from the insulation installer stating that the insulation has been properly installed. We prefer the building inspector to personally do the inspection, because then you don't have to worry about any conflict of interest.

✔ **Special inspections:** If your plans require special plywood or drywall nailing, those inspections occur next. Call the building department and find out whether they require such inspections if you're not sure.

✔ **Final inspection:** The last and most important investigation is the final inspection. You absolutely *must* have your project "finaled." This process completes the entire permit and inspection process.

The same inspection rules that apply to additions also apply to interior remodels. However, if an addition is not involved, you usually only have three inspections:

✔ Frame inspection (Remember, the inspector also checks the plumbing, heating, and electrical at this time.)

✔ Insulation inspection

✔ Special inspections

✔ Final inspection

A week or so after your project is complete, take a trip to the building department to make sure that your "final" is properly recorded in the community record book. Building departments have called us a year after a project was complete asking why we didn't final a certain project. In each instance, we had to bring the building permit card to them to prove we had been officially finaled.

Never, ever throw away your permit set of plans or the permit card. And be sure to pass them on to the person whom you sell your home to.

Greet the building inspector with open arms. He is your friend. So often a contractor attempts to lead a customer to believe that the building inspector is incompetent — a government official with nothing better to do than "write the job up." Not!

Measuring quality — who better than you

Good craftsmanship and material quality are yet another issue. Yes, building codes and ordinances do establish *minimum* standards. However, these standards are met by almost every manufacturer of construction products and materials. Just as you can buy compliant products that are durable and long lasting, so can you buy compliant products that are junky. The building department does not differentiate between a $39 faucet and one that costs $390 — as long as both meet established standards.

The government is anxious to ensure that you and the environment are protected to a certain extent, but the choice of level of quality is left up to you. Determining levels of quality will be one of your most difficult responsibilities — and you're going to be responsible for a lot — during your remodel.

Not every product manufacturer makes code-compliant products. Never purchase an item from a vendor unless they guarantee in writing that their product is code and ordinance compliant. If you can't get a written money-back guarantee, shop elsewhere. Also, remember that ordinances change from town to town and city to city. Get a guarantee that applies to the place where you intend to use the item.

Taxes

Getting a permit is not like sending an engraved invitation to the tax collector. If you significantly improve your property, you may face tax consequences — more or better real property usually does mean more taxes. However, in most areas, a typical kitchen or bath remodel does not necessarily cause your taxes to increase. Still, you may want to talk with the tax collector about possible tax consequences before you begin your remodel. Who knows, you may be planning a remodel just about the time the county is in bad need of revenue. You didn't like that joke — did you?

Thanks Ken, thanks Roger

Building inspectors don't go on witch-hunts or seek and destroy missions. We personally are thankful for building inspectors.

When we were new in the remodeling business — still learning how to do things the right way — Ken and Roger, a couple of really knowledgeable building inspectors, took us under their wings. While one of them explained the do's and don'ts of safe electrical wiring, the other donned his bright orange coveralls and crawled under the house to demonstrate the proper way to configure a sewer line. Their kindness, patience, and vast knowledge in all areas of the building trade helped us to advance and to become very proficient remodelers. Yep, we got lucky because most building inspectors don't have time to act as an assistant to your architect or job superintendent.

In-Law Units

If you are thinking about expanding your home to include private quarters for your parents, children, or another family member, then you need to know more about an *in-law unit*. Simply stated, an in-law unit exists when one residence has two separate sets of living quarters — each with its own kitchen — and a kitchen means anything built-in that cooks, including a stove or microwave.

A special zoning ordinance in many states, counties, and communities addresses this exact issue. The ordinance allows you to add a second occupancy to your single family residence in accordance with a special set of conditions that limit construction and use. An *occupancy* is defined as a living unit that has its own completely separate cooking facility. Having a second occupancy at a single family residence is sort of like having a duplex but without the extra parking places.

Single family zoning wasn't designed to prevent several generations of a family living at one address. In fact, we know that multiple generations of families have been living separately under the same roof in homes all over the United States for eons. Adult kids with parents, seniors with their children or siblings — and the list goes on. Unfortunately, at the same time, and in these same single family neighborhoods, other industrious residents have aspired to improve their income by becoming landlords. All without regard to zoning laws, crowded parking conditions, increased traffic problems, and the noise that often results.

Community planners wanted to root out these outlaw landlords to prevent them from unnecessarily overcrowding neighborhoods and to allow extended families to live together — within certain limitations. Unfortunately, people misunderstood our zoning forefathers, and in the late 1980s, building departments were overwhelmed with requests for approvals for in-law units. It seemed as though the would-be landlord had finally found a way to build an apartment on his single family lot. All he needed was a set of plans marked in-law quarters. Cities were approving such requests without questioning an applicant's intentions. It was finally discovered that many applications were fraudulent and that not every in-law unit was being used by a relative. That's when the rules started to get tough.

Now when you apply for approval to build an in-law unit, you can count on ample amounts of scrutiny from your local building official. In fact, some communities' restrictions are so stringent that in-law units are almost impossible to afford. Get this: Some places require a special notation on your home title that forces you to disassemble your in-law unit upon sale. Other building departments require you to agree to annual inspections to confirm that the unit is being used as family quarters.

On the bright side, many communities throughout the country still welcome in-law units. Most building departments in California, for example, have adopted the state's basic in-law unit guidelines. Here, the state has set forth the basic concept, and community building departments used those principals to create modified rules for use at the local level. For example, size is a primary limitation. Who said size isn't important? You can count on being restricted to a maximum floor area. In the county where we build, in-law units are restricted to 650 square feet or less — depending on the city. We don't know of any community that restricts area to less than 500 square feet. (By the way, 650 square feet is equal in size to the that of a roomy one-bedroom apartment.)

Some communities require that the secondary unit be attached to the primary dwelling. No, not with a long narrow hallway. It must be adjacent to the primary structure, on a second floor, or along a common wall on the ground floor. And to top it all off, some of these building departments require a door from the primary residence to the secondary one. Then again, other communities allow a completely separate structure.

Utilities are another big concern. Many communities simply do not allow a second electric meter or a separate water meter. However, the more you do to completely separate in-law quarters, the less management there will be and the less confusion.

Part III
Foundation and Framing

The 5th Wave   By Rich Tennant

What makes you think your foundation is sinking?

Well, for one thing, we're standing on the third floor balcony.

In this part . . .

We outline what happens during the first stages of a remodeling job: demolition, foundation building, floor framing, wall framing, and roof framing. Someone else may be doing all the work; we tell you what to look for so that you can be sure they do it right.

Chapter 16

Demolition: Out with the Old, In with the New

- -

In This Chapter

▶ Staying safe

▶ Tearing stuff apart

▶ Dealing (or not dealing) with asbestos and lead

- -

*O*ne of the most nerve-racking, but necessary, aspects of a home remodeling project is removing or dismantling existing finishes. It's called *demolition,* which, according to Webster's, means "to tear down, destroy, ruin." While that may be just exactly what you have in mind for your tired, old kitchen or outdated bath, hang on long enough to get through this chapter. We think that we can make your job a lot easier and maybe even save you money along the way.

Staging a Demolition Derby in Your Home

Demolition can range from removing something as simple as a door to — in the case of a full-blown addition or remodel — yanking out the following:

- ✔ Flooring
- ✔ Baseboards and interior trim
- ✔ Built-in cabinets and counters
- ✔ Plumbing and electrical fixtures
- ✔ Tile
- ✔ Wallpaper or other wall finishes
- ✔ Wallboard or plaster

✔ Windows and exterior doors

✔ Siding and exterior trim

✔ Roofing and gutters

✔ And much more

Less friendly, more complex elements of demolition can involve removing the following:

✔ Concrete paths and patios

✔ Concrete floors and foundations

✔ Wall, floor, ceiling, and roof framing

✔ Existing plumbing pipes

✔ Electrical wiring

✔ Heating and air conditioning ducts and equipment

Still, this disruptive process can be one of the most rewarding phases of a remodeling project for homeowners.

Many people want to participate in their remodeling work even though they have hired a contractor. Often, this interest stems from their desire to save money. Thus the term *sweat equity,* where homeowners provide their own time and physical labor in exchange for a reduced price.

Although some contractors have a strict policy of no homeowner involvement, most contractors do make exceptions when the sweat equity work doesn't expose them to undue liability or risk blowing the job schedule. If you want to contribute sweat equity, be sure that you choose a contractor who welcomes your participation — *before* you sign on the dotted line.

No experience necessary

If you are willing to roll up your sleeves and get your hands dirty, but are not inclined to take on tasks that require professional expertise, demolition is right up your alley. The fact that demolition doesn't require construction experience or expertise makes it especially appealing to the average layperson.

What's more, demolition can be quite therapeutic. Busting up concrete with a sledgehammer and pulling down plaster and wallboard with a hammer and pry bar usually get the blood pumping and, in turn, help to relieve stress and tension. So how do you spell relief? D-E-M-O-L-I-T-I-O-N!

Aside from saving money and relieving stress, "do-it-yourself-demolition" provides homeowners with a sense of accomplishment. Our experience is that most people take great pride and personal satisfaction in playing a "hands-on" role in their remodeling. They also take great pleasure in telling friends and neighbors that they had a personal hand in their endeavor.

Although it may appear simple, demolition involves more than meets the eye. Using improper tools and lacking safety information almost always guarantees a visit to the emergency room to mend a nasty wound. (We discuss other health hazards associated with demolition such as asbestos and lead later in this chapter.)

Danger, danger Will Robinson!

By nature, remodeling is full of surprises or unexpected events. Demolition is no less immune to surprises than is any other phase of construction. Indeed, demolition can account for the majority of the unexpected events that occur during a project. So, like a Boy Scout, always be prepared.

Yes, be prepared to find pipes, ducts, and electrical wiring in places where you would least expect to find them (such as right smack dab in the middle of a wall scheduled to be permanently removed). Ka-ching! Time to bring in a plumber, electrician, or sheetmetal contractor to reroute them.

Unless you have x-ray eyes, or know someone who does, you cannot positively determine what's waiting for you when you begin to tear out wallboard or plaster. Keeping your fingers crossed can be quite helpful; however, it can make the job of demolition a bit more cumbersome.

An ounce of prevention . . .

Before you run off to tear out your '50s kitchen or pre-World War II bath, a word about the importance of safety.

Construction can be dangerous and demolition is no exception. Indeed, demolition work can expose you to a host of injury-causing conditions. Having the proper safety gear is therefore essential. In addition, if you have a history of heart trouble, back pain, allergies, or other ailments that can be triggered or aggravated by physical activity or excessive dust, you should consult your physician before engaging in demolition work.

Nails, wire, wood splinters, broken glass, and sharp edges abound during the demolition process. Consequently, to avoid injury, you must protect as much of your body as possible when performing this kind of work.

Now, wearing a suit of armor is neither practical nor realistic. However, certain areas of the body deserve special consideration.

Your eyes, ears, nose, mouth, head, hands, feet, and toes are particularly vulnerable. Thus, we recommend that you have the following safety items on hand before attempting to remove even the first screw:

- Ear plugs
- Fabric breathing mask
- Hard hat
- Leather gloves
- Long-sleeved shirt and jeans
- Multipurpose fire extinguisher
- Safety goggles or glasses
- Steel-toed work boots

Although most of the aforementioned items speak for themselves, a bit of explanation may be useful for a few of the items on the list.

The fabric mask (much like a surgeon or dentist wears) is a disposable device that limits the amount of dust and debris that you breathe in through your nose and mouth. It helps cut down on sneezing and wheezing. Don't confuse this mask with a more sophisticated breathing apparatus such as a respirator that is designed to filter solvents, vapors, or other airborne particles that could be potentially hazardous to your health. Such a device is rarely used when doing demolition for a home-remodeling project.

A long-sleeved shirt and jeans offer better-than-average protection from scrapes and scratches, in sharp contrast to the minimal protection that a T-shirt and shorts provide. The long-sleeved shirt is particularly useful when removing wall and ceiling insulation. Along with a cold shower at day's end, it can help prevent frantic itching.

The prospect of a fire erupting always exists when working with power tools around construction. Therefore, it's a good idea to have a multipurpose ABC fire extinguisher handy. The multipurpose fire extinguisher suppresses grease, paper, and electrical fires. Chances are that you'll never need to use it, but Murphy's Law makes it a must.

Children and pets are both curious and fascinated by the goings-on of demolition. Therefore, you will want to pay special attention to their safety by keeping them away from the area where demolition work is being performed. Moreover, an area that has been demolished often contains gaping holes in floors, dangling electrical wires, and various other hazards. Accordingly, children and pets should be restricted from these areas at all times — or at least until they have been made safe. Furthermore, it's not a bad idea to limit adult access as well.

In fact, a rule that we have in our construction company is to "power down" whenever anyone (other than the work crew) enters the area. That means that all power tools are to be immediately turned off and other activity that could be potentially harmful is ceased until the area is clear and work can resume.

The Fun Part: Actually Demolishing Stuff

We present the next few sections as a scholarly exposé on the intellectually stimulating task of knocking stuff down.

Pass me the sledgehammer please

It's no secret that, skill aside, the key to performing a successful task has much to do with the quality or condition of the tools you are using. Accordingly, professional tradespeople are notorious for having the best tools. They know better than anyone that having the right tools makes a job easier, safer, and renders more professional results.

The same holds true with demolition. As a matter of fact, having the proper tools and equipment for this sometimes dangerous work can make your job infinitely easier and substantially safer.

We suggest that you have the following demolition tools on hand:

- Chain saw
- Chisel
- Circular saw
- Crescent wrench
- Framing hammer
- Hacksaw
- Pipe wrench
- Pry bar
- Razor knife and replacement blades
- Reciprocating saw (With the appropriate blade, this saw can cut through wood, wallboard, lath and plaster, iron pipe, copper pipe, sheet-metal, nails, roofing — you name it.)
- Screwdriver set
- Sledgehammer

This list is meant only as a guide. You may not need items such as a sledge-hammer or chain saw in the course of demolishing your bathroom. By the same token, if you're removing a concrete patio to make way for your new room addition, you may need a jackhammer, which is not on the list.

Don't feel inadequate if you don't have most of these tools. In most cases, you only need the power tools for a day or so to perform the majority of your demolition work. Consequently, you may want to consider renting the equipment from a local tool rental company. Renting costs a fraction of the price that purchasing does and is an especially good choice if you don't have a need for such tools down the road.

An easy job for most folks: Removing flooring

Most of this book focuses on tasks that you should hire professionals to do for you, but this section covers something that most people can do for themselves: removing finish flooring from a room, which happens to be the first step of demolition.

The carpet, pad, and tack strip (the strip of nails that holds the carpet to the floor) at the perimeter should be removed and taken out of the area. You can easily remove carpet by using a flat-blade screwdriver to pry it up in one corner. With a corner in hand, you pull the carpet up, releasing it from the tack strip. Once loose, you can roll up the carpet to get it out of the room. Since this may mean some really big rolls for large rooms, we recommend cutting the carpet into smaller, more manageable sections that can be easily transported out.

The carpet pad is next. Many people try to salvage the pad hoping that it can be reinstalled. Not a good idea. A carpet pad is designed to work in harmony with the carpet for the maximum level of comfort and wear. Most carpet pads are attached with staples and can simply be removed by peeling them back. Like the carpet, remove the pad in small, manageable pieces.

You can usually remove the tack strip by using a pry bar and a hammer. The tack strip is usually held in place with small nails, though on a concrete floor, it can also be glued. In either case, the pry bar and hammer will generally do the trick.

Keep in mind that the tack strip is filled with nails with tips as sharp as razors. You don't even want to attempt removal without a pair of leather work gloves.

With the carpet and tack strip removed, you're left with another layer of finish flooring or simply the subfloor or concrete slab. If it is one of the latter two, you don't have to take any special precautions. However, if another layer of flooring exists, you have a decision to make: Does it stay or go? Many people are pleasantly surprised to find hardwood flooring below their wall-to-wall carpeting. Often, you can preserve the hardwood floor and integrate it into the new plan. If this is the case, you should thoroughly protect it with at least one layer of 15-pound building paper and a layer of plywood, particleboard, or drywall. Seal all joints using duct tape. When the remodeling is far enough along, you can remove the protective layer and refinish the floor.

It you decide to remove the hardwood, like the carpet tack strip, you can remove it a piece at a time using a pry bar and hammer. Hardwood floor material can bring big bucks from salvage yards, so you want to be especially careful when removing it.

 There are other types of flooring that you may have to contend with such as vinyl tile, ceramic tile, or sheet vinyl. Keep in mind that some building products may contain asbestos or lead, which can be hazardous to your health. We suggest that you skip ahead in this chapter for this information to learn more about some of the precautions that should be taken during demolition.

Haste makes waste and can get you wet

Most people are sure that all demolition is done as the first order of business in a remodeling project. That may be the case when you're doing a small bathroom remodel or other minor remodeling project, but is certainly not the rule when adding on.

Many people are surprised to learn that the wall between the old and new space doesn't usually need to be "blown out" until the new space is weather tight. Thus, the excavation, foundation, floor, wall, ceiling and roof framing, windows, roofing, and siding are in place before demolition of the old wall takes place. Often, the existing siding or stucco can remain in place until the time comes to remove the wall. Typically, you only need to remove small patches of siding at the outset in order to make foundation and framing connections.

Removing a wall prematurely can expose your family, home, and furnishings to potential injury or damage from weather, dust, and construction activity. Your best bet is to leave the wall in place until you absolutely must remove it.

Delaying demolition has other benefits, too. Keeping the home intact for as long as possible makes the outside noise more tolerable, provides greater security, and keeps heating and cooling bills in check.

If you can't delay demolition, do the following to protect your home:

- ✔ Temporarily cover the opening left by a window or exterior door with plastic and/or plywood.

- ✔ Install plastic sheeting over any areas where siding or roofing has been removed to reduce drafts and prevent damage from rain showers.

- ✔ Put up plastic sheeting to act as a dust barrier between work areas and other areas of the home.

- ✔ Lay down plastic runners to protect flooring from potential damage caused by hauling debris outdoors.

To minimize debris traffic throughout your home, place a wheelbarrow or garbage can outdoors — directly beneath a window — and toss demolition debris into that. Wallboard, flooring, tile, and other material can be broken down into small pieces and thrown out a window, which saves you from hauling it through your home, and makes for fewer steps, too!

Keep in mind that although you may have the strongest foundation and the best-built frame, your remodel is only as good as the finishes. You need to be concerned not only about the quality of the finishes, but also how well they match the style and existing finishes throughout the rest of your home. A little care during demolition can mean all the difference in the finish.

Save the pieces!

You can partially, if not fully, salvage almost all the building materials that you remove. Among the many recyclable building materials you may have in your home are the following:

- ✔ Appliances

- ✔ Baseboard

- ✔ Bath accessories

- ✔ Cabinetry

- ✔ Carpet

- ✔ Chair rail

- ✔ Counters

- ✔ Door hardware

- ✔ Doors and trim

- ✔ Light fixtures

- ✔ Mirrors

- ✔ Paneling

- ✔ Plumbing fixtures and fittings

- ✔ Stone
- ✔ Windows and trim
- ✔ Wood flooring
- ✔ Wood wainscot

You may be wondering if we have altogether lost our marbles. Why in heaven's name would you want to salvage all of these items? After all, isn't the whole idea behind remodeling to replace most of this stuff? Well, yes, no, and maybe.

It would be ludicrous to suggest that someone spending tens of thousands of dollars on a new master bedroom suite install the variegated shag carpet that went out with the *Laugh In* television show.

By the same token, spending hundreds or perhaps thousands of dollars to re-create discontinued or otherwise unavailable doors, trim, and hardware is a poor use of resources. However, with a little care during removal, you can most likely rejuvenate the materials and reinstall them into your "new" space.

Dollars aside, another important reason to recycle building materials is the environment. Landfills from coast-to-coast and border-to-border are overrun with water heaters, stoves, and other building material. Moreover, recycling lumber and other building material places less demand on natural resources. How's that for being politically correct?

Queen Victoria may have had the money, but I don't

Re-creating the massive amounts of elaborate woodwork found in a turn-of-the-century Victorian home can cost a fortune. Most of this vintage trim is no longer standard stock material and, therefore, must be custom-made by a millwork company — that is, if you're lucky enough to find one in your area that can reproduce.

Most millwork companies that perform this work must shape the material with a series of millwork saws called *knives* to create an exact match. Setting up this machinery and creating this material can take a great deal of time in contrast to stock material, which is turned out by the truckload. Consequently, the cost to produce this custom material can be astronomical.

When Demolition Is Hazardous to Your Health

Earlier in this chapter, we discuss the importance of using caution when performing demolition work to avoid injury from things that you can see, such as nails or broken glass. Even greater caution should be taken in protecting your health from things that you *can't* see, such as asbestos and lead.

One of the unfortunate aspects of asbestos and lead is that you can't determine whether your home contains them just by making a visual inspection. Even though you may have an idea of which material or objects may contain asbestos or lead, the only means of positive identification is to have a laboratory analyze a sample of the suspect material.

Laboratories that do this work are usually listed in the Yellow Pages as *Laboratories-Analytical.* Testing fees can range from $75 to $250, depending on the number of suspect material samples being tested.

The cost to professionally abate (remove) lead and/or asbestos can range from a few hundred to several thousand dollars. Thus, health aside, it is critical that you determine — in advance — if either of these hazards exist. If they do, decide how you are going to deal with them and what the cost will be. You can then include this cost in your overall remodeling budget.

Everything works out for the asbestos

Asbestos is the name for a group of naturally occurring minerals that separate into strong, very fine fibers. The fibers are heat-resistant and extremely durable, which made asbestos very useful in the manufacture of building products. However, because of the health risks that it posed, the United States government banned its use nearly two decades ago.

Prior to 1978, asbestos was found in building products such as siding, roofing, wall and ceiling insulation, sheet vinyl (including the backing or underlayment), vinyl tile, pipe, furnace and boiler insulation and tape, and acoustic, "cottage cheese" style, ceiling treatment.

Asbestos was also used in the manufacture of some electrical equipment such as switch boxes, receptacle boxes, and old-fashioned "knob and tube" wiring. Until the mid-1970s, oven and in-cabinet dishwasher units were often wrapped in insulation blankets that contained asbestos.

If your home was built prior to 1978, it almost certainly contains some level of asbestos. Don't be alarmed. In the home, asbestos may or may not pose a health hazard depending upon the level of concentration and, more importantly, the condition of the asbestos-containing material.

Asbestos tends to break down into a dust of microscopic fibers. Because of their size and shape, these tiny fibers remain suspended in the air for long periods of time and can easily penetrate body tissues after being inhaled or ingested. These incredibly durable fibers can remain in the body for many years, ultimately causing asbestos-related diseases. An illness of this sort can take 10 to 30 years to appear, so what you don't see now really can hurt you later.

According to the United States Environmental Protection Agency (EPA), asbestos poses a health risk when the material is *friable* and fibers can be released — in other words, when the material can be crushed by hand pressure or the surface is not sealed to prevent small pieces from escaping. However, as long as the surface is stable, well-sealed against the release of its fibers, and not damaged, the material is considered safe. Treat material that could contain asbestos as if it does until reliable analysis proves otherwise.

Testing for asbestos is not something that you can do. Moreover, although you are not prohibited by law from removing asbestos-containing material, you would be smart (and healthier) by having the material professionally removed.

In as much as testing is concerned, only a qualified technician with sophisticated magnification equipment in a laboratory must do the testing. There are essentially two methods of gathering suspect material for testing:

✔ You can gather approximately a spoonful-size sample, place it in a sealed plastic bag, and send it to a testing laboratory.

✔ You can have a testing lab or consultant come out to your home to do sample collection.

In either case, the material must go to a lab for testing. The test results are usually available in approximately one to five days. The results will reveal to what extent asbestos is present in the suspect material (if at all). The average cost for a residential test is $25 to $50 per sample.

One of the best ways to find an accredited testing laboratory is to contact The National Institute of Standards & Technology. They maintain names and telephone numbers of accredited labs throughout the United States. You can also visit its Web site at ts.nist.gov/nvlap.

Although it may cost a bit more to have a professional collect samples in your home, there is a benefit, the most significant of which is the fact that the professional will be able to offer advice as to how the asbestos containing material should be dealt with. If tests demonstrate that asbestos exists, you can deal with it in three basic ways:

- ✔ **Encapsulation:** In this process, a liquid sealant is applied with an airless sprayer to seal the surface and ensure that no fibers are released. Encapsulation is appropriate when removal is not practical, the asbestos is firmly bonded to the underlying surface, and it is not readily accessible to the building's occupants. A qualified abatement contractor should perform this process.

- ✔ **Enclosure:** With this method, a barrier is installed over the asbestos-containing material. For example, you may have a wallboard-covered chase surrounding asbestos-wrapped heat ducts, or you may install a layer of wallboard over an asbestos "cottage cheese" ceiling. Enclosure is appropriate when the asbestos-containing material cannot be safely controlled via encapsulation but does not require removal. Most general contractors can generally perform this process provided that they are aware of the potential health hazard and are equipped with the proper equipment to capture potentially hazardous dust that may become airborne during the enclosure process. The safest means of performing this work would be by an abatement contractor.

- ✔ **Removal:** This step is appropriate when you cannot consider encapsulation or enclosure. This would be the case when removing insulation, ductwork, roofing, or siding that is in such a state where neither encapsulation nor enclosure will effectively arrest the material and prevent it from becoming a potential health hazard to your family.

When removal is the course of action, a professionally qualified and licensed abatement contractor should always perform the work. Most states maintain a certification or registration program for asbestos abatement contractors. One of the most effective means of locating a qualified abatement contractor is the Yellow Pages of your local telephone directory. In addition, some testing labs and/or consultants can often provide a list of qualified abatement contractors upon request.

Asbestos-containing material is considered for all intents and purposes hazardous waste, and, thus, must be disposed of accordingly. The material is collected, placed in specially marked bags by the abatement contractor, and transported to special landfill sites for safe disposal.

For more information on asbestos and how to deal with it contact your local branch office of the American Lung Association, or a regional office of the Environmental Protection Agency. You can also visit the EPA Web site at www.epa.gov.

Get the lead out!

Lead is limited primarily to paints (appropriately called lead-based paint). Public health officials rank lead as the number one environmental threat to children under the age of six — whether they live in public housing or neat, suburban homes. Lead from paint, chips, and dust can pose serious health hazards if not taken care of properly. The good news is that lead-based paint in good condition is usually not a hazard.

The United States government prohibited the use of lead-based paints in 1978. In 1996, federal legislation was enacted requiring that individuals receive information regarding known lead-based paint hazards before renting, buying, or renovating pre-1978 housing.

According to the U.S. Department of Housing and Urban Development (HUD), 74 percent of all private housing built before 1980 contains some lead paint. Three million tons of old lead line the walls and fixtures of 57 million homes. As if that weren't enough, one in nine children under age six has enough lead in his blood to place him at risk. Moreover, children with high lead levels are six times more likely to have reading disabilities. The fetus of a pregnant woman who ingests lead is especially vulnerable to brain damage. Not even our loving pets are immune to the health risks of lead.

People can get lead in their bodies by breathing or swallowing lead dust, or by eating soil or paint chips with lead in them. Furthermore, removing lead improperly can increase the hazard to your family by spreading dust throughout the house. Thus, when remodeling, under no circumstances should you dry-sand, dry-scrape, or heat existing lead-based paint. These actions create large amounts of lead dust and fumes. Lead dust can remain in your home long after the work is done.

In the case of lead, your home can be checked for potential health hazards in one of two ways (or both):

✔ **Paint inspection:** This inspection tells you the lead content of every painted surface in your home. However, it won't tell you whether the paint is a hazard or how you should deal with it.

✔ **Risk assessment:** This process tells you if any sources of serious lead exposure — such as peeling paint and lead dust — are present. It also tells you what action to take to address these hazards.

A paint inspection and/or risk assessment should be performed by a professional lead-testing lab. Many of the same labs that perform asbestos testing can also test for lead. Refer to the preceding section for information on how to locate a qualified lead-testing lab or lead-consulting firm.

Trained professionals use a range of methods to check your home, including visual inspection of paint condition and location, lab tests of paint samples, surface dust test, and a portable x-ray fluorescence machine.

Home test kits for lead are widely available, but, according to the EPA, recent studies suggest that they are not always accurate. Thus, you should not rely on such a test before doing renovations.

To permanently remove lead hazards you must hire a lead abatement contractor. Abatement methods include removing, sealing, or enclosing lead-based paints with special materials. Simply painting over the hazard is not enough.

Always hire a person with special training for correcting lead problems — someone who knows how to do this work safely and has the proper equipment to clean up thoroughly. If possible, hire a *certified lead abatement contractor*. Certified contractors employ qualified workers and follow strict safety rules as set by their state or by the federal government.

As with asbestos abatement, your best bet for finding a certified lead abatement contractor would be via the Yellow Pages in your local telephone directory or by obtaining a list of referrals from a testing lab.

Some cities and states have their own rules for lead-based paint activities. Check with your state agency to see if state or local laws apply to you. Most state agencies can also provide information on lead abatement firms in your area, as well as possible sources of financial aid for reducing lead hazards.

To find out more about lead, telephone the National Lead Information Center at 800-LEAD-FYI (532-3394) or the National Lead Information Center Clearinghouse at 800-424-5323. Also, we suggest that you contact your regional EPA office for a copy of their informative pamphlet, *Reducing Lead Hazards When Remodeling Your Home.*

Chapter 17

Always Begin with a Good Foundation

*W*hen talking about doing something the right way, how many times have you heard someone say, "You must always start with a good foundation?" This expression is especially true in construction because everything in a building rests completely on the foundation. A sturdy foundation means a stable structure. And in the long run, that means reduced maintenance costs. What better way to begin discussing the many aspects of home improvement construction than by starting with that upon which all other construction relies — the foundation.

History Set in Stone

The first home in a permanent community, outside the confines of a tree or a cave, was constructed about 11,000 years ago. Although these homes were made of reeds and mud, they had a stone base. About 1,000 years later (circa 8000 B.C.), in the town of Jericho, homes were built by using bricks made from baked mud. Wall and roof construction certainly had improved, but foundations were still made from stone. Later the Egyptians and the Romans used cementing materials to mortar joints and help stabilize things. However, the use of Portland cement — the kind that is used to make modern concrete — wasn't developed until 1824.

How's that for concrete information?

Ah, concrete. The modern contractor's wonder material. (We have a nephew who honestly thinks that Fred Flintstone invented concrete.) Many folks still confuse the terms cement and concrete, often using them interchangeably. Cement is not concrete. It is just one of four ingredients in concrete (the others are water and fine and course *aggregates* — fancy talk for sand and rock). The sand and rock are held together by a paste of water and cement — a mixture that dries concrete hard.

Where foundations were once a series of large stones cemented together, today's foundations utilize a blend of sand and small stones bonded together in a cement paste.

With the advent of concrete, the process of building a foundation became a relatively simple task. No more stacking and cementing large stones that were hard to lift and even tougher to transport. Once mixed, the pasty, gray substance is simply poured directly into an earthen trench or wooden forms. Imbedded steel bars are used to improve its strength, and a myriad of steel gadgets are strategically placed into the wet concrete to help make attaching the wooden structure easier and stronger. Sometimes masonry blocks are used for the foundation walls, but the base is always the same — concrete.

Concrete Strength

Concrete is available in several different strengths. By modifying the amounts of sand, stone, cement, and water, and by varying the size of the aggregates, you can radically alter concrete's strength. Concrete strength is measured in pounds per square inch of resistance (psi). The higher the psi, the stronger the concrete.

When it comes to a foundation, psi becomes a really important issue. The building code requires a foundation to cure (completely harden), within 28 days, to a strength of 2,800 psi, unless engineered otherwise. Even without engineering, we like to step up to 3,000 psi as a margin for error.

If you want to be sure that you are getting your money's worth, you can ask the concrete mixing plant (or your contractor) to provide you with steel test cans. They are about the size of a small coffee can and are filled with concrete during the pour. Usually, three cans are supplied. Enough for, you guessed it, three random samples. Later, the concrete they contain can be tested for strength by a testing firm of your choice. Hey, if you don't check, whose problem do you think it will become later if the foundation fails?

It's as easy as 1-2-3

By the way, you may want to know how to mix your own concrete for smaller home projects like walks and patios. It really is as simple as 1-2-3! By volume, use 1 part Portland cement, 2¹/₄ parts sand (no sea sand please — salt destroys concrete), and 3 parts rock (³/₄" to 1¹/₂" rock is okay). Everything you will need can be purchased at your local home center.

Don't buy "foundation concrete" by sack count. You've probably heard some old-timer say, "Hey bud, give me a five-sack mix — it's better than four sack." Well you heard good information all right. Five sacks of cement per cubic yard of concrete is stronger than four sacks. But neither one may be able to develop 3,000 psi — or more. Remember, all the components of concrete have a bearing on its ultimate psi rating. Not just the amount of cement. Tell the batch plant that you want to purchase concrete by psi rating. And as we mentioned earlier, don't forget to take samples while pouring the concrete. When you ask for cans to take samples with, the concrete plant knows you are seriously interested in getting what you ordered.

Forms — Shaping Things Up

Concrete forms are usually made of wood and are assembled with nails to "form" the desired shape of the concrete. The forms hold the wet concrete in place until it dries, in the same sort of way that a cake pan holds and shapes batter. The concrete is poured into the forms. They remain in place until after the concrete dries. At that point the forms are removed. The size of the lumber used to build forms will vary depending on the project. The lumber used for concrete forms can be purchased specifically for that purpose, but there is a less expensive way. Framing materials can be used. With an addition for example, the floor joist could double as foundation, forms. After the forms have been stripped away from the foundation, they can be cleaned and recycled. Being used as form material has no negative impact on framing lumber. Form oil can be sprayed onto the forms before they are used to make them easier to remove from the dried concrete.

Rebar — Not to Be Confused with Babar

Rebars (steel reinforcing bars) greatly improve the strength of concrete. The bars are usually placed horizontally within the foundation wall and run continuously throughout the entire structure. A foundation that costs $6,000 may only have about $300 worth of steel in it — lots of strength for a small amount of money. Incidentally, adding more reinforcing steel is yet another way to stretch your foundation dollar and get a better bang for your remodeling buck. Always check with the foundation's designer to determine exactly how much you should add to get the most increased strength for the least additional cost. Most simple, residential foundations only contain two or three bars of reinforcing steel. By adding an extra bar or two, you can substantially increase your foundation's strength without adding a great deal of cost. Remember, the foundation supports the rest of the construction. The stronger the foundation, the more solid the finished product will be.

Insist on steel reinforcing bars that are free of rust and oil. These conditions reduce strength and lasting quality. Rusty metal will continue to rust and eventually completely deteriorate. Reinforcing steel that has oil on the surface will not properly grip other pieces of steel it has been connected to — or the concrete it is imbedded in. Either of these conditions can weaken the entire foundation. Oil is sprayed onto the foundation forms to prevent the concrete from sticking to them. Naturally, this technique adds life to the forms, and it also makes them easier to remove — and clean — once the concrete hardens. But we are always amazed when we see some dope spraying form-oil onto the forms after the steel has been placed. At this point, oil can accidentally be sprayed onto the anchor bolts, earthquake connectors, hurricane ties, and — of course — the reinforcing steel. Even the slightest amount of oil on any imbedded steel is a definite no-no. If the condition were a song title it would be called "Strength Slips Away — When You're Oiled." If you or your contractor don't oil the forms before assembly, then don't oil them at all. The same holds true when cement blocks are used to build the foundation wall. The steel that is placed within them should be completely free of rust and oil. No rust, no deterioration. No oil, no slippage.

The Basic Foundation

A foundation has two basic design components: the footing and the wall. The *footing* makes up the foundation's base and is located underground — beneath the earth's surface. It is the first and most important link between the earth and your home. The footing size and depth is engineered to carry and evenly distribute the weight of the house onto the earth. Sometimes the footing is a continuous concrete beam that is wider than it is tall; sometimes it is a square or rectangular pad; and in other instances the footing is cylindrical. Here, a hole is dug straight down into the ground (diameter and depth vary). A deep, round footing is known as a pier footing or pier. In all cases, the footing is always built to rest below the frost line. The frost line is the point at which the earth freezes during the winter. Naturally, the depth of the frost line varies depending on the climate in a given part of the country.

The foundation *wall* resides atop the footing and continues upward, far enough above ground to safely separate the wooden parts of the structure from the earth. The wall protects the wooden parts from water damage (fungus and rot) and reduces the chance of a termite attack. You can construct the wall using poured-in-place concrete or blocks.

Any engineer will happily tell you that you can construct a block wall to be as strong as a wall that you pour in place. And we agree with that fact. Still, as far as we're concerned, nothing beats solid concrete. When mother nature decides to "roll over," causing the earth to shift, the mortar joints in a block wall are usually the first to go. Yep, poured-in-place concrete will crack, but in our opinion, solid concrete holds up better than the mortar joints in a block configuration.

Common foundations

Foundations consist of two parts: the footing and the wall. The two most common residential foundations are the T-foundation and the pier and grade beam foundation. The T-foundation looks like an upside-down T, and is most effective on flat ground. It's shown in Figure 17-1.

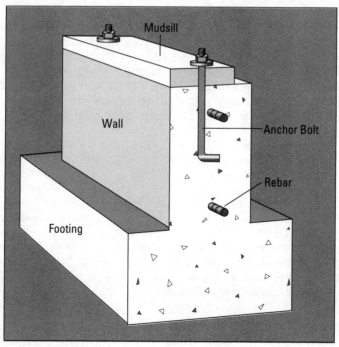

Figure 17-1:
A T-
foundation.

Termite tunnel vision

Whenever earth and wood are in contact with each other, termites can travel into a wood structure undetected. With a concrete wall separating earth and wood, termites must tunnel up the concrete wall to get to the wood. These tunnels make them easy to discover.

The pier and grade beam foundation consists of a series of cylindrical, concrete piers that traverse several feet into the earth. The foundation wall (also referred to as a *grade beam*) connects the piers together. Pier and grade beam foundations are used where surface soil is unstable or on hillsides where deep piers help to reduce the chance of slippage.

Structural features

You must ensure that your foundation is properly engineered. A weak foundation will crack under the stress of ground movement or under concentrated weight loads from above. Many remodeling jobs do not require foundation engineering. But you are always wise to have a civil or structural engineer review your plans. When the engineer quotes a fee that sounds a bit high, keep this thought in mind: If you try to make chicken salad out of chicken feathers — you can count on doing some serious choking. The engineer determines the shape and size of both the footing and the foundation wall. She also determines the size, amount, and placement of the reinforcing steel, along with the strength of the concrete in psi (see the section "Concrete Strength"). Finally, the engineer determines the size and placement of anchor bolts and other structural hold-downs.

Most folks believe that you have to "beef up the walls" to carry the extra load when adding a second story onto a one-story home. Actually, you don't have to strengthen the walls — a wall built with 2 x 4 studs spaced 16-inches apart will easily carry a second floor. Rather, it is the *foundation* that usually won't carry the extra weight. Take heed here: Upgrading a foundation can cost a pretty penny. With pier and grade beam foundations, adding a pier between each existing pair (of piers) usually does the trick. With a T-foundation, a thicker and wider footing is poured beneath the existing one. Check with a structural engineer to get the straight skinny on what will be required to support what you want to build. Once you know the cost you'll be able to make an informed decision.

Anchor bolts and hold-downs

Anchor bolts are imbedded into the top surface of the foundation wall — threads up — so that you can securely bolt the wood framing to the foundation (see Figure 17-1). When it comes to anchor bolts, the more the merrier. Your engineer may also suggest other imbedded connectors, such as *hold-downs,* to add strength and stability to your addition (see Figure 17-2). Hold-downs work in the same way that anchor bolts do. One part is imbedded in the concrete and another part connects to the wood. Some hold-downs look like straps with a bend at one end (kind of a flat anchor bolt), and some look like a wedge of Swiss cheese. In any event, don't be afraid to have the engineer specify the next size up from what she recommends — an upgrade if you will. If you live in tornado, hurricane, or earthquake country, you may appreciate the added strength firsthand someday. Yikes!

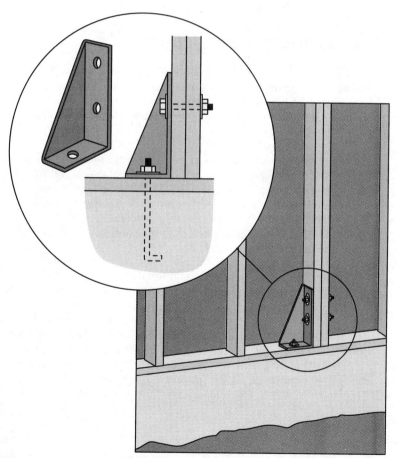

Figure 17-2:
A
hold-down.

Matching old and new for best results

With a room addition, the new foundation should exactly match the size and shape of your existing one in almost every case. Both the new foundation and the old one need to react to ground movement in the same way. Can you imagine your addition remaining solidly at one level while the old portion of the home rises or falls an inch or more? Can you spell "cracked wallboard?"

Using the same size and shape foundation doesn't mean that you have to sacrifice strength. Use the same shape and size but include stronger concrete, more steel, more anchor bolts, and modern hold-downs.

Matching the existing foundation shape is unwise when, for example, an addition extends the home from a flat portion of land to a hillside, or when the makeup of the soil changes.

Excavation: Can you dig it?

After you decide on the type of concrete, the shape and size of the foundation, and all the other incidentals, excavation can begin. Excavation is definitely not brain surgery. It involves nothing more than good, old-fashioned, pick-and-shovel work for a spread footing, or a gas-powered, two-man auger for piers.

Digging a footing is hard work. And it really is frustrating when someone kicks dirt into the trench after everything is clean and ready for concrete. Instead of removing the loose dirt from the bottom of the trench, occasionally, a lazy workman will try to hide the loose dirt by flattening it out with the soles of his boots. Flattened or not, it is still loose dirt. With a spread footing, all loose dirt *must be removed* from the trench. Loose earth below a spread footing can mean excessive foundation settlement, which in the long term, can mean big-time house damage.

Loose dirt spills into pier holes as often as it does in trenches. But piers are different. They normally don't get their support at the bottom like a spread footing does. Piers are designed to connect with the earth via friction between the vertical surface of the pier and the sides of the pier hole. Because loose dirt at the bottom of a pier hole isn't a major determent, we have a trick that you may find helpful. Simply dig your pier holes six inches deeper than required. Then, if a little dirt gets in the bottom, no harm done — the extra digging maintains the correct depth.

Drainage

As you excavate your foundation, keep in mind that you are building concrete walls that can act like a dam against irrigation or rain water. Your new foundation may very well have a negative impact on *lot drainage* (how water drains from one part of your yard to another and, finally, out to the storm drain system). You may have to install an underground drainage system to overcome such a problem. Homeowners commonly overlook drainage when building a room addition — especially on a flat lot. Trapped water can turn the earth below your foundation to slush. And endless damage can result when a foundation area floods.

To protect your foundation — and the area beneath your home — make sure that the grade around the foundation slopes away from the house. Concrete should slope away, too. Water flows downhill. If the foundation is on the downhill end of an adjacent grade, you are definitely in for trouble. If water is pooling beneath your home, you may need gutters and downspouts. And if you do have gutters and downspouts, remember that all rainwater should be released at least three feet away from the home. If water is puddling in the subarea, contact a geotechnical (soils) engineer for advice on fixing the condition.

Mudsill

Mudsill is the piece of wood that is bolted onto the top of the foundation wall. The building code requires that only pest and moisture resistant materials be used for mudsill because concrete is very porous and readily transmits moisture. Two common materials are used for mudsill: redwood and pressure treated lumber. We love using redwood for mudsill. It is lightweight, easy to work with, and has a natural resistance to damage by moisture and pests.

Sometimes you can't use redwood because it can't carry certain heavy loads. In those cases, pressure treated lumber is also quite good. However, this kind of lumber is hardened by a pressure treatment process and has a tendency to split at the ends. Consult with your engineer to determine the best material to use on your project.

Form inspection

After the forms are built and the reinforcing steel is in place, the building department must inspect everything before you can pour concrete. The building department wants to verify that the footing excavation was properly done, that the steel is in the correct position, and finally, that the hold-downs are installed accurately. (Anchor bolts are placed into the wet concrete and therefore aren't inspected until later — usually during the floor frame inspection.) Anyway, once the inspector has "passed" the work, you can pour the concrete. You may want to reread the earlier section of this chapter that relates to reinforcing steel. Furthermore, Chapter 15 includes a detailed description of how the building inspector is involved with the foundation process.

Getting the concrete from the truck to the foundation

The problem with many room additions is that surrounding landscape and existing structures may prevent a concrete truck from getting close enough to the work area for a direct pour. In this case, you can choose to manually wheelbarrow the load, or you can hire a concrete pump and operator. For small loads, a yard or so, the wheelbarrow is a great idea — the pump itself wastes about a half-yard of concrete in its hopper and hoses. However, for 8 to 10 yards or more, using a wheelbarrow can prove to be back-breaking work. You also have figure in the cost to repair a wheelbarrow tire or two — or more. Someone once asked us if we knew how much concrete weighs. Our answer: enough to flatten as many as four wheelbarrow tires in one day. And remember, concrete companies charge extra for waiting time. You pay extra for the additional time spent transporting the entire load by hand.

Pumping large loads of concrete puts you money ahead. With a pump, the concrete is poured from the truck directly into the pump hopper and sent through a large hose right into the forms. And you don't have to worry about concrete spilling in your flower garden, swimming pool, or driveway.

Concrete pumps come in two varieties: a gravel pump (capable of pumping concrete that contains gravel) or a rock pump (that can pump concrete containing rock). Gravel pumps are less expensive to hire than rock pumps, which may make you think that buying concrete made with gravel is a better option. Well, concrete that uses gravel is not as strong as concrete made with rock. You must use extra cement to create a gravel mix equal in strength to concrete that contains rock, which ends up making gravel mix more expensive. We prefer the rock mix and the rock pump. The rock mix is less runny and tends to stay in the forms better than a gravel mix.

Chapter 18

Concrete and Wood Floors

● ●

▶ Discovering pros and cons of concrete and wood floors
▶ Building a concrete floor
▶ Building a wood floor
▶ Dealing with squeaks

● ●

Three men die and go to heaven. St. Peter meets them at the pearly gates and tells them that they cannot enter because heaven is full. Because they have all been good, St. Peter says that they will be returned to earth as anything that they want to be. The men are asked to think about their choice and return, one at a time, with their final decision. The first man returns a while later and tells St. Peter that he wants to go back as a rich and famous movie star. "So be it," says St. Peter, and he returns the first fellow to earth. The next man comes back and tells St. Peter that he wants to go back as a "stud." "So be it," says St. Peter, and he returns the second fellow to earth. Finally, the third fellow returns to the pearly gates. "I can't make a decision," he complains to St. Peter. "What did the others want to go back as?" "They each had an extremely interesting request," reports St. Peter. "One wanted to go back as a famous movie star, and the other wanted to be a 2x4."

After the foundation is complete, you must construct the floor. With wood, each element of construction consists of a skeleton covered by a skin of plywood, siding, or wallboard. For an addition, the framing cost makes up approximately 20 percent of the total construction cost. Consequently, you need to be absolutely sure that the framer is highly qualified. By the way, our cost relationship for framing does not apply to interior remodel work.

Concrete versus Wood

One of us lives in a home with a wood floor; the other's home has a concrete floor. We each are very comfortable with our respective floors. And a wood floor is only slightly more expensive to build than a concrete floor. So, then, what's the difference? The real difference lies in how fast they can be built: A concrete floor takes a lot less time. By the way, a concrete floor is also known as a *slab floor* — short for concrete slab. A wood floor is sometimes built over a basement or cellar. Other times, the floor is built only a foot or two above ground. The area beneath the floor in the latter situation is known as the crawl space.

Construction basics

Constructing a wood floor involves more steps and time — the inspections alone can take three days or more — than a concrete floor:

1. **The area is excavated.**

2. **The foundation is formed, inspected, poured, and then** *stripped* **(forms are removed).**

   Piers (concrete supports within the foundation area) are also excavated, formed, inspected, poured, and stripped. Often, additional excavation is done to ensure proper clearances in the *underfloor area* (between the wood frame and the ground).

3. **The wood floor itself is built.**

   For a large floor this process may involve assembling hundreds of pieces of wood and using thousands of nails. And don't forget to include the construction of a crawl space access.

4. **The underfloor plumbing and heating are installed after the skeleton is complete.**

5. **The floor frame and the heating and plumbing are inspected.**

   With that okayed, the floor insulation can be installed and inspected.

6. **The subfloor is installed.**

With a concrete floor, things are different:

1. **The area is excavated.**

2. **The perimeter is formed.**

3. **The heating and plumbing are installed.**

4. **Everything is inspected in one trip, and after approval, the concrete is poured.**

5. **The forms are removed and excess concrete is hauled away.**

A concrete floor is a time saver — and therefore a money saver on larger projects. Builders like concrete floors because they save big time on the construction schedule. The other big plus — concrete floors simply don't squeak.

A penny saved

By saving one day of construction time on each home in a 100 home subdivision, a builder can end up saving hundreds of thousands of dollars in construction costs. If it weren't for such great savings, we don't think builders would use concrete floors. Concrete floors are hard to walk on and make some repairs considerably more difficult.

With a remodel, personal needs and comfort far outweigh the big dollar savings enjoyed at the subdivision level. Our suggestion — don't build a concrete floor if you can build one from wood. The extra cost is worth the added comfort.

Floor elevation: Keeping your floor on the level

Except in special instances, your best bet is to match floor type — and elevation (floor level) — when adding on. However, no rule says that you can't mix floor types when building an addition, but you should carefully weigh the architectural impact before you do so.

A floor level change in the wrong place can create confusion. On the other hand, a wood floor can be used in conjunction with a concrete floor to create architectural interest — a sunken room or a raised entry. Before making any decisions, consider your existing floor elevation first.

Concrete floors rest very near the ground. Building an addition with a wood floor means introducing a floor level change because a wood floor system rests higher off the ground. The thickness of a wood floor includes the thickness of the floor itself and the height of the foundation wall. If you build a wood-floor addition onto a home with a concrete floor, you'll have to put in a step or two to get up to the new level.

When the reverse is true, and the existing floor is wood, using a concrete floor for the addition creates a *dropped floor* (a floor that is sunken a step or two).

Cost and labor

Without the time variable, the combined cost of labor and materials to build a concrete floor is about the same as a wood floor. Including the time variable, building a new concrete floor is considerably more cost effective than wood. That's because a concrete floor takes less time to complete. The nice thing about concrete is that it never squeaks — like wood floors do.

It's not magic — it's a builder's trick

You may have been in a home where all the other floors were sunken — a step or two lower than the entry floor. Chances are, the other floors weren't sunken, the entry was probably raised.

It's kind of a regal feeling to look down into the rest of the home from a raised entry. And raised entries are simple and inexpensive to build: It's an old builder's trick — the designer knows that you probably won't realize that you took an extra step or two as you climbed the porch steps to get to the entry level.

Comfort

For some, a rigid concrete surface can cause joint pain and tiring. As you walk across a wood floor, it flexes beneath your feet. This "give" absorbs some of the shock that would otherwise have to be assimilated by your ankles, knees, and hip joints. If you frequently saunter from one side of the home to the other, your bones will be happier motivating on wood.

Access

An existing concrete floor can raise the cost of remodeling. For example, to access the sewer system, you have to cut and jackhammer the floor. Phone, cable, electrical, plumbing, and heating alterations are more difficult to perform when you don't have the ready access that a wood floor provides.

Moisture

A damp substrate can damage your flooring. The moisture causes hardwood flooring to lose its laminate and buckle. Vinyl and carpet mildew and smell musty. With a wood floor, you can often locate the moisture's source immediately by simply crawling through the subarea to take a look. Even when you can't find the source, you can eliminate the problem by pumping out ponded water, placing a layer of plastic on the ground, and increasing subarea ventilation.

When dampness makes its way under a concrete floor, finding the water source can become a real challenge. In many cases, the entire perimeter of the home becomes suspect. Because moisture under a concrete floor can be so unmanageable, make sure that your contractor does everything possible to prevent it when building the floor.

Foundation workers can build-in moisture problems

Be on the lookout for the concrete finisher who purposely punches holes in the plastic sheeting as the concrete is being poured. The moisture barrier should not be damaged in any way. The worker innocently perforates the moisture barrier so that the water in the freshly poured concrete will drain more quickly. As a result the concrete hardens faster and can be finished in less time. Also, the crew gets to go home earlier. Only problem is, you end up with a moisture barrier that looks like Swiss cheese and that won't stop moisture.

Building a Concrete Floor

You need to remember a few really important things when installing a concrete floor. First, make sure to incorporate at least *two* layers of plastic sheeting as a moisture barrier. Even though the building department only requires one layer, a good contractor uses two or more layers. We have used as many as four layers. The plastic prevents moisture from entering through the underside of the floor. Second, before the crew begins work, warn them that you will not accept the concrete if they trample the *steel reinforcing bars* (rebar) to the bottom of the pour. Rebar is normally mounted on concrete spacers called dobies, which ensure that the bars end up off the ground (hopefully between the top and bottom of the slab). Nevertheless, even with the dobies, as the workers spread the concrete, they must remember to lift the steel from time to time to ensure that it stays in the middle. This is not a problem with small jobs where the workers won't be required to walk into the pour area. On larger jobs — like floors — this is a serious problem.

Finally, for reinforcing, use rebar instead of *welded wire fabric* (looks like super-sized, heavy gauge chicken wire). Unless the engineer has specified otherwise, code allows you to use either one, but rebar is stronger. Concrete expands and contracts like crazy; you need plenty of imbedded steel to hold it all together.

Finally, be sure to *wet-set* a piece of 2x6 *mudsill* (lumber that is pressure-treated with pesticide) at each exterior door location. (Wet-setting is a process by which an item is placed into concrete while it is still wet.) Later, when the contractor installs the door, he can easily attach the threshold to the mudsill with screws.

Building a Wood Floor

The wood floor system consists of the foundation, interior piers, the wood framing, and the subfloor, and is somewhat more complex than the concrete floor. First, the concrete foundation and piers are constructed, then the wood framing, and finally the subfloor. By the way, the area created between the ground and the floor, within the foundation area, is known as the *subarea*.

Framing a wood floor usually begins about three days after the contractor pours the foundation walls and interior piers.

All concrete requires a minimum of 72 hours to properly harden, but it does not reach full strength for about a month.

Once the foundation is complete (see Chapter 17), the wood portion of the floor can be built. Installing the mudsill is the first step in the floor framing process. The contractor attaches the mudsill to the top of the foundation wall via anchor bolts that were previously wet-set into the top of the concrete. A mudsill block is usually wet-set into the top of each of the interior piers. Mudsill is used because of its resistance to fungus damage and pest attack. Redwood is also used because of its natural resistance to pest and moisture damage. Concrete has a tendency to retain water, and rising vapors can attack any wood attached to it. Mudsill acts as kind of a "moisture-resistant spacer" between the concrete and the rest of the framing materials. In fact, building code requires that all wood except mudsill be at least 1 inch away from any concrete surface.

Wood floor systems

You can choose between two basic wood floor systems: the girder system and the joist system. Both are shown in Figure 18-1. At a glance, they seem similar, but they are actually quite different. The girder system uses beams that are spaced far apart. In the joist system, each framing member is narrower, and they are spaced closer together. Often, the two systems are used together. A joist floor is built above and perpendicular to a supporting series of girders. The joist system uses more lumber and provides a better floor, but it takes up more height than girders do. The system to be used should be discussed with the project designer or architect.

When girders are used in combination with joist, the system it is still called a joist floor. (By the way, joist is both singular and plural — one joist, ten joist.)

Depending on the system you choose, you'll need different sizes of *subfloor* (plywood sheeting that covers the floor framing). The girder floor system is usually covered with sheets of $1^1/_8$-inch-thick plywood. The joist system uses thinner subflooring because the framing members are closer together. Solid wood planking was once commonly used as subfloor, however, plywood is now more common because it is stronger, less expensive, and more readily available.

By the sheer difference in mass, the girder floor can be far less expensive to build. Joist floors are more costly to build because of the added cost for the additional foundation wall, the increased amount of wood used, and the increased amount of labor to build it.

The building code requires that the crawl space clearance in a wood floor system be a minimum of 18 inches (see Figure 18-2). The 18-inch distance is measured from the *top* of the girder (or the *bottom* of the floor joist) to the earth below.

Create as much clearance as possible under a wood floor. You won't use the crawl space very often, but when you do, size counts. Remember the building code clearance is a minimum. You can build in all the clearance you want.

If your home already has a girder floor, you won't have room to use a joist system for your addition. Simply not enough clearance, Clarence! But, we have a trick that results in a stronger floor every time. To build a really sturdy girder floor, space the girders at 32 inches apart instead of 4 feet. The new floor's elevation matches up perfectly with the existing one, the sub-area clearance is plentiful, and the floor itself is unbelievably strong. Reducing the span between girders also eliminates the hollow sound associated with a girder floor.

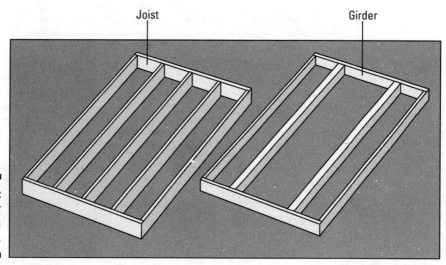

Joist   Girder

Figure 18-1:
A girder
floor and a
joist floor.

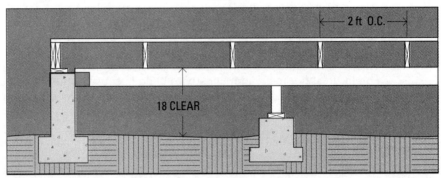

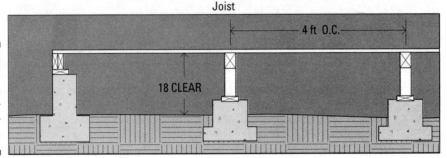

Figure 18-2:
A cross-section of a joist floor and a girder floor.

Choosing your materials

Southern Yellow Pine and Douglas Fir are the most commonly used framing materials in America. Depending on where you live, one or the other will be available. Other materials are also available for floor framing:

- ✔ **Plywood I-joist:** When plywood gets wet, it delaminates, and when plywood delaminates, it loses strength. We have used plywood I-joist with great success. However, we prefer to use them for between floor joist (second floor, third floor, and so on) where moisture problems are minimal. Also, we absolutely won't work with them in wet weather.

- ✔ **Steel joist:** Framing a floor from steel is an excellent alternative to wood. Here are some of steel's pros and cons:

  - Steel joist, unlike wood, do span long distances. Long spans mean fewer piers on first floors and larger rooms beneath second floors.

  - Steel joist don't attract termites; however, steel joist floors are always covered with a layer of wood subfloor. Whoops! Termite food.

- Steel doesn't rot, but it does rust.

- Steel doesn't burn, but it does melt.

- Steel radiates heat and cold like crazy. An Alaskan would not be wise to build a floor by using steel if warmth is in question.

✔ **Manufactured floor trusses:** Truss joist or *floor trusses* are another great alternative to a wood floor. A truss is an unusual looking building member. It has a top chord, a bottom chord, and a bunch of angled braces that travel between the chords, creating a series of triangles from one end to the other, kind of like a triangular spider web. Trusses are super for between-floor construction. Their openness allows heating ducts, sewer lines, and electrical wiring to travel any direction — even diagonally — from one corner of the floor to the other. But trusses have a down side:

  - To be large enough to allow 8-inch heat ducts, a floor truss must be at least 14 inches tall. Used on a second floor, this height requires an additional step in the stair run.

  - Trusses cannot be cut without involving an engineer. That's $200 worth of engineering to make a single saw cut. Yikes!

  - Trusses can't be drilled. You have no idea how much you will have to pay when the building inspector discovers the penetrations.

Figuring floor strength

Residential standards for wood-floor construction are not all they could be. Whether metal joist, wood joist or girders, or I-joist, the residential floor must be built to carry a load of 50 pounds per square foot (psf). We like to build our residential floors closer to 100 psi — the standard for office buildings — rather than 50. The stronger floor still flexes, but it's quieter and feels more solid.

Getting some underfloor ventilation

The subarea of your home stands a very good chance of becoming damp (or maybe even flooded) during the winter. Warmth from within the home radiates through the floor and into the subarea, warming the ground below. The moisture in the soil then evaporates. The vapors rise and condense on the floor framing and the underside of the subfloor. This condition can remain throughout winter and into spring, creating a feeding ground for yucky, smelly mildew. When condensation persists, wood rot also can occur.

The building code stipulates a minimum amount of ventilation for subarea by requiring so many square inches of perimeter ventilation (foundation vents) for a given floor perimeter. Whatever code requires in your area — *double it.*

Also, use more insulation than the code requires. Insulation is cheap protection against the cold. Insulation keeps you more comfortable, helps lower your utility bills, and reduces the transmission of heat from the floor to the earth, combating condensation and the mildew and rot that follows.

Whatever you do, don't ever block off foundation vents — especially during the winter. Reduced air flow exacerbates the problem of subarea condensation, mildew, and rot.

When adding a foundation vent, never install one beneath either side of a window or door opening. A substantial amount of weight bears on each of the wall studs that support the *header* (the beam that spans the top of the opening). If a foundation vent is cut in beneath either of the support studs, the opening will eventually sag. Subfloor alone — even thicker subflooring — is not sturdy enough to support such weight.

One way to reduce underfloor condensation is to place a thick layer of plastic on the ground in the subarea. With the plastic sheeting in place, condensation occurs on the ground under the plastic — not on the floor framing. If flooding occurs atop the sheeting, you must take preventive measures. Grade the ground surrounding the foundation — including planting areas and lawn, as well as concrete walks and patios — to slope away from the house. When it comes to preventing subarea flooding, nothing is sacred. A thick layer of plastic can last 10 to 15 years or more before replacement is required.

Check your irrigation systems. A leaking sprinkler pipe could be the problem. Rainwater from downspouts should be transported a minimum of three feet away from the home via downspout extenders. Alternatively, you can transport the water to the community storm drain system via underground drainage pipes.

Underfloor systems

After the frame of the floor has been built, but before the subfloor is installed, several things must happen:

- ✔ Sewer lines are installed.
- ✔ Water pipes are installed.
- ✔ Heating and/or cooling ducts are added.
- ✔ Electrical wiring is done.

By the way, each of these tasks is performed in the order just noted.

Generally, the contractor installs the floor frame followed by the plumbing, heating, and electrical. Then he calls the building department for an under-floor inspection. At this point, the inspector can easily view all systems. In larger cities, each phase of work (framing, plumbing, and so on) is often checked by a separate inspector who specializes in a specific aspect of construction. This process can delay construction for weeks at a time. In most communities, however, only one inspector is sent out to inspect remodels.

Subfloor

The contractor can finally install the subfloor after the insulation is in-spected. Plywood is our subfloor of choice these days. However, 2x6 tongue and groove (T&G) Knotty Pine planks make a magnificent ceiling when the underside remains exposed.

A contractor installs subfloor by doing the following:

1. **He always installs the long side of the subfloor (plywood or planks) at a 90-degree angle to the direction of the floor joist.**

   Each course of plywood must be staggered a minimum of 2 feet.

2. **He glues the subfloor to the joist (or girder).**

3. **He completely nails or screws the floor down before the glue dries (see Figure 18-3).**

   If the glue dries before the subfloor is firmly attached, the result is a lumpy, loosely connected floor.

We prefer screws over nails because, in our opinion, nails simply don't hold as well. The screws we love best are Grabber construction screws. They go in and stay in and the heads don't twist off. Automatic screw guns are available that can set a $2^1/_2$-inch screw faster than you can drive a 16d framing nail.

A general rule for screw length: When attaching subfloor, the fastener must penetrate at least 1 inch into the framing member. For example, if the subfloor thickness is $1^1/_8$ inch, the screw must be a minimum of $2^1/_8$ inches. For safety's sake, we use $2^1/_4$-inch screws. The slight extra length makes up for surface irregularities in the subfloor and floor frame. A good grade of plywood subfloor is free of knot holes and gouges. Insist that your contrac-tor use either *sturdy floor* or a grade of plywood that is plugged and touch sanded; that is, knot holes have been replaced with wood plugs after which the entire sheet is lightly sanded.

A secondary layer of flooring that is laid over the subfloor is known as *underlayment.* It is called underlayment because it is laid beneath certain types of finished flooring.

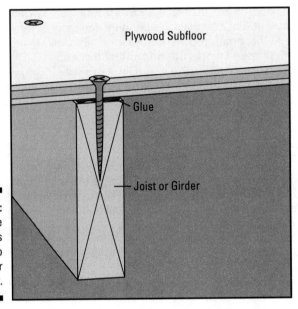

Figure 18-3:
How the
subfloor is
attached to
a girder or
joint.

Contractors use underlayment to provide a smooth, *removable* surface beneath finish flooring that must be glued in place (linoleum and ceramic tile, for instance). The underlayment is stapled to the subfloor and then the linoleum (for example) is glued to the underlayment. When it comes time to change the linoleum, you remove both the underlayment and linoleum at the same time.

Squeaks

Squeaks occur in a wood floor when the support system changes from its original position. This shift allows the floor framing members to *deflect* (move up and down) as you walk upon them. The movement causes the framing members to rub against one another. Also, nails loosen and rub against the wood, too, resulting in squeaks.

Boy have we got good news for you: You don't have to live with squeaks. Floor squeaks aren't difficult or expensive to repair, but without an extra measure of patience, the task can be frustrating. Yes, the key is patience and the rest is easy.

Diagnosis is first. Use a short length of garden hose — any old type will do — as a stethoscope with one end to your ear and the other end on the floor. Do this while someone else walks across the area in an attempt to make it squawk. Keep moving the stethoscope around the floor until the noise is so loud that you are sure that you have found "the epicenter." Once you locate the origin of the sound, the next step is to refasten the connection. All you have to do is install additional fasteners (nails or screws). We suggest that you make a subfloor repair with construction screws. We recommend Grabbers. Drilling a small pilot hole first makes the job easier. Most contractors will make squeak repairs for the first year. After that, you will probably have to pay them to make the repair, or you can try it yourself.

If the problem is a loose subfloor, the repair can get sticky depending upon the type of finish flooring. Table 18-1 shows what we do.

Table 18-1   Squeak Removal for Various Finish Flooring Types

Finish Flooring Type	*Recommended Repair Method*
Carpet	At the location of the sound, drive a *broad* head Grabber through carpet, pad, and subfloor directly into joist. Use the 3-inch length.
Linoleum	At the location of the sound, drive a *finish* head Grabber through linoleum, underlayment, and subfloor directly into joist. Use the 3-inch length.
Hardwood	Hardwood floor squeaks can often be stopped by sprinkling baby powder on the noisy area. If the powder doesn't work, use the repair suggested for linoleum.
Ceramic tile	Repair must be made from below the floor. Connect a Squeak-minder to the subfloor and the floor joist and tighten it until the noise stops. A Squeak-minder is a commercial repair devise sold in home centers.

A persistent squeak may mean that settlement has occurred in the foundation and piers. A major floor leveling may be in order. Leveling a floor is a difficult job. We suggest that you hire an expert to do the work.

Chapter 19

Wall Framing

• •

• •

Absolutely everything in a structure, in one way or another, connects to the frame. The roof covering connects to the roof frame via the sheeting. The floor covering connects to the floor frame via the subfloor. Heat ducts, plumbing pipes, and electrical wiring either hang from or attach to one part of the frame or another. A towel bar, door, window, or skylight — even the baseboard — all connect to the frame in some way. As the foundation makes up the structural base of an addition, the frame acts to "hold everything together." A sloppy frame can mean a weak structure. Internal settlement eventually can occur, translating into cracked wallboard and crooked doors and windows that don't operate properly. The frame doesn't need to have the detail and accuracy of a fine cabinet, but care must be taken during its construction.

What Walls Are and What They Do (As If You Didn't Already Know)

The wall separates the inside from the outside, the hall from a room, and the room from its closet. This design element defines the limits of a space. Walls contain doors to access other spaces, and windows act as the looking glass to the world outside. A wall may not seem poetic or even profound, but when you are naked or when you want your privacy, a wall definitely musters up a certain poetic virtue.

The wall frame

Framing constitutes a massive portion of any addition — about 20 percent. Even so, the wall-framing process seems to transpire in a shorter period of time than any other facet of construction. Arguably, nothing gets a novice more excited than watching the walls go up. At first, you see nothing but the floor. Then, all of a sudden, in a matter of hours, all the walls are in place. As the walls go up, separations between rooms, closets, and halls become apparent. Window frames capture the essence of the view to come, and door frames in exterior walls now have proximity to your favorite place in the garden. The wall-framing stage definitely is an exciting time. In an interior remodel, the framed wall is usually the first element to define the newly modified space. "Oh, that's how it's going to look?!"

Figure 19-1 shows a cutaway of a bathroom remodel with the wall frame exposed.

The wall itself is hardly more than several horizontal members called *plates* and a bunch of vertical members known as *studs*. All get nailed together securely with 16-penny (16d) nails. The basic elements that make up a wall are always the same:

- ✔ **Bottom plate** forms the lower-most horizontal element of the wall.
- ✔ **Studs** traverse vertically from the bottom plate and terminate topside at a second horizontal plate.
- ✔ **Top plate** comprises the second horizontal plate and attaches to the top of the studs.

Two nails hold each stud to each plate, for a total of four nails. If the framer uses only one nail at each end instead of two, the stud can spin. So no matter how many studs the framer needs to install, and no matter how close together, he or she needs to use two nails at each end: two through the top plate and two through the bottom plate.

To complete the basic wall configuration, a second plate needs to go to the top. The second top plate is the *double top plate,* or *double plate.* This second plate gets nailed onto the top plate and is used to connect adjoining walls by overlapping.

Framers need to be careful when nailing the double plate to the top plate, placing nails so that they clear stud bays. The center of a *stud bay* is a sacred location to the plumber, heating person, and electrician. This spot is where they must drill to feed pipes, ducts, wires, and other important stuff through the wall and into the ceiling or attic. (The stud bay is the space between the studs.)

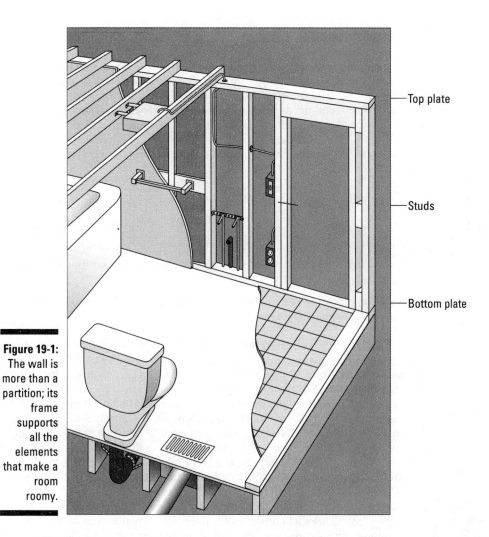

Figure 19-1:
The wall is more than a partition; its frame supports all the elements that make a room roomy.

Top plate

Studs

Bottom plate

Note: Workers normally frame walls for additions with the wall lying on the floor and then raise the wall into place when complete. With the wall on its side, the wall's top and bottom nailing surfaces are exposed, easy to reach, and accessible. Studs can be easily nailed to both plates by through-nailing (nails driven through the plate and into the studs). In an interior remodel, there usually isn't room to frame walls on their sides and then raise them. For this reason walls are often built in place. Framers nail a plate to the ceiling and one to the floor. Then the studs are installed.

Bearing walls

Framers follow a regular pattern when placing studs, no matter how many components are in a wall. Code requires studs to be spaced 16 inches apart for exterior walls and interior bearing walls. A *bearing wall* is one that supports a floor, ceiling, or roof. A partition that doesn't carry a load is known as a *non-bearing wall*. Non-bearing walls can be framed with the studs spaced 2 feet apart — no load, fewer studs needed. Some folks prefer to frame non-bearing walls with the studs spaced 16 inches apart. Not a bad idea.

How do you distinguish a load-bearing wall?

- ✔ If the ceiling joist run perpendicular to a wall, and the wall is located at the center of the span, it may be bearing.

- ✔ If the joist crossing it break — one ends and another continues — it's definitely bearing.

- ✔ If a roof support rests on the wall or if it supports rafters or a floor above, it is definitely a bearing wall.

Bearing walls can be removed but a support beam must replace it. When we remove a wall, we always "bury" the new timber above the ceiling line, thus hiding the beam. You can immediately recognize certain rooms as having been remodeled. Out of your peripheral vision you spy a beam that protrudes below the ceiling, all covered in wallboard and painted to match. The beam is right there in the middle of the room, for absolutely no apparent reason. Definitely tacky. Typically, beams protrude beneath ceiling level at the end of a room — but not in the middle of the ceiling. (And some folks wonder why their home didn't sell the last time it went on the market.) A remodel is like a computer — junk in equals junk out.

Beams that support ceilings, floors, roofs, and even large window and door openings create a special construction problem known as a *point load*. A little engineering terminology here: All of the weight carried by the beam equally transfers to either end and then down through its support posts. In a 20-foot-long wall, the load disburses to the floor (and foundation) evenly along its entire length — at each stud. In a 20-foot-long beam, each end post carries half the beam's load. In fact, the total weight carried by a beam transfers to the floor via a pair of skinny wood posts, which are usually 4 to 6 inches square. Now you know how the term *concentrated* or *point load* evolved — a lot of weight in a very small area.

Normal foundations and floors are not designed to support a point load. Floors and foundations are designed to carry evenly distributed wall loads. Therefore, the post that carries a concentrated load must have a special foundation. A typical point-load foundation can be 2 to 3 feet square and a foot thick. Some point-load footings are free-standing, and others are built beneath the existing foundation. When it comes to designing a point-load support, always consult with an engineer. Normal wall openings for doors and windows do not normally create unusual point loads.

Openings in walls

Building an opening in a wall for a door or window requires several additional framing components. To frame a door opening these components include a header, king studs, and trimmers (see Figure 19-2). Except for their special names — denoted by their particular placement in the wall — these components are nothing more than regular studs. Kind of like us. Thank you very much, you're a beautiful crowd.

- ✔ **The header** is a timber that carries the weight supported by the studs that must be removed to create the opening. A king stud and a trimmer support each end of the header.

- ✔ **The king stud** is a full-length stud that runs from the bottom plate to the top plate. However, this stud's only claim to fame is that it gets nailed directly to the end of the header. King studs prevent the header from twisting in the opening.

- ✔ **The trimmer** — also known as a *cripple stud* or *jack stud* — is cut to fit between the bottom plate and the underside of the header. Trimmers support the full weight of the header. Because the trimmer does the most work, we think it ought to be crowned the king stud.

Framing a window opening involves even more components — a sill and its supports (see Figure 19-2).

- ✔ **The sill** runs horizontally from trimmer to trimmer at what becomes the bottom of the window opening.

- ✔ **Window cripples** are short studs that support the sill along its length and at each end. These components are also known as *jacks, cripple studs,* and *jack studs.* We even heard one fellow refer to them as cripple jacks. Boy, was he confused. Note that the window jacks follow the same layout and spacing as the wall studs.

You may have noticed that our drawings show double trimmers at either side of the door and window openings with a double sill at the window. Larger openings require double king studs, trimmers, and/or sills. We think using doubles on all but the very smallest openings is a good idea. Openings built with doubles are stronger, quieter, and more secure. By the way, converting a window opening to a door opening is easy, as you can see in Figure 19-2.

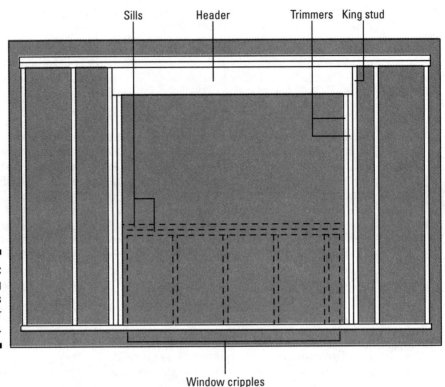

Sills Header Trimmers King stud

Window cripples

Figure 19-2:
The framing
components
for a door
or window.

When framers finish building a wall horizontally, they must then raise it into place. One or more helpers hold the wall upright while someone nails the bottom plate to the floor. Lengths of plates (or any long 2x4s) become temporary braces to hold the wall upright while other walls are framed and raised. One end of the brace gets nailed to the floor while the other end gets nailed to the top plate or the upper portion of a stud.

Carpenters can be babies!

Keep a close eye on the carpenters. If they bring baby oil or baby powder to work, it isn't to cure their chafing. Both oil and powder make easier work out of driving nails. If you drive nails all day long, your arm can get really tired. Unfortunately, the oil or powder that makes driving nails easier also causes those same nails to loosen even more easily. Talk about building in future problems everywhere. Wow! And, when the wind blows hard? Look out. Timmmberrrr! Don't let these short cuts be used. Make everyone aware that you object.

Framing materials

Various materials are used to frame walls. Solid wood, laminated wood, and steel. Wood has its problems: rot, twisting, cupping, splitting, and so on. But, it is still America's top building material: The material that most construction types are familiar with. With a wall, the stud is the most common component.

Normally, green wood is used for studs. As green lumber air dries, it changes shape (twists, warps, cups, crowns, etc.). However, there is a stud that we prefer hands down over all others: kiln dried, finger joint pine (*KDFJ* pine). KDFJ pine studs are just what the doctor ordered for straight walls every time. With kiln dried studs, the moisture is removed before they get to the job site. They aren't green, so they don't dry out and twist. They stay straight.

Finger joint studs are affordable because they are made from smaller pieces of wood. The short pieces are joined — end to end — with a glued, zigzag connection known as a finger joint (see Figure 19-3).

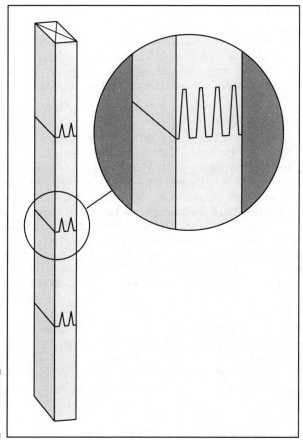

Figure 19-3:
A finger
joint stud.

Nails: Frame fasteners of choice

With subfloor and roof sheathing, we strongly recommend screws as the best method of attachment. When it comes to connecting the rest of the frame, we suggest nails, which carpenters can gun-nail or hand drive.

Choosing the right nail for the job can make all the difference in the world in holding power and appearance. Common practice calls for driving the nail through the thinner board into the thicker board. For maximum holding power, the length of the nail should be such that it passes almost, but not quite, through the thicker board. The most common framing nail is the 16d box nail. These are steel nails coated with a green vinyl that makes them easier to drive — and harder to get out. At the hardware store, carpenters ask for a 16d green vinyl sinker.

For finish work, when the nail head is to be recessed below the surface of the material and concealed with putty, a finish nail is the way to go. These nails have a small head that contains a dimple that readily accepts the point of a *nail punch* (a pointed tool used to countersink nails).

Ordinary nails are made of steel. Unfortunately, steel rusts. To avoid rusting, many types of nails are *galvanized* (coated with zinc). While zinc itself does not rust, zinc-coated nails sometimes do. The zinc often gets knocked off when the hammer hits the nail, thereby exposing some unprotected metal. Consequently, carpenters use a checkered head nail, which holds extra zinc or paint. Hammering doesn't chip off the protective coating.

Steel framing versus wood

Steel is unbelievably strong. Without a doubt, the single strongest frame that we have ever constructed is made of steel. And talk about straight. We have never seen finished walls look so good. And the floors — true and level end to end — completely lump-, bump-, and hump-free. Anyway, steel spans long distances, ends up straight as an arrow, and is solid as a rock. Unfortunately, when used for walls, builders need to apply a 1-inch-thick layer of insulation to the entire exterior surface. Steel stud walls must also be insulated in the same way as those constructed of wood — fully insulated stud bays. Steel doesn't rot, and it is impervious to damage by structural pests. But it does rust at every penetration or cut made at the job site. Will rusty walls last longer than fungus-damaged, termite-infested wooden ones? Only the future will tell.

For interior partitions, however, we can't think of a better material than steel. Hey, mixing wood with steel can provide all the advantages of each material. Here is how we would build our perfect frame:

✔ A solid wood joist floor (girders at 32 inches on center, if room is limited)

✔ 1¹/₈-inch subfloor

✔ Kiln dried, finger-joint studs for exterior walls

   ✔ Steel studs for interior partitions

   ✔ Plywood I-joist for the second floor

   ✔ Steel roof trusses with wooden tails for the eaves

You won't see any wolf blowing this house down!

Straightening and bracing walls

After the carpenter finishes framing the walls, and just before the ceiling and roof go on, he needs to straighten and brace the walls. The process of getting the walls to stand up perfectly straight is known as *plumbing and aligning* or *plumb and line*. Braces are used to hold each wall perfectly plumb (level up and down) and also to remove waviness at the tops of the walls. Nothing holds the tops of the walls except air — until the ceiling and roof are built. The bracing must be sturdy and plentiful, because workers will walk along the top plate as they build the ceiling and roof.

Blocking and backing

Partition channels attach intersecting walls and act as inside corner backing (a nailing surface) for wallboard. The first-timer doesn't usually discover the importance of installing backing until it comes time to hang the wallboard or a little later on, when cabinets, bath accessories, and shower doors go in.

Take a look at where carpenters should install wood blocks:

   ✔ Mid-height in the stud bay at each side of door and window openings. This strengthens the opening and reduces vibration.

   ✔ Wherever you plan to install drapery hardware.

   ✔ At mid-level platforms and landings where a foot may otherwise kick a hole in the wall.

   ✔ Where grab bars, towel bars, toilet paper holders, and coat hooks, will be installed.

   ✔ Where anything will be mounted on a wall, from a medicine cabinet to a shower door.

Each and every item will have a stronger and more solid connection. Wallboard alone doesn't have the strength to firmly hold much of anything. And, you certainly can't ever count on a stud being there. A block used for backing is nothing more than a short piece of wood cut to fit horizontally between two studs. The block is turned onto its side or "on the flat" so that its widest surface aligns with the face of the wall studs, as shown in Figure 19-4.

Blocking also make the home safer. Walls that are 9 feet or taller must be fitted with "fire blocks" that prevent the rapid travel of flames in a wall cavity. The blocks normally appear mid-height in the wall. Back when we worked on the ark, fire-blocking was a standard feature even in walls under 8 feet. Fire blocking also strengthens a wall. Some building departments require a fire block over each electric box in the firewall (the wall that separates the interior of the house from the garage). Fire blocks also prevent air from passing between walls and lowered ceilings. Building codes dictate that air must not pass from a wall into a floor, ceiling, or roof. When a wood chimney is built for a zero-clearance fireplace, *fire stops* are built in to inhibit the travel of flames. Here, the fire prevention device is built with wood blocks and wallboard. It often takes almost as long to install blocking and backing as it takes to build the frame.

Dealing with crooked studs

Nothing can be more frustrating than watching all your hard work twist in the afternoon sun. Don't say we didn't warn you. As wood dries, it changes shape (twists, bends, and buckles). In fact, this problem is so common that a repair procedure actually exists. Your contractor should know what to do, so be sure that all walls are checked for straightness before the wallboard goes on.

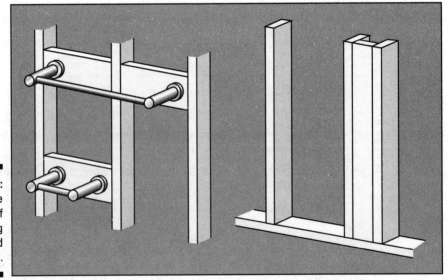

Figure 19-4:
Some examples of blocking and backing.

Chapter 20

The Ceiling and Roof

*W*e harp and harp about making sure that your remodel doesn't look like one. For example, you need to make sure that the pitch of your new roof matches the existing one. Also, the roof cover should match. So basically, you or the folks you hire need to use the same material and install it in the same way as the existing roofing. Make sure that the overhangs are the same length and that exposed rafter tails are the same size and that the ends are cut to match. The overhang sheeting and soffit sheeting should also match. And by all means — make sure that the gutters and downspouts match too.

This chapter outlines how roofs and ceilings are framed, and it also describes various roof and ceiling styles.

Framing the Ceiling and Roof

The final phase of framing a structure is known as *stacking* and includes construction of the ceiling and roof. Among carpenters, the *stacker,* or roof framer, is revered as one of the framing elite because working up high takes additional skill and coordination, and because cutting and assembling a roof is somewhat more complex than other kinds of carpentry. It is amazing to watch a roof framer glide across the top plates nailing here and sawing there.

Blocking the walls can take longer than the wall frame itself, and framing a roof can take twice as long as both together. Walking along the tops of walls is tricky at best and slows production considerably.

Framing the roof is an interesting process. First, the stacker lays out his work by transferring the joist layout from the plans onto the double plate. Here, he uses a pencil to mark the position where each ceiling joist and rafter will rest. Next, the spans between bearing walls are measured for each section of roof. These are compared to the plan for accuracy and then ceiling joist and rafter lengths are calculated and pre-cut. After everything is cut, assembly begins.

The roof is framed in two steps. First, the ceiling joist are installed followed by the rafters (roof framing members). The ceiling joist are stood on end all around the perimeter of the structure. Then the stacker climbs onto the double plate and begins to pull each joist up to his level. Once all the joist are positioned, the stacker starts at one end of the ceiling and begins nailing each joist into place. With the ceiling joist installed, braces are nailed across the top to hold them in place and prevent them from twisting as they dry. Once complete, the stacker can then use the ceiling joist as a platform to frame the roof. An almost identical process is followed to install the roof rafters (roof framing members). First, the framing pieces that make up the peak of the roof are installed on temporary posts. Next, rafters are placed at an angle to connect the walls and the peak.

No matter what style the roof is, when the roof is completely framed, it must then be *sheathed* (covered with a layer of wood planks or plywood). The type of sheathing depends on the type of roof covering selected.

Roof Styles

The most common roof styles are the gable roof and the hip roof (see Figure 20-1). The gable roof looks like a big upside-down "V" with peaked walls at the end — more wall, less roof. The hip roof sheds down at every wall like the folded down brim of a hat — no peaked walls, more roof, less wall.

Gable and hip style roofs can be combined to make a house look more interesting. However, it is important to match what exists. If a full hip roof is already in place, build the addition using a hip roof. The same holds true for a gable. Where both styles top off the same house, the choice becomes yours. A gable roof is less expensive to build than a hip roof. The more ridges, hips, and valleys that are used to build a roof, the more expensive it becomes.

A major consideration in roof construction is *pitch*. Pitch is the term used to describe the amount of slope a roof has. Pitch is expressed as a ratio of rise to run. For example, a 4:12 (4 in 12) pitch indicates that for each 12 inches of horizontal measurement, the roof pitches, or slopes upward, 4-inches. Higher pitched roofs cost more to build.

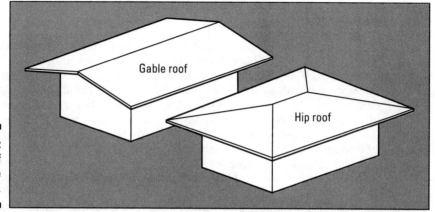

Gable roof

Hip roof

Figure 20-1:
A hip roof
and a gable
roof.

Sometimes the ceiling joist and the rafters are one in the same. On a flat roof, for example, the ceiling joist are the roof rafters and vice versa. Flat roof architecture gained popularity for this exact reason. One layer of framing construction instead of two. Also, the monolithic, tar and gravel roof was less expensive than the types used on pitched roofs. To hide the dismal looking flat roof, architects and designers continued the exterior walls above the roof line and topped them off with all kinds of neat gingerbread details and fancy decorations that gave the home character and interest.

Earlier this century, it was considered "shi shi" to have a home with a flat roof. For a while it was the rage. Today, we find our customers asking us to build pitched roofs over their flat ones. This is a very cool thing to do because most homes with flat roofs have amazingly interesting overhang details. They consist of massive joist or large exposed beams sometimes topped off with knotty pine and sometimes finished on the underside with an attractive wood siding or plaster. The focus with flat roofs always seemed to be on the overhang detail. So take one of these super overhangs and build it into an new pitched roof system, and you can be sure that you will end up with a finely finished pitched roof that will look stunning. The other nice thing about building a pitched roof over a flat one is the additional floor space that can be created. Hey, and don't forget storage. With the addition of an attic, you can improve insulation as well as access to electrical wiring, alarm wires, telephone wires, cable, plumbing pipes, and even heat ducts. In fact, access is *the* major difference between the flat roof and a home with an attic — inexpensive energy efficiency and access to all the home's systems. Now you know why attics aren't just for storing suitcases.

But pitched roofs aren't always accessible. Sometimes people eliminate the flat ceiling, and the pitched rafters become a cathedral or shed ceiling (described later in this chapter). And as energy inefficient as they are, pitched ceilings are in high demand. Anything that will make a home seem larger or make it look more dynamic is "in." You can't make something go away when folks yearn for it.

Ceiling Styles

A ceiling is an awful lot like us: It never looks like it's doing anything! In most homes, it is simply a plain, flat surface consisting of wallboard and paint — or maybe a layer of spray-on acoustic material that looks like someone splattered it with a container of cottage cheese. A ceiling collects grease in the kitchen, dust in the garage, and mildew in the bathrooms and laundry. Sound familiar? But a ceiling really can have a major impact on a room. In a really large room, an 8-foot ceiling looks long and low and tends to compress the room's size and make it feel cramped. In a really small room, a tiny powder room for example, a high ceiling can give you the feeling that you are in a wind tunnel. You feel like the floor is dropping out from beneath you.

Ceiling lines are soffited, coffered, raised, lowered, and otherwise changed to add impact and interest to a room. (These terms are covered in the next few sections, and they're shown in Figure 20-2.) Some ceiling designs are used to disguise construction elements such as heat ducts, second floor sewer lines, structural timbers, and even changes in the roof line.

Turns, twists, corners, and protrusions in a ceiling do increase its cost. Higher scaffolding, a slowed work pace, and more intricate detail management are a few of the reasons for the added expense.

The following sections describe flat, cathedral, shed, soffited, and coffered ceilings. We also cover barrel vault (rounded) ceilings, which are popular in more expensive homes.

Asbestos in ceiling materials

Getting rid of that cottage cheese ceiling isn't difficult, but it could be dangerous. Way back when, the bumpy stuff was made with asbestos. In 1978, the federal government outlawed the use of asbestos in all construction products, including spray-on acoustic products. Even so, what had already been manufactured was allowed to be sold. So if you have a home that was constructed in the early eighties, your acoustic ceiling may contain asbestos.

You should remove a sample and have it tested. To find a testing lab, contact your local chapter of the American Lung Association.

Once you know that removal is safe, here is what to do:

First, fill a spray bottle with warm tap water and spray a 3- to 4-square foot area. It doesn't take much, so be careful not to overdo it. Wait for a moment or two while the water soaks in. The acoustic material will turn a wet gray. Use a 4- to 6-inch putty knife to scrape the ceiling clean. The average bedroom will take about two and a half hours. Hire a drywall finisher to retexture the ceiling to match the walls. Figure about $50 per room.

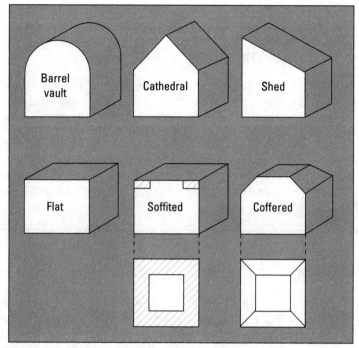

Flat

The typical flat ceiling travels horizontally across the house from room to room at one level.

Cathedral and shed

Some folks are confused by the difference between the cathedral and shed ceiling. The cathedral ceiling rises, peaks, and then returns downward at an angle opposing the rise. The shed gradually rises, at one angle, from one end of the room all the way to the other. You might call it a half cathedral. These ceilings are usually very high and are the worst energy wasters of all. Heat rises and is trapped in the high ceiling area where it can't be used.

Cleaning spider webs off a high ceiling can be a chore. If you don't have a pole long enough to reach and don't know what to do, try this: Drop a tennis ball into a pillow case, tie off the end, and hurl it at the spider web. Hey, it's David and Goliath. Give yourself a Kewpie doll. You got it clean!

TIP

Waste not, want not

A great way to enjoy high ceilings and not waste so much energy is to have cold air returns mounted as high as possible. Cold air ducts draw tempered air out of the home and back through the central heating unit. Placing the return register near the ridge is best. If you don't have a central heating system, then you won't be able to take advantage of cold air return ducting.

However, as an alternative, you can install a decorative ceiling paddle fan. Running the blades in reverse will force hot air first up against the ceiling and then down the walls. The room temperature will be more even — and therefore more comfortable — and the air circulation will reduce condensation, and resultant mildew, at windows and sliding glass doors.

Soffited

In some homes, very high ceilings are dropped at the perimeter to a height of 7 to 8 feet so that cabinet tops won't end in mid air. These perimeter drops are known as *soffits*. You can find soffits built anywhere from 1 to 2 feet (or more) away from the wall. Often, soffits are used in a room to hold recessed light cans — for accent and mood lighting. You can find soffited ceilings in living rooms, dining rooms, family rooms, bedrooms, you name it.

One common use for a drop ceiling is as a light well. You leave a void in the middle large enough to house several, long, fluorescent light fixtures. Then cover the void with an aluminum or wood frame filled with plastic lenses. Essentially, one could call a ceiling with a light well a wide, flat soffit with a light in the middle. Who knows?

When is a soffit a different soffit?

We haven't ever seen a cabinet mounted on the underside of a roof overhang, but roofs also can have a soffit. When the overhang is finished so that the rafter tails are concealed, the concealment detail is known as a *soffited eave*. Soffited eaves are finished with stucco,

plywood, wood planks, vinyl siding, you name it. Whatever the covering, it is still a soffit. Be sure to include ample ventilation when building a soffit, as you need to maintain free flow of air to the attic.

We once bid a kitchen remodel that included the removal of several soffits. The demolition took place, and we discovered that one of the soffits contained a beam. We were able to modify the structure so that the soffits could be eliminated, but a small portion of the new cabinetry had to be used to hide the timbers. Fortunately, we had warned the owner, and she had no problem with a partial loss of the additional cabinet space. The moral to the story is simple: When it comes to soffit removal — be flexible. Often, ceiling changes disguise things that can't be moved.

Coffered

Coffered ceilings are like soffited ones except the transition from the wall to the ceiling is accomplished with an angled change instead of a 90-degree corner. The coffer is a relatively inexpensive remodel that can add interest to a ceiling. The coffer adds depth and interest and doesn't involve major modifications. However, expect the wallboard contractor to charge a little more, as angled corners are a bit more difficult to finish.

Barrel vault

A barrel vault is nothing more than a round ceiling, and it is very expensive to build. It kinda looks like half a barrel on its side. Curved rafters for a barrel vault are normally made by cutting them to shape out of plywood or by bending steel rails. Wallboard is applied in $1/4$-inch thick layers. This thin material flexes without cracking, but you can use thicker wallboard if you wet it first. Yep, all it takes is a garden hose. You end up with an extremely heavy, very hard to handle, extraordinarily fragile sheet of wallboard that will form perfectly to the contour of just about any curve.

What about the Attic?

The perfect remodeling situation gets you the ceiling lines you desire with the roof you love and an attic to spare. The attic really is an important place. The ceiling is insulated to hold in the heat, while the attic is ventilated to maximize air flow and reduce condensation. Condensation results when inside and outside air meet at the ceiling. So insulate your ceiling to the max and ventilate your attic to the max and your home will be comfortable, energy efficient, and dry.

For best attic ventilation, maximize eave vents and add ridge ventilation. Thermostatically controlled electric attic fans can improve energy efficiency by increasing the flow of air in the attic.

Part IV
Closing It All In

"First of all, the stupid elves never return my phone calls and now I find out they put the roof on without the nougat sealer."

In this part . . .

A remodeling project really begins to take shape when the walls, doors, windows, and ceiling, and siding go up. We provide all the details you're likely to need during this exciting stage of remodeling.

Chapter 21

Windows, Skylights, and Exterior Doors

. . . .

In This Chapter

▶ Considering building codes

▶ Peering into windows

▶ Scouting out skylights

▶ Discovering doors

. . . .

*I*f you think about it, without windows and doors, a house is nothing more than a big box — with no light, no ventilation, and no way in or out.

With that thought in mind, we take a look at the basic principles of what is required to first turn this big box into a safe and functional house. And then we explore some of the many options available that provide greater aesthetics and/or improved function, which turns a basic house into a beautiful living space and a cozy home.

The Big Picture

As with many of the elements that make up today's high-tech lifestyle, homeowners often take their homes' windows and doors for granted — barely aware of their presence — while depending on them heavily for everything from light and ventilation to shelter and security from weather and intruders alike.

However, before delving into the specifics for some of today's truly amazing products, we thought it may also help to first give you some idea as to just how big the market for these products has become.

Within the entire spectrum of home improvements, windows and doors by far command the lion's share of total products sold and remodeling dollars spent. A recent survey of remodeling contractors revealed that between 75 percent and 87 percent of all residential projects they completed in 1997 included either windows or patio doors and/or exterior doors with new locksets.

In 1998, 45 million new windows were sold, and by the year 2000, that number is expected to top 60 million — a 33 percent increase and nearly double the 35 million sold only ten years earlier. Today, as in the past, the majority of all windows sold are used for remodeling and replacement. Skylights also have become a serious consideration for many homes, with more than 1.5 million sold in 1998. Again, the majority are used for remodeling projects. Currently, more than 12 million residential entry doors are sold annually — and this figure is expected to reach or exceed 13 million by the year 2000.

Granted, these numbers are huge and mind-boggling, but they do serve to let you know that you are not alone in having to purchase these items for your particular project. More important, shifts in the sales of certain options and types of material may prove helpful as indicators of which types of product have become more popular — and thus, indicate which ones also may deserve special consideration in your project planning as well.

For the moment then, let's just say that today, one heck of a lot of windows and doors are being sold, and the majority of them are being used in remodeling and replacement — versus new home construction. And it has been that way for a decade or more.

Are We Playing by the Rules?

With regard to windows and doors, the building codes are very important to your safety and well-being, as they determine the light you receive, the air you breathe, and your safe exit in an emergency such as a fire. We've all heard horror stories of people who have died needlessly because an exit was blocked, locked, too small, or simply not there at all when fire broke out.

Thus, we strongly suggest calling your local building department for information regarding what is required in your area and what may be needed for your project. First, find out whether you need a permit for your specific project, and then ask for suggestions and insights to prevent possible problems down the line.

Building officials are not allowed to recommend contractors. However, here's a way you can learn plenty using another approach. Let's say you find a contractor you're interested in using. Or perhaps you have three bids and you're in the process of choosing one. You can ask your local building official if she's ever inspected work done by this contractor (or contractors). If she say's "no," it means the contractor is either new or he performs unregulated projects — probable cause for a pass. If she says "yes," you can then ask if the contractor's finished work normally meets code and is generally up to snuff. While not an out-and-out endorsement, the official's response is certainly a good indicator of who does acceptable work and who is not responsible to anyone.

Always hire the contractors who play by the rules. As it says in Section 102 of the Uniform Building Code: Your "life, limb, health, physical property, and the public welfare" depends on it. Enough said?

Basic light and ventilation codes

As far as the current UBC is concerned, here are some of the minimum requirements for turning a big box into a code-worthy house. Basically, most mandates are just based on common sense.

- All habitable areas — living rooms, dining areas, and bedrooms — require windows. These windows must total at least 10 percent of the total floor area. For example, a 10-x-15-foot room (150 square feet) must have a minimum of 15 square feet of windows. However, no habitable room can have less than 10 square feet of total window area. Also, 50 percent of the total window area must open directly to the outside to provide natural ventilation.

- Kitchens and bathrooms — not considered habitable areas — do not require windows *per se,* but do have mechanical ventilation requirements based on fans and air-exchange ratios governed by room size. Where windows do exist, you must meet requirements. For example, in bathrooms, windows must be at least $1/20$ of the floor area with a minimum of $1^{1}/_{2}$ square feet that opens.

- Bedroom windows receive special attention for safety reasons. On average, most codes require that all windows in sleeping rooms below the third floor have 5 to 6 square feet of openable area, and are at least 22 inches wide, with a sill no more than 44 inches above the floor. Why? Because, (1) that's how high a fire truck's ladder can reach, (2) that's how wide a window must be for a fire ladder to rest on the sill, (3) that's how wide and high it must be for a fireman in full gear to climb in, and/or (4) that's how low the sill must be for you to easily climb out.

See. If you stop to think about it, it's all just common sense. However, we often don't stop to think about it . . . until it's too late. And that's why codes — which have been carefully considered, long and hard, and well before your project came to light — are a necessity and not to be taken lightly.

A few more codes to worry about

While we can't offer codes for every possible situation, here are a few more worth noting . . . and hopefully, it'll be enough to get you thinking that it's worth a call to your local building department before buying or installing any window or door.

Glazing, or the type of glass used, is also regulated based on very logical issues pertaining to safety. As an example, any glass used overhead — in skylights, recessed lights, or even mirrors — must be safety glass. By this, the code means tempered glass, which has been heat-treated to shatter into a million pieces when broken (like side windows in a car), laminated glass, which is actually two layers of glass with a film sandwiched in between that holds the broken pieces in place (like the windshield in your car), or a variety of approved high-tech materials, such as Lexan, a clear plastic-like panel that is tough and shatterproof.

Other glass or glazing restrictions pertain to anywhere you may find slippery surfaces — such as in bathtubs (shower doors), in bathrooms (windows, mirrors, and so on), and near swimming pools (to name but a few) — and in rooms where window heights are low and in reach of knees, feet, or anything else, such as heads and elbows, if one were to stumble and fall. Again, common sense.

State, county, or local energy-efficiency standards may exist that dictate the amount of total allowable window area. One such standard in the state of California is called Title 24 — which mandates window size as it relates to energy efficiency.

Basically, huge picture windows, single glazing, and all-glass houses are fast becoming a thing of the past. Such structures are massive energy wasters and could soon be about as popular as smoking in an elevator.

Through the Looking Glass: The Wonderful World of Windows

Gone are the days of the old-fashioned, clunky, wooden window that gets an extra boost from heavy weights — suspended on ropes — concealed within the frame. This style of window peppered the home that we grew up in, a two-story Mediterranean-style home that our grandfather built around the turn of the century. The windows needed constant repair because of peeling paint, stuck frames, and deteriorating ropes from which weights hung. Can you guess how dad spent most of his free time?

Today's windows are highly engineered systems based on scads of testing and research. They are designed for optimum climate control and management, and maximum energy efficiency. Modern windows comprise a host of both traditional and new space-aged materials interwoven for unbelievable durability, safety, and longevity. And that's just for starters! You think you know windows? Come along. . . .

In our "big box/house" theory, windows are the single most important element in turning that box into a habitable dwelling. But when your contractor finishes with the basics regarding the windows, according to the building code, you find you've really only just begun. Windows represent the greatest single design influence of anything you can do to your home. When remodeling, windows represent the greatest — and most exciting — opportunity to change the architectural impact, overall function, and livability of your home. The amount and type of light that your windows admit even govern how colors and fabrics look in your home and how you may feel psychologically.

Window styles

You can choose from more styles of windows than ever before. Models that slide open do so either vertically or horizontally. The good, old, standard window that we all know and love is a vertical slider — called a double-hung window — where both windows slide up and down. A variation of this type of window is called a *single-hung window* — with a fixed top and a bottom that you can raise and lower. However, today's model comes loaded with features, benefits, and options that, although hidden from the eye, add amazing performance characteristics.

Next comes a myriad of variations on this same, basic, vertical slider theme: double single (or double)-hung (two windows side-by-side), triple single (or double)-hung (three windows), and multiple operable units with fixed panels (or lights) in between. You can find even more variations such as single (or double)-hung units with fixed tops that are rounded (radius or circle top) or angled (gable style), *ad infinitum*. The same varieties apply to horizontal sliders beyond the standard half-vent model, in which one half slides open to one side or the other. Here, too, you can add numerous panels that either open or are fixed, in near endless combinations, varying from manufacturer to manufacturer.

Three additional types of windows are *casement windows,* side-hinged to swing open horizontally from either left or right; *hopper windows,* bottom-hinged to swing open vertically; and *awning windows,* top-hinged to swing open vertically. Generally, all three types operate with hand-cranking, with the entire frame swinging open. Figure 21-1 shows some examples.

Figure 21-1:
All kinds of
windows.

Don't forget the *fixed widows,* which range from square picture windows (in nearly any size imaginable), to you name it: circles, half-rounds, angles, arches, quarters — and in any combination thereof, to name but a few. Again, nearly every manufacturer offers a dazzling array from which to choose and which are truly an architectural wonderment not to overlook.

On top of this already huge selection, you can also find a wide variety of unique specialty windows that offer a combination of both dramatic beauty and improved function. These windows range from box and bay window units of all sizes (some offering built-in bench seats), to small garden greenhouse kitchen windows, to complete prefabricated greenhouse additions that serve as spectacular solariums and additional living space. If your budget and design allow for it, these greenhouse additions may be worth considering.

The bottom line: Review every type available before you decide.

First the doughnut . . . and then the hole

While most people think the main consideration of a window is its glass, any professional will tell you that the *frame* is really where the action is. But any mutual agreement on window frames abruptly ends here. As far as determining which type of material is better, or best, you'll find opinions are like noses — everybody has one, and no two are alike.

When discussing the merits of various types of window-framing material, you may as well be discussing the virtues of Fords versus Chevys, picking lottery numbers, or arguing which horse will win tomorrow's race or who will win the Super Bowl. Beforehand, everybody's right. When it's over and done, you either made the right choice or you didn't. Unfortunately, unlike the lottery or a horse race or the big game, you can't just walk away afterwards and forget it. This is one arguable decision you're going to have to live with for many years to come. Thus, window frames deserve special attention and lots of informed analysis before zeroing in on the frame material that's right for you.

Frame materials

The basic types of window-frame materials currently used are metal (aluminum), vinyl (PVC), wood, and hybrid combos such as vinyl-clad wood. And within these classifications are numerous design technologies — such as aluminum frames with thermal breaks — that greatly affect performance and efficiencies. Before looking at each individually, let's review respective market shares and detect any projected changes for possible trends.

In very broad terms, vinyl windows are rapidly gaining popularity. In 1998, for the first time ever, vinyl surpassed wood windows — the traditional number-one seller. Vinyl sales represented more than 43 percent of all windows sold. While vinyl continues to gain, wood remains popular (with 41 percent of sales), and any increases for both are being gained at the expense of aluminum — now at only 14 percent of sales, down from 27 percent as recently as 1991. Industry projections for the year 2000 show vinyl continuing to grow, wood holding steady as a popular choice, and aluminum continuing to decline — to almost 10 percent.

Another projection is that more high-tech composites could soon surface (such as the new fiber-reinforced polymer material called *pultrusion* and composite wood hybrids) that may gain market share and further erode earlier leaders, such as aluminum.

Aluminum

Aluminum frames, light and sturdy, were once the industry standard. These frames offered many benefits over wood, ranging from low cost to low maintenance, and for years were considered high-tech. Today, this framing material continues to experience a steady decline in sales while manufacturers scramble to introduce new wrinkles and innovations to bolster popularity and usage. Thus, you will rarely see a plain, old, aluminum, mill finish these days. Rather, units are now anodized and feature spiffy bronze, gold, and copper tones — or have painted and powder-coat finishes to offer traditional-looking white frames.

One of the primary reasons aluminum frames are steadily declining in popularity and usage — even with double and triple glazing — lies in the fact that metal readily and easily conducts hot and cold temperatures. Thus aluminum has a tendency to promote condensation and, ultimately, mildew growth much more so than any other type of frame. And while aluminum continues to be attractive from a price standpoint, this tendency has helped pave the way for other types of framing materials to quickly gain market share.

This high conductivity of both hot and cold is also why aluminum frames are some of the least energy-efficient frames available today — and certainly not the best choice for homes in severe weather climates.

A recently developed technology that helps offset this negative aspect of aluminum is the thermal-break aluminum frame. Either an air space or non-conductive material, or both, are designed into an aluminum frame to eliminate a direct path of conductivity from the outside in or vice versa. While this technique does help, not all manufacturers offer thermal break designs, making them hard to find. When you do strike it rich, these frames are quite expensive when compared to run of the mill aluminum windows, which puts them on a par with more pricey windows such as vinyl and wood. Now, if you already have aluminum frames on your home, then we suggest using thermal-break frames for any replacements or additions — even though they're much more expensive. The new frames will match those you already have and solve the condensation problem to boot.

Vinyl

Vinyl — the new kid on the block — is gaining rapid popularity, much of which is being driven by high usage in new home construction and heavy marketing efforts. But while better than aluminum, vinyl is still not as good as wood. In many ways similar to metal, vinyl transmits heat and cold. You still get condensation, but not to the same extent as wood. Vinyl manufacturers also use thermal breaks that reduce both conductivity and resultant condensation but with varying degrees of success.

In certain instances, some manufacturers' frames are also flimsy, made simply of extruded plastic — actually PVC (polyvinyl chloride). If not properly or generously designed, PVC flexibility becomes a pesky problem. And while vinyl frames look great when they're new — with maintenance-free finishes touted as a big selling feature — from day one PVC continually gives off free chlorides, and over a period of time can become brittle, with surface pitting and/or staining, and the frame may even crack.

For this reason, while vinyl does offer many benefits, it is not at the top of our list for ultimate best framing material. However, future vinyl extrusions may prove us wrong as manufacturing technologies gear up to beat down any and all negatives for these popular, up-and-coming, space-age window frames.

Wood

We love wood, but it is also maintenance-intense. Wood is beautiful, warm, and luxurious. Because it doesn't conduct heat or cold, wood therefore does not present a condensation problem. However, there's no getting away from the high degree of maintenance needed for raw wood windows. Raw wood must be primed and painted. And as with any painted finish, it must be scraped, sanded, puttied, and painted every few years. In addition, the glass in wood windows is held in place with putty which, over time, will shrink, harden, and crack — requiring replacement. If you've ever tried painting a wood window, you know what we're talking about. On the other hand, they also offer, by far, the most stunning design options and overall effects from an architectural standpoint.

Hybrids

The framing materials of choice for the Carey Brothers are the new hybrid combinations and composite windows featuring wood that is clad with either aluminum, vinyl, or fiberglass. There are also the combined hybrids whereby one type of framing — such as aluminum — is melded with another type of window, such as wood.

These new concepts offer the best of all worlds and are our choice for durability, efficiency, low maintenance, and downright beauty — with tough surface materials outside and natural wood warmth inside, where maintenance isn't nearly as high.

Overall, we suggest that you comparison-shop to see what is available and best for your specific type of project. And don't forget to compare product warranties while you're at it.

Types of glazing: Old and new

Window glazing simply means the addition of glass to a frame. For decades, this meant putting a single pane into a frame, or *single glazing*. But in recent years, energy costs and energy savings became top issues. Windows turned from a simple product produced by woodworking craftspeople into high-tech fenestration systems designed and produced by highly degreed college grads armed with computers, space-age materials, clipboards, and wind tunnels. The result: products that look like windows but perform like a sleek new Porsche, in terms of energy efficiency. Varooom!

The old stand by, single glazing, has given way to a new industry standard. *Double glazing* (also called *dual glazing* or *insulated glass*) is where a hermetically sealed air space exists between two panes of glass. The air space provides insulating properties and helps reduce condensation. Many energy-based building codes — especially in severe hot and cold weather climates — specify dual glazing.

As manufacturers, contractors, and homeowners alike discovered the merits of dual glazing, the folks with the clipboards sought new plateaus of energy efficiency with the addition of still another pane of glass — thus creating the super-efficient *triple-glazed window*. If two was good, three is better — and a worthy consideration, for obvious reasons, in severe weather situations. Triple-glazed windows are also great for reducing sound infiltration in noisy areas, for example, near highways, airports, and commercial areas.

Storm windows are a separate issue, and not to be confused with dual glazing as they do not create a sealed/dead-airspace environment between the main window and the add-on storm unit. Basically, storm windows are but glorified window shutters, which were occasionally closed to protect against the most severe weather situations. But when shuttered up, one's home had the ambiance of a cave. Thus, storm windows came into vogue to help defeat nasty weather while still admitting natural light.

You should always remove storm windows during warm weather. First, they are hard to remove in the event of an emergency, like a fire. Second, your windows and frames need to breathe — especially if they develop a leak — or mildew and rotting could occur.

Souping-up glass performance

In recent years, a new, optional, high-performance glass technology has emerged. *Low-E glass* (for low-emissivity) has a thin metallic coating that reflects radiant heat back to its source, out of a home during summer and back into a home during cold weather.

While allowing 95 percent of natural light to pass through, energy costs are dramatically reduced by blocking radiant heat loss or gain. Ultraviolet rays also get blocked, cutting down on the fading effect that intense sunlight has on drapes, furniture, and carpets. Low-E technology can be added either as a coating applied directly to the interior side of insulated glass, or as a film suspended between two panes. What's amazing is that many of these energy-efficient additives are virtually undetectable. It is, however, still possible to have a window that looks like a mirror from the outside, but this condition occurs primarily when using highly reflective film — more than what is needed for most residential applications.

Another new innovation is dual glazing filled with argon gas. This colorless, odorless, inert gas — when pumped into the sealed airspace of a dual- or triple-glazed unit — replaces atmospheric air, giving the window a 30 percent greater resistance to energy loss through conductivity.

Keep in mind that anything other than a simple single pane of glass is going to be more expensive to replace. Thus, the more features (such as multiple panes, low-E coating, and gas-filled windows), the more expensive the replacement cost. Unfortunately, a crack in the gas-filled glass will void its effectiveness, thus requiring replacement.

Together, the addition of low-E glass and argon gas nearly doubles the energy-efficiency performance of standard, dual-glazed, sealed insulating glass.

Another window performance enhancement is tinted glass and reflective coatings that reduce both heat gain and fabric fading — somewhat like the benefits of low-E glass — and serve to create striking architectural accents with both colors and/or mirrored surfaces. Tinting can be either done by a glass manufacturer, or installed afterward — on site — as an interior surface film. Both technologies look good, work well, and are gaining popularity coast-to-coast.

Tempered and laminated safety glass should always be used in applications where safety from impact is important. *Tempered glass,* super-heated in the manufacturing process, is four times stronger than standard glass. When broken, tempered glass shatters into tiny, dull-edged fragments to reduce risk of injury. *Laminated glass* has film sandwiched between two layers of glass to keep it from splintering and to prevent pieces from falling out — like an auto windshield. Both types of safety glass, as well as various other clear plastic panels and glass with wire or fibers embedded — are specified by building codes for many specific circumstances and installations. Always check codes to be sure.

Plastic tinting films, installed on-site, also have a hidden safety benefit in that when a pane breaks, the film helps hold shards of glass in place, much like laminated glass.

U- and R-values = efficiency

The letters U and R are not two episodes of television's *Sesame Street.* Rather, the letters pertain to ratings for energy efficiency and the thermal performance of windows — and any in-depth explanation would certainly cause one's eyes to glaze over.

Basically, R-values indicate how well a material *resists* heat from passing through it. The higher the number (for example, R-38 versus R-19), the better it is at slowing heat transfer. This system is used to rate the effectiveness of home insulation.

When more than one material is used, the individual R-values are added together — and the inverse of the sum total R-value becomes the U-value. Thermal resistances (R-values) must first be added and the total resistance (Rtotal) divided into 1 to yield the correct U-value. For you eggheads out there: U=1/Rtotal. For the rest of us, and as it pertains to windows, the U-value rates thermal conductivity of a total window system — frames, glass, and all — and the lower the number, the better it is at saving energy.

This information is available on a square label overseen by the National Fenestration Rating Council. The data can be most helpful in comparing overall window performance.

Retrofit versus new installation

Basically, a remodeler can choose from three different ways to replace a window.

✔ **Buy a retrofit window that fits inside the old wood frame.** While there are many variations on this process, the basics are the same: A new frame — generally of aluminum or vinyl — is custom built to fit into the old one. In retrofit installations, built-in wooden flashings reduce any water infiltration between the old and new frames. Basically these flashings work well but don't always offer the best esthetics.

✔ **Saw the old frame out and install the new window in a thick bed of caulking and/or foam on all four sides.** This technique is used primarily for aluminum and older-type steel windows. With windows, leaks are always a primary concern, and this process has the most potential for developing leaks because caulk may shrink or separate from the frame as a result of normal house movement and settling over the years.

✔ **Install a new window.** This is the most desirable technique. All exterior wall covering gets removed; the old window is taken out completely (including the flashing) down to the studs; and the new window and flashing is nailed in place, covered with siding paper, and caulked and sealed from face of stud to exterior trim. This way, you have three or four layers of protection between the outside elements and the interior of the house.

Of these three options, installing a new window is the most expensive form of replacement — but also the most dependable, and certainly the best looking. We vote for door (um, window) number three.

Additional considerations for additions

For planning purposes, the general rule for insulated (dual-glazed) windows is to figure no more than 16 percent of your room's floor area for optimum energy efficiency. Even if your community does not have existing standards, this rule provides a normal and acceptable window configuration. If your remodeler exceeds 16 percent of total floor area, he may then need to consider additional requirements such as more room insulation or special glazing options to maintain good energy efficiency.

When you do a room addition, it is also very important that your remodeler match the new windows to the existing windows used elsewhere in your home. If your house has wood frame windows, you also want wood frame windows in your new addition. If you've got aluminum frames, go aluminum in your new space. Otherwise, your addition will look like just that — an addition.

Now, your remodeler certainly can employ all sorts of technological upgrades, like dual glazing, low-E glass, tinting, and so forth. You just don't want him to mix apples and oranges visually.

We've seen numerous jobs where a homeowner decided to use wood windows in an addition for a home with aluminum windows throughout — with the intention of replacing the home's metal windows with wood ones at a later date.

Well, as human nature often has it, these plans never materialize, and years later — when the home was sold — its mismatched exterior caused a lower selling price, much to the owner's dismay. Keep this in mind when selecting windows for your new addition. Matching is a good thing.

Skylights and the Fifth Wall (Look Up)

The history of skylights traces all the way back to ancient Egypt and the pyramids, where long, slender shafts brought daylight hundreds of feet into the dark inner chambers. Skylights as we know them today really came into vogue much later in larger European cities, where buildings — often butted up against each other — had only roofs left unobstructed with direct access to abundant natural light. Thus, skylights became a ready and immediate solution.

One primary note is that skylights have different characteristics than regular windows or exterior doors, and special attention must be paid to bringing together the right glazing material, the right flashing system, and a good installation for optimum performance and leak-proof wear.

Types of skylights

Skylights come in two basic types: (1) flush-mounted, installed directly on the roof surface, and (2) curb-mounted, installed either on a site-built, 2-by wood frame with sheetmetal flashing or as a self-flashing model, with a one-piece integral curb built into the unit and a prefab flashing kit included. Flush-mounted units are used only on sloped roofs where there is water run-off, while curb-mounted units are used more widely due to their suitability for both flat and sloped roofs.

Curb-mounted units, which have been around longest, cost less to buy but require building a curb and adding a flashing. Newer, self-flashing models cost more initially but are easier to install and go in faster — thus offsetting the higher price. Basically, roofers (who are good with flashing fabrication) prefer curb-mounted units, and self-flashing units are the choice of remodelers and builders, making this type the current number-one seller.

Another, newer European concept, is the roof window skylight with an operable ventilating sash and frame (much like a conventional window) which can be either flush- or curb-mounted.

Glazing issues

With regard to glazing, skylights use both glass and plastics, which generally governs the unit's profile. Glass units are usually low and flat, and plastic skylights are generally domed. Unlike regular windows, skylight glazing is often high-tech plastics, like acrylic, Lexan, and Uvex, among others. Domed plastic units can be round, square, or pyramid-shape, and are offered single-, double-, and triple-glazed in clear, bronze-tints and various shades of translucent white.

With both glass and plastic glazing, most of the same options offered for windows are generally available in skylights — ranging from low-E to tints — and for glass units, safety glazing is a given. Some glass units are also custom sand-blasted by contractors to achieve an opaque translucence. There is also a wide variety of fixed and operable shade, screen, and light filtering options available for skylights to manage light volumes and heat gain.

Framing materials

Framing materials for skylights are much the same as those used for windows — wood, vinyl PVC, aluminum, and with some combinations, hybrids and variations such as fiberglass. And as it is with windows, wood and vinyl are increasingly popular framing choices because of higher thermal efficiencies.

We suggest comparison shopping to check quality and to then establish which particular product will perform best on your roof and in your region of the country. Compare seals, gaskets, and weather stripping — as well as special features and options. Small variations can make a big difference in long-term performance. For example, aluminum frames with an anodized finish will look nice longer versus those that are simply spray-painted, which can chip or peel over time.

As with windows, skylights have become highly engineered systems blending framing and flashing technologies with a myriad of glazing options to create a near-endless array of products to choose from. Thus, one must ask lots of questions and review many models before making a final selection that will perform best in your particular situation.

Light shafts

The roof of your home is not always directly adjacent to the ceiling of the room where you want more light. Thus, a light shaft must be constructed to channel daylight from the roof to the room's interior. Ancient Egyptians used light shafts in the pyramids. It's the same idea — 3,000 years later. Most are constructed of lumber and drywall and can add as much as 20 to 50 percent to the cost of the job.

But many new concepts have been introduced that offer prefabricated light shafts that bring in more light while saving both time and money with fast and easy installation. Called *tubular skylights* (or *rooflights*), outside units are round and have prefab round shafts to bring light in through attics and dead space.

Tube lights install quickly, thus economically, and come in two types:

✔ Flexible, accordion, fan-folded versions have a silver metallic interior. These tubes can twist, curve, and bend for tricky installations.

✔ Rigid tube shafts have highly polished metal interiors for straight-shots.

Where possible, we prefer the rigid style as fan-folded surfaces refract too much light, often preventing light from reaching the business end with full force.

Leaking

To put an old myth to bed — once and for all — skylights do not leak, especially today's high-tech, highly engineered units. Rather, leaking is the result of poor installation. Improper flashing and shoddy workmanship allow water to penetrate between your new watertight skylight and the home's roof.

Make sure you hire an experienced contractor who is knowledgeable in skylight installations.

Exterior Doors: Open Sesame

Not unlike windows and skylights, innocent-looking exterior doors have now become — in reality — high-tech, energy-efficient entry systems with all sorts of new concepts and interior engineering built-in and hidden from sight. But the technology is there, and it's doing everything from providing more beauty and security to less maintenance and lower utility bills.

Basically, exterior doors today are either wood or metal, and in some cases, new materials are being introduced with surprising success, such as fiberglass. As with windows and skylights, the annual share of market sales-figures serve to indicate the true popularity of these products.

Industry figures show that today about three out of every four residential entry doors sold and installed are metal, more specifically, steel (70 percent). The remainders are primarily wood doors (27 percent), with a small portion being fiberglass (3 percent). Currently, about 12.5 million entry doors are sold annually, which is expected to increase about 10 percent by the year 2000, to nearly 14 million.

At the turn of the century, it looks like about three out of every four residential entry doors will still be steel.

An overview of today's doors

A closer look at today's entry doors reveals (1) they are not always what they seem on the surface, and (2) not unlike windows and skylights, they, too, have become highly engineered systems offering both beauty and energy efficiency.

For example, steel doors are really only a metal outer shell — stamped or formed into various surface designs — which is then injection-filled with a lightweight polyurethane-type foam core that is highly energy efficient. Some steel doors feature a composite-type, high-density fiberboard or engineered wood inner core instead.

You can also choose from foam-filled metal doors using wood, or a composite-type, inner framing (called rails and stiles) to create a thermal break, thus further reducing the transmission of heat or cold through the steel surface.

Steel doors are usually shipped with a primer coat ready for painting by the contractor or homeowner. This factory primer coat is generally white and is often left as is without additional painting.

Wood doors are often not (as you would think) solid wood doors. Today, they, too, have become highly engineered products filled with various composites and/or highly energy-efficient materials. In many cases, a beautiful wood veneer (such as mahogany, ash, or oak) provides a gorgeous exterior surface over a hollow center — filled with insulating foam or other material — or it is used over a core of high-tech, engineered lumber for added strength, warp prevention, and efficiency.

However, many of these high-tech cores and fillers used are susceptible to moisture and can swell or warp, causing problems. So how and where you plan to use a wood door is another consideration. Even prolonged direct sunlight (versus full or partial shade) should factor into your decision on wood.

Fiberglass doors are a more recent product, and they combine many of the best features of both metal and wood doors. The fiberglass outer skin is grained to look like wood and offers greater weatherability, which has less transmission of heat or cold through its surface than steel. Fiberglass can be painted or stained to look like wood.

The best bang for the buck

As far as our preferences and recommendations, we still like good, old-fashioned oak or fir, solid-wood exterior doors. We also prefer simple, plain exteriors — versus lots of inset panels and surface detail — where joints and seams become an invitation for moisture to penetrate between the panels and frame, causing warping, splitting and/or separation. Generally, the more detail the door has, the more maintenance you'll have over the long haul. So, in our opinion — for overall beauty and elegance — a solid wood door is still your best bet.

So why have metal doors become so popular? Primarily because of lower maintenance and home security concerns. But unless the replacement door also uses a new steel frame, the old wood jamb is still just as vulnerable to break-in as it was before the new steel door was added.

Because metal doors are one piece of formed steel sheathing, surfaces can be highly styled with intricate panels and designs that do not offer moisture entry points as can be the case with wood. But while offering more durability and lower maintenance overall, metal doors still do not have the pizzazz of natural wood. Thus, in many cases, homeowners opt for metal doors on all exterior entrances except for the front door — where they want beauty, elegance, and a great first impression. To underscore this point, just ask any real-estate agent how much a new entry door boosts "curb appeal" and thus a home's salability. Then ask if they'd rather see wood or metal.

Now, while the world continues to beat a path to metal doors (due much in part to high usage by new home builders), here are just a few of the down sides that keep metal doors from being our number-one choice. Many of these doors are made with no thermal breaks between the outer and inner metal cladding, so you have heat and cold conduction and/or condensation. Also, steel doors cannot be planed, therefore jambs may need to be adjusted when any settling or swelling occurs. Steel can also rust, scratch, and dent.

As far as security is concerned, don't kid yourself. Basically, almost any door can be easily breached. A hunting knife can readily cut through the surface of a metal door, just like wood veneer or a fiberglass panel. Also, setting the door itself aside, the frame, hinges, and how they're all put together are just as susceptible to incursion and break-ins. If a burglar wants in, a steel-skin door won't make much difference.

Now, after all that, and to prove that we're not slamming metal doors (pardon the pun), they are — in reality — the best bang for the buck. Low maintenance is a big plus, and we like a pre-hung steel door with a wood or composite core that adds weight and reduces denting, with a factory-engineered metal frame for maximum security and high thermal efficiencies. But if you want sheer beauty and don't mind the maintenance, go with wood.

The 15-inch-square hole

A standard door has a total of 232 inches of edges (top, sides, and bottom) where air can leak. Thus, putting these sides all together, they have a total equivalent to a 15-inch-square hole that is open to the great outdoors — year round, 24 hours a day, seven days a week. Without a proper seal between the door and frame to close this hole, you have major energy inefficiency.

This is the primary reason that we always recommend (1) installing a pre-hung door, and (2) checking and/or upgrading weather stripping on all existing exterior doors.

Prehung doors, of all types, are highly engineered systems designed to provide the best weather seal and tight fit between the door and frame. When delivered, just install the entire unit, add hardware and paint (if needed) — and you've got the best of the manufacturer's design capability and energy-efficiency engineering.

In addition to factory engineered, prehung door and frame systems, there are a wide variety of esthetic options to surround a new entryway with beauty and light. These include both sidelights and overhead transoms that turn a simple entry into a spectacular welcome. These units come in a wide variety of matching framing styles, with energy-efficient glazing options ranging from insulated glass and tints to beveled/leaded crystal and custom stained-glass designs. They are, and can be, the crowning touch that garners "ooohs" and "aaahs" and sets your home apart from all others. Most manu-facturers offer these elements and, if your budget allows, give 'em a look. They're beautiful.

Hardware notes and options

Many of today's doors and door systems come bored and ready to receive the hardware of your choice. This bore is a $2^1/8$-inch hole through both faces of the door, for knobs or handles, with a 1-inch bore on the edge for the lock throw mechanism. If not prebored, a builder can easily bore the holes to ready the door for hardware.

Backset is a door term to remember. This is the distance from the edge of the door to the center of the knob, and there are two basic measurements used: $2^3/8$ inches and $2^3/4$ inches. The latter is better, as it provides more clearance for knuckles between the knob and frame, but the frame of your door must also be wide enough to accept both the bored hole and the knob escutcheon — without hanging over the edge above a recessed panel. Granted, this is a small point, but one that becomes a huge (and constantly annoying) eyesore if it happens to you. The remodeled door should measure both for bore and the escutcheon, or you could be sorry. Also, adding fancy escutcheon plates — inside, outside or both — can add incredible character and beauty to an otherwise plain door and utilitarian lockset.

Here are a few issues to keep in mind:

✔ With regard to separate deadbolts, they must be able to be opened from the inside without a key. If they have a key lock on both sides, it can be dangerous (in the event of an emergency) and is most definitely illegal according to the Uniform Building Code.

✔ A door viewer (peephole) is a true necessity. Unless you have a clear sidelight or a window nearby that affords you a clear look at what's outside — within 4 feet of the door — then you should install a viewer, and after deadbolts, door and hardware manufacturers report viewers are the number-one requested option.

✔ Hinges should be reviewed and considered before proceeding. Some hinges are steel and plated with brass, which rust. Meanwhile, solid brass may discolor due to oxidation, but it won't rust and possibly freeze-up. Thus, a solid brass hinge is a far superior choice. You can also use chrome-coated brass when coordinating hinges with chrome hardware. An even better choice is the newer roller bearing hinge that operates more smoothly and handles heavy doors with ease. Another tip: Four hinges on exterior doors and three hinges on interior doors reduce warping.

✔ Doors between the garage and home require a special kind of hinge and special inner construction. Building codes require a solid core, fire-rated door — as part of what is called a *one-hour firewall* between the garage and residence — and it must have a strong, self-closing hinge.

For additional, and maximum, fire protection, have your remodeler screw a piece of galvanized sheet metal onto the garage-side of the fire door. You'll prolong the time it takes fire to burn through and perhaps give you and your family precious extra minutes in the event of an emergency.

Replacement doors

When considering a replacement door, the process can be as simple as just putting a new one in the same place. Your remodeled door uses the same frame and hinges but upgrades weather stripping. This approach is a "match up." The remodeled door can either reuse or replace the old hardware and — presto — you'll have better energy efficiency with more curb appeal.

But if you do opt to simply replace the old door with a new one, using the existing frame, be sure to install the absolute best weather stripping you can get. Here too, high-tech aftermarket systems of all sorts are now available that interlock, overlap, and/or magnetically latch for a tight weather seal.

Chapter 22

Roof Coverings and Gutters

*W*e refer to the roof as "the fifth and forgotten wall" because, for most people, it seems only to generate interest when something is wrong with it — such as when water is pouring into the home during a storm.

A roof is like a serious illness — ignored and untreated, it only gets worse with time. Consequently, what could have been a few hundred dollars in maintenance and repairs often balloons into thousands of dollars. A roof leak is not only bothersome but can also result in significant damage to insulation, walls, ceilings, flooring, and personal property. Worse yet, if left undetected, the leak can even cause rot that attacks the structural integrity of the roof framing system, resulting in even more costly repairs.

However, with ongoing care and preventative maintenance, the average roof lasts in the neighborhood of 20 to 25 years, depending on the material with which it is made.

When choosing a new roof for your home, never be penny-wise and pound-foolish. A bit more money up front can literally save you thousands in the long run.

Evaluating Your Current Roof

Before deciding to buy a new roof, you may want to take steps to prolong the life of your existing roof.

According to the National Roofing Contractors Association (NRCA), an industry trade association, you should have your roof inspected at least twice annually — once in the fall before the rains arrive, and again in the late spring to determine how the roof fared during winter (the period during which a roof is subject to the most abuse).

Most homeowners can inspect the roof for trouble areas and, if handy around the house, can even make the required repairs. If, on the other hand, you have a fear of heights or feel uneasy about attempting such a project, then many professional roofing companies provide free roof inspections and provide a written estimate that outlines needed repairs.

Keep in mind that home improvement/repair scams rank second only to auto-related complaints that the Better Business Bureau receives each year. What's more, roof scams are high on the list when it comes to home improvement consumer rip-offs. Therefore, be wary of a roofing company that comes to the door with an invitation to inspect your roof because they "just happen to be in the neighborhood." Like clockwork, these unscrupulous companies will make their way onto your roof, find several hundred (or perhaps thousands) of dollars of repair work that must be done. What follows is an "unbelievable" offer (typically a savings of 10 to 20 percent) if they can do the work "on the spot" for payment in full upon completion of the work. Sadly, some will insist upon advance payment without ever setting foot on the roof — never to be seen again.

So remember our planning credo: Never be in a hurry to begin any remodeling work without doing lots of planning. Now might be a good time to have a look at Chapter 7 for more detailed information on the planning process.

If your roof is in need of repair, you should have an inspection and estimate made by at least two (or preferably three) licensed roofing contractors. You can then compare inspection reports and cost estimates to determine which repair route to take. Finding a roofing contractor can be a chore. The Yellow Pages of your local telephone directory, a local consumer referral service, references from friends, neighbors, or a local real estate professional are all good resources for finding a reputable roofing contractor. Once you have made a list of roofing contractors, use the information on how to hire a contractor in Chapter 9.

If the thought of climbing on the roof brings on high anxiety, consider keeping your feet planted firmly on the ground and using a pair of binoculars for a closer look. Even if you're not bothered by heights, limiting traffic on the roof is a good idea to prevent damage to shingles or tiles. Use the binoculars to look for loose shingles or wood shakes, or, if you have a tile or slate roof, look for missing or cracked pieces.

Looking for trouble

On shingle roofs, look for curling, fraying, and tears at the edges. And don't forget to check the flashing around chimneys, vents, skylights, and other roof penetrations — they should be tight and in good condition. Flashing is a solid waterproof barrier that prevents water from entering an area that cannot be completely sealed with a roofing material. Although most flashing is constructed of galvanized sheetmetal, lead and copper are also frequently used. Copper and lead are more flexible than galvanized sheetmetal. This makes them the better choice for use with other-than-flat roofing material such as clay or concrete S-tile. Good flashing, especially that at roof edges and penetrations are crucial to roof system performance. Many roof leaks are actually flashing leaks. Clean up rusted flashing by using a wire brush, repair with a high-quality caulking, and paint with a rust-resistant paint. Replace severely deteriorated flashing and vents with new material.

Leaves, pine needles, and other debris on the roof inhibit your roof's ability to properly shed water, which can cause water to back up between shingles or around flashing, resulting in a leaking roof. Clogged gutters and down-spouts are another cause of leaks. Clear sticks, leaves, tennis balls, and other debris from drains, scuppers, and gutters. Bad drainage is only slightly better than no drainage. A scupper is typically constructed of galvanized sheetmetal and is used as a short trough to discharge water off of a roof and into a downspout. Scuppers are used in lieu of gutters for many flat roofs. However, downspouts apply in either case.

Locating a leak

Often, a visual inspection of the roof isn't enough to determine where a leak exists. In that case, a water test is in order.

You need to venture atop the roof to do this test effectively. Use a firmly braced or tied-off ladder equipped with rubber safety feet, and wear rubber soled shoes to avoid slipping. Affix a safety harness to an anchor on the roof, tree, or other solid object on the other side of the roof to give yourself further safety protection.

Using a garden hose, run water onto the areas where a leak is most likely to exist. For example, if you have a water stain on the ceiling just in front of the living room fireplace, concentrate your water test on that general area. The chimney flashing may be the culprit in this case, and a water test is likely to expose it. Have a helper in the attic when performing this test. The helper should be able to readily identify where the water is making its way through the roof and help isolate the problem.

When performing a water test, always work in an area no more than 4 feet wide, starting from the lowest part of the roof and working up to the ridge on dry roofing. Thus, you will be working in sections about 4 feet wide from eave to ridge. Once you reach the ridge, you begin at the eave at the next 4 foot section. Doing so allows you to easily tackle one area at a time and prevents you from working on a wet roof, which can be a slip hazard.

After you find the source of the leak, you can either attempt the repair yourself or call in a professional roofing contractor. Sometimes all that's required is a dab of roofing adhesive, a touch of caulking, or a small shingle patch. Other times flashing, vents, or sections of roofing must be torn out and replaced, in which case you should definitely hire a roofing professional.

So You Need a New Roof

Even with the best of maintenance, a roof inevitably reaches the end of its useful life, which means that you need to shop for a replacement. If you haven't been roof shopping for a while, you may be pleasantly surprised at the wealth of material choices available. On the other hand, you may find that having so many choices can make the process confusing.

You can eliminate much of the confusion or frustration that you may be feeling by understanding that not all roofing material choices work for every roof. For instance, some materials are designed specifically for flat or low-slope roofs, while others are designed specifically for pitched roofs.

Some types of roofing material are designed to be installed in high wind areas, while still others may be too heavy for your existing roof structure. Therefore, the process of elimination has a great deal to do with choosing roofing material.

Of course, if you are tired of your flat roof and like the looks of pitched roofing material, you may consider converting your structure from flat to pitched. (This increasingly popular improvement can have incredible impact on the appearance of a home.)

The down side to pitching your roof is cost. The labor and material cost to pitch a flat roof can be as much as (more in some cases) the cost of a new roof. However, this improvement can pay big dividends when it comes to resale. Keep in mind that the most cost-effective time to consider such an improvement is when it is time to install a new roof.

If the material that you choose is too heavy for the structural limitations of your roof framing system, you can often beef up the system to support the added load. Simply contact a structural engineer to determine what your roof requires in the way of additional support to allow you to install the material of your choice.

Keep in mind that the real cost of a roof is the initial cost divided by the life expectancy (in years). Thus, if the material that you choose has superior life expectancy, your average annual cost may be less than if you were to use a cheaper product — even after including the cost of any structural upgrading. So a roof costing $10,000 with a life expectancy of ten years has an average annual cost of $1,000. On the other hand, a roof with a price tag of $15,000 with a life expectancy of 20 years has an average annual cost of $750. In reality, the one with the higher purchase price is, in fact, the better value.

Other considerations that influence most folks' decision to opt for one style or brand over another are cost, durability, aesthetics, and architectural style.

Roofing is sold in *squares*. A square of roofing covers 100 square feet of area. Therefore, if the roof area of your home is comprised of 2,300 square feet of area, you will need 23 squares of roofing. You should include a small additional amount for waste.

Prices range from about $40 per square for asphalt shingles to well over $700 per square for slate (labor and material). And you have an almost infinite number of choices and prices that fall within that range. Your only limitations are the size of your pocket book and the amount of weight your roof will hold.

Fretting about fire resistance

For most people, a factor that makes one style of roofing more appealing than another is its fire resistance. We witnessed, first hand, the devastation caused by the 1991 Oakland, California, firestorm. The sight of so many once beautiful homes reduced to rubble in the course of a few hours was astounding. Even more astonishing, though, were the sporadic, unscathed homes. Interestingly, these lone survivors were almost always constructed of materials with greater fire resistance.

The Underwriter's Laboratory (UL) assigns roofing material one of three classifications (A, B, or C), which rate its fire resistance. The best rating, Class A, indicates that the roof will resist severe fire exposure. Classes B and C are rated to resist moderate and slight exposure respectively.

Some materials (untreated wood shakes, for example) do not qualify for a rating because they don't pass the UL test — they simply burn too rapidly. Face it, wood burns easier than concrete. Moreover, the type of roof sheathing (or decking) below the roofing can impact the installed fire rating of a roof. We recommend that you stay away from unrated roofing materials. See Chapter 20 for more information on roof sheathing.

Selecting the roof that's right for you

Roofs are made from shingles, masonry, metal, tar and gravel, bitumen, and foam. Some of these options are shown in Figure 22-1.

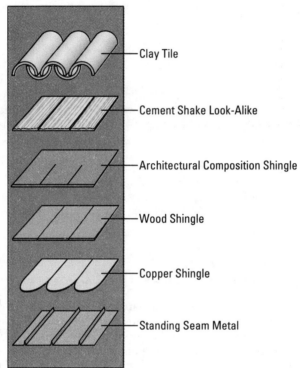

Clay Tile

Cement Shake Look-Alike

Architectural Composition Shingle

Wood Shingle

Copper Shingle

Figure 22-1:
Types of
roofing.

Standing Seam Metal

Shingles

Eighty percent of homes in the United States have asphalt shingle roof covering, according to statistics prepared by the National Roofing Contractors Association (NRCA), a roofing industry trade association. The two types of asphalt shingles are organic and fiberglass.

Organic shingles consist of a wood-fiber base that is saturated with asphalt and coated with colored mineral granules. To fight fungus growth in warm, wet climates, these shingles are available with special algaecide granules.

Fiberglass shingles consist of a fiberglass mat, top-and-bottom layers of asphalt, and mineral granules. Like organic, they are available with algaecide granules. The bonus is their fire rating — UL Class A (organic shingles are UL Class C).

Asphalt shingles come in two basic styles: *three-tab* and *architectural grade*. The three-tab is the oldest style and consists of a flat piece of material with two slits that create three equally sized shingles or "tabs." Architectural grade asphalt shingles consist of several layers, which gives them a three-dimensional look that closely mimics a wood shingle roof. This material usually contains more than one color to create shadow lines that further enhance the roof's appearance.

Because architectural grade shingles are heavier, they are rated to last longer. In our opinion, this style of roofing material is one of the best choices available. It is attractive, reasonably priced, and long lasting. When given the choice, go for the 40-year material. It is worth the small additional cost.

Wood shingles and shakes are made from cedar and sometimes redwood, Southern pine, and other woods. They are a handsome roof cover but have become increasingly less popular due to their poor fire resistance. Wood shakes typically have a UL rating of either B or C or none at all.

To qualify for a UL fire rating, wood roofing material must be pressure treated with a fireproofing material prior to installation. This treatment hikes material costs and makes the material more brittle, reducing its useful life to as little as ten years.

By the way, we know of no after-market application that can be made to a wood shingle or shake roof that improves its fire resistance. Be wary of such claims by snake oil salesmen who will take your money and leave you with a roof that has no better fire rating than before they began.

A roof that's set in stone

Masonry roofing materials are, by comparison, more costly than other types of roofing, but are regarded as among the most attractive and longest lasting materials available. Among the choices of masonry roofing are natural slate, ceramic tile, fiber cement, and concrete tile.

When it comes to roofing, it doesn't get any better than slate. It also doesn't get any more expensive. Slate is a natural stone quarried in New England and in other countries. Its color and grade depend on its origin.

A skilled craftsperson must install slate (unlike other roofing materials, which a skilled do-it-yourselfer can attempt to install). Keep in mind that slate is one of the heaviest materials available and, therefore, may necessitate beefing up the roof framing system. An added bonus is its Class A fire rating.

Tile — clay or concrete — is a durable but fairly expensive roofing material. Mission-style and Spanish round-topped tiles are widely used in the Southwest and Florida, and flat styles are available to create French and English looks. Like slate, tile is heavy and may require upgrading the roof support system. Clay and concrete tile roofing have a Class A fire rating.

Fiber cement roofing materials have quickly become one of the most popular choices. They are especially appealing to people who want the look of wood shakes or shingles without worrying about fire. Some styles even mimic the look of natural slate. They are lighter in weight than their slate, tile, and concrete cousins, making them a popular reroofing choice.

Fiber cement roofing consists of portland cement and wood fibers. This combination produces a product that is attractive, durable, and more fire resistant with a Class A or B fire rating. When shopping for these kinds of roof cover compare the following details:

 ✔ Strength

   To compare strength, lay a wood block on the floor. Put one end of the shingle on a wood block and the other end on the floor. Stand in the middle of the shingle. If it breaks, you don't want it on your roof.

 ✔ Dry and wet weight

 ✔ Exposed surface finish

Metal roofing can be a "steel"

Many people regard metal roofing as the new kid on the block when, in fact, it is one of the oldest types of roofing used in the United States. All you need do is visit Charleston, South Carolina, or Savannah, Georgia, for a taste of the beauty of traditional metal roofing.

Metal roofing comes in three styles:

 ✔ **Tile:** Metal tiles generally consist of panels constructed of galvanized steel or aluminum that is coated with several layers of primers and sealers along with a baked-on acrylic topcoat. Some variations have a granulated mineral finish.

 ✔ **Standing seam:** Standing seam metal roofing comes in sheets that have a self-sealing, raised seam that is crimped after it is in place. Although standing seam panels are available in aluminum or copper, the vast majority used for residential roofing consist of a baked-on factory finish. Although this style of metal roofing is used primarily for commercial applications, its use on upscale homes continues to grow, providing a unique and interesting architectural element.

 ✔ **Shingle:** The most common style of metal shingle is copper — and, by comparison, it is quite rare. Typically, copper is laminated onto asphalt-fiberglass shingles that yield a copper roof at a fraction of the cost of their solid counterpart. If you like the look of shiny copper, don't go with a copper roof because it turns a blue-green or *verdigris patina* — which can be absolutely stunning — soon after you install it.

Most metal roofing has a Class A fire rating when installed on new roof sheathing; however, when installed over an old roof, they receive a Class C rating. Minor installation techniques such as adding a layer of thick building paper between the old and new roofing or a layer of drywall atop the roof sheathing can upgrade a Class C roof to a Class A or B.

If you've already begun comparing prices, you probably know that metal roofing is among the most expensive choices. Bear in mind, though, that the cost of a roof is the initial investment divided over the life expectancy. The fact that metal can last 40-plus years makes it among the more cost-effective choices. Also to its advantage, metal is one of the lightest roofing products available and thus does not require upgrading the existing roof structure, which is a cost that must be considered with some heavier roofing materials.

When the slope is low

Roofs with a pitch of 2 inches in 12 inches (2 in 12) or less are considered low slope or just plain flat. Of all the choices in roofing, the material designed for these applications must be the most waterproof due to potential ponding.

One of the oldest and most pervasively used types of flat roofing material is *tar-and-gravel* or *hot-mopped*. It is also often referred to as *built-up roofing* (BUR). All three are appropriate titles because they each describe the process that is used to create this roofing system.

The typical built-up roof consists of several layers of fiberglass-base asphalt sheeting, which is flooded with molten bitumen.

An asphalt that's ancient

Here's an interesting bit of history: Bitumen was an asphalt of Asia Minor that was used in ancient times as a cement and mortar.

After the uppermost layer is coated with asphalt, it is covered with gravel, which acts as insulation and protects the roof from damage as a result of prolonged exposure to the sun.

A recent variation to the use of gravel involves installing a granulated mineral cap for the uppermost layer. This option is becoming increasingly more popular because it is lighter than a gravel topped roof. However, where the roof is visible from the street, the gravel is regarded as a more attractive installation because of its seamless appearance.

When it comes to price, think layers. The greater the number of layers, the more expensive the roof and the longer it will last. Most modern, residential built-up roofs consist of at least three layers (often four) and have a Class A fire rating.

A relatively new type of roofing material is *modified* bitumen. In contrast to BUR, modified bitumen is a pre-manufactured replacement for the old, hot tar, built-up systems. This material is installed in one of two ways — mopped with asphalt or heated with a torch. The result is a durable and handsome finish.

One of the biggest advantages to this system is the fact that the membrane is manufactured in a factory under uniform quality control standards. On the other hand, a BUR system is manufactured right on your roof, so the quality is in the hands of the installation crew.

The material is called *modified* because the asphalt or bitumen has indeed been modified with rubber and/or plastic to make it substantially more elastic. The additional elasticity allows it to expand, contract, and move with the structure, thus avoiding tears.

Though a bit more pricey than BUR, modified bitumen warranties are vastly better than the warranties offered for their BUR counterpart. A professionally installed modified bitumen roof commonly comes with a 12-year warranty on labor and material from the manufacturer. In contrast, the standard warranty for a BUR is three to five years on workmanship only.

Foam: It's not just for shaving

Polyurethane foam is another relatively new residential roofing system that was previously used almost exclusively for commercial roofing projects.

As with a BUR, the quality of the installed product is left in the applicator's hands because the polyurethane foam (a liquid plastic) is sprayed onto a roof's surface. As the material dries, it expands to form a dense, seamless, rigid material. If you have ever used spray foam in a can to eliminate drafts around the house, you have some sense of what the roofing material is like.

Once the spray foam dries, a special sealer is applied that acts as a waterproof barrier and protects the foam from deterioration caused by the sun.

In our opinion, foam is not designed as an appearance product and should, therefore, be used on roofs that are not visible from the street. Polyurethane foam does, however, have a few advantages that are unique to it:

- ✔ The polyurethane provides a layer of insulation that can significantly reduce the temperature of the roof and, in turn, the attic and living space below. You don't have to be a scientist to realize that this insulation converts into increased comfort and a lower utility bill.
- ✔ Polyurethane foam can be sprayed onto virtually any surface, regardless of the configuration. Curves, corners, and intricate details are difficult to roof, making them prime sources for roof leaks. Such is not the case with foam roofing.

✔ Foam roofing is extremely lightweight and, therefore, does not require beefing up the existing roof structure.

✔ The foam can last indefinitely provided that the waterproof sealer is applied as needed (every five years or so).

Keep in mind that a foam roof is no more difficult to remove than other types of roofing should you decide at some future date to replace the foam with a different style of roofing. However, as with any roof removal project, it can be done by an ambitious do-it-yourselfer.

Potential disadvantages are that the waterproof sealer is quite thin and is subject to puncture by a falling tree branch or traffic on the roof. A puncture can ultimately result in a roof leak. In addition, the waterproof sealer must be reapplied every so often in order to protect the foam and maintain its integrity. The sealer should be applied by a professional with the proper application equipment. Anything less will void material and/or application warranties.

Removing the old roof

If you decide to install a new roof, you have two alternatives: *re-covering* — installing a new roof on top of the existing one — or *replacement,* wherein the old roofing is removed. Although some building codes allow the application of up to three layers of roofing, we strongly recommend that all existing roof cover be torn off before the new roof is installed.

We suggest this process for the following reasons:

✔ **Rot:** The roof sheathing or wood decking below the roof cover is frequently rotting as a result of leaks or excessive condensation due to poor attic ventilation. The only way to effectively inspect and repair this damage, should it exist, is by removing all the existing roof cover.

✔ **Protrusions:** Exposed roof sheathing offers a prime opportunity to look for protruding nail heads, which can damage roofing and become the source of future leaks.

✔ **Weight:** Multiple layers of roofing place additional weight on the roof structure. Too much weight can cause rafters and other roof framing members to sag or even fracture.

✔ **Waviness:** Removing the existing roof also eliminates any waviness of the new roof and makes flashing and roof jack repair or replacement infinitely easier.

Choosing a roofing contractor

When you're ready to select a roofing contractor, remember that all roofing contractors are not alike. A new roof is a big investment — take your time and make a smart decision. Use good common sense and follow these guidelines:

- Ask friends and neighbors for recommendations of contractors they have used.

- Look for a company with a proven track record. Make sure that the contractor has a permanent business address and phone number.

- Make sure that the contractor is licensed (where required) and check with the licensing agency to check the status of the license.

- Get three to four written estimates.

- Call your local Better Business Bureau to find out if they have any complaints on file against the contractor.

- Ask for a list of customer references and make sure to take the time to check them out.

- Make sure that the contractor carries liability and worker's compensation insurance — ask for certificates of insurance.

- Insist on a warranty for both materials and workmanship — and, at contract time, get it in writing.

- Make sure that everything is in writing — scope of work, materials, warranties, price, and start and completion dates.

- Be wary of contractors with very low bids. They may have to cut corners to make a profit.

Time to Put Your Mind in the Gutter . . . and Downspout

Gene Kelly would probably not be remembered as well for his part in *Singin' in the Rain* if the movie set had been equipped with rain gutters. As a matter of fact, the producers would probably have changed the title to *Staying Dry While Singin' Near the Rain.* We agree — it would probably have been a flop.

But when it comes to the place you live, the last thing you'll be doing is singing if you don't properly manage watershed at the perimeter of your home. You control *roof water,* the water that hits the roof, by using rain gutters, downspouts, and sub-surface drainage pipes.

Choosing materials

Roof gutters have been made from stone, copper, wood, metal, and plastic to name just a few materials. Their cost versus their value differs, to a great extent, on the architecture of your home. For example, a turn of the century Victorian would not have as much value with plastic gutters as it would if it were retrofitted with the wood type that were originally installed on the eaves.

Naturally, unless you have a European castle, stone gutters are out. But the rest are all viable alternatives.

Copper and wood are among the most expensive types, but the copper is the longest lasting of all the types. Yes, all metals oxidize, but copper does so more slowly than most. However, copper does have its shortcomings. As it oxidizes, it produces a by-product that is poisonous to insects, fungi, plants, and yes, people too. Although wood lasts several decades, it is extremely expensive to replace.

The most common gutters in use today are made from galvanized sheetmetal. The sheetmetal is made from a heavy gauge tin that is galvanized on both sides to retard rusting.

Aluminum is less prone to rust than galvanized sheetmetal, but it is not as strong as its tin alternative; therefore, the aluminum is more easily damaged. Aluminum gutters are most commonly referred to as *seamless gutters* because the metal is so soft that it can be formed on the job site in lengths that traverse from roof corner to roof corner without joints (seams) in between.

Plastic gutters and downspouts are the least expensive to buy and the easiest to install, but, unfortunately, they have the shortest life expectancy of all the different types that are available. The material is fragile and can't be painted. As with all polyvinyl chlorides, plastic begins to oxidize from day one.

If plastic is all that your budget allows, go for it. You'll cut down on the cost of other repairs and will, hopefully, be able to upgrade to a longer-lasting alternative sometime in the future.

In our opinion, you get the best bang for your buck by installing galvanized sheetmetal gutters and downspouts. They should be painted to ensure lasting quality, and you will have to control rust from time to time.

Dealing with drainage

Gutters and downspouts are only two of many elements that make for effective watershed surrounding a home. What happens beyond the downspout and the conditions that exist around the perimeter of a home can either act in harmony with gutters and downspouts to protect a home or negate their value entirely.

Winter rain and excess water due to poor drainage and excessive landscape irrigation change the condition of the soil beneath your home — expanding it in some places and making it mushy in others.

If you can prevent water from getting under your house, the dirt thereunder will very likely remain stable, and house movement will be minimal. Moreover, you can prevent the wood framing members under your home from becoming damaged by fungus and rot by keeping the crawl space dry.

You can control *surface water* (the water that hits the ground) by shaping and grading the earth, concrete, brick, and other surfaces around your house so that they shed water away from your foundation. This can be as simple as using a garden rake or as complex as replacing concrete, depending upon the conditions that exist.

Rainwater that your gutters collect (and subsequently downspouts transport) should be discharged away from your home.

Geotechnical engineers (soils engineers) recommend that roof and ground water be diverted to at least 3 feet away from the perimeter of your home. We think 20 feet is better.

The best means of transporting this rainwater is to tie all the downspouts into a solid 3-inch plastic drainpipe that is buried below the surface of the soil. The drainpipe should then discharge into a municipal storm drain system or drainage culvert.

If budget or other circumstances do not allow for this configuration, at a minimum, place pre-cast concrete or plastic splash blocks that divert water *away* from the foundation. In addition, a host of temporary pipes and tubing material can be placed above ground to carry water from downspouts and away from the foundation. Disadvantages to these devices are that they are temporary and can be a trip hazard.

Chapter 23

Exterior Siding

*R*e-siding a home's exterior is one of the top ten most popular home improvements. The material that makes up the exterior wall covering of your home serves two very important functions: It acts as a weather barrier and enhances the home's curb appeal.

Curb appeal depends mostly on a home's architecture, but the success of the architecture relies much on the choice of siding. Have you ever seen a Mediterranean style home with clapboard siding? How about an English Tudor with vinyl lap siding? Certain types of architecture are meant to be surrounded by very specific exterior finishes.

Siding also acts as a weather barrier, but that does not mean temperature control. Some siding companies claim that their siding provides better insulation. Properly installed, siding prevents wind and rain from getting into your home, but it does not prevent the transmission of heat and cold. That particular task is accomplished with insulation. By the way, the insulative value of most siding materials is minimal — nearly zero.

During re-siding, you can install a layer of insulation between the old and new surfaces — regardless of the type of siding you're using. Just don't be sold down the river by a company that promises "added comfort" with their brand of siding. If added insulation is an important factor, compare prices apples-to-apples by asking all of the bidders to include it in their proposal.

The type of siding you choose does not depend on the climate or geographic area — only the architecture and your good taste.

Wood can rot and stucco has a tendency to crack, but you can frequently — depending on the severity of the damage — repair the existing siding less expensively than you can replace it. If your siding is currently in good condition, you can reduce future damage with a well-managed maintenance program.

This chapter covers three siding-related areas: making the best of your existing wall covering, what to consider when building a room addition, and re-siding.

Making the Best of What You Have

Before we cover the various kinds of siding and how to maintain them, we ought to show you a picture of what we're talking about. Figure 23-1 shows all different kinds of siding.

Water can attack and damage wood siding. Stucco walls crack when the house shifts as winter rains expand soil. Metal siding dents easily. Vinyl siding pits as it oxidizes. Even bricks chip and crack with winter freezes and summer ground settlement. No surface is perfect; no material perfectly withstands the rigors of nature and the force of the elements. But you can do some things to your existing home that add life and beauty to its exterior.

Wood siding

When wood's moisture content reaches 20 to 30 percent, fungi deep within its fibers begin to grow and flourish. The end result is known as *wood rot*. Fortunately, unless the exterior of the home has been completely neglected for decades, rot is normally confined to just a very few isolated locations. Don't let rot scare you. It's like bad breath. Everyone has it once in a while. The only thing that can get expensive here is overreacting to the problem. Small areas of rotted siding can be easily patched or replaced. With wood siding, only a few nails hold any 1- or 2-square foot area. If you tear the paper below as you are replacing the siding, simply caulk the tear. Partially replacing or patching wood siding is not a big deal. Clean and protect the wood after the rotted areas are repaired so that the rot doesn't return.

Preventing rot

Wood siding should be treated with an application of oil, stain, or paint to prevent water attacks. These materials act as a barrier, preventing water from coming into direct contact with the wood and reducing the chance for rot to recur. Oil, stain, and paint are all effective, but they each work quite differently.

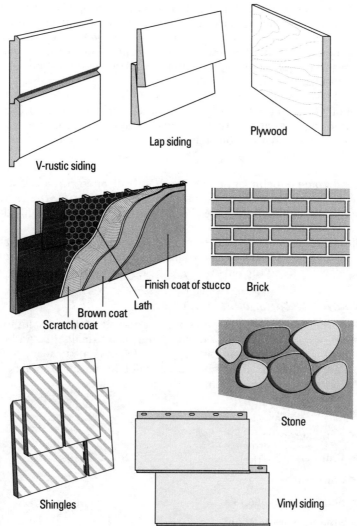

V-rustic siding

Lap siding

Plywood

Finish coat of stucco

Lath

Brown coat

Scratch coat

Brick

Stone

Figure 23-1:
Siding,
siding,
everywhere!

Shingles

Vinyl siding

✔ Oil is absorbed into the wood, filling all pores and voids, thereby displacing water that would otherwise be absorbed.

✔ Stain is the same as oil except the oil is filled with colored particles of pigment.

✔ Paint protects by coating the surface of the wood with a thin, durable, waterproof hide.

Oil is easier to apply than paint, and if the oil is clear (or almost clear), mistakes are nearly impossible to detect. Oil is very forgiving. When the oil contains stain, the added pigment makes application slightly more difficult. But the added pigment helps to filter out the sun's damaging ultraviolet rays. Unfortunately, clear oil has a tendency to evaporate, and within a year or two, you must apply a new coat. Adding pigment causes oil to last longer by creating a quasi-hide on the surface. Unlike paint, oil stains do not split, chip, or blister.

With oil you won't ever have to sand, scrape, or chisel the surface to make it ready for another application. But be prepared to reapply a new coat every couple of years. With an oil stain, figure about three to five years of lasting quality.

A good grade of paint, applied to a properly cleaned surface, lasts 7 to 10 years or more. Paint certainly lasts longer, but it is by far the most difficult to apply. Be careful not to use cheap paint. Cheap paints simply don't last.

Follow this general rule to determine lasting quality of oils and paints: The more wood-grain that you see when the job is complete, the more often you can expect to redo the finish.

Preparing wood for oil, stain, or paint

Paint experts agree that 80 percent of a good oil, stain, or paint job is in the preparation. But the exterior of your home is no small area. And when it comes to preparation, you can expect to do some major work. Fortunately, tools are available from home centers, paint stores, and rental outlets that help make the job almost fun:

- Sand blasters
- Hand scrapers
- Chippers
- Soda washers
- Sand-water blasters
- Steam cleaners
- Hot water cleaners
- Pressure washers
- Chemical strippers

All these tools involve some degree of work on your part, but they are a breeze to use compared to a hand-scraper, a hand-chipper, or a blow-torch.

You prepare oiled surfaces for refinishing differently than painted ones. You must first properly clean the surface. Sanding down to new wood is one way, but we understand that most folks would opt to move if given only that choice. Can you imagine trying to sand a building sided with shingles — yikes!

Another way to get the surface clean is to dip a scrub brush in a concoction of laundry detergent and water ($1/2$ cup detergent per gallon of water). This technique is certainly effective, but is second only in difficulty to sanding, and it does not remove the dead, gray cells on the surface. Bristle brushing detergent onto a house is a lot of work. Kind of like scrubbing 35 delivery trucks — all at once.

For an oiled surface, a pressure washer is far more effective and much easier to use — especially when used in combination with our detergent formula, followed by an application of a wood bleach. The pressure washer uses the detergent and high pressure water to dissolve away surface dirt, exposing the pores of the wood. With the surface of the wood completely clean, the bleach can dissolve away the gray layer of discolored cells. A pressure washer is often powerful enough to remove gray wood cells. If not, bleach brightens things up in no time.

Most folks don't realize that a fine layer of stuck-on dirt will prevent wood bleach from doing its job. Clean the wood with a detergent, rinse with a pressure washer, apply a coat of wood bleach, let it stand (per manufacturer's instructions), and pressure wash again. Your oiled siding will look so good you won't believe you did it yourself.

After your siding is finally oiled, stained, or painted, your home will not only look better, but the siding will last longer, too.

Hardboard siding

Hardboard siding is made by binding wood fibers together with glue. In both planks and sheets, it has been the focus of more class action law suits than Carter had little liver pills.

Attack by moisture makes the material swell radically, causing it to crack, buckle, and bend. Sounds like the title to a song. We're all for products that are inexpensive and easy to install, *if* they last!

The hardboard manufacturer's installation instructions include a require-ment that all six sides of each piece of siding be *sealed* (painted), making it impractical to use. Painted or not, we don't have a real high comfort level with hardboard. If you have to make repairs, be sure to paint every edge — especially saw-cut ends — and use the best paint you can buy.

Stucco

Stucco is really cool stuff. It doesn't rot, and, best of all, it hides building flaws like crazy. A half-inch too high here, a quarter inch too low there — hey, stucco it. Truthfully, no one will ever notice.

Stucco is made of a cement and sand mixture that is troweled or sprayed on. It dries incredibly hard, making it highly resistant to damage. Because it is applied as a paste, stucco can be troweled on in various thicknesses. Therefore, during application you can gradually taper it to hide lumps and bumps in the structure. Is it any wonder why stucco is such a very popular siding material among new-home builders?

However, the fact that it dries to become rigid is also one of its greatest drawbacks — maybe its only drawback. When the house shifts, rigid things crack. Stucco is a rigid surface that often cracks as the house shifts.

3-coat, 2-coat, or 1-coat

Three popular application processes are in use today: 3-coat, 2-coat, and 1-coat. If you have an older home, chances are you have a 3-coat application. The 2-coat system wasn't widely used until the early '80s, and the 1-coat method didn't become popular until the '90s.

The only way you can tell if you have a 2- or 3-coat system is to have a sample analyzed. The 3-coat system contains only cement and sand and includes a thick base coat (scratch coat), a thinner middle coat (brown coat), and a thin, colored finish coat (color coat). The final texture is achieved with the color coat. Cellulose fibers are added to the cement and sand for the 2-coat method. The fibers allow for a thicker application, hence the first and second coats are combined. The finish coat is the same in both applications. We have successfully used both of these systems and like them a lot. The 2-coat system is especially nice for a room addition because less time is involved start to finish.

The 1-coat system is very different. With the other systems, you apply plaster to *paper-backed wire lath* (chicken wire over building paper) that is attached directly to the studs (or plywood). With the 1-coat system, a special 1-inch thick foam backer-board is applied first. The board looks like rigid insulation, but has tongue and groove edges. It is attached to the studs and then covered with wire-lath (no paper backing is needed), followed by a quarter-inch thick coat of material, which is applied with a spray gun.

The 1-coat system is more pliable — and not prone to cracking. As a matter of fact, it rarely cracks. On the other hand, the 1-coat system is a great deal more susceptible to damage than the 2- and 3-coat processes. The 1-coat system trades flexibility — and the absence of cracking — for reduced resistance to damage from blows and scrapes.

Maintenance

Barring house movement and the cracking that results (see the next section), stucco is truly an easy surface to maintain that lasts just about forever. Stucco really is extremely low maintenance. When it cracks, caulk is all that you need to repair it. If it discolors, all you need to do is paint.

Stucco, being very porous, holds onto paint better than most other finishes. We so often see folks who are angry because the "color coat" in the stucco failed. Hey, all exterior surfaces fail eventually. Fortunately, stucco is one of the easiest surfaces to prepare and paint. So, if you have stucco — count your blessings.

We don't recommend that you re-side stucco unless you want to change the look of your home or you have tried everything to prevent it from cracking and failed. Remember, once you cover stucco, you have lost a most durable and easy-to-maintain exterior surface.

By the way, some folks think that the only way to spruce up a stucco finish is to re-side. Wrong! Talk to a designer or an architect. You can spiff up a plain exterior in dozens of inexpensive ways, including the following:

- Shutters
- Planter boxes
- Decorative appliqués
- Interesting trim options
- A multicolored paint job

Comparatively speaking, almost anything you do to the exterior of your stucco home is less expensive than re-siding.

Caring for cracks

The 2- and 3-coat stucco systems have great strength and rigidity — almost 1-inch thick. A youngster with a baseball bat probably wouldn't damage either finish. But even the best stucco job can crack. Most homes remain in a constant state of movement, which is caused by soil that heaves and settles as its moisture content changes. When house movement is extensive, stucco cracks. Isn't it interesting that stucco is damaged by water? The same culprit that ravages wood! The attack may be in a different way, but attack it does. Water in wood causes fungus damage, and water under the house causes wall movement that cracks the stucco.

You can easily repair stucco cracks:

1. **Clean all loose debris from the crack.**

2. **Use a paintable silicone caulk — and your finger — to make an invisible repair.**

   The caulk will probably shrink as it dries. When this happens, simply add another coat. Don't use a putty knife. You achieve a proper repair when your finger forces the caulking to align with the highs and lows in the surface you're repairing.

Don't use just any caulk; use the 50-year kind, which really does hold better and longer. You can repair gouges with a latex patching compound. Follow the instructions carefully. The amount of water you use can change the properties of the patching compound. If this happens, it probably won't hold for very long.

Painting

Really porous stucco absorbs gallons of paint. If you're painting stucco for the first time and the surface is really porous, completely wet the surface with a water hose just before getting ready to apply paint. The water fills the pores and prevents them from absorbing excess amounts of paint.

You don't have to paint stucco. You can apply another color coat of stucco instead. If your stucco has been painted before, a new color coat may not hold. The best bond occurs when you apply the new coat of stucco directly to a previously unpainted coat of stucco. A new color coat can make an old, tattered exterior look brand spanking new again. If your stucco has been painted and you want to add a new color coat, then remove as much paint as possible first. A pressure washer or sand blaster are the right tools for this task.

Brick, block, and stone

Brick, without a doubt, is revered by many as *the* exterior wall finish. Besides being exceedingly beautiful, a brick wall doesn't burn, doesn't decay, is impervious to insect attack, and it is one of the lowest maintenance surfaces. Brick is readily available in most parts of the country, and it is reasonably easy to install. Don't get too excited — it is still expensive. You literally have thousands of choices, but those most frequently used are

- New brick
- Manufactured used brick
- Slump stone

Whether your choice of masonry is stone or brick, a foundation is necessary to prevent sagging and shifting. Most folks like to think that a lip at the base of a spread footing foundation is all they need. Wrong! If you want your veneer to be strong and sturdy, and if you want it to stay in place without shifting or cracking, you need to consider a separate foundation. Your engineer may suggest that it be connected to your home foundation, but in any case, the home foundation may not support a full-height masonry wall.

A new and interesting finish

A neighbor had a brick facade, painted white, on either side of his garage door. It traveled from the driveway up to the roof overhang. One weekend, he rented a pressure washer and took off about 95 percent of that white covering. Specs of paint remained in the brick's pores, and a lot remained in the mortar. We rarely see new and interesting finishes, but this was definitely one for the record books. The look was astonishingly beautiful and interesting.

Stone is also quite beautiful, having all the virtues of brick. Unfortunately, stone is more difficult to install than brick and isn't always available in every area. Also, not every kind of stone is acceptable for use. Some are soft and wear too easily. Others are highly porous and become nests for all sorts of little crawly things.

We absolutely love stone; however, when it comes to cost, stone tends to be reserved for folks who have more money than they know what to do with. One absolute truth about stone: You simply cannot make a mistake putting it up. No two stones are alike, which means that there will never be two walls that are alike.

Cultured stone is an alternative that offers the look of real stone without the high cost. Cultured stone is made with cement and sand and includes a colored surface that looks just like the real thing. With cultured stone, the variety in size and shape is limited. With rock and stone, mother nature never makes two pieces alike. By rotating a piece of cultured stone, you can make it appear to be different than others like it. Mapping things out on the ground before installation is also smart. We must admit, some of the products on the market today are incredibly real looking.

Then you have concrete block. What can we say about concrete block?

- ✔ Concrete block is reasonably inexpensive and quick to build.
- ✔ When the wall is fully standing, the only thing you have to do is paint — inside and out — to finish it.
- ✔ Start to finish, concrete block is the easiest material from which to build a wall.
- ✔ Almost anyone — assuming he or she is reasonably strong — can build a concrete block wall.

✔ Electrical wiring, heating, and plumbing can be difficult at exterior walls, but you can easily handle most of these tasks by using framed interior walls. All you need is a bit of creative planning.

✔ Insulated block is now available. That's right, the interior of the block contains insulation. In fact, the interior and exterior sections of the block are completely separated by the insulative material. Insulation makes all the difference.

A few flaws worth mentioning

Like every other exterior wall cover, brick, stone, and block require ongoing maintenance. They are all porous materials. In cold country, where freezing temperatures are a common occurrence, real problems can result. Water seeps into the pores, freezes, and expands. This freeze-expand process is powerful enough to cause severe cracking and chipping. So water rots wood, indirectly causes stucco to crack, and also causes brick, stone, and block to crack and chip. Do you see a pattern here?

Because masonry materials are porous, water enters the material, and then later, when the water evaporates, leaves behind a mineral deposit. The white powdery material that lays on the surface is known as *efflorescence*. Sometimes cleaning is easy; however, if buildup occurs over a long period of time, you must take extreme measures:

1. **Mix a cup of vinegar into a quart of water.**

2. **Scrub with a wire brush.**

   If this doesn't work, try a 10 percent solution of muratic acid (one part acid into nine parts water). Again, scrub with a wire brush. Muratic acid is very dangerous. Absolutely do not breath fumes and do wear eye protection, gloves, and other protective clothing.

3. **If the first two techniques don't do the trick, try renting a soda blaster or a pressure washer.**

   The soda blaster will do a better, quicker job but is not available everywhere.

Some protection

No matter how good the masonry is on your home, if you want to protect it from mother nature, then clean and seal it. Pressure wash with detergent, repair mortar cracks, and then use a high-grade masonry sealer. Contact your local masonry contractor or chimney sweep for the sealant that works best in your climate.

If you use stone, other conditions may need your attention from time to time. Moss and mildew love taking up residence on stone, block, and brick. The pores trap water, which become mini feeding grounds for all sorts of microscopic little buggars. Scrubbing with detergent and bleach works great to remove what exists, but unless the surface is sealed, the growth returns immediately. Some surfaces are so porous and irregular that sealer doesn't prevent new growth. In such cases, the solution to the problem requires finding out where the moisture is coming from — and then eliminating it.

A layer of brick, stone, or block is impervious to attack by structural pests like termites. However, most masonry walls in this country are a single thickness (veneer) added to the surface of a wood frame wall. Having stone or brick attached to a wood wall absolutely will not prevent the adjacent wood from being ravaged by termites. If anything, veneers of all kinds provide easier access for structural pests. If you have a masonry veneer on your home, be sure to order annual, structural pest inspections. A proper inspection requires accessing wall cavities, which means removing and replacing wallboard. This process is far less expensive than replacing an entire wall eaten away by a hungry pack of termites.

Vinyl and aluminum siding

One author we know of refers to vinyl siding as "one of the greatest innovations in home construction . . . in this century." Yes, vinyl siding is easy to put up, low maintenance, and quite beautiful. But it is also flimsy.

A vinyl siding salesperson will tell you that vinyl doesn't rust or corrode, that it lasts forever, and never needs painting. The fact is that vinyl siding is actually *polyvinyl chloride (PVC),* the same stuff used to make sprinkler pipe. PVC is a great material, but it does deteriorate — just like every other kind of siding. From the moment it leaves the factory, PVC begins to give off free chlorides. As a result, the material becomes more brittle as it gets older. Brittle plastic is okay for underground sprinklers — not for siding. Once vinyl siding becomes brittle, it can easily crack and split when swiped by a wheel barrel or whacked by a speeding basketball.

We have also seen vinyl siding that has become badly pitted. So much so that a new piece could not be used to make a repair. The old piece was dull and the new piece shiny. They didn't look anything alike. Yuck!

We attended a remodeling contractors' round-table discussion where it was unanimously agreed that the worst thing about vinyl siding is the trim — windows, doors, and corners. Everyone agreed that it was bulky, flimsy, and hollow sounding; using real wood trim would improve the end result.

Some claim that vinyl siding can be painted. They are correct. You can paint vinyl siding. In fact, you can paint anything. Unfortunately, paint does not stick to plastic. Therefore, if you paint vinyl siding, you may end up with the shortest lived paint job in history.

In the '50s, there was the great discovery of that decade — aluminum. At one point it was estimated that aluminum siding covered the exteriors of almost 20 percent of American homes. When vinyl siding hit the market, the popularity of aluminum siding diminished. Even though rot wasn't a problem, consumers came to realize that aluminum dented, faded, oxidized, and had to be painted — just like wood. If you have aluminum siding, you can get a new paint job to last by painting it like you would a car. Sand off oxidation and old paint, spray with a metal primer, and finish with a good grade, zinc oxide-based metal paint. Remember, the paint used to adhere to wood is different than what is needed for a good finish over metal.

Asbestos siding

If you have asbestos siding and want to keep it looking bright and new, try a good coat of latex paint. Asbestos siding is nothing more than finely ground asbestos particles mixed with cement. Products made from asbestos were popular because they were strong and inexpensive. Mixing cement and sand produces a similar product but it isn't nearly as strong.

However, you probably know that asbestos is dangerous to your health (see Chapter 16 for more information); you must take measures to make your home safe by removing or encapsulating it. Asbestos is not considered dangerous unless it becomes *friable* (crumbles when pinched). Minor cracks here and there do not pose a danger in asbestos siding materials unless the cracked edges are friable.

Siding an Addition

As it relates to a room addition, siding can be challenging. For example, one couple just couldn't figure out how we knew that the bay window at their kitchen was added after the house was built. The window matched all the others, and you certainly couldn't tell that a remodel had been done from the inside. On the outside of the house, the built-out area beneath the window was covered with a really good grade of resawn plywood siding. And to top that off, the size and finish of the corner trim perfectly matched the rest of the exterior.

So how did we know? The biggest hint was that we could not find plywood siding anywhere else on the home's exterior, not even beneath the eaves. It was a dead giveaway. The outside of the house was beautifully finished with cedar lap siding. The plywood under the window stuck out like a sore thumb. During the remodel, someone had decided that the price to exactly match the siding was just too high. Big mistake!

Forgive us for repeating ourselves, but matching old and new exactly is so important when remodeling your home. If a potential buyer can, in fact, tell that a remodel has been done, then obviously, that buyer has already ascertained that the job wasn't done to the highest standard. This situation is exactly the kind that opens the door to other questions about the quality and integrity of your home.

If you are like most people, your home is your biggest single investment. Therefore, its resale value should be one of your biggest single concerns. You never know when some unforeseen circumstance will cause you to list your home for sale.

Matching siding: The importance and the expense

Matching exterior wood siding can sometimes cost a small fortune. One of our remodeling customers had a home covered with grooved plywood siding. The grooves were vertical and spaced every two inches. None of the lumber yards in our area carried such siding, so we purchased solid sheets and used a router to cut the grooves ourselves. Each sheet took an hour or more to make. The custom work almost tripled the cost of the siding.

Another interesting problem that we often face involves horizontal lap or tongue and groove siding. Even with years of shrinkage, older siding usually is much wider and thicker than the siding that is available today. Lacing horizontal siding together requires that old and new be exactly the same size. We often find it necessary to purchase custom milled pieces to achieve a perfect fit. Again, all this special attention is given so that no one can tell that an alteration has taken place.

Another problem occurs when strips of old and new siding meet at a corner. Obviously, the siding doesn't have to be laced together. But a minor mismatch in plank height can grow into a major problem. A 10-foot-high run of siding has approximately sixteen 1 x 8 courses (horizontal runs). If each new piece is only $\frac{1}{8}$ inch shorter than the old material, then you'll have a 2-inch error in alignment by the time the last course is installed. A 2-inch error is really easy to spot. Even by widening the space between each course $\frac{1}{16}$ inch, the misalignment at the end is still a highly visible 1 inch or so.

What's our point you ask? Why all the stories about siding and how it often has to be custom made? Exterior wall covering really is one of the most costly finishes to match correctly — and one of the most visible when done incorrectly. Your contractor may tell you not to worry, that no one will notice the minor difference. Don't believe it.

Matching and patching stucco

Stucco is another exterior wall covering that requires painstaking attention to achieve a good match. If you intend to add an addition onto a stuccoed home, you need to remember some really important things:

✔ **Ragged edges:** The secret is *ragged edges.* You may prefer to describe the condition as jagged, but in either case, the connection between any existing and new stucco — patch or addition — must not be straight (as in saw-cut edge). The irregular edge staggers the connection, provides "tooth" between old and new, and even helps in aligning the new surface to the old one.

✔ **Matching texture:** This is where a penny saved can prove to be pound foolish. If you don't have the time or tools to match the texture, then hire someone to do it for you. Plasterers are hard to find and the process is expensive, but the finished product lasts forever.

✔ **Patch paint:** Be prepared to patch paint. You absolutely cannot match an old stucco finish every time. Chances are, this time you won't find a match. Paint makes things so much easier to match.

Matching brick, stone, and block

Matching most block is easy. And more often than not, you can find matching brick as well. Matching stone is another story. Even if you find the correct stone, it may be a slightly different color. If you are planning an addition and patching or matching stone will be involved, first, contact a mason for advice. You may have to alter your project design depending on the availability of matching material. Often a designer or architect will suggest that a certain material is available by including a note on the plans stating that the contractor should "match the existing masonry." However, the contractor can only match the material if it is available.

Figure 23-2 shows some examples of masonry patterns. Note that many require multiple types of bricks, stones, and blocks. Your contractor will have to find all the materials in the pattern to get a workable match.

Re-siding

We aren't big advocates of re-siding. We believe in making do with what you have unless the exterior of your home is completely rotten.

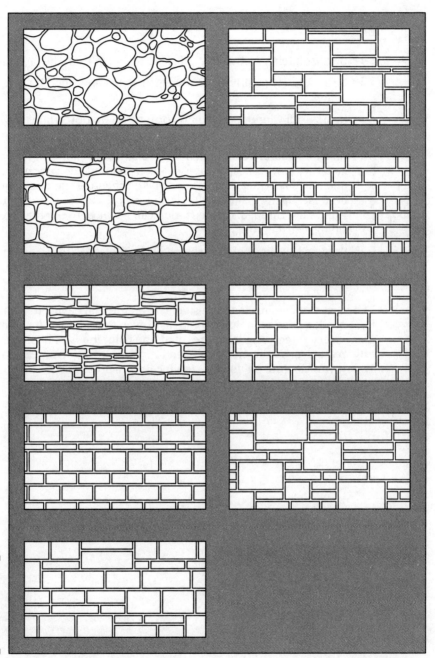

Figure 23-2:
Brick,
stone, and
block
patterns.

If you do decide to re-side, here are a few tips that may result in a better end product:

- ✔ Be absolutely positive that all rot is removed from the old siding.

- ✔ Be absolutely positive that the earth clears any wood by at least 8 inches.

- ✔ Remove all window, door, and corner trim that protrudes beyond the face of the existing siding.

- ✔ Apply a moisture barrier. A moisture barrier — not a vapor barrier. A moisture barrier keeps water droplets out and lets vapors pass. This difference is critical. Do not use plastic sheeting such as visqueen because plastic is impermeable and vapors cannot pass through it. If vapors are trapped, condensation can occur between the layers of siding, causing rot.

- ✔ Prime all six sides of the trim and seal in place with a high-quality, 50-year caulk. (With some types of siding, the trim is applied before the siding and with others the trim is applied last.)

The most common reason to re-side: "We are tired of having to paint so often." First of all, a good paint job should last seven to ten years. If you have to paint every three years, or more often, the paint job isn't being done properly. Years ago, all the methods used to remove paint involved a lot of work. Today, you can tool on down to the local paint store and rent a pressure washer or a soda washer that is powerful enough to cut wood for a hundred dollars a day or less.

Part V
Energizing the Walls

The 5th Wave   By Rich Tennant

"To preserve the beauty and durability of the dental molding, we put fluoride in the trim paint."

In this part . . .

We cover the stuff that goes in and on the walls: everything from the drywall to the insulation to the electrical wiring.

Chapter 24

Plumbing, HVAC, and Electrical

*A*while back, one of our remodeling customers called our office to complain that no work had been done to his project that day. "I just got home from work," he said, "and it doesn't look as though anyone has been here." He was polite but tense. The wall framing for the tiny bath modification had been completed the day before, and we promised him that the plumbing and electrical alterations would be done the following day. We couldn't figure out why he was so nervous. We had been there — ourselves — all day long. We had completed the plumbing, vent-fan installation, and all of the electrical work. We had even called for a rough inspection for the next day. We told him what had been done and that we had done it ourselves. He just couldn't believe it. "Let me go look," he said. When he returned to the phone we could tell that he was a little embarrassed. "I'm sorry, guys," he said, "I had no idea that anyone had been here." We explained to him that his reaction was very normal.

Folks typically are amazed by the speed at which demolition, foundation, and framing are done, but they seem to become frustrated quickly during the plumbing, HVAC (heating, ventilation, and air conditioning), and electrical phases. Much of this work gets done below the floor and in the attic — not as highly visible as demolition and carpentry work. Also, HVAC and electrical work is slow and tedious; it can take almost as long as the floor and wall framing combined. The work could go faster if all three phases were done simultaneously, but doing so would be more dangerous than sensible. You'd have workers from all three trades present at the same time. Crowded conditions and working over each others' mess is reason enough to separate the tasks. Regardless, workers need to follow an *order of installation* process. The success of each phase depends on proper coordination of that order.

First, the plumbing gets done. Yeah, we know, plumbers can route water lines around just about anything. But you can't say the same for sewer lines. A sewer line must run in as straight a line as possible (with as few turns as possible) and all at a gradual downward slope away from the fixtures, and ultimately, the building. Downhill is the only direction that certain stuff flows. A waste line wouldn't work very well if it had to skip heat ducts and hop electric wires. So plumbing gets to go first because the freedom to route sewer lines in any direction is so important.

HVAC comes next. Even though heat ducting is sometimes rigid, it can be routed around obstacles with only minimal negative impact to the system. With heating systems, there is a bit more flexibility associated with the installation.

Finally, the electrical gets installed. As it is probably apparent by this point, a material's flexibility is pretty important during installation — and wiring is the most flexible of all. Electricians can bend, twist, turn, and wrap electrical wire around, through, above, or below just about any building component.

Well, now you know why workers follow a definite order of installation.

Plumbing

A plumbing system consists of four elements: the water supply pipes, the sewer lines, the plumbing fixtures, and gas lines. The fixtures (faucets, tub, sink, toilet, and so on) are the most important as far as appearance is concerned. The water supply lines are the most important when it comes to good water pressure and plenty of volume. And don't forget the gas line if you want to stay warm. But when it comes to importance, the sewer line takes the cake. Hey, the sewer line is one system that you don't want to be around when it fails. The sewer line is definitely an important part of a plumbing system. So let's talk about each of the elements of the plumbing system beginning with the water lines.

Water supply lines

If you have municipal water, you write a check to the city or the county for the service. With a well, you bear the cost of operating and maintaining your own system. There may be one difference: City water undergoes regular testing for dangerous elements. If you have a well, testing should be a regular part of your operating procedure. You never know when some idiot will pour something toxic into the groundwater in your area.

Consider a filter system

With all the junk floating around in the environment today, it makes good sense to do a little of your own water management too. Take a look at some of your choices:

- ✔ **Whole-house, activated-charcoal filter.** The filter attaches outside the home at the main water inlet. Such a filter removes larger particles, including rust-causing metal and some of the elements that smell as well. Outside faucets and irrigation lines can be bypassed so that only water used inside the home is filtered.

- ✔ **Water softeners.** Salt based water-softeners eliminate lime deposits and other minerals that leave white, powdery stains all over your expensive plumbing fixtures. We don't think that salt based water-softeners ought to be connected to the faucets that you use for drinking water. Salt residue can be dangerous for heart patients. Also, as far as we are concerned, the jury is still out on magnetic water-softening devices. At the writing of this book there are no "official," "government approved" tests that indicate the effectiveness of magnetic water softeners — or that they work at all!

- ✔ **Point-of-use filters.** Point of use filters are installed onto the fixture where they will be used (icemaker, kitchen sink, and so on). Activated charcoal and reverse osmosis are the two most popular point of use filters. Activated charcoal filters vary in size and quality. The bigger they get the better they work, the longer they last, and the more they cost. Although they are more expensive, we like reverse osmosis. Reverse osmosis filters do waste some water, but no other filter purifies water as well. With reverse osmosis, everything gets filtered, bacteria, aluminum, chlorine, minerals, herbicides, pesticides, and even heavy metals. Point of use filters can be used in combination with whole house filters. In fact, we recommend it. With a combination of filters (whole-house and point-of-use), minerals, rust, and smells are reduced at all locations. Plus, filtration at the point of use is better, and the point of use filter-cartridge lasts longer.

By using a combination of all three water management systems, your drinking water tastes sweet and is safe, your dishwasher and clotheswashers work more effectively, you enjoy cleaner clothes, cleaner dishes, and better showers (and your shower doors have fewer spots). You can minimize pipe deterioration, or, in some cases, prevent it. We can name even more benefits, but we think you get the point.

Watch your water pressure

If you plan to remodel and you want to get an edge on water pressure, then replace as many pipes as possible while they are exposed and easy to change. Replace the pipes in the walls before the wallboard is repaired.

The causes of poor water pressure can vary. For example, a local golf club dug a giant well to fill a lake on its course. Surrounding residents complained of reduced water flow, forcing the golf club to modify the use of its well. The giant pump was sucking the community dry. What a way to lose water pressure. Simultaneous use — when everyone in the community needs water at the same time — can also reduce water pressure. In the summer, for example, thirsty lawns and dry gardens mean you and all your neighbors are watering your landscapes. You know the drill.

You may not be able to control water pressure based on how it is being used in the community, but you can at least be sure that the problem doesn't result because your own lines are clogged. Keeping water lines clear and free-running is important. We have seen pipe nipples clog to the point where a $1/2$-inch line was so corroded on the inside that it had been reduced in diameter to less than $1/8$ inch. (A *pipe nipple* is a very short length of pipe threaded at both ends and used mostly to make connections.) The nipples that we see clogged most often are those located at the water heater and under the sink where the pipes come out of the wall. Dissimilar metals coming into contact with each other cause *electrolysis* to occur, resulting in corrosion buildup. We call this buildup "arterial pipeosis." Hey, it works for us. A galvanized iron pipe nipple that connects to a copper water line and a brass faucet isn't uncommon. Talk about dissimilar metals — that's a three banger.

A *dielectric union* is a connector used to join water pipes made from dissimilar metals (see Figure 24-1). This connector eliminates the possibility of electrolysis and the corrosion buildup and metal deterioration that results. Also, a special galvanized nipple is available that is coated on the inside with plastic. It also eliminates electrolysis. Remodelers can use these fittings to replace the ones that come out of the walls and those located at the water heater inlet and outlet ports.

Finding a water leak

Want to find out if you have a water leak? Turn off every faucet and fixture in the house — and don't forget the ice maker. Go outside and read the water meter. Return in an hour and read the meter again. If the needle has moved, you have a leak somewhere. With all the faucets off, chances are, the leak is underground, under the house, or at a toilet. To see if a toilet leaks, place a few drops of food coloring in the tank. If the color shows up in the bowl within 10 to 15 minutes, then you have a bad flapper. If the toilets are okay, a trip beneath the house is in order. If nothing is discovered by this time, you need to call a leak-detection company. These companies have sounding equipment that can pinpoint a leak through concrete.

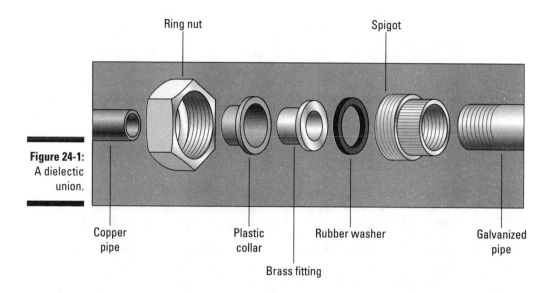

Figure 24-1:
A dielectic
union.

Ring nut

Spigot

Copper
pipe

Plastic
collar

Rubber washer

Galvanized
pipe

Brass fitting

In a remodel, water lines can be connected to the water source before the walls are covered with wallboard. This is a significant advantage. With the new pipes under pressure, leaks can be found. Also, if a pipe is damaged during construction, the problem is quickly discovered.

With a bathroom remodel, there is always the question about how you will bathe, shower, and just generally stay clean. Where a tub or a molded shower unit can be installed in a few hours, showers that will be tiled can be unusable for weeks. What we do is tear out the bath with the tub going first. We then get a new tub in place and operational. Then we complete our demolition. By doing this, a tub and toilet are available at all times. We have found that, given the choice, most consumers prefer to walk on an unfinished subfloor in their own bathroom rather than use a portable toilet.

Heat me up, baby!

It isn't a hot water heater. It heats cold water. Therefore, it is a cold water heater or simply a "water heater." Now that we have that straight, we would like to say that we Americans do not use our resources in the same way the Europeans do. We use hot water tanks and they use coils (instant hot water systems). We heat water and store it in a tank so that we can get gobs of it all at once for nice, long hot showers. Or, if we have a large family — several nice, long, hot showers. The Europeans heat their water as they go. Coils are filled with a few gallons of water and then quickly become super heated. If water is used sparingly, you can get one or two brief, navy-style showers. (Navy-style shower: Wet down for a few seconds and then immediately turn the water off. Next, lather up everywhere. Finally, turn the water on again, just for a moment or two, and rinse off.)

Regardless of which type of water heater you own, someone must pay for the energy used to operate it. If you are the one with the deep pockets and want to reduce your hot water bill, then make sure to keep your water heater clean, operate it at about 130 degrees Fahrenheit, and wrap it and all your hot water lines in insulation. These are easy, inexpensive tasks that can be especially easy to do during a remodel when there is access to pipes in walls, ceilings, and subareas.

Aren't sewers a gas?

When you finish taking a bath, washing the floors, or brushing your teeth, where does all that water go? The water goes down the drain and into the sewer.

Did you ever wonder why they call it the sanitary sewer system? Think about it for a moment. Unlike water lines that are pressurized, a sewer system depends on gravity to work properly. And although sewage can be pumped up hill, there are far fewer problems with a conventional gravity line that constantly slopes downward from the fixture — all the way to the street. The more slope the better. Lots of stuff can clog a sewer line: baby diapers, toys, grease, tree roots, you name it. But nothing will cause a sewer line to clog faster than when there is not enough slope. The plumbing code says $1/8$ inch per foot is minimum fall. We suggest $1/4$ inch per foot or more as the minimum. Be sure to keep this in mind as you expand or modify your sewer system.

A sewer system has three parts:

- ✔ **The drain line** transports waste to the main sewer system. That's a no-brainer.
- ✔ **The vent line** provides equalizing air pressure to the drain system. The concept is similar to opening a can of oil. You punch two holes, one opposite from the other. You pour out from the first hole, and the second hole allows air into the can so the oil can flow freely. Look at the vent lines in your homes as the second hole in the oil can. Air gets in, sewage flows freely. You may think you have a clogged drain line when, in fact, a vent is clogged.

The vent travels from the drain line, up the wall, through the attic, and out through the roof. Birds and rodents can easily nest, or even get stuck and die, in a vent pipe. If this happens, air pressure in the drain line cannot be equalized and water flows ever so slowly. When snaking a sewer line, don't forget to snake the vents as well.

✔ **The trap assembly** is the most important part of the sewer system. Every plumbing fixture has one. You may not see it, but it's there. As shown in Figure 24-2, the trap for the shower is under the floor. With a toilet, the trap is built into the base. The trap you are probably most familiar with is the one under the sink: the *P-trap*. This trap is nothing more than a water door that prevents sewer gases from escaping into the home. Without the trap system, your home would smell . . . different. Where the "P-on-its-side" shape of the trap holds water, it also is a major clog point. Silt, grease, hair, and other yucky things gather in the trap and clog it.

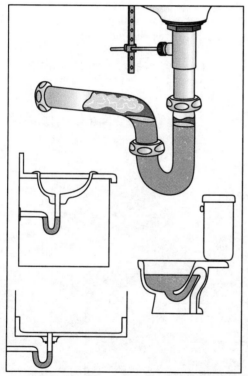

Figure 24-2: Trap assemblies.

If you will be tying into an old cast iron drain, use a hack saw or a recipro-cating saw with a metal-cutting blade to make the incisions for the tap. With older lines, a snap cutter may crush the pipe. No-hub rubber couplings are perfect for making the transition from new ABS (black plastic) to old cast iron lines. Do we suggest ABS for your sewer line? You bet. It is inexpensive, easy to work with, and easy to repair — and the insides are as smooth as a baby's butt. Smooth inside means less friction and freer-flowing waste. In English, that means less chance of clogging.

Storm drains and sewers

It was over a decade ago and we were doing our radio show on KCBS in San Francisco. A caller wanted to know what to do with leftover paint thinner. One of us instructed him to pour it into the storm drain. Hey, even the best of us make mistakes. Anyway, after being chastised by at least a half dozen callers, we learned that the storm drain system and the sewer system are completely separate from each other and that both systems eventually end up in our waterways — and in our drinking water. "Say, Bub, give me a paint-thinner cocktail, will ya'?"

A storm drain system controls water runoff and rainwater overflow. The rains drip off the roof, over the lot, across the curb, and into the storm drain where it travels through a large pipe that spills into the local waterway or settling pond. Sewer lines, on the other hand, carry waste directly to a sewage treatment plant before it is dumped into the local waterway (see the following figure). By the way, if the water source in your area has toilet paper in it, your community may not have a sewage treatment plant. Swimming therein would not be recommended. In both cases, storm drain and sewer system, be careful how you use them. The water they transport will eventually end up in your drinking glass.

Fixtures

We asked Morris' wife Carol what could be said about plumbing fixtures. She quickly replied, "Don't buy a cheap one. They don't last." We said that we were looking for a comment that was a little more all-encompassing. "Oh, okay," she said, "how about this . . . there is a butt for every seat." That was it. She hit the nail right on the head. The styles, shapes, and colors of plumbing fixtures are infinite. There is one — or more — for every taste. Where the water and sewer pipes do all the work, the fixtures seem to get all the credit. But you need to know a couple of things before you go shopping.

Faucets

When it comes to a faucet, anything beyond a solid brass body and a plain chrome finish is all pomp and circumstance. A solid brass plumbing fixture with a chrome finish is as good as it gets. Split finishes, polished brass, brushed finishes, antique, and painted finishes are all designed to appeal to your taste — and don't increase the life expectancy of the faucet. We think plastic faucets suck. How's that for direct?!

Toilets

If you are planning a bath remodel or addition, the toilet must be an *ultra-low-flow* model. These units are now required by federal law and must not use more than 1.6 gallons of water per flush.

In the late 1980s, the first of the low-flow toilets came onto the market. Public response could be described as "outrage." Everyone who did a bath remodel was required to throw out their perfectly good 7- to 10-gallon-per-flush toilet and replace it with a 3.5-gallon unit. As it turned out, these first low-flow toilets were generally badly engineered and often had to be flushed twice to work. You got it. 3.5 x 2 = 7. The 3.5 gallon toilets took us one step forward and then two steps back. Will we now have to flush four times? How in heaven's name, you ask, are the new 1.6 gallon units going to work? Actually, pretty well so far — especially, if you get one of the pressure-assisted models. With one of these units, air pressure assists the flush. It's quick and clean. And it only takes *one* flush. The same water that refills the bowl also operates a compressor pump that refills the pressure-assist tank.

Want the best bang for your buck? Plan to spend somewhere in the neighborhood of $350 to $450 for a pressure-assisted model. Some cost as much as a $1,000, but here we take you back to our comment about faucets. As the price goes up, the fixture looks prettier, but doesn't work any better.

Showers

For the shower, look into a pressure-balancing valve that will keep you from being scalded. By the way, you don't have to change your existing valve. The regulating valve unit can be connected to the shower pipes beneath the floor. Are we creative or what?

Plastic shower units vary widely in quality. If the walls feel thin and flimsy at the plumbing store, then they are sure to feel thin and flimsy once the unit is installed in your home. You may have to pay more to get a thick-walled unit, but then you won't have to worry about falling through it.

 Fiberglass plumbing fixtures, such as tubs and shower pans, should be installed over a bed of plaster of paris. Doing this guarantees full, even support at the base of the fixture — regardless of the irregularities in the floor or the bottom of the fixture. Put the fixture in place and check to insure that it will mount properly. Once you are sure everything is ready, pull the fixture out and set it aside. Mix and spread about 25 pounds of plaster onto the floor in the center of the area where the fixture will be installed. Immediately install the fixture. Be careful not to stand inside the unit. Doing so will compress the plaster. Wait until the plaster has had plenty of time to dry (about 30 minutes) before screwing the unit to the studs.

How natural is gas?

Can you imagine how confusing it could get if you mentioned that your beans were cooked with gas? Whether it is propane or natural gas, it has to be piped into the house. And when that happens, someone who knows exactly what they are doing should be present. Of all the systems in the home, the gas line is the least forgiving. One leak and it is all over, baby! We don't recommend that you do your own gas line unless you realize how dangerous a sloppy job can be. Even the smallest leak can create enough gas buildup to level your home if the gas ignites.

A gas line's size is normally determined by an engineer. The distance between the house meter and the fixture, as well as the amount of gas required by the fixture, are used to calculate the diameter of the gas pipe. The pipe is "sized" to provide only enough gas for a specific fixture to operate. Oversizing the gas line so that additional fixtures can be added later is rarely done. Therefore, tapping into "just any gas line" could substantially reduce the gas flow to a fixture. This is dangerous because it could cause a "flame out" at the fixture. A flame out is where the pilot light and burner shut off due to lack of fuel. Once the flame is out, gas continues to flow. Talk about potential for an explosion!

Heating, Cooling, and Ventilation

When the plumbing is complete, then it's on to the next phase: heating, cooling, and ventilation. HVAC includes the heating system, the air-conditioning system, and air ventilation system. Each works with the other to make the environment in your home not only habitable but more comfortable, as well. During the last decade, major strides have been taken in the development of super energy-efficient equipment that can do a better job for less money. We can remember well those room additions in the '60s where baseboard heating was added because it was so inexpensive and easy to install. We saw those same families replace gas appliances for a "modern electric kitchen." If we had only known how wasteful electricity is.

Heating systems

Heating systems come in an amazing variety. There are wall- and floor-mount units, ceiling-mounted units, central units, and window units. There are units that heat with steam, heated air, and warmed water. And the energy source that fires each can vary from electricity to gas, coal, or oil. But regardless of which type exists, when it comes to a remodel or a room addition, most folks want to know how to get the best bang for their heating buck. Should the existing furnace be reused, or should it be upgraded or replaced with something new?

We feel that it is extremely important that we all do our share to comply with new energy-conservation laws. They are designed to reduce energy waste. However, we think it would be wasteful for us to suggest that you throw out your old heating system before it has outlived its usefulness.

For room additions, you are normally allowed to keep your existing heating system. If it is a central, forced-air unit, then ducting is simply extended to the new space. Duct size should be determined by a qualified mechanical engineer. Whenever space is added to a home, wall and floor furnaces become less efficient, but they will still work. Floor furnaces have been outlawed and are dangerous. If you have one, we suggest that you convert to a different type as soon as possible. If you have a wall furnace, we strongly recommend that you replace it with one that has a circulating fan. The fan distributes the heat more evenly and reduces the "hot spot" created by such a system.

A modern, forced-air furnace system can cut your heating bill nearly in half. If you currently pay $100 per month (five months per year), then a new system can save you almost $250 per year. At $200 per month, $500 per year could be saved. However, if the cost of a new system is $4,500, then it could take from 5 to 10 years to amortize the savings. On the other hand, the minute that puppy has warmed its last room and gone to that big, warm furnace heaven in the sky, then replacement with a more energy-efficient system becomes a must — not only to comply with the law, but because it makes good economic sense as well.

If you own a forced-air heating system that isn't working efficiently enough (hot spots here, cold spots there), you may want to look into adding more cold air returns. Most forced-air systems are installed with only one or two cold air returns. However, to improve efficiency, add more cold air returns. Hot spots can be completely eliminated. How many cold air returns is enough? One in every room is plenty.

Gas versus electric heating

Gas-fired heating systems are far more cost-effective than electric units. If you have natural gas piped into your home, then you are one of the lucky ones who can enjoy more warmth for less money. The initial installation cost of a gas-fired, forced-air heating unit is quite a bit higher than for an electrically fired one. But in the long run, you will actually save money and precious energy by going with gas.

A gas-fired heater doesn't have to be a central heating unit or even a full-sized wall furnace with an expensive exhaust flu that has to be installed up through the roof. Small, energy-efficient gas-fired wall-mount heaters can be purchased that will easily heat 400 to 600 square feet. And they can be installed in a weekend.

Gas-fired forced-air-units (central heating) and wall units use gas burners to heat a large metal chamber. With central units, air is fanned over the chamber, warmed, and then forced through ducts to various rooms by an electrically operated fan. With wall units, the chamber is heated and radiates naturally into the room. Some wall units can be fitted with low-energy-use fans that distribute heat more readily than radiating naturally. Units that use fans, such as gas-fired central heating units, bring outside air into the house. This can cause two problems because dust moving from outside to inside can create (1) a cleaning problem, and (2) sneezes, sniffles, and swelling for allergy-prone folks. The good side here is that gas-fired units are comparatively inexpensive to purchase, install, maintain, and operate.

The only requirement is that the unit be mounted on the inside of an exterior wall. This is because the exhaust for the unit is on its rear side, so it can exhaust directly to the outside air. No fancy flues or ducting are required.

Steam-heating

Old fashioned steam heating (still in use today in some places) utilizes steam to warm a metal container (called a radiator) and the steam-heated radiator, in turn, warms the air in the room. The steam is created by heating water in a boiler. Coal, coal oil, and other oils are still used to fire the boiler in a steam heating system. Coal is dirty, and oil is expensive — not the best of systems. If you are considering purchasing a home with a steam heating system, remember, they can be extremely expensive to maintain and repair, with a lot of hardware involved. But there is a good side: Folks with allergies like steam heaters (and hydronic and radiant heaters too). This is because air from the outside is not drawn into the home to get the system to work, as is the case with some other types of heating systems.

Gas-fired hydronic heating

Another type of heating system, gas-fired hydronic heating, is based on the same principal as a steam heater. But instead of sending steam from an oil or coal boiler to a few radiator locations, the hydronic heating system sends heated water from a gas-fired boiler to several long, narrow baseboard-style radiating units. Less intense heat is distributed (radiated) over a greater area. A hydronic system is cleaner, safer (steam units have exploded), more energy efficient, and easier to decorate around than its obsolescent steam-snorting ancestor.

Radiant heating is another form of hydronic (water) heating. Here, a gas-fired boiler heats water that is then distributed through a series of metal or plastic tubes. The tubes are formed into a hidden pattern that covers the area within an entire wall, ceiling, or floor, or a combination of them. Since heat rises, the floor is usually where you will find the radiant heating tubes hidden. Generally speaking, radiant heat is even and subtle. Unfortunately, it can be very expensive to install and maintain.

By the way, all types of hydronic heating are based on the same principle: Heated water is distributed to radiating units that gently heat an area. The better the distribution of the water, the more even the heating. The good side? You get allergy-free heat because no air from the outside is needed. The bad side? Whenever a device contains water, then you can expect corrosion and leaks to happen eventually. Over the long haul, this kind of maintenance can be expensive compared to other types of heating systems.

Heat pump

A heat pump is a somewhat more complex heating alternative (that, by the way, can also double as an air-conditioner). Although a heat pump runs on electricity, it should not be confused with energy-consuming electric resistance-type heating devices. Heat pumps are far more energy efficient than they are.

The electricity used in a heat pump operates an electric motor (not a heat coil) that runs a compressor and a blower fan (far less current is used here than in an electric-coil-type heater).

First, you need to know an interesting fact about Freon. Freon will either absorb heat (and cool a room) or give off heat (heat up the room) depending on whether it is in a liquid or gaseous state. Simply put, Freon can be used to heat or cool by altering its physical state. A heat pump contains mechanical devices that can change Freon from a liquid to a gas and vice versa. The Freon is contained in copper tubes, and air is fan blown across the tubes. So even though electricity is used to run a heat pump, heat comes more from the action of the Freon and less from electricity.

Imagine a room and two sets of Freon-filled copper tubes (one set of tubes inside the room and the other set of tubes outside the room), both interconnected through a compressor and a series of check valves located some-where in between the two sets of tubes. A switch inside the room controls check valves that can selectively assist in liquefying or vaporizing the Freon in either of the two sets of connected tubes. Vaporize the gas on the inside set of tubes; heat is released into the room; pump the gas to the outside tubes, liquefy it, and heat is absorbed. Pump it back into the house, vaporize it, and heat is again released. Reverse the process and you have a refrigeration type air-conditioner. And yes, given proper insulation, a refrigerator as well!

And you always thought your cat liked to lie next to the refrigerator because of hunger. Yes, sometimes it's because of food, but most of the time it's because of the warmth output by the cooling-warming cycle of Freon. Isn't it a small world?!

Thermostats

Whatever kind of heating system you have, don't be shy about upgrading to the most modern thermostat available. There are digital thermostats that take a college education to operate. And there are simple ones too. Look until you find one that is versatile and easy for you to operate. Speak with a local heating contractor, or find a vendor who has various units on display. You want a unit that is sophisticated enough to automatically turn your heating or cooling system on and off based on your particular lifestyle and work schedule.

Air conditioners

To own a dwelling that is equipped with an air conditioner is only part of the equation. The way an air-conditioning system operates is a lot like an automobile: Efficiency depends greatly on the way it is maintained and operated. Cars give better mileage and last longer when they get proper care and attention and are driven moderately. The same is true of air-conditioning systems.

If you have a system and can locate the manual, it is a good place to start finding ways to operate your system most efficiently. Tips on maintenance and efficient operation are usually an integral part of these manuals.

Air-conditioning systems do more than just cool the air. They lower humidity and also remove dust and dirt by moving the air through filters. When these filters become clogged with dirt, the system must work harder to do its job. This wastes energy and can make utility bills rise. Disposable filters should be checked every two months (once a month during peak use) and replaced when necessary. Permanent filters should be cleaned in accordance with the manufacturer's instructions.

Some people like to "help" their air conditioner by opening doors and windows on warm days. But doing so just lets all the cool, dehumidified air rush outside and lets in the hot, humid air. The more your home seals out heat, humidity, and dust, the more efficiently your system will do its job.

The useful life of an air conditioner can vary greatly. Factors such as climate, maintenance care, and quality and capacity of the original equipment can increase or decrease the service a system will give by months and even years. On the average, a residential central air conditioner will last from 10 to 15 years. When a unit begins to show its age, it is usually major components such as the motor or the compressor that wear out. In the short run, replacing failed components usually costs the least amount of money. But in so doing, an opportunity to greatly improve the overall efficiency of the system may be lost.

In recent years, air conditioner manufacturers have made dramatic progress in increasing the efficiency of the units they produce. Therefore, it may make more economic sense to put the cost of repair into a new, more efficient unit which will immediately bring down operating cost. Eventually, the more efficient unit should pay for itself through decreased utility bills. What's more, the new unit will be more reliable and offer warranty protection.

The size of an air-conditioning unit is best determined by a local heating and cooling professional contractor. A properly sized unit can ensure maximum comfort and efficiency. Too large a unit will cool the space but will not run long enough to remove humidity. The result will be a cold, clammy feeling within the home. A unit that is too small may mean that you will not attain the degree of coolness you want on very hot days, no matter how long the system runs. Hence, a thermostat set at 78 degrees may only be able to reduce the temperature to 85 degrees on especially hot days.

If you walk into your home and find it stifling hot because the air conditioner was turned off, don't be tempted to move the thermostat to a very low setting to cool the house faster. Setting the thermostat lower than usual will not produce more or colder air. It's best to leave the thermostat alone while the system is running. Constantly setting the control up or down may waste significant amounts of energy.

At night, or when you'll be away from the house for extended periods of time, you probably will want to make energy-saving adjustments to the thermostat setting by raising the desired temperature. But for normal daytime activities, find a comfortable level and leave the thermostat at that setting. A "smart" or programmable thermostat is an element that can help you get the most from your heating and cooling system.

For more money-saving air-conditioning tips write the Air-Conditioning and Refrigeration Institute (ARI), 4301 N. Fairfax Drive, Suite 425, Arlington, VA 22203. Include a self-addressed, stamped, business-size envelope, and they'll send you an information-packed 31-page booklet for free!

Ventilating systems

Getting ready to do a bath or kitchen remodel? How about a new inside laundry? Well, there are a few considerations you may want to make!

Sweaty windows, peeling wallpaper, mold-covered walls, and a musty odor are just a few of the symptoms of a poorly ventilated home. The clothes washer, clothes dryer, shower, wash basin, and stove are just a few of the many sources in the home that produce water vapor. It is an excess of this water vapor that causes the maladies we mentioned.

The most effective method of dealing with excessive moisture in the home is to properly exhaust it to the exterior via an automatic exhaust fan. These fans come in various shapes, sizes, and styles that correspond to their specific application and the size of the area in which they are to be used.

Let's take a bathroom, for example. We use this example because, if you're like many folks, you're constantly fighting the mildew battle. This may have a great deal to do with those long, hot showers the teenagers in the family enjoy. When does a teenager know that his shower has been long enough? When there's no more hot water. Sound familiar? Seriously, the high concentration of water vapor produced by a shower will not only produce a fabulous environment for mildew to prosper, it will peel wallpaper and paint, damage wallboard, and can even cause framing members to rot.

Building codes in many parts of the country require only a vent fan in a bathroom that does not contain an operable window. This fan is required to fully exchange the air five times in the course of one hour. We believe that an exhaust fan in the bathroom is a must for every bathroom, window or not!

There are several aspects of installation and operation which will produce maximum fan efficiency. Whenever possible an exhaust fan should be installed at the high point in the ceiling. This applies to rooms with ceilings that are vaulted or contain soffits or drop ceilings. Also, the fan should be centrally located and close to the shower, which is the single biggest source of water vapor in the bathroom. When we design a bath remodel, we usually locate the fan between the shower and the toilet. The fan must double as an exhaust for sewer gases as well. Usually, one fan is all it takes no matter how large the bath is.

Having a fan is only part of the equation. Properly exhausting the fan is a major part of its successful operation. Most bath fans consist of a metal housing with a dampered exhaust port. Rigid or flexible plastic or metal pipe should attach to the exhaust port and terminate at a jack located on the roof or, in some cases, at an exterior wall. The ducting should be secured to the housing and jack with at least one screw and thoroughly wrapped with duct tape. An exhaust fan should *never* be discharged into an attic or crawl space. This could result in major damage within these areas. Moist air driven into the attic or subarea can create excessive condensation which can lead to mildew and fungus growth and eventually wood rot. Furthermore, sewer gases can become trapped — an unsanitary condition at best.

The range hood

Answer this question: Is it a requirement of the building code to have an exhaust hood over a range or cooktop? The answer is no. Surprised? Although an exhaust system is not required in the kitchen, once one has been installed, it must measure up to codes and regulations. For example, a range hood used above a gas cooktop must be rated to exhaust more air than one over an electric cooktop. If you plan on converting to gas, it may be a good idea to consider the cost of a new hood as well.

If at all possible, don't use a recirculating range hood in lieu of a ducted one. That's right, there are range hoods that draw the air in from below the hood, filter it, and then send it back out into the room. This gets rid of a lot of the grease and some of the smell, but humidity remains high and your home can end up smelling like a dirty garbage can if you forget to clean the filter. The ducted-type hood exhausts everything to the exterior — where it should be.

Electrical

Grandma's kitchen was nothing like yours. She didn't have an automatic dishwasher, a compactor, a disposal, a blender, an electric mixer, undercounter and in-cabinet lighting, or a juicer. If grandma had anything that was electric, it was probably a refrigerator and a range.

In those days, a home's electrical system was a modest 60 amps in size, a tiny system by today's standards. Subdivision homes now come standard with 100- and 125-amp services. And custom homes have services that range in size from 200 to 400 amps and more. The more amperage, the more power available to run several appliances simultaneously — and safely.

Know what's required

If you have an older home and decide to do a remodel — any kind of remodel — your local building department will probably require you to upgrade your electric service to at least 100 amps. The idea is to ensure that you have enough power in your home to serve all the modern conveniences — *without* causing a fire. That's right, too many appliances on too few circuits equals serious consequences.

When the wire in an old circuit is overloaded it heats up. That's when a fuse blows or a breaker trips. We honestly think that many people believe that fuses blow because they aren't any good. Wrong! A breaker doesn't trip until it overheats.

When a breaker continually trips, don't replace it. Find out the reason why it's tripping. An electrician can easily find every outlet or light on a given circuit. Once it is known what the circuit is powering, a simple calculation can determine what is overloading it. Breakers trip for other reasons, but overload is the biggest single cause. If the circuit is not overloaded, then the electrician will check for shorts, bad fixtures, and faulty outlets. It is important to be aware that your electrical system is trying to tell you something when fuses blow and breakers trip. "Help, I'm being overworked!"

Another problem occurs when a circuit is continually overloaded. Each time the wiring heats up, it *fatigues*. As fatigue continues, the wire becomes brittle and it cracks. And a small crack is all it takes for *arcing* to occur. How can we best describe arcing? A wire arcing within a wall cavity is like pointing a blow torch at a barrel of gasoline. A fire is imminent.

But wait, there's more

The electrical system in your home consists of more than just house wiring. The electrician is also charged with the installation of the door chime system, the thermostat wire for the furnace, the telephone wiring, and even cable TV. Wiring for a computerized "smart house" management system, a stereo system, an irrigation control system, a home security system, and other specialized wiring is usually done by a specialist. These specialized wiring tasks *must* be coordinated with your electrician. The electrician's high-voltage wiring and the stereo company's low-voltage wiring must be kept separated in the walls by at least several inches. Running them too close together can cause problems with low-voltage equipment. If the electrician has the opportunity to speak with other persons who will be wiring, she may elect to wire differently to specifically accommodate their needs.

Essentially, the electrical system in your home is nothing more than a bunch of extension cords tied together within the walls and ceilings. The electric code specifies which materials are allowed to be used and how they can be safely connected. However, without hiring a second electrician to test every wire, it is nearly impossible to determine whether a proper job has been done. But, there are some things you can look out for. So keep your eyes peeled to see that the electrician is doing his job properly.

What breakers do

Breakers are nothing more than reusable fuses. When the circuit overheats, the breaker *trips,* or disengages and interrupts power to the circuit. When the wiring cools down, the breaker can be reset to the *on* position. The breakers are contained in metal housings known as *breaker panels.* Housings come in these basic types:

- ✔ **The main panel** always contains at least one breaker, the one that turns *everything* off.

- ✔ **The subpanel** is wired to the main panel and contains the breakers that fuse each circuit in the home. Did you ever wonder why there are so many breakers in an electric panel? The answer is easy. When a circuit gets overloaded, it doesn't shut down power to the entire house but only the items connected to that circuit. Also, determining the reason for the overload is quicker and easier when only a few outlets are connected to a given circuit.

In some instances, there is no subpanel. In these cases, all the breakers are contained in the main panel. When the main panel also houses all the circuit breakers, it is known as a "combo" (combination main and subpanel). Small panels such as those mounted near air conditioners and heat pumps contain individual fuses dedicated only to the specific appliance.

In larger homes it is often wise to separate the main and the subpanel. Remember, every circuit must eventually end up at the subpanel. By adding one or more subpanels, the *home runs* (wires that run from the last receptacle in a circuit back to the panel) are reduced in length. Larger homes can have three or four subpanels.

A proper ground may save you from losing your footing

The wiring in your home may not be grounded. The results can be shocking. When a short occurs, the current travels toward the best conductor. Water is a super conductor, and your body is full of water. In many instances, the ground wire, in a grounded circuit, will absorb enough of the current to leave you standing.

Upgrading a receptacle by adding a ground is easy.

1. **Remove the cover and replace the old two-prong receptacle with a new three-prong grounded model.**

2. **Reattach the black and white wires to the receptacle.**

3. **Slip a new, bare copper ground wire into the box and connect it to the ground lug on the receptacle.**

   If you are doing an addition, you can connect the other end of the ground to any ground wire in the newly added system. If no new system exists, then simply connect the other end of the wire to a water or gas line. Special connectors are made for this purpose. No, the gas line won't blow up.

The main electric panel will have to be grounded as well. This can cost several hundred dollars. So be prepared because most building departments require an upgrade to a grounded service — regardless of what size it is.

The lazy way to upgrade a non-grounded circuit is to replace the old two-prong receptacle with a GFCI receptacle (covered later in this chapter).

Get to know the Ground Fault Circuit Interrupter (GFCI)

An electrical short occurs when a pair of hot (electrified) wires come into contact with each other. When electric current is allowed to flow through a path other than the one that it was originally intended to follow, it, in essence, takes a shortcut — thus the term "short." Worn out wire casings, cuts, and other damage to the wire insulation are just a few of the causes. When a short occurs, current overloads in the circuit causing immediate overheating in the wiring. What usually follows is a blown fuse (or tripped breaker).

When a hot lead touches a ground source such as a grounded appliance motor housing, a ground wire, or some other grounded device, the resultant condition is known as a *ground fault*. In this case, the current is redirected from the hot wire to the ground. This is because the ground has less resistance to electricity and therefore becomes an easier path for the electricity to follow. It is safer for us to use an appliance or tool that is grounded. When a short occurs, hopefully, the electricity will travel in the direction of the ground instead of our body.

Theoretically, when a ground fault occurs, the electricity is supposed to travel via the ground wire to the ground source — not through the body. This theory is valid to some extent. However, if moisture is present, the facts change. Water is the world's best-known ground source. And water makes it easier for electricity to pass through the body. When wet, people actually become a better ground than the ground wire in a three-wire circuit. This is why the Ground Fault Circuit Interrupter (GFCI) was developed. Normally, there is an equal balance between the current that travels in both the black hot lead and the white neutral lead. When a short or ground fault occurs, an imbalance results that can be detected. When this happens, a message is sent to the GFCI and it is tripped in one fortieth of a second — a short enough period of time so that most healthy persons would not be injured.

In the home, one of the safety features that many of us take for granted is the GFCI. Now you can see how important they really can be.

You can find three kinds of GFCI devices:

- ✔ **The plug-in type** is easiest to install and very portable. This makes it great for use in the garage and outside.

- ✔ **The built-in outlet type** guarantees that the GFCI protection will be used at that location. One is shown in Figure 24-3.

- ✔ **The breaker type,** which is installed into the breaker panel, can be used to protect an entire series of receptacles.

GFCI protection should be provided at all receptacles within 4 feet of a sink (or other water source), at all exterior and garage receptacles, and at all electric fixtures (lights, fans, and so on) over showers and tubs.

The average GFCI receptacle in a subdivision home is rated at 15 amps. Two hair dryers plugged into the same circuit will trip a GFCI breaker. The tendency is to remove the receptacle and replace it with a non-GFCI type. Don't do it. Spend $75 to $200 with an electrician and have the circuit upgraded to meet the demand you are putting on it. Removal of this safety device is just not worth the danger it poses to your loved ones. And have a happy holiday.

Figure 24-3:
An outlet with GFCI protection.

Considerations for kitchens

If you plan on doing a kitchen remodel, then prepare for some big time electrical upgrades. The kitchen uses more electrical power than any room in the home. That is, unless you have an arc welding shop in the garage. Today, you must provide a *dedicated* circuit to every built-in appliance in the kitchen. Disposal, dishwasher, instant hot water dispenser, compactor, microwave, you name it. If it is to be built in, it must have its own circuit. No, a dedicated circuit is not necessarily loyal. A dedicated circuit is one where a single appliance is wired to a single breaker. The circuit is "dedicated" to that appliance. Nothing else can be connected to a dedicated circuit except the appliance for which it is intended.

If you have a countertop microwave or a free-standing dishwasher and intend to build them in, then plan on adding two, new, dedicated circuits. One for each. We despise contractors who don't include electrical upgrades in their pricing. They know very well that the work will have to be done, but they don't advise their clients in advance to expect the extra cost. Cheaping out on the electrical system in a kitchen is a serious mistake. If you are selling your home, a prospective buyer carefully studies two areas of your house before making that all-important decision to plunk down a deposit: The master suite is one, and the kitchen is the other.

Chapter 25

Insulation

- ▶ Understanding the benefits of insulation
- ▶ Knowing what insulating materials are available
- ▶ Finding out where to insulate
- ▶ Reducing drafts
- ▶ Adding insulation for sound absorption

*W*hen one of your little ones is cold, chances are, you wrap the child in a blanket. What you may not know is that you can do the same thing for your home. We don't suggest that you commission Grandma to create the world's biggest quilt. Actually, the blanket we recommend is home insulation. And, in fact, the insulation doesn't need to be a blanket at all. Insulation comes in many forms.

Insulation has an unusual and unique characteristic. In addition to keeping you warm when it is chilly outdoors, it also helps prevent you from sweltering when temperatures rise. This may come as a surprise, but the same cold air that chills your bones also warms you up when combined with insulation. Here's how it works: Insulation is nothing more than a lightweight material filled with hundreds of thousands of tiny air pockets. Each pocket traps a small portion of air and holds it motionless. Motionless air is a dynamite insulator. Isn't that interesting?

You can increase the comfort of your home while reducing your heating and cooling needs by up to 30 percent by investing just a few hundred dollars in proper insulation and weatherization products.

Three's Company

You reap three major benefits when you insulate your home — comfort, energy savings, and improved value. And who can't stand to have a little more of each of these precious benefits?

Most people insulate their home to make it more comfortable. Studies show that drafts and air currents strongly affect our bodies' comfort. A well-insulated and weather-stripped home is comfortable with an inside temperature of 65 to 68 degrees Fahrenheit during the winter. Interestingly, the same home, poorly insulated, requires an inside temperature that is at least 3 degrees higher to maintain the same level of comfort under the same weather conditions.

A well-insulated home is an energy-efficient home. What's more, an energy-efficient home is good for both the environment and your pocketbook. It helps our environment by diminishing our dependence on fossil fuels used to heat and cool our homes. Consequently, it helps our pocketbooks by lowering our utility bills. Less demand equals big savings in energy _and_ money.

There's another bonus: Insulation is one of the few home improvements that is completely politically correct. Think about it. Liberals are in favor of insulation because it's good for the environment. Conservatives are behind insulation because it's easy on the pocketbook.

We've decided that if we ever run for public office, we'll run on the insulation platform. A chicken in every pot, insulation in every home! We can't lose!

View each and every proposed remodeling project with resale in mind. The best remodeling projects are those that improve your lifestyle and pay big dividends when it comes time to sell. Using these criteria, insulation ranks high on the list. Remodeling industry analysts report that an attic insulated to minimum levels in a given area will, at resale, yield 200 percent the cost of a do-it-yourself job.

To Insulate or Not to Insulate

Most home insulation appears in four areas — attic/ceiling, walls, crawl space/floor, and the basement. One of the most prudent and least costly times to install insulation in any of these areas is during a remodeling project. Often, wall, ceiling, and floor areas will be exposed, making the installation process significantly easier and hence, less expensive.

Should you insulate your home? Although building codes will dictate minimum levels of insulation for new construction, older homes have no such requirements. Thus, the decision ultimately is your own.

✔ Do you have an older home and haven't added insulation? In a recent survey, only 20 percent of homes built before 1980 were well-insulated.

✔ Are you uncomfortably cold in the winter or hot in the summer? Adding insulation creates a more uniform temperature and increases comfort.

✔ Are you adding on or installing new siding or roofing?

✔ Are your energy bills excessive?

✔ Are you bothered by noise from the outdoors? Insulation helps to muffle sound.

✔ Are you concerned about the effect of energy use on the environment?

If you answered yes to one or more of the preceding questions, your home may be a perfect candidate for an insulation upgrade. You be the judge.

Many local utility companies perform free home-energy audits. This test uses infrared technology to reveal locations throughout the home where energy may be wasted.

Insulation R Us

The efficiency of insulation is expressed as an R-value. R stands for resistance to heat loss and heat gain. A higher R-value means more resistance to heat loss and, again, that is more insulation. Keep in mind that with insulation, more is better. You can't use too much.

However, there is a point of diminishing return: Insulation loses its effectiveness when compacted. Thus, if you believe that you are improving energy efficiency by cramming R-19 into a wall designed to accept a maximum of R-13, you could actually end up with about R-5. In moderate climates R-38 is more than enough in the attic. However, in extreme climates R-60 makes more sense.

The U.S. Department of Energy (DOE) recommends ranges of R-values based on local heating and cooling costs and climate conditions in different areas of the nation. Figure 25-1 shows a map of the eight climate zones in the United States as designated by the DOE. Table 25-1 shows the DOE R-value recommendations for each climate zone. State and local codes in some parts of the country may require lower R-values than the DOE recommendations, which are based on cost-effectiveness.

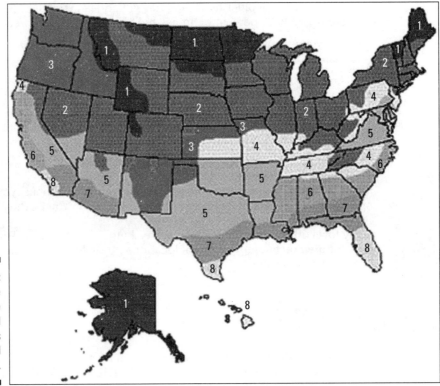

Figure 25-1:
The climate
zones of the
United
States as
designated
by the DOE.

Table 25-1			DOE Recommended R-Values					
	Ceilings below Ventilated Attics		Floors over Unheated Crawl Spaces, Basements		Exterior Walls (Wood Frame)		Crawl Space Walls	
Insulation Zone	Gas, Oil, or Heat Pump	Electric	Gas, Oil, or Heat Pump	Electric	Gas, Oil, or Heat Pump	Electric	Gas, Oil, or Heat Pump	Electric
1	49	49	19	19	11	11	19	19
2	38	49	19	19	11	11	19	19
3	38	38	19	19	11	11	19	19
4	38	38	19	19	11	11	19	19
5	30	38	19	19	11	11	19	19
6	30	38	–	19	11	11	19	19
7	30	30	–	–	11	11	19	19
8	19	30	–	–	–	11	11	11

Insulation: Not Just Another Blanket

You may already have discovered that insulation is available in a variety of forms — especially if you or your remodeler have torn out a wall or pulled down a ceiling. Chances are the insulation in the wall was a blanket while the attic insulation came down on your heads like snowflakes.

Although there are many types of materials used to manufacture insulation, the four most widely used include fiberglass, cellulose, rock wool, and rigid foam. Fiberglass usually is available in rolls, blankets, batts, or loose fill. Rock wool (also referred to as "mineral wool") is most commonly found in loose-fill form. Cellulose is exclusively a loose-fill insulation. Rigid insulation is produced in boards or panels that are nailed, stapled, or glued in place.

Each type is made to fit in a different part of your house. Batts fit between the studs in your walls or between the joists of your ceilings or floors. Blankets can be laid over the floor in the attic, while loose-fill insulation is blown into the attic or walls.

Fiberglass

Fiberglass, also known as "glass wool" or "spun glass" is regarded as among the most versatile insulation material available. The material consists of sand and recycled glass and generally is either yellow or pink. Its uses are almost infinite. Aside from being found in attics, walls, and crawl spaces, you can find fiberglass used in the manufacture of water heaters, automobiles, refrigerators, automatic dishwashers, and wherever one wishes to insulate from heat, cold, or sound. Economy is another reason for its popularity. Fiberglass is among the least costly choices.

Fiberglass is non-flammable and resists damage from water. The fibers can irritate your skin; therefore, precautions must be taken while handling. Gloves, breathing apparatus, protective clothing, goggles, and a hat can reduce an itchy aftermath. A cold shower can remove tiny fibers that make their way to your skin. Be careful — a hot shower opens the pores of your skin and allows the pesky fibers more opportunity to make you uncomfortable.

Cellulose fiber

Cellulose fiber is essentially recycled newspaper that is chemically treated with borax or aluminum sulfate powders to make it less attractive to insects and to enhance fire resistance. In addition, the chemicals help the material travel through the blower hoses that are used in the installation process.

Cellulose fiber insulation is generally used for horizontal applications such as an attic; however, the product is being manufactured with a special adhesive that allows for its use on vertical applications such as walls.

To its credit, cellulose fiber has a moderately better insulation value than its blown fiberglass counterpart, and it's a bit less pricey. Unfortunately, although chemically treated, it is not totally insect-resistant and can be a sponge when it comes in contact with moisture. Moreover, we have yet to hear of cellulose fiber insulation that isn't subject to rapid deterioration when wet.

Rock wool

Rock wool, or mineral wool, is very similar to fiberglass insulation. This material is a little more expensive, but doesn't usually provoke the itchy reaction that fiberglass causes. Rock wool is made from basaltic rock (there's a term that goes back to high school geology) and recycled material from steel mill wastes. It looks a great deal like lint from a dryer and can be equally dusty when handled. Rock wool is typically used for attics — blown in like fiberglass or cellulose fiber. It is also available in bags that allow it to be poured into place.

Unfortunately, as with cellulose fiber, rock wool can cake when wet and naturally settles over time, both of which diminish its insulating value.

Rigid foam

Rigid foam boards are made of polyisocyanurate (try saying that three times fast), extruded polystyrene (XPS or blueboard), expanded polystyrene (EPS or beadboard), or other materials. These boards are lightweight, provide structural support, and generally have an R-value of 4 to 7 per inch. Rigid board insulation is made to be used in confined spaces such as exterior walls, basements, foundation and stem walls, concrete slabs, cathedral ceilings, and below roofing.

Where to Insulate

The next few sections tell you how and where to insulate your home. Some people think that a little insulation in the attic or blowing a bit of insulation in the walls will solve all their energy and comfort problems. WRONG! If you are really serious about eliminating drafts, improving comfort, lowering your utility bills, and saving energy, you will insulate every area of your home that can be insulated and bring already-insulated areas up to snuff. The attic, walls, and floor (where a crawl space or basement exist) are the three primary areas that should be insulated. Doing one without the others is like putting on an overcoat without buttons.

Insulating the attic

The easiest and most cost-effective means of insulating your home is to increase the insulation in the attic. To determine if your home contains enough attic insulation, measure the thickness of the existing insulation. If there is less than R-19 (6 inches of fiberglass or rock wool or 5 inches of cellulose) you can likely benefit by adding more. According to the U.S. Department of Energy (DOE), most homes should have R-38 insulation in the attic.

You can add insulation to the attic in several ways. Blow loose-fill insulation into the attic, pour rock wool over the existing material, or lay fiberglass batts or blankets over the existing insulation.

When choosing batt or blanket insulation you will find that some material contains a kraft paper or foil facing. This facing acts as a vapor barrier to prevent moisture from passing through the insulation and collecting inside walls, ceilings, and floors.

A general rule when installing a vapor barrier is to always put the vapor barrier toward the warm-in-winter side. Under no circumstances should a vapor barrier be installed over existing insulation in an attic. When adding insulation, use unfaced material. If unfaced material is not readily available, you can use the faced type — provided you remove the paper or foil.

By not following this "warm-in-winter" rule and installing a vapor barrier where it doesn't belong, you can create conditions that can result in some serious moisture problems. Keep in mind that insulation must breathe in order to be effective. Thus, a vapor barrier on the cold-in-winter side will prevent free ventilation that, in turn, will allow condensation to collect. This condensation will cause the insulation to become damp and, thus, anything that it comes into contact with such as wood framing and drywall or plaster. The result is mildew, fungus, and rot.

Ventilation plays a key role in determining whether or not a vapor barrier is necessary. If a crawl space or attic is properly ventilated, a vapor barrier may not be necessary. If attics and crawl spaces are not properly ventilated, problems with moisture are likely to develop. Eave vents — openings under the eaves — combined with roof vents or gable vents are effective ways to create a positive movement of air out of the attic.

When installing insulation, be certain not to cover vents. Consequently, insulation should be held back from vents about 4 to 6 inches. This works especially well with batt insulation because once it is in place, it almost takes an act of God to move it. However, this is not the case with blown insulation (such as in attics). A strong gust of wind through the attic can cause the insulation to block eave vents. Therefore, it is a good idea to install baffles at all eave vent locations. Although insulation baffles can be made of cardboard (gourmet dining for insects), we suggest that you use manufactured baffles that can be found at most places that sell or install insulation. In either case, the baffle acts as a dam of sorts to prevent the insulation from blocking the eave vent. Nifty contraption!

Insulating walls

If your investigation reveals that there is plenty of insulation in the attic, but your home still feels drafty and cold in the winter or too warm during the summer, there's a good chance that you need to add insulation to the exterior walls of your home.

Insulating existing walls is more complicated and, consequently, more expensive than adding insulation to an attic. Thus, most people hire a professional to tackle this job. The added cost is well spent if you live in a very hot or cold climate.

Aside from the labor, part of what makes the job of blowing insulation into existing exterior walls difficult is the need to drill holes into the exterior siding or stucco. Holes get drilled at each stud bay (typically at 16-inch centers) into which the blower nozzle is inserted. If wood blocking exists at mid-stud, two holes must be drilled into each bay — above and below the block.

Unfortunately, many pros and do-it-yourselfers (who attempt to retrofit insulation at exterior walls) make one common mistake that negates any potential value improvement. They do a poor job of patching the hole in the exterior skin of the building, and the patch stands out like a sore thumb. Therefore, when hiring a professional to perform this service, make sure that the contract stipulates the method that will be used to patch access holes. If plastic plugs are specified, run the other way.

Holes in stucco siding should be patched using a portland cement, stucco patching compound tooled to match the existing finish. Holes in wood siding should be filled with a wood plug and sanded or filled with an epoxy wood-patching compound that will bond with the existing material.

If your home's exterior is brick, stone, or vinyl or aluminum siding, the insulation should be installed either by drilling a hole in the top of the wall in the attic or by drilling holes in the interior drywall or plaster. Here again, pay special attention to ensure that patches are made to match existing finishes as closely as possible.

Insulating floors

Cold floors are a major complaint among owners of homes built before 1973. Prior to that time, insulation was not required in the floors of new construction.

The U.S. Department of Energy recommends R-19 insulation for floors over unheated crawl spaces or basements in most homes. Installing floor insulation can be quite tricky, especially if your crawl space is relatively shallow. If you suffer from claustrophobia, arachnophobia, or insulaphobia (we made that one up), this is a job best left to someone else.

In contrast to adding insulation to the attic, the floor is a location where you will want to use kraft- or foil-faced batt insulation. Keep in mind, the vapor barrier is installed toward the warm-in-winter side. Thus, the paper would face the underside of the subfloor.

Curing Air Infiltration: A Little Can Go a Long Way

Insulating floors, walls, and attics can go a long way in solving your personal comfort and energy crisis. However, there are other steps that you may need to take to make your home a real peak performer. *Air infiltration* is a fancy way of describing drafts — the drafts that make their way in through cracks around windows, doors, pipes, and electrical switches and outlets. The best way to deal with drafts around windows and doors is to caulk around interior and exterior window and door trim. Another excellent means of cutting down on drafts is to weatherstrip doors and windows. An adjustable door bottom (door shoe) can make all the difference in cutting off the draft at the base of exterior doors. Just think, no more towels at the bottom of your doors.

A great way to cut drafts in your home is to install foam gaskets at all electrical switches and outlets. The foam gaskets are manufactured to size with the proper cutouts and cost less than 25 cents each. The best part is installation — it's easy. All you need is a screwdriver and about two minutes for each outlet. Simply remove the switch or outlet cover plate, place the gasket over the plug or switch, and reinstall the cover plate. It's that simple.

Insulation: A "Sound" Investment

Insulation can improve comfort by affecting another of your senses. You are well aware of the benefits when it comes to feeling, but are you aware of the benefit it has on your hearing? No, insulation won't improve your hearing; indeed, it will cause you to hear less — less of the things that you don't want to hear, such as the flush of a toilet, the pitter patter of feet from the room above, or tunes emanating from the boom box in your teenager's bedroom.

Wall soundproofing in frame construction is usually accomplished by insulating with $3^1/_2$-inch unfaced fiberglass insulation and installing resilient channel perpendicular to the framing. Wallboard is then applied directly to the resilient channel using drywall screws. This same detail holds true when creating a sound-resistant floor. Thicker and more layers of wallboard also help control sound.

Chapter 26

Drywall

● ●

In This Chapter

▶ Deciphering drywall jargon

▶ Knowing what's involved in drywall installation

▶ Understanding how drywall can reduce noise

● ●

*O*kay, time for a construction quiz. Here's how it works: We describe a construction material and you try to guess what it is. No cheating!

Here's your clue. You paint it, wallpaper it, drive nails and screws into it, use the infamous "molly screw" in it, and occasionally patch holes in it. Give up?

Is the material in question (a) gypsum, (b) plasterboard, (c) gypboard, (d) drywall, or (e) wallboard?

(Hum *Jeopardy* jingle here.) Time's up!

If you guessed a, you are right. As a matter of fact, had you guessed b, c, d or e, you would have also been correct. Don't you just hate those trick questions?

Actually, each of the terms is an accurate description of the most common names for the material that can be found as an interior wall finish in most homes built since the 1950s. However, when all is said and done, the appropriate industry term is *drywall*. Let's all say it together — drywall. There, now that wasn't so hard after all.

The drywall phase of a remodel can be one of the most exciting times during a project. The drywall conceals a maze of studs, plumbing pipes, electrical wiring, and mechanical apparatus with a uniform and uncomplicated surface. It is during this time that rooms begin to take shape and most people are able to visualize what previously was only a dream.

The excitement around this time must be tempered with the reality that, in most cases, a remodeling project moves at a pretty good pace until the drywall is installed, at which time things begin to slow until the job is complete. This is because finishes such as trim, paint, cabinets, counters, and flooring are, by nature, more time-consuming than "rough" work. But don't be discouraged. The frustration that you may feel will be temporary and will be all but forgotten as you experience all of the beautiful pieces of your dream come together.

What Is Drywall and Why Did It Replace Plaster?

Drywall is made of gypsum, a material that has been used in construction for thousands of years. What makes gypsum so popular as a construction material? Relatively speaking, it is durable, inexpensive, and user-friendly. We like user-friendly.

In the 1940s and '50s, gypsum drywall replaced plaster as the material of choice for interior wall cover. Until that time, most American homes had a portland cement plaster that was painstakingly hand-troweled onto wood slats (lathing) nailed to the wall and ceiling framing. Our grandfather used redwood lath and plaster as the interior wall covering in our old family home he built circa 1910.

Plaster is still an excellent wall covering but is no longer practical because it is so labor intense and hence, far more costly than drywall. Cost aside, there are other advantages to using drywall as an interior wall covering.

For example, in order to achieve a high quality, finished product, a skilled technician must apply plaster. On the contrary, professional hangers, carpenters, or a well-prepared do-it-yourselfer can hang drywall. Plaster is one of the last tasks that we suggest a do-it-yourselfer attempt.

Moreover, plaster leaves a building saturated with moisture which must first evaporate before painting or trim work can begin. Drywall requires far less moisture for application. Thus the name — drywall. The wall is covered with a dry material that can be finished shortly after application is complete.

Drywall can be more fire resistant than comparable building materials, depending upon its thickness, and can also act as an excellent means of controlling sound due to its high density.

Run-of-the-mill drywall is sold in sheets that are four feet wide, eight feet long and one-half inch thick. You can also get 10-, 12-, 14-, and whopping 16-foot lengths. Can you imagine trying to hang a sheet of drywall that is 4 feet high and 16 feet long? Definitely not a one-person project.

Ashes to ashes, gypsum to drywall

The familiar white boards that we have come to know and love, which can be found at almost any home center, didn't just appear. We all know that lumber comes from trees, but many of us don't know that gypsum comes from the ground. The mother of all manufacturers, Mother Nature, manufactures it.

Gypsum is a mineral consisting of hydrous calcium sulfate — whatever that is. Interestingly, it can be found in virtually every part of the world. It is mined and in its purest form is white, though in the earth, it can be gray, brown or sometimes pink. The color comes from impurities in the earth such as iron oxides and clay.

After the gypsum is mined, it is pulverized and heated to about 350 degrees Fahrenheit to eliminate almost all moisture. What remains is a dry powder (it looks like coarse flour), which is combined with aggregates, fibers, and other additives to add strength and moisture resistance.

To complete the process, water is added to this concoction to enable it to be molded and shaped into the desired form: more often than not, a flat sheet of uniform thickness. These sheets consist of the gypsum core between two layers of paper. When dry, the mixture turns into a rock-hard mass that, on occasion, is the beneficiary of a shoe, fist, head, or various other body part. Thank God for patching compound.

The biggest sheet that we can remember hanging was 4 by 12, and that was quite a challenge. Unfortunately, we've been known to make better use of our backs than our heads. Consequently, at the end of a day of hanging drywall, we discovered muscles we didn't even know we had.

You want thick? Take your pick!

In addition to the $^1/_2$-inch thickness, there are five other standard thicknesses: $^1/_4$-inch, $^5/_{16}$-inch, $^3/_8$-inch, $^5/_8$-inch and 1-inch. Although the two most commonly used thicknesses in construction are $^1/_2$-inch and $^5/_8$-inch, you may find it useful to know how the various other thicknesses are used since they are frequently used in remodeling.

- ✔ **$^1/_4$-inch:** This, the thinnest type of drywall, is used primarily as a covering over an existing finish such as plaster, paneling, or even drywall. It is especially useful in covering a blemished surface that would otherwise be difficult to remove. You can use $^1/_4$-inch drywall in combination with other material or in multiple layers to create radius or curved walls and ceilings. It is not designed to be used as a single layer unless installed over a solid surface.

- ✔ **$^5/_{16}$-inch:** Rarely used in residential construction or remodeling, this material is reserved primarily in the construction of mobile homes due to its light weight. You can use it as a single layer provided the framing members are spaced accordingly.

✔ **³/₈-inch:** The thickness of this material makes it especially useful when remodeling a home that contains plaster as an interior wall covering. Two layers of ³/₈-inch drywall can be combined to plane into existing plaster that measures about ³/₄ inch. Sometimes, ³/₈-inch can be layered with ⁵/₁₆-inch to create a match for plaster that is slightly less than ³/₄-inch. The point is that one can use various thicknesses in combination to achieve a desired thickness.

✔ **¹/₂-inch:** This is the material that most of us are familiar with and it is, by far, the most widely used in residential construction and remodeling on walls and ceilings. This material can be installed in multiple layers to achieve greater fire resistance and to suppress sound.

✔ **⁵/₈-inch:** As with two layers of ¹/₂-inch drywall, this material provides increased fire resistance and sound deadening characteristics. Because it is thicker, it is less likely to sag and, thus, can be used on framing with greater spans.

✔ **1-inch:** Some thick stuff! These panels, known as *coreboard,* are available in two forms — as a single thickness or as two half-inch panels glued together. This material is typically used where solid drywall partitions are needed (generally commercial applications) or where a high fire rating is required. We can't recall ever having worked with 1-inch drywall.

One type of drywall that is steadily growing in popularity is gypsum lath or *blueboard.* It is used in lieu of traditional wood or metal lathing as the base for skimmed plaster on walls and ceilings. Gypsum lath consists of a gypsum core covered with rough paper that creates a good bond with the plaster. This material acts as a cost-effective alternative for people with an appetite for plaster on a drywall budget.

Water and fire resistance

Drywall provides more than just a smooth and uniform surface on which to apply paint, paper, or other decoration. With special construction, it can protect your home from damage by fire or water — two of the biggest threats to any home.

Fire-resistant drywall

Where the possibility of fire is a concern, such as the wall between an attached garage and living space, the Uniform Building Code (UBC) requires a "one-hour" firewall. In theory, this configuration will hold off fire for up to 60 minutes by using one layer of ⁵/₈-inch Type X drywall. Although Type X drywall resembles standard drywall, its core contains glass fibers that give it the fire resistant characteristics. Type X comes in two thicknesses — ¹/₂-inch and ⁵/₈-inch — and is clearly stamped "Fire-Resistant" or "Type X" on the back of each panel.

Water-resistant drywall

When moisture resistance is a concern, such as in a bathroom, kitchen, or laundry, water-resistant (WR) panels should be used. This brand of drywall is frequently referred to as *greenboard* due to its light green facing paper. Both the paper covering and the core material used in the fabrication of WR drywall are said to be water-resistant. We believe that this is stretching it a bit — to say the least.

It is our experience that WR drywall provides marginal protection to any surface (other than itself) from excessive moisture. We have had the unfortunate displeasure of tearing out countless shower and bathtub walls that fell prey to water damage when they were alleged to be "water-resistant."

The most offensive use of this material is where tile is glued directly to the panels. This poorly designed detail is one of the best examples of planned obsolescence that can be found in residential construction. Water-resistant drywall is a remodeling contractor's dream. He knows that he can look forward to repeat business three to five years down the road by having to tear out tile, drywall, framing, and perhaps even flooring and siding in order to put this Humpty-Dumpty bathroom back together again.

Water-resistant drywall might be fine for moisture-prone areas where the biggest threat is steam in the air. However, it offers little or no real protection from exposure to water — such as that in a tub or shower. Thus, whenever a contractor suggests installing tile directly over drywall, run the other way. The contractor that insists on installing tile in a bed of mortar is the sign of a real pro.

Hanging Drywall

Once you have chosen the appropriate drywall for the job, the next step is to install it. In the industry it is known as *hangin' the board*. Paneling is *installed* but drywall is *hung* — go figure.

The tools you need

There are two primary devices used to fasten drywall to the framing: nails or drywall screws. We prefer drywall screws for a variety of reasons, the foremost of which is damage control. Using a hammer to pound a nail into a wall consisting of aged, dry framing can crack plaster, pop existing drywall nails, and knock tile off nearby walls and ceilings. This chaos can be avoided by simply using drywall screws and an electric screw gun.

Drywall screws also go in easier, hold tighter (350 percent more holding power than nails), and don't work loose like drywall nails do when the wood framing dries out. What's more, it takes fewer screws than nails to hang a board because the screws can be spaced farther apart.

Some of the basic tools for hanging drywall include a utility knife with a battery of sharp blades, a pencil, and a measuring tape. A hammer or an electric screw gun will also come in handy depending upon the method of attachment you choose. If you decide to use a hammer, a drywall hammer is your best choice. It looks a lot like a hatchet and has a round, oversized, slightly convex face that leaves a dimple in the drywall when driving a nail. The dimple will be filled with drywall joint compound to conceal the nail head during the finish phase of the process. The hatchet blade, which isn't sharp, is used for wedging and prying.

Depending upon the complexity of the job, other tools that may come in handy include a chalk box, framing square, T square, key hole saw, saber saw, and a router.

How things go together

Essentially, drywall is hung like a puzzle is put together. In most cases, the panels are installed with the long side running horizontally — perpendicular to the wall studs. The ceiling panels are installed perpendicular to the ceiling joist. If the wall or ceiling is framed with proper spacing, (typically 16 inches or 24 inches on center) the end of each panel should align with the center of a stud or joist. Thus, there will be ample bearing for fastening with nails or screws. In addition, joints are also staggered to provide maximum strength and to prevent cracks at joints.

There is a definite method to the madness of hanging drywall. Ceiling material hangs first and wall material follows. The primary reason for this order is to make a super neat corner configuration, which makes the finishing job easier. This order also makes the wall panels cover the entire wall down to the floor, leaving only a small gap — otherwise a larger gap would exist.

Since most homes have 8-foot ceilings, two panels (one above the other) cover the wall from floor to ceiling. What do you do if the ceiling is greater than 8 feet high? Here's what the pros do: Rather than hanging two full sheets high and adding a partial strip at the bottom, they hang the strip in the center of the wall with one full sheet above and one below. This places the joints at a comfortable working height for fastening and finishing. This technique reduces the need to bend over and thus saves time, money, and back pain.

Hanging the board is as simple as measuring the required length, transferring the measurement to the panel, cutting the panel with a razor knife, and snapping the panel in both directions for a nice, even edge. Special care should be taken to measure for and mark electrical boxes, pipes, and other penetrations that will require cutouts to be made in the panels. These cutouts can be made using a drywall saw, jigsaw, or router.

The trim

After the board is hung, but before the joint compound is applied, corner trim (called *corner bead*) must be installed at outside corners. Corner trim is designed to provide a straight, smooth, and uniform corner. In addition, it protects the corner from future damage.

There are essentially two types of corner styles — square and radius (called *bullnose*). The corner bead for square corners is made of rigid galvanized steel. There is also a *taped metal corner* wherein the metal is encased in thick paper and embedded with joint compound.

The second style, a bullnose corner, is becoming increasingly popular as people are looking for methods of making their homes look less mainstream. The bullnose corner provides a soft, less structured look and can act as a significant architectural element to a home's interior. As with square corner material, bullnose corners can be metal, taped metal, or even plastic.

Bear in mind, bullnose corners are considered an upgrade because they require more labor and, hence, add to the bottom line.

The finish

In the final analysis, when it comes to drywall, it all boils down to the finish. After all, the finish is the part that everyone sees. The finish is what makes the pieces of the puzzle come together. It is what makes drywall look like a wall. There are three steps to the finishing process: taping, topping, and texture.

Taping and topping

Taping is done using joint tape and drywall joint compound. The tape is made of paper of a fiberglass mesh and is wide enough to easily cover the joints. The tape is embedded with a coat of drywall joint compound. Appropriately, the first coat is called the *embedding coat*.

Professionals apply joint tape with a tool called a *bazooka*. It's a nifty mechanical tool that dispenses tape and joint compound at the same time. It makes the job a heck of a lot easier and renders far more professional results. Do-it-yourselfers use a 10-inch drywall taping knife, joint compound, and something to hold the compound in — a trough.

Once the initial coat of joint compound has dried (typically overnight, depending upon temperature and humidity), at least two successive coats (called *skim coats*) are also applied, which transform the surface into something more uniform and monolithic. Each coat is about two inches wider than the previous coat to make the joints less noticeable.

Texture

Wall texture is designed to hide blemishes and imperfections in the surface. Texture is to drywall what peaches and cream are to one's completion — it can make or break the appearance of a wall or ceiling. When it comes to selecting a wall finish, there are two basic types and within which there are several styles.

The two basic types of finish are textured and smooth. If you opt for a textured finish, be prepared to choose between a heavy, medium, or light application. Texture can be applied by hand with a taping knife, sponge, or paint roller. It can also be sprayed on for a completely different look.

A smooth finish is, as the name implies, smooth. Thus, no texture is applied. Some rooms need a smooth finish while others look best textured. The kitchen, bathrooms, and laundry room are most suited for a smooth or stipple finish. A stipple finish is often referred to as an *orange peel* finish due to its striking resemblance to a skin of an orange. Walls and ceilings must be left smooth for a stipple finish, as the stipple application is a paint process, and not a function of drywall.

Why smooth finishes in these rooms? Smooth walls and ceilings are less likely to collect the airborne dust and dirt that these high-traffic rooms are generally subject to. Also, ease of cleaning is an issue. A smooth wall is substantially easier to scrub than a textured one.

There are two types of smooth wall finish: smooth for paint and smooth for wallpaper. Smooth wall for paint is the more expensive of the two because it requires hours upon hours of work eliminating the slightest imperfections. Wall finish that is smooth for paper doesn't require the same level of detail but is more complex than a textured finish.

When preparing to install wallpaper, unpainted drywall or latex-coated surfaces should be painted with an oil-base primer/sealer. The oil-base primer will seal the walls and minimize the amount of moisture absorbed by the drywall from the paste. Thus, the wallpaper is more manageable, easier to install, and is substantially easier to remove at a later date.

When you want the finished surface to look like a plaster wall, choose a trowel finish. There are several variations to choose from. You can vary the depth of the texture coat and the amount of troweling done. You can use a very light texturing compound or a heavy one.

If you prefer a surface treatment that is similar to a trowel finish but with more random texture, use skip-troweling. Skip-troweling is also known as skip-texturing or a brocade finish. It is one of the most common hand finishes.

Spray texture is the most widely used method today. Its popularity, like many other aspects of construction, has more to do with the bottom line that its appearance. It is a more expedient process that requires less labor and is, therefore, not as costly as hand-applied finishes.

Texture material is blown onto the walls or ceiling through a nozzle attached to a hose supplied with compressed air. The texture, applied in varying degrees of intensity, can be *knocked-down* or flattened slightly using a trowel or taping knife depending upon the desired affect.

Drywall: Helping to Keep the Peace

Privacy: It's a condition that's becoming more rare around many homes. Sometimes the disturbing noise comes from your teenager's stereo in the next bedroom. Other times the noise comes from the teenager's stereo in the bedroom in the home that is attached to yours by a wall, ceiling, or floor. Heaven forbid!

In the days when the interior walls of most homes were constructed of large studs, covered with wood lath and several layers of plaster, noise was less of an issue. As you can see in Figure 26-1, the walls and floors prevent the sound waves from moving from room to room. However, the interior walls in most modern homes consist of nothing more than a two by four stud (the 4-inch side actually measures $3^1/_2$ inches) covered with one layer of $^1/_2$ inch drywall on either side.

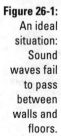

Figure 26-1:
An ideal situation: Sound waves fail to pass between walls and floors.

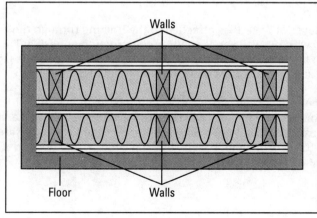

Controlling noise between floors

The worst condition of all has to be a two-story home or downstairs flat wherein you are painfully able to monitor each and every move above. The most effective solution to this problem is to increase the density of the material between floors. One of the simplest ways to do this is with a thicker carpet and pad upstairs.

If you've tried the thick carpet and pad trick, your best bet is to install a resilient channel (RC) along with a layer of $5/8$-inch drywall onto the ceiling downstairs. RC is a Z-shaped metal channel that is acoustically engineered to reduce vibration and, hence, the transfer of noise. It can be attached with drywall screws right over an existing drywall or plaster ceiling. The channel is applied in a direction perpendicular to the ceiling framing and should be screwed into the framing.

Keep in mind that light boxes, heat registers and other ceiling-mounted devices must be extended to align with the new ceiling surface. And, needless to say, the new drywall will need to be finished and painted.

Due to the complexity of this project, you may want to hire a professional drywall contractor. We are hard pressed to think of a task that requires more physical stamina than hanging those monstrous sheets of wallboard overhead. In this case, we suggest that you use your head instead of your back and call a professional.

Controlling noise between rooms

The solution for dealing with noise from room to room is similar to the one for floors. Again, the operative word is density — or thickness of the material separating the spaces. The addition of one layer of $5/8$-inch drywall can have a profound impact on noise reduction. Adding a layer to both sides of a wall can make it virtually soundproof.

The new layer of drywall is attached to the framing through the existing wallboard with drywall screws and/or construction adhesive. The drywall must then be finished and painted, paneled, or papered. Again, if you'd rather be sailing, then a drywall contractor can help.

As with the ceiling scenario, electrical outlets, switches, and other mechanical components and finishes will need to be extended. Electrical box extenders are inexpensive and are readily available at the local hardware store or home center. Crown mold, baseboard, and window and door trim may also need to be replaced.

Part VI
Interior Finishes and Final Touches

In this part . . .

So the walls are up, a roof is keeping out the rain, and you've got plumbing and electricity. Is the project done yet? Not by a long shot. You need to worry about the painting, the flooring, the final inspection, and even what to do before making your final payment. Don't worry though: We can get you through it.

Chapter 27
Painting: A Job for All Seasons

- -

In This Chapter

▶ Prepping for interior painting

▶ Buying the paint and tools

▶ Painting the interior

▶ Painting the exterior

▶ Cleaning up

▶ Storing your paint

- -

*P*ainting is the one home improvement project most people feel they can handle. For good reason: It doesn't involve any of the house's mechanical systems. You don't need power tools, and it seems simple to do. But the fact is, most people don't do a very good job.

Most folks go out to the nearest home center, pick up a gallon or two, grab the cheapest brush or roller they can find, drive home, and start painting. They forget to do the most important thing: prepare the surface to be painted. Does this sound like you?

Although paint and application tools are important, preparation is the real key to a beautiful, long-lasting paint job.

Paint is designed to be applied to a clean, smooth surface. Luckily, in most cases, getting to this ideal state requires simple preparation.

Preparing for Interior Painting

First, remove all the furniture, lamps, and knick-knacks from the room. Or, if you can't do that, remove anything that is irreplaceable or easily broken. Push whatever is left to the middle of the room and cover it completely with drop cloths. Don't be lazy — you don't want to break anything or get dust or paint on your stuff, and you're going to need as much clear space as you can get.

Also remove anything attached to the walls, including pictures, window treatments, and switch/outlet plates. (Put the screws and plates together in plastic bags.) Take off all the hardware from windows and doors. Cover radiators with newspaper. Loosen ceiling light fixtures and cover them with plastic trash bags. Cover every inch of the floor with canvas or heavy plastic drop cloths.

Then get to work: Wipe away fingerprints, crayon, pen marks, dirt, and dust from walls, trim, and doors with a spray cleaner and a damp cloth. Smooth out uneven, brushmarked, and bumpy walls by lightly sanding them with light-grit sandpaper.

Knock down the shine on glossy trim by lightly sanding it. Fill nail holes, cracks, and other imperfections in the walls and ceiling with patching compound (spackle), let dry, and then sand smooth.

Scrape any loose or flaking paint on windows and sills and then sand the bare areas. Fill gaps between the trim and the walls, especially along the baseboards, with caulk. Vacuum the room, including the windowsills and trim, to remove the sanding dust. Wipe down everything with a tack rag or barely damp cloth.

Prime any bare wood and all patched areas. Water stains and children's "murals" must be primed with a special sealer/primer to prevent bleed-through.

Got lead paint? Leave it alone!

The manufacture of lead-containing household paints has been banned since 1978. And production was restricted for five years before the ban. But millions of American homes — 40 million, according to the U.S. Environmental Protection Agency—contain at least some lead paint on their exterior and interior walls and trim.

There is no completely safe way for a do-it-yourselfer to remove lead paint. Sanding generates a cloud of lead dust that can hang in the air for years. Burning it off with a propane torch creates breathable lead vapor. An electric heat gun generates no dust but often leaves a hard-to-control pile of lead paint scrapings. Dry scraping results in a sprinkling of poisonous flakes and dust. Though chemical paint strippers create pernicious lead gunk, they are among the safest choices.

Because lead paints have been prohibited for more than 20 years, most lead-containing paint was long ago covered by fresh layers of non-lead-based paint. But if you buy an old house, or one that hasn't been painted in a very long time, follow these guidelines:

✔ When lead-suspicious paint is in good shape (or even pretty good shape), it's best to leave it undisturbed. If it's inside your house, seal it in with a new coat of non-lead-based paint. If it's outside, paint over it or cover it up with new siding.

✔ When suspect paint is widespread and chipping/peeling too badly to paint over (especially if it is inside the house), the least dangerous way to remove it is with a chemical paint remover. But ultimately, say the experts, the very best way to deal with this situation is to call in a lead-abatement specialist.

Interior paint-removal tools: Knives, guns, and strippers

Sounds like the plot for one of Hollywood's latest blockbusters! Seriously, most interior painting requires little paint removal. Unless your house is 90 years old, a putty knife and sandpaper will take care of any peeling spots.

But if you do own an old house, you could have 20 layers of paint on your walls and woodwork. Getting rid of the paint and finding the smooth, original wood will require more than a two-dollar putty knife and a twenty-cent piece of sandpaper.

✔ **Scrapers** come in a wide range of styles. Some are pushed; others are pulled. Some are designed for flat surfaces and others for moldings. Some have comfortable, ergonomic handles, and some do not. All require a great deal of what your grandmother called "elbow grease."

✔ **Propane torches** burn paint away. They allow for fast work but can char the wood you're trying to save and have the potential to start a fire. They're dangerous in the wrong hands.

✔ **Electric heat guns** soften thick paint so it can be scraped away. They're much slower but much safer than a propane torch, and they're cheaper on big jobs than chemical paint strippers.

✔ **Chemical paint strippers** also soften paint and allow it to be scraped off in sheets. They're fast (especially when large areas must be cleaned), but smelly, messy, and depending on the product, potentially hazardous. On the other hand, chemical paint strippers have come a long way. One such product that we are familiar with comes complete with a canvas-like fabric that is placed over the chemical stripper after it has been applied to the surface. The chemical compound dissolves the paint and the fabric absorbs the compound and the paint. The fabric is then peeled away, and with it can come a dozen or more layers of paint.

Primers

To most people, priming seems unnecessary. But it really does make the final paint job look better.

Here's why: When you patch a spot or scrape down to bare wood, you create a rough, porous area that absorbs more paint than the area around it. If you paint the spot without priming it, you'll end up with uneven gloss and an area that is a slightly different color than the surrounding wall.

And primer comes in handy as a first coat when you need to cover a much darker or lighter color. (And primer can be tinted to match!) Plus, primer creates a stronger bond between the paint and the wall, helps resist moisture, fills small cracks, and smoothes and seals the surface so that finish coats are more uniform and lustrous.

What should be primed? On the outside, bare wood and patched areas. On the inside, bare wood, patched areas, new drywall, new trim, strange dark marks that don't wash off, water stains, and places where kids have used crayons, markers, or pens.

 By the way, interior windows, trim, and doors that are already painted with enamel are okay to paint as is, although it would be a good idea to wipe them with a damp cloth and knock down the shine with some sandpaper or a liquid deglosser.

Which primer to use? It's probably best to use the same brand as the paint you will be using because manufacturers design their paints and primers as "coating systems." Be aware that some primers are specifically designed to seal in and prevent potential bleed-through and staining problems.

Oil-based primers are among the finest available. Keep in mind that latex can be applied over oil, but it is not recommended that oil be painted over latex because bubbling and peeling can result.

The bottom line: Check the label on the paint can — it'll tell you what to do. And if you're still confused, ask one of the experts at the paint store.

Scrub, scrub, and scrub

Kitchens and bathroom surfaces require all of the prep work mentioned in the previous sections plus something extra: a thorough washing beforehand.

You may not realize it, but your kitchen cabinets, fixtures, walls, and ceiling are covered with a micro-thin coating of grease and gummy dust. If you cook, it's there. And it needs to go before you do anything.

Bathroom walls get their own coating of crud, including hairspray, cleaning products, and stuck-on dust. All that stuff has to be washed away before painting.

In newer homes, a thorough wipe with a damp sponge and a mild detergent solution will do. In older homes, you may need to bring out the big gun: washing with a synthetic TSP solution. Short for trisodium phosphate, synthetic TSP cuts through grease and gunk like nothing else. When you're done, a bucketful of brown water will show you how well it works, how slimy your walls were, and how important it is to wash before painting. Remember to rinse the walls with clean water, as a leftover film of TSP prevents proper paint adhesion.

Synthetic TSP is more environmentally friendly than the TSP of yesteryear.

Buying Interior Paint and Painting Tools

These days, latex paints are the top choice for interiors, especially walls and ceilings. Here are their advantages:

- ✔ They're water-based, so soap-and-water clean-up is easy.
- ✔ They dry quickly.
- ✔ They are relatively odor-free (for paint).

Latex paints do have disadvantages, though:

- ✔ They dry so quickly that brushmarks and lapmarks are hard to avoid.
- ✔ On baseboards and trim, they do not stand up to scrapes and clunks as well as oil-based paints do.

But overall, the advantages far outweigh the disadvantages, particularly when you consider that latex paints contain no toxic solvents. In latex paint, the solvent is water.

Oil-based (alkyd) paints are the best choice for doors, trim, and damp areas such as a kitchen, bath, or laundry. They also have a few advantages:

- ✔ They dry slowly, so brushstrokes have time to smooth out and disappear.
- ✔ They dry to a very hard, durable finish.

Oil-based paints do have disadvantages as well:

✔ Clean-up requires solvents.

✔ As the paint dries, it releases volatile organic compounds (VOCs) into the air. The Environmental Protection Agency has limited the amount of VOCs that oil-based paint can contain, so it is safe to use. However, the low-VOC paints tend to dry far more slowly than their solvent-rich counterparts. Thus, the paint will be tacky and "vulnerable" for up to a couple of weeks after being applied.

In addition to latex and oil-based paints, there is a wide variety of specialty paints, including some for painting cement, brick, floors, and metal; and multi-color and textured paint for interesting, arty finishes.

Buy the highest-quality paint you can afford unless you like to paint. Poor quality paint means that you'll need at least two coats, and you'll have the chance to do it all over again in just a few years.

How much paint should you buy?

Get out your calculator! To figure the wall area of a rectangular room, measure the length and width of the room (rounding to the nearest foot), add the two numbers together, multiply that total by the room height, and then double the result. The formula: (L+W) x H x 2.

When a room is not a rectangle, you have to measure the height and width of each section, multiply to get the area of each, and then add them all together to get the square footage.

Trim paint has to be figured separately. For example, a door has about 22 square feet on each side. The average window has about 8 square feet of paintable area, and you can roughly figure the area of a baseboard by dividing its total length by half a foot.

The label on the paint can tells you how much area it can cover. Then divide your square footage figure by that amount. Voilà! Now you know how much paint to buy. Now that wasn't hard after all.

With that said, here are some general guidelines: It takes a gallon to paint the walls of an average-size room, half a gallon for the ceiling, and a quart for the trim. Buy extra if the surface is rough, porous, or unpainted.

When it comes to estimating paint, it's better to err on the high side. You can always use the extra for touch-up painting down the road.

Painting tools: Brushes, rollers, and sprayers

You have a few choices when it comes to applying paint. The next few sections should help you choose the right tools for the job.

Brushes

There are three things to consider when it comes to buying brushes: quality, size, and purpose.

For both interior and exterior painting, a quality brush is a smart investment. But don't go crazy. Remember that it's the magician, not the wand, that does the trick.

What makes a brush good? The handle should feel good in your hand. The ferrule (the metal piece that holds the bristles) should be securely attached. The bristles should fan out, not separate, when you press them against your palm. The bristles should be smooth, straight, and have *split ends.* The bristles should stay put when you tug lightly on them.

The size of the brush depends on what you're going to do with it. Frankly, most people use too small a brush for big jobs. It's best (and fastest) to use as wide a brush as possible, but not one that is wider than the surface to be painted.

So for large, flat areas like the side of a house, a 4-, 5-, or 6-inch brush is the fastest way to apply a lot of paint. For trim painting and cutting in, use a 2- or 2.5-inch angular sash brush for windows and 2- or 2.5-inch brush for everything else. For skinny window dividers, go with a 1- or 1.5-inch brush.

The shape of the brush is determined by the job, too. For painting a flat surface (like siding) and cutting in corners, a square-cut brush is perfect. When you need precise edges and clean lines (like for trim), a beveled brush is best. The awkward angles of windows, door frames, and shutters require an angular brush.

Finally, latex paints require polyester (best) or nylon brushes (good). Oil paints can be applied with a polyester brush (nylon bristles are softened by the solvents), but the best results come with using a natural "Chinese" bristle brush.

What about foam brushes? Quick touch-ups are the best use for these relative newcomers. But many people like the smooth finish they provide when using gloss and semi-gloss paints and polyurethane coatings.

Rollers

Rollers consist of two parts: the roller cover and the roller frame. Rollers come in a variety of sizes from 2 inches to 18 inches, but 7 and 9 inches are the most popular and useful. To the average do-it-yourself painter, one roller is pretty much the same as any other. WRONG! Just as there are several levels of quality with paint brushes, the same holds true for rollers. Cheap, poor quality rollers shed fibers, leaving behind a painted surface marred by fur. When it comes to choosing a roller cover and roller frame, let price be your guide. Better roller covers and frames will cost a few bucks more, but will be well worth the investment. In a nutshell, just don't buy the very cheapest.

Roller covers are selected based on the surface to be painted. Smooth surfaces like drywall and plaster walls require a short-nap ($^1/_4$-inch) roller. Bumpy surfaces like concrete and textured walls are best painted with a medium-nap ($^1/_2$-inch to $^3/_4$-inch) roller. Rough surfaces like concrete block and stucco demand a long-nap ($^3/_4$-inch to $1^1/_4$-inch) roller. There are other, even hairier rollers, but extra-rough and irregular surfaces usually are best painted with a brush.

Roller covers are made of a number of materials. Synthetic covers are fine for almost any paint, but experts will tell you that wool is best for oil-based paints and mohair is tops for enamels.

Sprayers

Sprayers come in two types: conventional and airless. Conventional sprayers use compressed air to turn liquid paint into a mist and shoot it through a nozzle. Professional-quality rigs require a portable air compressor, but a number of companies make low-pressure spray guns that operate with just a small electric compressor.

Airless sprayers atomize liquid paint by forcing it at great pressure (up to 3,000 psi!) through the spray nozzle. Fast and efficient, this equipment can be dangerous, as the spray pressure is high enough to inject paint into your skin, so be careful!

Applying Interior Paint

Okay. You've bought the paint and you've prepped the room. It's time to actually do the painting.

Before you do anything, stir the paint thoroughly. It will perform and look better if the components are well mixed from the start. Need a guideline? Stir for three minutes.

Now get to work! Always paint a room from top to bottom. The job will go faster—and turn out better—if you follow this plan:

1. **Paint the ceiling.**

   Use a trim brush to *cut in* the edges of the ceiling where it meets the walls. Paint a 2- to 4-inch-wide strip that feathers out toward the middle of the room. Begin painting the ceiling immediately. Start in a corner and paint across the narrowest dimension of the room.

2. **Paint the walls.**

   Start when the ceiling is dry. Do one wall at a time. Use a trim brush to cut in where the walls meet the ceiling, around doors and windows, and along the baseboards.

3. **Paint the windows.**

   Use an angular sash brush and, if you like, a smaller brush for the dividers.

4. **Paint the doors.**

   Use a trim brush. Work quickly but carefully. Don't forget to paint all six sides. Don't paint the hinges.

5. **Paint the door and window trim.**

   Use a sash brush. Paint the edges and then the face.

6. **Paint the baseboards.**

   Use a sash brush. Protect the floor or carpet with painter's tape and/or a paint shield.

 It's best to work with a partner. One of you can cut in the edges, and the other can follow along with the roller! Another tip: Use a roller wherever you can. One more tip: Use plenty of paint. Most do-it-yourselfers try to make a brush-full or roller-full go too far and end up with a lousy-looking room that desperately needs a second coat.

Using a roller

For ceilings, it's best to work in a 3-foot-square "W" pattern. For walls, an "M" is the way to go. Here's why: A zigzag pattern spreads the paint evenly over the section and lets you fill in without lifting the roller.

Use even, medium pressure, and stop when the section is evenly covered. Then move on to another section; you can move sideways or up/down (it doesn't matter). You can avoid lap marks if you overlap a bit of the section just painted while it is still wet. An extension pole enables you to paint the ceiling and the high sections of the walls without a ladder.

Painting a window

First, decide whether to mask off the glass, or paint carefully and scrape off any paint when you're done. If you want to mask, you can do it with tape or by using a peel-off film you apply with a roll-on applicator (like deodorant).

Instead of using masking tape, use a wide-blade putty knife (6 to 10 inches). Insert the blade between the glass and the frame and paint that section of trim immediately adjacent to the blade. Move the blade and continue the process from section to section. You will occasionally need to wipe off excess paint that collects on the putty knife. Another tip: strips of damp newspaper work well as an alternative to masking tape.

Start in the middle of the window and use a little brush to paint the dividers in double-hung windows or the inside edge of the frame if it's some other type. Switch to a 2.5-inch sash brush and paint the window frame and the trim.

Finally, paint the sill and the trim below the sill.

Painting a door

If your door has panels, work from the middle outward. Follow this sequence: (1) panels, (2) the horizontal areas between the panels, (3) the vertical areas between the panels, (4) the edges, (5) the horizontal areas at the top and bottom, and (6) the vertical areas on the outside.

If your door is flush or plain, start at the top and work your way to the bottom.

Be careful, but work quickly. You'll get brush marks if you try to brush wet paint over paint that is already partially dry.

One of the quickest ways to paint a flush door is to apply a nice even coat with a roller and then brush the paint out for a smooth and uniform finish. This process is called *back-brushing* and is used after applying paint with a roller or sprayer.

Painting metal

The secret to good results is, once again, preparation. You have to remove the dirt and rust from metal to get the paint to stick.

New metal should be cleaned using a metal etching solution or simply by wiping on good old fashioned vinegar — undiluted. This will remove surface oils that go part and parcel with the manufacture and fabrication of metals.

No matter what metal you're going to paint, the first step is to wash with TSP or paint thinner to remove any dirt and grease. Then take a wire brush and scrub away any rust and every bit of loose paint. You also can remove rust with products that either dissolve rust or convert it to a paintable surface. Ask your paint store for the one that's right for your purposes. Regardless of how you remove rust, the next step is to prime any bare metal using an alkyd or oil-based metal primer for aluminum and steel, or galvanized steel. Primers that contain zinc-oxide or red-oxide are your best choice. Note that some metal paints are self-primers and can be applied directly to bare metal.

Finally, finish the job with an alkyd house paint or alkyd exterior enamel or high-quality exterior latex house paint.

A semi-gloss luster will provide a more durable, easy-to-clean finish.

Painting Outside the House

Much like the inside of your home, the outside requires quite a bit of cleaning and preparation before you can apply paint.

Cleaning

Once again, paint doesn't stick to dirt. So it's important to properly prepare the outside surfaces of your home. A thorough washing is the first task. The experts recommend one of two methods: hand washing or pressure washing.

- Hand washing is the best way to remove dirt, and it requires nothing more than a ladder, bucket, sponge (or nylon truck brush), and TSP. But it is time-consuming and creates a potentially dangerous situation by combining soapy water and a ladder.

- Pressure washing is faster than hand washing, and today's machines are powerful enough to remove most loose paint at the same time. But the high-pressure stream can damage the surface and force water behind siding, which will ruin a new paint job as it works its way out to the surface. Therefore, it's important to use this equipment carefully.

In real life, most people try to get by with washing the house using a garden hose and nozzle. You could really be short-changing yourself by using this method. Unless the surface is perfectly clean, the paint simply won't stick. Thus, we suggest renting a pressure washer for a day. It is well worth the cost of 50 to 75 dollars.

Whichever method you choose, remember to let the house dry before you move on to surface preparation and painting.

Doing other prep work

Remove anything attached to the exterior, including shutters, mailbox and address numbers. Light fixtures can be loosened and covered with a plastic trash bag. Scrape and brush any painted areas that are peeling, flaking, blistered, chalky, or thin.

Resolve any mildew problems by treating the area with a bleach solution and removing the cause: usually sprinklers or thick vegetation close to the house. The best mildew removal solution that we have found consists of one-third cup of powdered laundry detergent, one quart of liquid chlorine bleach, and three quarts of warm water. Add the bleach to the water first and then the detergent. Even though the solution is mild, be sure to wear safety goggles and rubber gloves and have plenty of ventilation.

Apply the solution with a sponge, spray bottle, or pump garden sprayer. Allow the solution to sit for about ten minutes, but don't let it dry. Rinse thoroughly with fresh water.

Once the surface is clean, the next step is to countersink exposed nail heads, and patch old nail holes, cracks, and knots. Caulk cracks, gaps, and the butt ends of clapboards, plus the trim around windows and doors. Sand and prime any bare wood and all patched areas. You may need special stain-killer primers to seal in brownish surface discoloration caused by *cedar bleed*. This condition results from the natural tannins in the wood leaching through to the surface.

Scrape and brush rust and peeling paint from downspouts, gutters, and railings. Clean old paint and efflorescence (that powdery white stuff) from any brick or masonry surfaces to be painted by scraping and brushing. One cup of vinegar in a gallon of warm water works great for removing efflorescence.

Removing paint

The scraper, wire brush, and sandpaper are the most useful exterior paint-removal tools. They are excellent for removing dry, peeling paint from siding, trim, stucco, and metal railings. However, these tools require more physical exertion and ladder-climbing than other methods, but they leave a thoroughly cleaned, paint-ready surface.

Pressure-washers blast away loose paint pretty well but can force water into places it doesn't belong. A pressure washer works great for giving a house the all-important, adhesion-improving washdown.

Sand blasters, soda blasters, and similar machines use compressed air and tiny granules to pulverize paint layers. These tools are designed for fast paint removal from hard surfaces such as brick, stone, steel, and concrete. These devices can seriously alter the surface appearance and texture of the material being cleaned, so they are generally not for a do-it-yourselfer.

Chemical paint strippers soften paint and allow it to be scraped or brushed off. They are best for difficult-to-clean exterior materials like brick, stone, steel, and concrete.

Propane torches burn paint away quickly. But they can burn siding and trim, singe your hair, and start a fire. While one of the finest methods of paint removal, we suggest that this method be left to the pros due to the dangers associated with its use.

Drill-mounted rotary strippers flail away at painted surfaces with stiff (usually wire) bristles. They work especially well on metal surfaces to remove rust and dislodge old paint.

Choosing and using caulk

There are about 20 different kinds of caulk and sealants. But unless you have a special need, you can get by with three: latex, silicone, and polyurethane or latex foam.

- ✔ Latex caulk is perfect for interior uses such as filling the cracks along baseboards or around windows. It's paintable, it dries quickly, and it lasts a long time.

- ✔ Silicone caulk can be used indoors or out for almost any purpose. It bonds to almost everything and does not become brittle with age. It is amazingly flexible and offers outstanding water- and weather-resistance. In short, it is the top performer of the sealant world. Be sure to buy a *paintable* silicone caulk.

  A hybrid, latex with silicone, combines the qualities of both products and is thus one of the best, most user-friendly products available. It will stick to almost any surface — provided it is clean.

- ✔ Polyurethane foam (expandable spray foam in a can) is ideal for sealing around pipes, ducts, and vents, and for filling voids and gaps inside the walls. There are two kinds: high-foaming (HF) and minimum expansion foam (MEF). MEF is designed for use around windows and doors. (HF can cause the frames to bow.)

✔ Latex foam is the new kid on the block. Like latex paints, this innovative product is user-friendlier than traditional solvent-based products. Unlike its polyurethane counterpart, the latex foam does not expand beyond the size of the material that comes out of the can. What you see is what you get! Another difference is that latex foam can be tooled using a putty knife. Try doing that with polyurethane

For latex and silicone caulk, application is simple:

1. **If the caulk comes in a soft tube, knead it with your hands to mix and warm the material.**

   You will have a better product and it will flow more easily.

2. **Push (not pull) the cartridge tip along the crack or gap to lay down a nice even bead. Smooth the caulk with the best tool not even money can buy — your finger.**

If you're tired of your caulking jobs looking like a failed finger painting project, try this: Apply a strip of masking tape to the surface on either side of the joint to be caulked. Hold the edge of the tape back about $1/8$ inch from the joint. Apply the caulk and smooth it using your finger. Remove the tape by carefully peeling it away from the joint. You'll be amazed at the results!

To apply foam, just shoot it out of the can, and it rapidly expands to fill the crack or gap.

Choosing exterior paint

As for interiors, the most popular choices are latex and oil-based (alkyd) paints. Latex cleans up with water; oil-based cleans up with paint thinner. Latex dries faster; oil-based dries smoother. Latex lasts longer; oil-based covers better. Latex "breathes" better; oil-based adheres better.

A high-quality, 100-percent acrylic latex house paint is your best choice. The acrylic resins make the paint more abrasion-resistant, reduce chalking, and improve adhesion.

We said this earlier but it's worth repeating: Buy the best-quality paint you can afford. A good-quality paint will last longer than a cut-rate paint.

Determining how much paint you need

To roughly figure the paintable area, measure the perimeter of the house and multiply by the height. Then subtract the area of the doors (about 22 square feet each) and the window frames (about 15 square feet each). The formula: $(P \times H)$ – total trim.

You can estimate the amount of trim paint needed by adding up the area of the doors, windows, railings, and shutters. If you're going to paint the gutters, you can assume that each linear foot represents a square foot of area.

To figure out how much paint you need to buy to give all the surfaces one coat, divide your area estimates by the number of square feet each gallon of paint can cover. (It's on the label.) Double the amount if you plan to use a sprayer, as sprayers put the equivalent of two coats on with one pass.

With all that explained, here are some general guidelines: For most houses, you need one gallon of trim paint for every six gallons of siding/wall paint. You may need to fudge your estimate a little if the exterior of your house has a rough texture or was previously unpainted.

Buy a gallon or two more than you think you'll need. If the paint is not custom-tinted, you can usually return it provided it has not been opened. And if it is a custom color, you may find a need for the leftovers: touch-ups, missed spots, trellises, decks, patio furniture, fences, and so on.

The hardest thing to figure out is how long the job will take. Most people can cover 60 to 120 square feet in an hour, depending on the surface being painted. Rough shingles take a long time to do; smooth clapboard siding paints relatively quickly. Don't forget to include time for daily setup and cleanup.

Applying exterior paint

Always paint from top to bottom. Begin on the shady side because you want to avoid painting sides that are in direct sunlight. Wait until any surface moisture evaporates. The outside temperature must be higher than 50 degrees Fahrenheit, and don't start if the weather is threatening. Follow this sequence:

1. **Paint the gutters and eaves (if they will be the same color as the siding).**

2. **Paint the siding.**

   Work moving sideways, not up and down. Clapboards should be painted all the way across the width of the house. Paint the underside (where the boards meet) first and then paint the face.

3. **Paint the windows, doors (including the surrounding trim), and shutters.**

4. **Paint the railings, stairs, and foundation.**

The Finale: Cleaning Up

Latex paint cleans up with water. Wash the brush under warm water, making sure to work any paint out of the base of the bristles and the ferrule. Shake or snap the brush to get the water out, and hang it to dry (bristles down).

Oil-based paint cleans up with paint thinner. Luckily, you only need to clean your brushes once — at the end of the job.

A dirty little secret: Many do-it-yourselfers throw out their brushes at the end of a job rather than go to the trouble of cleaning them. A good brush is an investment that will lend itself to a professional job — throwing it away would be like trashing a good hammer.

TIP

Saving your paint brushes

One of the quickest ways of ruining a good paint brush is by placing it in a bucket or can of thinner. In just a matter of a few hours, the bristles will become permanently bent — ruining the brush forever. You can avoid this problem by using our brush-saving solution that requires only a clean, empty coffee can complete with vinyl lid.

1. Using a razor knife cut a small X in the center of the lid.

   The X should be just large enough to allow the brush handle to be inserted through it.

2. Pour some thinner into the can.

3. Push the brush handle through the X in the vinyl lid and place the lid on the can, as shown in the figure.

Like magic, the brush is suspended in the thinner without the bristles ever touching the bottom. When it's time to paint again, simply squeeze out the thinner against the side of the can and blot the brush on newspaper. This process should be used only during the painting process — brushes should not be left to soak in thinner for more than a few days.

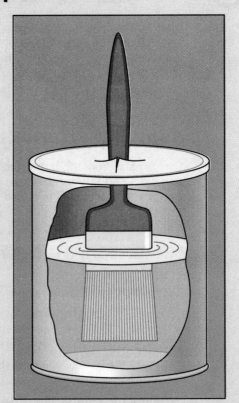

If you find yourself doing lots of painting around the house, consider investing in a brush and roller spinner. All you need to do is mount your brush or roller cover to the device and crank away as you would with a child's top. Your brushes will remain like new forever. Oh, don't forget to hold the brush or roller inside a bucket or barrel. Otherwise you'll have paint splatters all over your neighbor's car. We provide this valuable insight firsthand — enough said!

Some Paint Storage Tips

One aspect of the painting that is often overlooked is the proper storage of paint. Why is proper storage important? You'll understand when it's 2:00 in the afternoon and you discover that little Jamie has decided to practice pencil art on the hallway walls and dinner guests are coming at 6:00. In a panic, you run to the garage or storage shed, rummage through can after can of paint to finally find what remains of the hall paint. You throw an apron on, arm yourself with a brush, throw down a drop cloth, and open your paint to find that it is no longer a liquid — it's hard as a rock. To add insult to injury, you remember that the hallway paint was a special peach tint that takes at least 24 hours to match. OOPS!

You can avoid this scenario by taking a few steps that will keep your paint labels easy to read and the contents of the cans fresh for the next time you need to do some touch-up — crisis or not. For most people, after a painting project, it's tough to tell where most of the paint ended up — on the item being painted or on the outside of the can. This typically comes from running the paint-loaded brush against the inside rim of the can. The rim fills with paint and overflows, allowing paint to trickle down all sides. While it's true that coating the outside of the can with paint might assist with quick color identification, it also covers really important information such as color match formulas and application instructions. Here are a couple of ways to prevent this problem:

- ✔ Punch small drain holes in the rim of the paint can by using a hammer and a medium sized nail. One hole per inch will provide plenty of drainage. A couple of added bonuses: You won't waste as much paint, and the lid seals tighter, keeping the paint fresher.

- ✔ String a heavy-duty rubber band across the center of an open paint can. Anchor the rubber band under both of the knobs that the can handle is attached to. When painting, strike the fully loaded paintbrush against the rubber band instead of the rim. Try it, you'll love it!

Tired of dried paint when it comes time to touch up or repaint a wall or ceiling? Next time you get ready to store a can of paint, place a sheet of plastic wrap over the open can before putting on the lid. Tap the lid into place (using a small wood block between the hammer and the lid) and store the can upside down, as shown in Figure 27-1. This technique makes for airtight storage that will allow the paint to last for eons. Just remember to turn the can right side up before opening the can or you'll have a real mess on your hand . . . and feet . . . and floor.

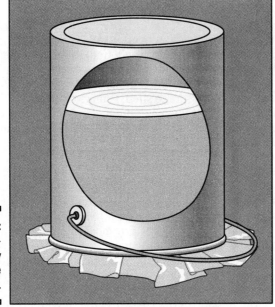

Figure 27-1:
The paint-
saving way
to store
paint.

Chapter 28
Tile

*W*hether you use it in the kitchen, bathroom, or foyer, on the countertop, wall, or floor, ceramic tile is one of the most beautiful and durable surfaces you can have in your home.

This shouldn't be news to you. After all, the Egyptians and Mesopotamians invented tile way back in 4000 B.C. These early civilizations used tile to decorate the exterior of their houses, and tile has been an important interior and exterior decorative element ever since. For proof, all you have to do is look at the intricately decorated wall tiles of ancient Persia, the colorful and complex 500-year-old mosaics of Spain and Portugal, and the magnificent floors of Renaissance Italy. And don't forget your grandparent's bathroom!

Although manufacturing methods have been improved, perfected, and automated over the centuries, the basic recipe remains unchanged from ancient times: Take clay, form it into thin squares, bake at high temperatures, and apply glaze.

You end up with a tough, colorful material that offers many design possibilities. That result is what makes tile so timelessly appealing.

Choosing Tile

Because it can last almost a lifetime and because it can be expensive, you can't afford to goof up when you select tile. Take the time to look beyond the pattern or design. Think about how and where you want to use the tile and other key considerations.

Floors or walls

Floor tile is different from wall tile. Floor tiles have tougher glazes, and the tile itself is harder and stands up better to foot traffic, abrasive grit, and impacts. Good-quality floor tiles are designed to look sharp for eons — no matter how much abuse they endure. Floor tiles come in a variety of functional, but mostly neutral, styles (unless, of course, you take the custom-design route). On the other hand, wall tiles, because they get much less wear and tear, are available in an enormous variety of designs, patterns, and colors.

Glazed or unglazed

Choices abound: high gloss, semigloss or low gloss (matte). Would you like the glaze to fully or partially cover the surface? (The *glaze* is the protective barrier that lies between you and the tile itself.) No glaze, no protection against staining and moisture absorption. Yes, you can purchase unglazed tile and apply your own protective surface out of a can. Good luck! We've tried unglazed tiles, and their surfaces don't hold up. However, you can use such tiles successfully in areas like exterior patios and walks where it won't matter.

 When the time comes for you to decide on a tile, keep in mind that the key considerations are abrasion resistance, slip resistance, and cleanability. A tile with low abrasion resistance is best for areas that receive only light traffic, such as bathrooms. High abrasion resistance is vital in areas with a great deal of gritty traffic, like foyers. By the way, contrary to popular belief, most floor tiles are no more slippery than any other hard floor covering. Many tiles now feature an abrasive grit on their surface to make them even more slip resistant. As for cleanability, glazed tiles win hands-down — they are well-suited for otherwise high-maintenance interior applications like kitchen backsplashes and bathroom walls and floors.

Classifications

When it's time to pick tile, use common sense and take your cue from the classifications that manufacturers use:

- **Group I.** Light residential traffic — bathrooms or bedrooms
- **Group II.** Moderate residential traffic — residential areas, except kitchens, entrance halls, or areas subject to direct outdoor traffic
- **Group III.** Residential traffic — kitchens and all other high-traffic areas
- **Group IV.** Commercial traffic — public areas such as hotel lobbies, restaurants, banks, and so on

We suggest Group III for your floors, unless you have kids. In that case, we suggest Group IV.

If you really want durable tile — with a surface that is as hard as a rock — look into Japanese porcelain. This is great stuff, and it really does hold up. We built a home nearly 20 years ago that had porcelain tile, and it looks as good as new today.

Size

Tile dimensions range from as small as 1 inch to as large as 24 inches and can be square, rectangular, octagonal, and various other shapes. The "right" size is a matter of personal taste. These days, 12-inch tiles are the most popular size for floors, and 4-inch tiles (actually $4^1/_4$ inches square) are the standard for bathroom walls and kitchen backsplashes.

Color

Tile offers a virtually infinite variety of colors. You can match anything you want — the drapes, the dog, the color of your best friend's eyes . . . and you can mix several colors to create a unique look. The only limitation is your imagination.

Cost

Prices start at less than $2 per square foot for basic, plain-white tile. Solid colors and simple patterns range from $3 to $10 per square foot. More sophisticated European-made tiles go for $15 to $50 per square foot. We feel that here's no reason to pinch pennies, as most bathroom floors and kitchen backsplashes contain less than 40 square feet of space that you can tile.

Give plenty of consideration to American-made tile, especially for the bathroom. Matching trim and accessories abound: soap dishes, towel-rod hangers, clothes hooks, and toilet-paper holders. Hey, when it comes to lasting quality, American and Japanese tile is at the top of our list. Mexican tile is at the bottom, and European tile falls somewhere in the middle.

Preparing to Install Tile

After you choose the tile that's right for the job (and right for you), you need to think about installation. Although experienced do-it-yourselfers use the word "challenging" to describe tile work, tiling is really more tedious and time-consuming than difficult. Plan on the work taking anywhere from three or four (long) days to several weeks to complete. Naturally, this time frame depends on the size and complexity of the project. Tile can be laid in a myriad of patterns. The more complex the pattern, the longer the project takes. If you hire someone to do the work, expect the bid to skyrocket when the pattern begins to get intricate! But of course, tile really doesn't look stupendous until the pattern gets intricate.

Thinking about the surface

Tile installation is only as good as the surface upon which it is installed. Whether the tile is going on the countertop, wall, or floor, the surface must be flat, dry, smooth, and structurally sound. The best substrate for wet installations (tub, shower, kitchen counter, vanity tops, and so on) are those that are "finished in place" using mortar. Mortar is a lot like cement without the rock and gravel. Thus, a thin (about an inch), uniform, and smooth surface can be achieved with maximum strength. Mortar is finished in place as is a concrete patio — the mortar is mixed on site and applied to metal lath over a layer of building paper. When dry the tile is attached to the mortar using an adhesive (another mortar) called *thinset* mortar.

A cost-effective do-it-yourself alternative to mortar is a pre-cast mortarboard. Instead of the mortar being "finished in place," the mortarboard is produced in a factory and sold in sheets — like drywall. Mortarboard has essentially all the same properties as the finish-in-place stuff, except mortarboard is not seamless, and it will take the shape of the surface to which it is being applied. Thus, if you have a wavy wall, the mortarboard and tile will be wavy when complete — unless you straighten the studs before proceeding with your tile work. These surfaces hold up if water leaks through the grout or a cracked tile. Mortar that is finished in place is the very best. Walls and floors in a home are wavy. Tile doesn't do well on wavy surfaces. Finished-in-place mortar is waterproof, adds strength to the configuration, and, when done properly, provides a perfectly flat substrate.

Never, never, never install tile for a shower wall directly onto water-resistant wallboard (see Figure 28-1). Call this wallboard what you want — "waterproof Sheetrock," "green board," "blue board" — it is all the same stuff. Water-resistant wallboard is the worst backing that you can glue tile to. We have seen tile that had been glued to wallboard come completely off the wall in three years. That's not much of a lifespan for an expensive home improvement!

Figure 28-1:
Don't
install tile
directly on
wallboard.

Selecting the tools

To do the job right, you must have the right tools. Some you have in your toolbox. Some you will need to buy. Others you can rent.

- Buckets
- Carpenters square
- Chalk line
- Dust mask
- Knee pads
- Level
- Pencil
- Rags
- Rubber gloves
- Safety glasses
- Scraper
- Sponges

- ✔ Square-notch trowel
- ✔ Squeegee
- ✔ Tape measure
- ✔ Tile cutter
- ✔ Tile nippers
- ✔ Toothbrush
- ✔ V-notch trowel

Selecting tile adhesives and mortars

The type of adhesive to use depends on the area you want tiled. Thinset mastics (Type I and II), mortars, and epoxies are your options — and each has its place in the tile world.

Ask your friendly neighborhood tile expert for help in selecting the right adhesive for your job, but here are some guidelines:

- ✔ **Type I mastic** is good for bathrooms and kitchen walls and floors.
- ✔ **Type II mastic** is fine for low-moisture applications. Guess you won't want to use this one to do a shower.
- ✔ **Dry-set mortar** is good for low-moisture floor applications.
- ✔ **Acrylic mortar** is great for bathroom walls and bathroom and kitchen countertops.
- ✔ **Epoxy** is by far the best for countertops. Epoxy is great for everything, but it costs a fortune.

A couple of things you should know: Thinset mastics aren't suitable on top of wood underlayment, atop plastic laminate, or on ceramic tile. Thinset mastics just don't adhere well to these surfaces. Acrylic mortar doesn't stick to laminate, but it does stick to everything else. Epoxy adheres to everything and is perfect over plywood substrates in wet areas.

Installing Tile

How you install tile depends greatly on where you install tile. The next few sections discuss installing tile on walls, floors, and countertops. Then we discuss grouting — the stuff that goes between the tiles — and finishing.

Installing tile on walls

Remove the existing wall tile. (A pry bar and a broad scraper work well.) Then remove everything — drywall included — right down to the studs. Before proceeding with replacement, repair or replace all moisture-damaged wood. Next, staple building paper (one course at a time) onto the studs. The first course should overlap the lip on the tub or shower pan. From this point you must install wire lath and mortar or mortarboard. In non-wet areas, replace the wallboard, apply the adhesive, and start setting tile. If the removed wall surface was plaster, wallboard can replace it. However, don't forget about waviness. Whenever finished-in-place mortar is not going to be used, shimming and stud straightening are always the order of the day — before the wall covering can be applied.

The installation looks better if the walls are as plumb and square as possible.

Some prep work

Find the lowest part of the wall. Use a level to mark a line and measure down from there. From that point:

1. **Measure up one tile. Mark the spot, and draw a horizontal line at that height.**

2. **Find the center of the wall and mark a vertical line that intersects the horizontal line you just drew.**

3. **Do a *dry run* by placing a horizontal row from the center line to a corner.**

   If you need less than half a tile at either end of the row, move the center line until you end up with a full tile at the most visible end.

4. **Continue the dry run by stacking a row of tiles along the vertical line, as shown in Figure 28-2.**

5. **Mark the upper line.**

The application

Now you're ready to begin setting the tile. The following steps describe the procedure.

Apply only as much adhesive as you can tile in 15 minutes. Also, when installing, select tiles from different boxes to make sure any color variation among the boxes is spread throughout the installation.

1. **Start in the center where you drew the vertical line.**

2. **Apply a ¹/₄-inch coat of adhesive over a small area using the flat side of the V-notched trowel; then use the notched side to "comb" the adhesive into rows.**

Figure 28-2:
Doing a dry
run of
installing
tile on a
wall.

3. **Lay the tile just as you did in the "dry run."**

   Work upward from the center line, placing the tile directly into the adhesive; wiggle the tile slightly and gently to make sure it has good contact.

4. **Keep going until the wall is done.**

At some point during the process, you need to cut some tiles. To make straight cuts, it's best to use one of the following tools:

- **A snap cutter.** This hand-operated tile-cutting tool scores the tile. The scored line makes easy work out of snapping the tile in two.
- **A tile saw.** A tile saw is expensive to rent but makes the job a breeze.

Cutting is one of the most difficult parts of tile installation. If you intend on using the snap cutter, get about 10 percent extra tile — for bad cuts. To make irregular cuts, use a tile nipper to take small bites until you get the cutout you need. Or better yet, if you have a miniature roto tool, purchase a tile cutting bit. You can use it to cut a circle out of the center of a piece of tile. Really neat.

Wait until the end to install soap dishes, towel bars, paper-towel holders, and other accessories. Don't forget to leave the spaces for them!

Installing tile on floors

Installing floor tile is very similar to installing tile on walls, except that your choice of a starting point (and the need for a dry run) are much more important.

Dealing with the existing floor

You can save a great deal of time and trouble by tiling over the existing floor, but here's a huge caveat: The existing floor must be in rock-solid structural condition — no rot, no flex, no nothing. If the floor is not in good shape, you need to pull up the finish flooring and replace the underlayment or repair the subfloor.

If the existing floor is tile, make sure it is sound by looking carefully for rot. Mildew, deteriorating grout, mineral deposits in grout, loose tiles, cracked tiles and floor movement are dead giveaways. Firmly rap any suspect areas with a rubber mallet to make sure they are solid (and find out if they're not). If you think the subfloor has water damage (and in many bathrooms, it will), you need to tear out the tile and replace any damaged subfloor. If everything looks okay, you can simply sand down the glaze until the shine disappears and move on to the next step. If the existing floor is vinyl, simply sand it down and move on to the next step.

When you have a good rough surface on your tile or vinyl, you need to clean it. Tile adhesives don't stick to dirt, dust, and grease, so you have to do a thorough vacuuming. The next step is a good, old-fashioned, hands-and-knees floor wash. If the substrate is a new layer of plywood, particleboard, or mortarboard, then a thorough vacuuming is all that's necessary.

Finding the place to start tiling

You can choose from several fairly complex ways to find the right place to start tiling the floor. However, in bathrooms, the easiest place is to start at the front of the bathtub and along an adjoining wall. Do a dry run to see how it looks. In kitchens, your best bet is to start in the middle of the room and adjust the tiles until you get a full tile along the most conspicuous wall (see Figure 28-3). You may need to experiment with different starting points until you get a uniform layout with a minimal amount of cut tiles. Make sure that the layout places cut tiles in the most inconspicuous places.

When you have to cut tile, Figure 28-4 shows you how to measure exactly how much to cut.

The bigger the tile, the less grout you have to apply, and the less grout you have to clean.

Figure 28-3:
When
laying out
tile in a
kitchen,
start in the
middle of
the room.

Getting the tile down

When you have the starting point figured out, grab the can of adhesive and get to work! Here's how:

1. **Start in the center of the room.**

2. **Spread a $1/4$-inch coat of adhesive over a small area using the flat side of the V-notched trowel, and then use the notched side to "comb" the adhesive into rows.**

3. **Lay the tile just like you did in the dry run.**

   Maintain uniform spacing. Work toward a wall, placing the tile firmly into the adhesive. Make sure you have good contact between the tile and adhesive by gently thumping each one with rubber mallet. Keep going until the floor is covered.

You can expect lots of cutting to work around pipes, fixtures, cabinets, and so on. Use the right tools — a tile saw or a snap cutter and a tile nipper. Be patient. Be careful.

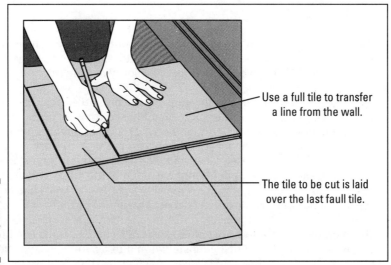

Use a full tile to transfer a line from the wall.

The tile to be cut is laid over the last faull tile.

Figure 28-4:
Measuring tile for cutting.

Installing tile on countertops

Countertops require the same basic prep as floors and walls — remove the old tile, install the substrate and clean it, and do a dry run to eliminate unneeded cuts. Then begin: Always start at the front-center of the countertop.

1. **Spread a $1/4$-inch coat of adhesive over a small area using the flat side of the V-notched trowel; then use the notched side to "comb" the adhesive into rows.**

2. **Lay the tile just like you did in the dry run. Maintain uniform spacing.**

3. **Start with the trim tiles. Work first from the center line to one edge, and then along the center line from the front to the back.**

4. **Set the rest of the tiles in the same pattern.**

5. **Place the tile firmly into the adhesive. Make sure you have good contact between the tile and adhesive.**

6. **Keep going until the countertop is covered.**

   Look over the tiling carefully and make any adjustments before the adhesive sets. Remove any excess adhesive as soon as possible.

Do the backsplash last, after all the countertop tiles are set:

1. **Spread adhesive on the wall and set the tiles in place.**

2. **Align the joints to match the joints in the countertop tile.**

3. **Leave a grout line between the countertop and the backsplash. Small plastic wedges are available for this purpose.**

Grouting

After all the tiles are laid, the next step is grouting. But you have to wait 24 hours (48 hours for floors) before you can do it. You have to give the adhesive that holds everything together plenty of time to cure.

Grout is the stuff that fills in the gaps between the tiles. You can choose from two different kinds of grout: cement-based (dry-set, unsanded, latex-portland, and sanded portland) and epoxy-based. Cement grout is the most popular because it is the least expensive and easiest to work with. For thin ($\frac{1}{8}$-inch) grout joints, use plain grout. For wide ($\frac{1}{4}$-inch) joints, use sanded grout. Unsanded grout should not be used for wide joints and vice versa. Epoxy grout is the best because it remains flexible and holds like iron. Unfortunately, epoxy grout is extremely expensive and very difficult to work with.

Grout comes in a rainbow of colors, and your choice can have a big effect on the appearance of the finished installation. But as you may expect, dark grout shows dirt less — and is easier to clean — than light grout. Regardless of which grout you choose, the process is the same:

1. **Mix the grout (it comes as a powder) — but only as much as you think you can use in 30 minutes.**

2. **Apply the grout to the surface using the rubber float or squeegee held at a 45-degree angle to the joints.**

   Spread the grout around liberally and force it into the joints. Remove excess grout by wiping it with the float as you go along.

3. **Let grout set for 20 minutes.**

4. **Wipe entire surface with a damp sponge, and keep wiping until all the grout lines are even and the joints are smooth. Rinse the sponge frequently.**

5. **Let the grout dry for another 20 minutes.**

6. **Polish with a rag or cheesecloth. Use an old toothbrush to get into the corners and other hard-to-reach areas.**

7. **Mix fresh grout.**

8. **Move on to another area.**

9. **Continue until entire tiled area is grouted.**

10. **Remove the haze on the tile with a 10-percent solution of vinegar and water.**

Finishing

The worst part is over. All that's left to do is a little caulking and sealing:

- ✔ **Walls:** Caulk the gap between the bathtub and the bottom edge of the tile, and around the bathtub soap dish, grab bars, or other wall fixtures (see Figure 28-5). Caulk can be purchased that exactly matches the color of your grout.

- ✔ **Floors:** Caulk where the floor meets the wall, and protect unglazed tile with a sealer.

- ✔ **Countertops:** Caulk where the countertop meets walls and/or splash and around the edge of the sink.

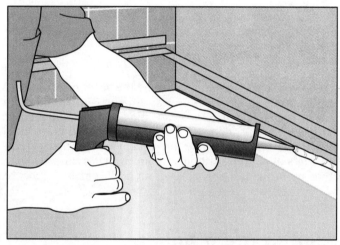

Figure 28-5:
Caulking.

After about three weeks, it is a good idea to seal all grout lines and tile with a high-quality tile and grout sealer. The sealer goes a long way toward preventing stains and keeping your beautiful new tile and grout looking good. Actually, it couldn't hurt to do it twice!

Some Cheap Advice

We've compiled some all-purpose, tile-related advice that didn't seem to fit anywhere else. Here goes:

Cleaning grubby grout

If you haven't ever sealed your grout, and it is still clean, then do so right away. Cleaning dirty grout is a breeze using 3 percent hydrogen peroxide. You know, the stuff you use to disinfect cuts. Use it straight and scrub with a nylon bristle brush.

Replacing grubby grout

If you find you can't clean your grout, the best solution may be to replace it. Start by removing $1/8$ inch of your existing grout with a grout saw. Rinse the area thoroughly to remove dust and loose bits. Apply a new layer of grout. And this time, remember to seal the grout so you won't have the same problem again!

Staining grubby grout

A lazy alternative to regrouting (provided the grout is in good shape) is to apply a grout stain. Grout stains are essentially paint applied with a small brush. To ensure lasting quality, the existing grout should be thoroughly cleaned using TSP (tri-sodium phosphate) and a small brass brush. Rinse, allow to dry overnight, and apply the stain in accordance with the manufacturer's directions. Although grout stain is a time- and energy-saving alternative, it doesn't last as long as grout replacement. Expect to restain again in a year or two.

Preventing tile trouble

Clean the entire tile surface frequently. Use abrasive cleaners sparingly, if at all. You can also try cleaning grout with a mild solution of bleach and water — a toothbrush works well if a bristle brush isn't available.

Chapter 29
Finish Flooring

. . . .

. . . .

If you are considering a room addition or a major remodel, then you need to begin thinking about the floor covering as soon as possible. Even though flooring is normally the very last finish to be installed, you need to select the flooring type early on so that doors, cabinets, and other finishes can be properly installed. For example: Door frames are installed directly onto the underlayment when vinyl flooring is used. When carpet is to be installed, the door and frame are held to the top of the opening — to clear the carpet and pad.

More important than anything, when it comes to choosing the best floor — or any finish for that matter — make sure it makes you feel good. It doesn't make any difference which one lasts the longest or which is most durable or easy to clean. You will have to look at that floor every day of your life, and regardless of what makes best economic sense, it is important that you are comfortable with it. This chapter not only helps you make the right flooring decision, but it also presents some tips on maintaining your floors.

Flooring Options

Flooring options abound: sheet vinyl, vinyl tiles, hardwood planks, wood parquet, carpet, ceramic tile, brick, slate, stone, granite, plastic laminate, and more. So rather than spend a great deal of time comparing and contrasting the different types of flooring, we thought we'd cut right to the chase and simply look at the pluses and minuses of each type:

Carpet

Plus: Absorbs noise like no other floor covering.

Minus: Absorbs dirt and water like no other floor covering.

Plus: Makes a room cozy and warm.

Minus: Does not last in high-traffic areas.

Plus: Easy fluff up with a vacuum.

Minus: Retains dust and pollen particles, which is bad if you have allergies.

Ceramic tile

Plus: Easy to keep clean, although grout does take some cleaning and sealing management.

Minus: Hard surface reflects household noise.

Plus: Lasts a long, long time.

Minus: Cold to the touch and hard on the feet.

Plus: An almost infinite number of color, texture, design, and style combinations.

Minus: Grout and tile are brittle and will crack if the subfloor is not sturdy.

Sheet vinyl

Plus: Offers good value, good looks, and durability.

Minus: Cheaper vinyls collect dirt and stain easily.

Plus: Easy to clean.

Minus: Cheaper vinyls need replacing every five to seven years or so.

Plus: High-end vinyls last 15 to 20 years or more.

Minus: Caution must be taken to prevent cutting and gouging.

Vinyl tile

Plus: Very inexpensive.

Minus: Can look cheap if not carefully installed.

Plus: Do-it-yourselfers can do a good installation easily.

Minus: Doesn't last as long as sheet vinyl.

Hardwood

Plus: Long lasting (with proper care).

Minus: Easily scratched and easily dented by high heels.

Plus: Offers a warm, natural look.

Minus: Does not stand up to water and is expensive to maintain (that is, refinish).

Plastic laminate flooring

Plus: Available in a myriad of colors and styles.

Minus: Looks like vinyl but is more expensive.

Plus: Costs less than real hardwood.

Minus: Lasts about as long as vinyl but is almost impossible to repair.

Plus: New floating style floor made for DIY installation.

Minus: Warranty does not cover scratches.

Brick, slate, and stone

Plus: Unusual look.

Minus: Easy to stain, hard to clean.

Plus: Unusual look.

Minus: Expensive.

Linoleum and sheet vinyl flooring: The right stuff

Linoleum became an affordable flooring at the turn of the century and immediately went into wide use. Almost 100 years later, its stepchild, sheet vinyl, remains one of your best flooring choices. The Carey Brothers take pride in awarding a very special trophy to the sheet vinyl industry: "Best Bang for Your Flooring Buck" award. Nothing lasts longer, with as little maintenance, as does sheet vinyl flooring.

Our advice

In the old days (10 to 15 years ago), people put sheet vinyl in the kitchen and bathroom, hardwood or carpet in the living room, and tile in the entry. Those time-proven guidelines still make sense, but homeowners are taking a more flexible approach. Today, the "right" flooring can be just about anything.

For example, sheet vinyl is still the most popular choice for kitchens, bathrooms, and the laundry, but other materials have made inroads. Ceramic tile is now a close number two in the bath. Hardwood floors, previously limited to dry areas, are showing up in kitchens. Plastic laminate and wood floating floors, which hit the market in the early 1990s, have quickly gained acceptance for use in a variety of areas, including the kitchen. However, we strongly suggest against using hardwood and floating floors in any wet area. But with the proper care, almost any flooring material can be used almost anywhere.

 And in case you're feeling frisky (in a home-improvement kind of way), floor installation, except for the new floating floors, is not the kind of job most do-it-yourselfers care to tackle. Pick your floor covering and hire a professional installer to put it in — you'll be happier with the end result.

Hot Installation Tips

We don't have the space to cover the ins and outs of every kind of floor installation, but we can give you the following helpful tips:

- ✔ If you decide on vinyl, buy the highest-quality product that you can afford, preferably one in which the pattern goes all the way through the material. It will last longer and look better.

- ✔ The only types of hardwood flooring that can be glued down to a concrete substrate are parquet and laminated planks. Because parquet floors are actually made of thousands of little pieces, they aren't prone to cupping, twisting, and buckling caused by dampness that can attack the top of a concrete floor slab. Laminated floors are made of thin, cross-laid courses of wood (like plywood), so they also are not affected by moisture.

✔ Some elderly (20-plus years old) vinyl flooring may have asbestos in it. Don't worry. It is the least dangerous type of asbestos-containing product we know of, and removing it (if done correctly) will not release a dangerous amount of fibers into the air. Here's how to do it: Simply pry the underlayment and vinyl up together. Fold it over and bend/break it into manageable pieces. Never, ever sand a vinyl floor that may contain asbestos. Be sure not to separate the vinyl from the underlayment. Doing so could release a dangerous amount of asbestos. If the vinyl is glued to concrete, have the material tested. If it contains asbestos, we suggest a call to a licensed abatement contractor. For more on asbestos removal, see Chapter 16.

✔ Be aware that if you install a new floor over an old one, you lock appliances like built-in dishwashers, refrigerators, and trash compactors into place. The new material can block the lower portion and prevent them from being slid out of their spaces.

Cheap Advice: Keeping Your Floors Looking Good

We thought we'd end this chapter with some tips on floor maintenance.

✔ Got scuff-marks on a vinyl floor? Get an art-gum eraser (one of those grayish-tan ones you used in high school) or borrow a Pink Pearl eraser from your favorite kid. Just rub the mark and voilà!, the mark is gone. For tough scuffs, use a little paint thinner. Pour a spare amount on a rag and rub the spot clean. Be careful not to go nuts with the thinner. Here, less is more.

✔ Got a stinky carpet? You can try a commercial carpet deodorizer or you can go to the pantry and arm yourself with a box of baking soda. Sprinkle it into the carpet, leave it for several hours, and then vacuum it up. For less money and a little extra work try sprinkling grated potato (yes, potato) throughout the area. Let it stand for several hours and then vacuum. The extra work with the potatoes is in the grating. If none of these methods work, call a carpet cleaning company, you cheapskate.

✔ Got dirty hardwood floors? The cleaners you can buy at the store work fine. But if you want to save money and like to play chemist or just prefer to do things the old-fashioned way, mix yourself a 5 percent solution of vinegar and water. Measure carefully, and don't use any extra vinegar — the acid can eat through the finish. Remember that water and wood don't mix. When you mop, use as little water as possible. Your mop should be damp, not wet. Wipe the floor and dry immediately with a towel. Never let the floor air dry — you can damage the wood, and you can end up with more water marks than you know what to do with.

✔ Got scratches on your hardwood floors? There is nothing you can do except refinish. So for future reference, be sure to use a welcome mat or rug at the outside and inside of each exterior door to catch the grit that might get tracked in. And don't be embarrassed to ask workers, children, and women wearing spike heels to take off their shoes before coming in.

✔ Want to keep ceramic tile from looking lousy? Don't use abrasive cleansers. They literally "sand" off the finish. Check the labels of the products you use — it will amaze you how many contain abrasives.

✔ If you have a damaged section of carpet or vinyl flooring, here is a suggestion that will save you plenty. If you don't have a scrap piece of flooring lying around to make the repair, then grab a piece from a closet floor, from under an appliance, or from beneath a piece of furniture. It may not match perfectly, but our experience is that most of your guests will never know "the real truth" about your floor.

✔ There is only one way to properly repair a damaged section of hardwood floor. Be prepared to replace any stained or damaged wood and then sand and refinish the entire floor. In the greatest percentage of cases, any other solution will leave a noticeable "patched" area.

✔ Is your carpet dirty around the edges? That "dirt" may actually be mildew, but it probably is dirt deposited there as air migrates from room to room and from outside to inside. The carpet is filtering dust, soot, and dirt out of the air. Solve the problem by caulking the joint between the baseboard and the subfloor. This will require removal of the carpet at its edges. Finally, call a carpet cleaner — and your carpet will look as good as new. Well, at least it won't be pin-striped any more.

✔ Here is a great one for eliminating bubbles in your vinyl floor. If the bubble is small, take a large sewing needle and poke a tiny hole in the center of the bubble all the way through the vinyl. Lay a thick towel over the area and use a hot iron to soften and flatten the flooring. Then stack several large books onto the repair to keep the former bump in close contact with the adhesive while it cools and rebonds to the substrate. Larger bubbles (6 to 8 inches or more) require more sophisticated solutions and are best left to flooring experts.

Chapter 30

Wrap-Up

. . . .

. . . .

After days or weeks (or months) of dust, disruption, noise and inconvenience, your project is nearly complete. All that remains is the little stuff — an outlet cover here, a towel bar there.

You also need to worry about an official final inspection, your own final walk-through, cleaning up, moving in, and releasing final payment. This chapter helps with all those details

Final Inspection: For Your Safety

From a building code standpoint, the final inspection is the one that tells you "everything works, everything is safe, and now you can use the space."

A good final inspection doesn't necessarily depend on you, but you can improve it by your presence — if you know the right questions to ask. Therefore, some vigilance and participation on your part should be planned. Time-pressed building inspectors sometimes overlook important things that you'll want checked. If in enough of a hurry, the inspector might skip checking something, assuming that your contractor did it correctly because "he has always done it properly in the past." Make sure that you get the thorough inspection you paid for and the thorough inspection you deserve.

In some instances, you will also have to get past your contractor's anti-inspector and anti-inspection bias. Some builders see the inspector as someone who swoops down on a broom to snoop around, find mistakes, and create a lot of unnecessary work — all unpaid of course. In short, a pain in the butt.

Don't get sucked in. The inspector is your friend. And in case you're wondering, they aren't there to hassle your contractor or slow progress; they are there to protect you by making sure your project is safe for your family — safe to use and safe to live in.

You need to know what should be inspected. The building inspector should make sure to check the following:

- Grading around the house provides proper drainage.
- Exterior materials meet code, and workmanship is satisfactory.
- Lock sets work and meet code. (Deadbolt locks should have a thumb turn on the inside, not a key.)
- Attic/crawlspace access is adequate/safe.
- Gas lines are connected properly (with flex tubing from valve to appliance).
- Smoke detectors work and are installed where required.
- Electric connections are proper throughout the house and at the service panel.
- Electrical circuit breakers are labeled correctly on service panel.
- Electrical outlets and switches work properly.
- Ground-fault circuit interrupters (GFCIs) work.
- Light fixtures are installed properly and work.
- Appliances (especially cooktop and vent hood) are connected properly.
- The water heater is strapped down.
- The water heater pressure relief valve works.
- There are no penetrations through the firewall between the garage and house.
- Penetrations throughout house are sealed or finished properly.
- Roof, gutters, and roof vents are properly installed and flashed.
- Plumbing and fixtures work and are installed properly.
- Sliding glass doors, windows in or near doors, shower doors, and enclosures and mirrored closet doors are made of tempered glass.

It's a lot to check. But each item is important. A loose gas connection can lead to an explosion. An ungrounded switch can start a fire. An improperly constructed roof can leak and ruin thousands of dollars of interior improvements.

Safety aside, nothing will bug you more than a sink drain that isn't water-tight, an outlet that doesn't work, or a vent hood that doesn't vent. Do yourself a favor: Protect your family and your sanity by insisting on a thorough and complete final inspection.

We mentioned it earlier in the book, but we feel it is important enough to run it by you again. The building department does not warrant their inspection and they aren't responsible for their mistakes — economically or otherwise. Essentially, this means is that you have a share in the responsibility if something goes wrong. Be aware of your position, ask questions, read, learn, and provide input. Even if you are wrong once in a while — who knows — you may find a mistake that could cost big time to fix later.

The Final Walk-Through: A Check for Quality

Becoming a remodeling contractor is pretty easy. Some trade experience, a little estimating background, and a pickup truck are a few of the basic ingredients. But the contractor who *finishes completely* is the true expert. And in our opinion, the contractor isn't finished until every minute detail has been attended to.

Some folks assume that the building inspector is the one to count on when it comes to getting your job completed properly, especially if you are having difficulty getting your contractor to cooperate. Wrong! Don't you remember? The building inspector is only concerned with *health and safety issues*. Level of quality is an issue between you an your contractor.

When we first began as remodelers, we were told that we needed to charge more to doctors and lawyers because they were more picky than other folks. What we decided to do was charge the amount that it took to do each and every job correctly and thoroughly — no matter who was paying the bill. We felt that getting the job done *completely* should be a matter of attitude on our part — not that of our customers. Unfortunately, this is not how every contractor thinks. So as usual, you end up being the one to look out for you.

Nail holes, hammer marks, gaps and voids, mismatched finishes, crooked switch covers, and more are all a part of the items that must be corrected before the project can be tagged "complete." In fact, there are so many items that we created a "Final Walk-Through Checklist" that we use on every project we do. We hope it will help your project as much as it has helped us complete ours.

Plumbing

✔ All plumbing fixtures and trim are in good condition. No chips, cracks, or scratches exist.

✔ The ice-maker is connected, and so is the air gap for the dishwasher.

✔ The tub, shower pan, and toilet are all silicone-caulked to the finished floor covering.

✔ Faucet aerators have been cleaned at all faucets and showerheads, and they are clear and work properly.

✔ Gas appliance shut off valve(s) have been soaped (checked for leaks), and the appliance(s) are operational.

✔ The disposal is fully operational.

✔ The dishwasher is fully operational, and it is properly mounted to the cabinet.

✔ Towel bar(s), toilet paper holder(s), shower rod(s), coat hook(s), towel ring(s), and other bath accessories are firmly and neatly mounted and are free of nicks and scratches.

HVAC and sheetmetal

✔ Heat ducts have been vacuumed, register covers are installed correctly, and air flows properly when the system is turned on.

✔ The vent hood duct is correctly connected, and it operates properly.

✔ The thermostat is working properly.

✔ The furnace is operational and working properly.

✔ Gutters flow properly and are free of leaks, and they are not dented or otherwise defaced.

✔ Downspouts are installed and are free of dents, and splash blocks are in place (or they are properly connected to a drainage system).

✔ All exhaust fans, light fans, and heat-light-fans are operational and working properly.

Electrical

- ✔ All electric outlets and switches work properly (including 3- and 4-way systems); cover plates are straight and level and tight to the wall.

- ✔ The wallboard is free of gaps at all plugs and switches and other electric fixtures.

- ✔ All GFCI outlet plates are properly marked "GFI" or "GFCI".

- ✔ The electric panel is labeled to show which breaker controls which circuit or appliance.

- ✔ All light fixtures have bulbs that are the correct size for the fixture, and they operate properly.

- ✔ Smoke detector operation lights are on, and the detectors have been tested and operate properly.

- ✔ All electric appliances are properly installed, and every function on each is fully operational.

- ✔ The whirlpool tub operates properly.

Finish carpentry

- ✔ All wood trim including baseboard is completely installed and free of hammer marks, gouges, and other flaws.

- ✔ Kitchen cabinets are installed and complete. There are no scratches or chips, and the cabinet finish is acceptable.

- ✔ All countertops are in good condition, and there are no scratches or chips.

- ✔ All door hardware is installed, free of scratches, and is working properly.

- ✔ All exterior doors have been weather-stripped on all four sides and are operating smoothly.

- ✔ Exterior decks, porches, and steps are complete and free of flaws.

- ✔ Interior doors operate smoothly, are free of flaws, and have been trimmed to clear the finish flooring.

- ✔ Shelves and closet poles are installed, level, and adequately braced.

Finish flooring

✔ Grout is cleaned from tile, and there are no scratches or chips.

✔ Mastic is cleaned from all vinyl floor coverings, and there are no scratches, tears, or other flaws.

✔ The cove mold cap in the bathroom is sealed to the wall with caulking (not normally sealed in other rooms).

✔ All hardwood flooring is free of scratches, and the finish is acceptable in every way.

Other finishes

✔ The stucco is free of excessive cracking; the texture and color match, and it is complete and in good condition.

✔ The wallboard (or plaster) matches the existing and is free of flaws.

✔ All plastic laminate work is complete, free of scratches and chips, and is in good condition.

✔ All butcher block top work is complete, free of scratches and chips, and is in good condition.

✔ All Corian work is complete, free of scratches and chips, and is in good condition.

✔ All ceramic tile work is complete, free of scratches and chips, and is in good condition.

✔ All cultured marble, onyx and granite work is complete, free of scratches and chips, and is in good condition.

✔ All marble tile work is complete, free of scratches and chips, and is in good condition.

✔ All slab marble/slab granite work is complete, free of scratches, and chips and is in good condition.

✔ All mirror work is complete, free of scratches and chips, and is in good condition.

✔ All tub/shower enclosure work is complete, free of scratches and chips, and is in good condition.

✔ All exposed roof metal and all exposed plastic of all kinds are painted.

Painting

✔ All interior and exterior doors are painted on all six sides.

✔ All painted and/or stained interior wood work is free of gouges, scratches, and hammer marks, and is acceptable in every way.

✔ All painted and/or stained cabinetry is free of gouges, scratches, and hammer marks, and is acceptable in every way.

✔ All exterior painting and/or staining is acceptable in every way.

✔ Over-spray, as well as splashes and spills, have been completely cleaned up (including door hardware and window glass).

General

✔ Contractor sign has been removed, and any damage it may have caused has been completely repaired.

✔ All window and door glass inside and out has been closely inspected, and no cracks or scratches exist.

✔ All screens are installed at all doors, windows, and sky windows. No tears or flaws exist.

✔ All parties involved with the work have cleaned up and hauled away their debris, construction materials, and equipment.

✔ The attic and underfloor areas are clean and free of all debris and construction materials.

✔ The yard is clean and free of even the slightest debris, including cigarette butts.

✔ Excavated soil left on the property is free of debris and has been placed in the location designated in the construction agreement.

✔ All interior areas have been completely cleaned. (Only applies when "final janitorial" is a part of the construction agreement.)

✔ All damage caused during the project has been properly repaired.

Make sure that you check above and below, inside and out, and anywhere else you can think of as you make your inspection. Take notes as you travel from one location to another. Use blue painter's tape to mark flaws. It is easy to see and easy to remove once the repair has been made. If you have a computer, type the notes into a spreadsheet sorted by location (kitchen, bath, family room, north exterior, and so on). Re-sort the data by category of work (plumbing, heating, electrical, and so on) and make another printout. Provide a copy of both to each and every person associated with the project. You will really be surprised how positively everyone will respond.

Don't move in before the job is entirely complete. Moving in prematurely can shift responsibility for paint scratches, nicks in the wallboard, and other damage, to you. "Look lady," the contractor said, "that tile wasn't chipped when you moved back in!" Sound familiar? And besides, moving in can slow things down. And you want corrections done as soon as possible, don't you?

Clean-Up and Move-In

Remodeling makes a mess. And when your contractor is done, your entire house will need a major cleaning. No joke.

Dust will be everywhere. Carpets will be dirty. Walls will have smudgy handprints. And that's in the rooms that weren't remodeled! The rooms that saw all the work will be a disaster area. The point is, no matter how careful your contractor is or how good his intentions, your house will need to be thoroughly cleaned. And not by you.

Post-remodeling clean-up is a job for professionals. It doesn't add much to the cost of the project ($150 to $300, depending on house size). And after you've made it through two months of construction, you deserve a present, so let someone else clean the screens, wipe the baseboards, wash the walls, scrape up greasy plumbers putty, shine the sinks and faucets, wash off the grout haze, clean the carpet, and grab all the roofing nails out of the gutters.

Construction clean-up can be tricky. If you were to do it, you could do damage to your beautiful new space. For example, did you know that tempered glass is easily scratched if you use a paper towel to wipe off drywall dust? Did you know that you will ruin your household vacuum cleaner if you use it to clean new carpet? Do you know which solvent is best for removing construction adhesive from a countertop? We thought not.

So if your contractor offers to let you do the clean-up, tell him no.

What a janitorial contractor does

A janitorial contractor knows the secrets to a thorough clean-up, or at least knows people who know the secrets. These days, post-construction janitorial is a trade in itself.

Here's what happens: A big crew shows up with giant boxes of clean white cloths, huge commercial-grade vacuums, and dozens of special cleaners, buckets, squeegees, and mops. Then they swarm all over your house, cleaning the heck out of every room. Pretty good deal!

What you shouldn't do

Don't even think about trying to use your new space until all the work is done and the clean-up is complete.

We know how exciting it can be to have a new kitchen, new bathroom, or new master suite. But if you start bringing furniture, you'll slow down (or even prevent) completion. Plain and simple, your furniture and stuff will be in the way. And things won't get done right.

For example, if you put a bed against the wall, the outlet behind it won't get checked and the baseboard won't get cleaned. If you put dishes in kitchen cabinets before the electrician hooks up the under-counter work lights, he will have to move them or work around them, and they will get dirty or broken. If you fill your new bathroom cabinets with fluffy towels before the plumber is done working on the drain, your towels might end up covered with greasy, grimy, sticky plumber's goup.

Avoid these and other problems by being patient. It's difficult to resist jumping the gun. But if you can refrain from moving in too soon, you'll end up with a better job, one that is more thoroughly detailed and entirely complete.

Final Payment

You would think that once the final walk-through and clean-up are completed that you can relax, write the final check, and enjoy your new digs. But there are a few more things that you still need to do while the last bits of touch-up work are being done. First, if you don't already have one, you definitely need a list of the subcontractors who worked on your home. Next, you also want notarized lien releases from everyone who worked on your project. And finally, you must be sure to get copies of all warranties and operating manuals.

Get the list of subcontractors

When a warranty repair is needed, the normal course of action is to call your general contractor. He in turn contacts the party responsible to make the repair. But sometimes, the contractor isn't there to answer the phone.

We don't want to unnecessarily alarm you, but now and then, general contractors do become *permanently unavailable*. It could be their desire to follow a new field of endeavor, go back to school, move the business to another location (out of state), or sometimes, they simply just go broke. In most instances, the general contractor is your only link to the subcontractors. Not a good idea. You should take steps to insure that you will be able to get warranty work done later — no matter what happens to your general contractor. Reduce your risk by asking for a list of all subcontractors including their name, address, phone number, and exactly what tasks each performed on your project. A good contractor requires each subcontractor to warrant his or her work for at least one year. Having the subcontractor's phone number may just get an item repaired even if the general contractor has become unavailable.

Get copies of all warranties and manuals

Make sure that you get copies of all warranties and operating manuals. If the alarm guy gets paid and you don't have the system operating manual, you might never get one. That actually happened to us once.

Get lien releases

There is a funny thing about the final payment. Once the contractor has been paid in full, things can sometimes kind of slow down. When you make a final payment to the contractor (with some of them) it's almost the same as telling them, "Okay treat me like I don't exist anymore." It doesn't have to be that way.

It is an industry standard to hold back a 10-percent retention (10 percent of the contract sum) for 30 days after absolutely everything on the project is entirely complete. You don't need to withhold the retention payment if all subcontractors and the contractor provide you with notarized *full releases of lien*. You may want to go back and review the chapter on mechanic's liens (Chapter 12) to be sure that you are clear on how to proceed with the final payment as it relates to final lien releases.

By the way, obtaining lien releases is another good reason to make sure that you have a list of everyone that worked on your project. Otherwise, how will you know for sure that everyone has provided their release. Just a reminder, you could pay twice, once to the general contractor, and once again to the subcontractor, if you don't get the proper releases.

Part VII
The Part of Tens

The 5th Wave   By Rich Tennant

"You said you wanted me to add space to the kitchen."

In this part . . .

Every ...*For Dummies* book ends with top-ten lists, and this one is no exception. We close with some succinct tidbits of advice that will save you money and keep you sane.

Chapter 31

Ten Things to Remember about the Remodel Process

- ✔ Prepare for several disagreements with your spouse during the planning phase.

- ✔ When you see the estimate for the first time, remember, cars now range in price from $16,000 to $200,000. And they really haven't changed much since the '70s.

- ✔ After you have signed the construction contract, you may feel slightly depressed about all the money you spent. Keep a stiff upper lip. You can't take a U-Haul to heaven.

- ✔ Immediately after ground breaking, you will experience tremendous exhilaration and joy. Go out and buy something to celebrate.

- ✔ Your pets will be traumatized when strangers arrive at your home. Don't let them bite your new guests, as it could result in a lawsuit.

- ✔ Let your neighbors know that a home improvement project is underway at your place. Don't be surprised if you receive calls from their attorneys about the noise and traffic problems.

- ✔ Excitement will continue through the completion of the framing. Then things will slow down as the plumbing, HVAC, and electrical are being installed. You will begin to feel slightly depressed with the slowdown. Write your contractor a nasty letter and send it along with your next payment. He'll understand but feel good because he was paid.

- ✔ You will be overjoyed when the drywall, doors, and millwork go in. But then you will discover that everything is scratched and needs touch-up or replacement. Write another letter to your contractor and send it along with the next payment.

- ✔ After the flooring goes in and as the janitorial contractor completes the final stage of cleaning, you can see that it was all worth it. Make a walk-through with the contractor. Tell her how pleased you are, but don't send her the last check until everything is entirely complete and to your full satisfaction.

- ✔ The job is entirely complete. It is just you and your family now. And your dream that has finally come true. If you are happy with the work, write the contractor another letter. Now you can send the rest of the money. Then go out and buy yourself something to celebrate.

Chapter 32

Ten Remodeling Tips That Will Save You Money

- Planning: It's the single most important part of your project. Keep in mind that it is much easier (and less expensive) to move a wall on paper using an eraser than to relocate a real wall using a hammer and a crowbar.

- Overbuilding can turn your hard-earned money into poorly-spent cash. Check the values in your neighborhood and choose projects wisely to get the best bang for your buck.

- Always get more than one bid. Three seems to be the magic number. Be prepared to call ten contractors in order to end up with three bids.

- Hiring a contractor: Don't do it until you have read our chapter on this subject in this book. It's Chapter 9.

- Communication: It can make or break a project. Be available to answer questions and never be shy about asking them.

- Permits are *not* an engraved invitation to the tax collector. They are for your protection. Doing a job without a permit is asking for trouble.

- Change Orders: Two words that you want to avoid like the plague. Your best defense is a strong offense. See the very first bullet point.

- Make sure that everything is in writing: If it isn't, chances are, you won't get it.

- Lien releases are *your* protection from having to pay twice. Be certain that you have received lien releases from anyone who has furnished labor and/or material to improve your home before making final payment.

- "Haste makes waste" and "Patience is a virtue" are words to live by when remodeling. Don't be in a big hurry to begin your project until you have done all of your planning. And once underway, keep reminding yourself that the circumstances are temporary and that you know you will love it once the dust has settled.

Index